MW00440678

The *Legenda aurea*

In the thirteenth century a young Dominican friar, Jacobus de
Voragine, compiled the book that came to be known as the *Legenda
aurea,* a collection of medieval lore about the saints and holidays of
the church. Through the centuries this noted book has had a
conspicuously uneven reputation: enormous popularity in the late
Middle Ages, a precipitous decline during the Renaissance, and a
gradual rehabilitation in the modern era. Sherry L. Reames's study of
the *Legenda aurea* offers the first comprehensive account of the
book's history and of the qualities that differentiate it from earlier
and less controversial works about the saints. The fresh perspective
introduced by this study will provide new insights and challenge old
myths for historians, literary critics, theologians, and students
concerned with medieval culture and hagiography.

The *Legenda aurea*

A Reexamination of Its Paradoxical History

Sherry L. Reames

THE UNIVERSITY OF WISCONSIN PRESS

Published 1985

The University of Wisconsin Press
114 North Murray Street
Madison, Wisconsin 53715

The University of Wisconsin Press, Ltd.
1 Gower Street
London WC1E 6HA, England

First printing

Printed in the United States of America

Library of Congress Cataloging in Publication Data
Reames, Sherry L., 1942–
    The Legenda aurea, a reexamination of its
paradoxical history.
    Bibliography: pp. 305–311.
    Includes index.
    1. Jacobus, de Voragine, ca. 1229–1298. Legenda
aurea. 2. Christian saints—Biography. 3. Fasts
and feasts. I. Title. II. Title: Legenda aurea.
BX4654.R32 1985   270'.092'2 [B]   84-40502
ISBN 0-299-10150-9

Contents

Preface   vii

Introduction   3

Part I. The Meaning of the Renaissance Verdict

1. The Modern Legend of the *Legenda aurea*   11

2. The Fall of the *Legenda* Reexamined   27

3. Towards a Reasonable Standard for the Evaluation
   of Medieval Hagiography   44

**Part II. The *Legenda* and Gregory's *Dialogues:*
The Differences Examined**

4. The Richness of Gregory's *Dialogues*   73

5. The Impoverishment of Gregory's Narrative in
   the *Legenda aurea*   85

6. Jacobus as a Teacher: Supplementary Evidence
   from the Sermons   101

Part III. Jacobus's Work in Its Historical Context

7. Saint Ambrose and the Enemies of the Church   117

8. Saint Augustine and the Holy Life   135

9. The Legacy of the Founder   164

10. On the *Legenda* as a Medieval Best-Seller   197

Notes   213

Principal Works Cited   305

Index   313

Preface

This book might best be described as an introduction to the study of the *Legenda aurea.* I have not written it for great experts on medieval hagiography, but for students and scholars in related fields who need some help in disentangling the historical reality of the *Legenda* from the popular myths and misconceptions that have grown up around it. My work is also introductory in the sense that it is intended to encourage and facilitate future studies of the *Legenda,* rather than to make them unnecessary. Since my research has been confined almost entirely to printed sources, and indeed to printed sources mentioned by earlier investigators, it obviously represents no more than a bare start on the kind of modern scholarship the subject deserves. I have simply reexamined the documents in the case and attempted by showing their implications to banish the myths and point out some promising directions for further study.

A few editorial decisions need to be explained at the outset. For the sake of readability, virtually all the quotations in the text itself are given in English. I have borrowed from previously published translations whenever I found them exact enough for my purposes, but for most of the principal sources—including the *Legenda* itself—it was necessary to produce English versions of my own. Readers can easily check the accuracy of my translations by consulting the endnotes, which give the original versions of the Latin and Italian quotations and all but the very simplest of the French ones. With regard to proper names, I have used the most familiar forms—some of them anglicized, some not. Thus my central character is called Jacobus de Voragine, as he has been for centuries, rather than James of Varazze or even Jacopo da Varagine, which is probably closer to the authentic form. For Biblical references I have used the Clementine Vulgate and the Douay-Rheims translation.

It is a pleasure to acknowledge all the help I have received in the course of this project. The Graduate School of the University of Wisconsin sponsored the first stages of my research, in the summers of 1978 and 1979, and a year-long fellowship at the Institute for Research in the Humanities provided the leisure and the intellectual climate I needed to pull things together and write the first draft. Giles Constable and Jerome Taylor were both kind enough to listen and give advice as my ideas took shape. Robert Kingdon took the time to answer numerous questions on post-medieval church history. Standish Henning read an early draft of one chapter I was particularly uncertain about. A. N. Doane, E. Catherine Dunn, Douglas Kelly, Fannie LeMoine, Eric Rothstein, and Donald Rowe read the entire typescript, at various stages, and suggested ways of improving it. George Goebel made transcriptions for me from two medieval manuscripts, one of them so worn as to be almost unreadable on the microfilm; and if my translations from Latin are acceptable, he and Matthew Hogan deserve most of the credit. I am also indebted to Linda Sokolowski, who cheerfully tackled the problem of translating some purplish Italian prose; to Patricia Stirnemann, who went repeatedly to the Bibliothèque Nationale in Paris to get microfilms I needed; to Richard Kieckhefer, who directed me to some important sources I would otherwise have missed; to Dee Briley, who patiently typed the manuscript submitted to the Press; and to a host of wonderfully helpful librarians, most notably those of the Inter-Library Loan service at the University of Wisconsin, the Vatican Film Library in Saint Louis, the Marquand Library of Art and Archaeology at Princeton, and the rare book departments at Harvard, the New York Public Library, Notre Dame, and the University of Virginia. Special thanks are due to my careful and perceptive editors, Betty Steinberg and Carolyn Moser; to the dear colleagues and friends who provided moral support all along the way; to Matthew, Kent, and Martin, who helped with proofreading and other chores at the end; and especially to my husband, Fred, who not only cheered me on but also sacrificed a great deal of his own time to get this book done.

The *Legenda aurea*

Introduction

It is entitled the *Golden Legend*; but how justly do others call it the *Iron Legend*, others, the *Leaden*, others, the *Legend* of *Glass* or *Straw*! In it good is confused with bad, and truth with fables.

Casimir Oudin, 1722

Even from the perspective of twentieth-century America, where a book can sell millions of copies before it fades from the scene, there is something awesome about the rise and fall of the *Legenda aurea*. This thirteenth-century work about the saints and celebrations of the church, compiled by the Dominican friar Jacobus de Voragine, was not just a popular book in our sense; it was almost a cultural institution. By the time the first printing presses were established in Europe, the *Legenda* had already been something of a best-seller for 175 years. There is doubtless some exaggeration in the old claim that late-medieval scribes produced more copies of the *Legenda* than of any other book except the Bible, but the manuscripts which have survived until our own time leave no doubt about its dominant position in a very popular genre. A number of abridged legendaries were compiled in the thirteenth and fourteenth centuries; and two of the earliest ones, the *Abbreviatio in gestis et miraculis sanctorum* attributed to Jean de Mailly and the *Epilogus in gesta sanctorum* by Bartholomew of Trent, achieved a good deal of currency, as attested by the survival in each case of at least twenty manuscripts of varied provenance.[1] But the success of these works, the *Legenda*'s predecessors and closest rivals in the genre, is completely overshadowed by the massive success of the *Legenda* itself. Manuscripts of Jacobus's Latin text are still so common that modern catalogers have

3

found some 55 of them in the public libraries of Paris alone, 27 at Oxford, 46 in the Staatsbibliothek at Munich, and so on. All told, over 800 extant manuscripts containing all or part of the Latin *Legenda* have been identified within the last century,[2] and the Latin text is just the first of its numerous incarnations.

As impressive as the number of Latin manuscripts is the multiplicity of forms in which the *Legenda* flourished. By the end of the Middle Ages the influence of the original text had been supplemented by that of condensed Latin versions, expanded ones containing material on dozens of additional saints, and an extraordinary variety of offshoots in the vernacular. To cite the languages into which the *Legenda* is known to have been translated or adapted—French, Spanish, Italian, Provençal, English, Dutch, High and Low German, Bohemian—is just to scratch the surface of the subject, for there was not just one version per language. In French, for example, the version by Jean de Vignay in the second quarter of the fourteenth century seems to have been just the best-known of a long series of medieval translations.[3] In English there were only two full translations, the anonymous prose version of ca. 1438 and Caxton's more famous one some forty-five years later; but among the less obvious progeny of the *Legenda* must be included such earlier works as Mirk's *Festial,* Chaucer's Tale of the Second Nun, and significant portions of several popular verse legendaries.[4]

With the advent of printing in the second half of the fifteenth century, the status of the *Legenda* becomes easier to document. The popular success of Caxton's version, which went through nine editions between 1483 and 1527, is almost too well-known to need mentioning. The noteworthy fact is that the experience of the *Legenda*'s publishers in England was just a small echo of what happened on the Continent. For a time Jacobus's book was a staple of printing houses almost everywhere in Western Europe. By one careful reckoning, that of Robert F. Seybolt, the thirty years between 1470 and 1500 saw the publication of at least 156 editions of the *Legenda,* and perhaps as many as 173; the more conservative figure, omitting questionable identifications, includes 87 Latin editions and 69 vernacular ones: 10 Italian, 17 French, 10 Dutch, 18 High German, 7 Low German, and 3 Bohemian, as well as the 4 earliest editions of Caxton's English version.[5] Seybolt notes that the comparative figures for printed Bibles before 1501 are just 128 editions all told: 94 in Latin, 4 in Hebrew, and 30 in vernacular translations.[6]

Seybolt did not go on to survey the evidence for the *Legenda*'s fall from this pinnacle of success, in the course of the sixteenth century; but one can derive a meaningful, if rough, calculation of its shifting fortunes from the dates of the printed editions held by the British Library, the

Bibliothèque Nationale, and the American libraries surveyed for the *National Union Catalog*. Using this method, one finds 72 different Latin editions for the years between 1470 and 1500, and 49 translations. The figures are naturally lower than Seybolt's; but the geographical distribution of the editions is similar to that in his lists, and there is at least one representative of each of the seven vernacular versions he cites. For the next thirty-year period (1500-30), one finds considerably fewer editions: 21 in Latin and 28 in the various vernaculars.[7] Thereafter the decline becomes very dramatic indeed. For the years between 1531 and 1560 just 13 editions are attested—7 in Latin, 4 in French, and 2 in Italian; for the next forty-five years, just 5, all in Italian and all printed in Venice. And then, with the Italian edition of 1613, the publishing history of the *Legenda* comes to a stop. Only one new edition seems to have been issued, in any language, during the next 230 years.[8]

In the past century and a half, the *Legenda* has enjoyed a considerable revival. Many of the medieval versions have been republished, and new translations have appeared in French, German, Spanish, Italian, English, Dutch, and Polish. Some authorities have hailed Jacobus's work as a forgotten classic of popular devotional literature; others have described it more soberly as a characteristic expression of the medieval mentality. But there has been wide consensus on two points. The *Legenda* has been almost universally regarded as a kind of *summa hagiographiae,* a book presenting the essence of what medieval people knew, or thought they knew, about the saints. And its spectacular fall from esteem during the Renaissance has been explained in effect as a mistake, the result of critics' prejudices or reformers' zeal. The two premises are virtually inseparable, and together they sound so plausible that they have been accepted without much scrutiny. To probe their foundations, however, is to discover that they rest on illusions and half-truths instead of solid facts. The real story behind the rise, reign, and fall of the *Legenda* seems to have been much more complex than the version modern readers have heard, and more instructive as well. The goal of the present study is to reconstruct at least the general outlines of that story, thus correcting the major misconceptions about this famous medieval book and providing a more accurate picture of its literary and historical significance.

Recovering the truth about the *Legenda* is not a simple matter, of course. The complexities of the case are reflected in the very structure of my argument, as well as in its limitations of scope. Of necessity, I begin with the questions on which the evidence is clearest and most accessible, rather than with those that come first in terms of chronology, and try as the argument proceeds to resolve more difficult questions by applying my findings on the easier ones. Thus the argument bears little resemblance to a complete, neatly ordered history of the *Legenda*. It consists instead of three large, interconnected parts which proceed more or less backwards in time, and whose general logic is worth emphasizing at the outset.

The purpose of Part I is to discover the real import of the Renaissance reaction against the *Legenda*. As my first chapter demonstrates, the modern version of this story is not history but a sort of pious legend which has rehabilitated the *Legenda*'s reputation at the expense of its Renaissance critics and has obscured most of the crucial facts in the process. The second chapter weighs the historical evidence on the book's fall from esteem, attempting above all to establish the identities and credentials of its principal opponents. The third chapter, which examines the actual testimony of these early witnesses, lays the essential groundwork for my own reappraisal of Jacobus's book. Besides clarifying the nature of the old charges against the *Legenda,* this chapter is designed to rediscover what Jacobus's early critics knew about the evaluation of hagiographical sources. As commentators on the genre, these witnesses naturally have certain limitations. But they begin with the signal advantage of having lived and written while the medieval tradition in hagiography—and the issues it raised—were very much alive; and their testimony, when combined with that of recent historians who have reexamined the cult of the saints, yields criteria for saints' legends that are both realistic and surprisingly universal. The same kinds of themes and patterns that had central importance for late-Roman participants in the festivals of the saints seem to have retained their special value, if not their precise shades of meaning, throughout the Middle Ages; and they are reaffirmed not only by sixteenth-century critics of the *Legenda* but also by the book's most prominent twentieth-century defenders. What emerges from my third chapter, then, is a broad historical consensus on the qualities a saint's legend ought to have.

Part II explores the differences between the life of Benedict in the *Dialogues* of Gregory the Great and Jacobus's treatment of the same legend. Gregory's work provides a logical standard of comparison for a number of reasons, including the fact that it was highly recommended by the same Renaissance critics who condemned the *Legenda;* and the contrasts between the two works turn out to be very illuminating indeed. My fourth and fifth chapters demonstrate in essence that Gregory's account of Benedict deserves its perennial reputation as a classic and that Jacobus radically impoverished it in his abridged version, almost systematically removing the qualities valued by all our expert witnesses on hagiography. An examination of Jacobus's surviving sermons on Benedict and other important saints, in Chapter 6, confirms that this departure from tradition was no accident; instead of preserving the essential content of the old legends, Jacobus seems to have been using them for some special purpose or purposes.

Part III is designed to shed some additional light on the problems raised by Jacobus's treatment of the Benedict legend. Since it makes no systematic attempt to demonstrate that the patterns of selectivity in the Benedict chapter typify the *Legenda* as a whole, I ought perhaps to explain that I have studied some forty chapters of Jacobus's book, comparing each of them with at least one probable source, and have found the presence of those patterns in nearly every one of them. Detailed accounts of my findings on two cases, those of Cecilia and Martin of Tours, can be read elsewhere.[9] Here I have focused on three legends—those of Ambrose, Augustine, and Dominic—whose treatment in the *Legenda* is particularly illuminating. I chose them primarily because these three saints were of special significance to Jacobus himself—Augustine, manifestly his favorite theologian; Ambrose, the supposed author of the Milanese liturgy he repeatedly quotes in the *Legenda;* Dominic, the founder and exemplar of his religious order—and because he handles the sources concerning them with unusual thoroughness and care. For the purpose of proving Jacobus's consistency, these are the hardest cases, the chapters which should come closest to preserving the kinds of essential content he omits elsewhere. And for the larger purpose of understanding the human logic and historical circumstances behind the peculiar selectivity of the *Legenda,* these relatively personal chapters of the book are indispensable.

It is obviously not possible in a study of this scope to give a definitive answer to any of the questions raised by the *Legenda.* I hope simply to make it evident that Jacobus's famous book deserves a different kind of attention than it has generally received in this century. The book is not, in fact, a splendid representative of its genre, or even a very adequate one. This point has some importance even for beginners in the study of medieval literature or church history, since they are often encouraged to rely on the *Legenda* as a handy substitute for all the older works about the saints. If such students are not to read the real classics of hagiography, they ought at least to know that such works are significantly better than the *Legenda*—richer and more believable in human terms, more balanced and humane in their teaching. For more advanced students of the Middle Ages, on the other hand, the very omissions and biases which lessen the literary value of the *Legenda* make it worth pondering as a historical phenomenon. As I attempt to show in

Part III, those omissions and biases seem to make sense in terms of the particular problems that confronted a friar like Jacobus around the year 1260. But what is one to make of the book's prodigious success in the next two centuries? Exactly who used it, and for what purposes? Was its character changed appreciably, either for better or worse, when it was enlarged, translated, or otherwise adapted for particular audiences? And what kind of effect did it actually have on the generations of layfolk who must have been taught from its pages? To answer such questions with any certainty will require an enormous amount of further research, including a study of the evidence in the hundreds of *Legenda* manuscripts that have survived. But I hope to persuade some historians of the period that the answers are worth finding.

I. The Meaning
of the Renaissance Verdict

1
The Modern Legend
of the *Legenda aurea*

I have submysed myself to translate into englysshe the legende
of sayntes, which is callyd legenda aurea in latyn, that is to say
the golden legende. For in lyke wyse as gold is most noble
above al other metalles, in lyke wyse is thys legende holden
moost noble above al other werkys.

William Caxton, 1483

The modern notion of the *Legenda aurea* as an exemplary piece of
medieval piety or learning, or both, has surprisingly little behind it.
There is Caxton's statement, of course, and other evidence of the book's
popularity in the Middle Ages. But the opposing verdict from the
Renaissance has been cancelled out by the misinterpretation or oversimplification of what a few later authorities actually said on the matter.

The key document in the whole case for the *Legenda*'s rehabilitation is
a prominent passage in the first volume of the *Acta Sanctorum* (1643).[1]
Here, in the general preface introducing the Bollandists' monumental
work of hagiographical scholarship, the eminent John Bolland himself
paused to defend the *Legenda* against its critics—and especially against
two Christian humanists of the previous century, Georg Witzel and Juan
Luis Vives. It is obvious, when one reads the argument as a whole, that
Bolland did not regard the *Legenda* as a particularly valuable work of its
kind. For example, he responds with some heat to Witzel's contention
that many monastic libraries contained no other source on the history of
the saints: "And how false is that claim, that in the average monastery
libraries there exist no histories of the saints but this *Legend!* On the
contrary, there is no ancient monastery to be found—provided it has
escaped the fury of the heretics of this age—in which there are not several
excellent volumes of the deeds of saints, and many of them written in an

early hand."[2] By insisting on the antiquity and excellence of the other sources held by monasteries, Bolland concedes in effect that Jacobus's compilation would be a poor substitute. In the next few lines he concedes another point, agreeing with Witzel that the *Speculum* of Vincent of Beauvais is preferable to the *Legenda*.[3] But the relative merit of Jacobus's work is not the important issue, so far as Bolland is concerned. What he is really defending, throughout this section of his preface, is the respectability of the saint's legend as an object of scholarly attention. Hence his emphasis on the many ancient and authoritative manuscripts preserved in those monastic libraries. And hence, more centrally, his emphasis on Jacobus's own credentials as a man of learning. Characterizing him as a very learned and holy professor of theology, Bolland attempts at the outset to dissociate him from the most obvious peculiarity of the *Legenda,* the fanciful etymologies of the saints' names that preface many chapters.[4] After citing a few examples, Bolland goes on to explain that such material is objectionable because it causes learned men to ridicule and despise the lives of the saints themselves: "I pass over other things no less absurd, which ignorant men used to repeat continually from the pulpit; and thus, exciting the disgust and laughter of the learned, they brought both themselves and the stories of the saints into the greatest contempt."[5]

This is the context within which Bolland takes up the harsh judgments meted out against the *Legenda* by Witzel and Vives. The two humanists are used to exemplify learned men who look down on hagiography,[6] and Bolland sets himself to show that their opinions are founded on insufficient knowledge. He is particularly severe with Witzel, whose brief and rather cryptic comments on Jacobus, taken from the preface to the *Hagiologium,* he subjects to a good deal of ridicule. That Witzel compared Jacobus unfavorably with one "Petrus Lombardus, qui post Voraginem scriptitavit," leads Bolland to wonder loftily whether the Peter whom Witzel mistook for a late-medieval hagiographer was the Peter Lombard of the *Sentences,* who wrote no history and died 140 years before Jacobus, or Peter Comestor, whose *Scholastic History* long predates the *Legenda* and mostly covers different subject matter.[7] Witzel's complaint that the *Legenda* had been preferred to the acts of the saints in Eusebius's *Ecclesiastical History* is also met with scornful incomprehension.[8] Only when he turns to the charge that Jacobus had given himself up to fables ("Mythologiae ille impensius indulget") does Bolland dignify Witzel's attack with a substantive response. To make such a charge, he suggests, is to expose one's ignorance about the traditions behind the *Legenda;* he himself has confidence that Jacobus was a faithful historian, not an innovator: "But where, my dear Witzel, does Jacobus indulge in fables? I certainly do not endorse everything he wrote; I have no doubt, however, that he followed old sources, and I know for a fact that many of his stories agree with old and genuine ones, though I have not read through them all; there is no need, when I have found the source, to follow the streams."9 Lest the lesson be missed, Bolland goes on to underline it. The credibility of authors like Jacobus cannot fairly be judged except by comparing their work with the sources—a basic principle which, he implies, has not been grasped by most recent critics of the *Legenda:* "I estimate the trust to be put in abbreviators and paraphrasers by comparing their writings with those of earlier writers. I think therefore that the criticisms of the moderns are unjust, for the most part, when they knock the *Legenda* about."10

When Bolland turns to the condemnation of the *Legenda* as bad history in Vives' *De disciplinis,* his tone moderates noticeably, but the general line of the argument remains the same. He expresses wonder that such a man as Vives should have condemned poor Jacobus for what he himself obviously regards as inaccuracies routinely encountered elsewhere: "I have always valued Luis Vives very highly, as a man of singular learning, seriousness, and prudence, and I entirely agree with him that the preeminent deeds of the saints ought to have been more accurately committed to writing than is usually the case. I am frankly amazed that such a serious and reasonable man should go so far in his abuse of the author of the *Legenda* as to call that wise and holy man 'leaden-hearted and iron-mouthed.'"11 The famous jest that the *Legenda,* far from being golden, was the work of a man with a leaden heart and an iron mouth, Bolland ventures, was perhaps not originated by Vives at all but by his (and Witzel's) mentor Erasmus, whom Bolland characterizes as a critic impossible to please.12 His discussion of the *Legenda*'s attackers ends with the suggestions that Erasmus often criticized things he did not understand ("hoc etiam ridiculus quod ea arroserit saepe quae nec intelligebat nec didicerat") and that he and his followers might have underestimated both Jacobus's scholarly merits and his piety because of the relative inelegance of his Latin style.13

Bolland's delicately nuanced reply to the critics of the *Legenda* has been so often misinterpreted that there is good reason to emphasize what he does not say in its defense. Nowhere does he suggest that Jacobus's work ought to be judged by any other standard than that of fidelity to good sources; that is the standard he himself uses, rendering the verdict that it is generally respectable but inferior to at least one other compilation from the same century. Bolland does not claim, however, to have made any systematic investigation of the matter; in fact, his response to Witzel includes a telling disclaimer on this very point ("I have not read through [all his stories]; there is no need, when I have found the source, to follow the streams''). Nor does he pretend to understand, much less to refute, most of what Witzel and Vives were trying to say about Jacobus's work. For Bolland seems to have had no particular interest in the *Legenda,* save as a symbolic victim of contempt from supposedly knowledgeable men. His own major research, and that of the society that bears his name, is directed elsewhere: toward discovering the earliest and most authentic versions of the stories told about the saints, dispelling confusion about their origins, and appraising their degree of validity as historical documents. Derivative collections like the *Legenda* are of little use in such a program. If their compilers tend to follow reliable sources and to preserve the historical element found in them, Bolland implies, they have achieved as much as can reasonably be expected. The true scholar will not rely on them, since better sources are available; but neither will he condemn them without a full and fair examination of the evidence.

For the next two and a half centuries the most prominent defenders of Jacobus were the historians of his own religious order, who tended to modify Bolland's argument in a very interesting way. The commentary in the first volume of Echard and Quétif's *Scriptores Ordinis Praedicatorum* (1719) lays out the basic positions that would become standard in Dominican sources.[14] Certain critics of the *Legenda* are implied to have gone too far; Adrien Baillet is cited as the prime offender, although Echard also presents two colorful stories about Renaissance critics who publicly recanted their attacks. The previous popularity of the book is emphasized, with the conclusion that it was very much in tune with what medieval audiences liked.[15] But Echard's own estimate of the *Legenda* is revealed by the fact that he devotes very little attention to its defense, striving instead to dissociate it from Jacobus. Extending the argument Bolland used against Witzel, Echard insists that Jacobus was not really the author of the *Legenda* at all but only the collector and editor of earlier sources, for whose lapses he cannot justly be blamed:

Furthermore, a fair argument in Jacobus's defense is that at which he hints himself: that he did not write these saints' lives but, as he said himself, compiled them; that is, he collected lives which had been written long ago by various authors and scattered in their various works, arranged them in order, supplemented them from the sacred histories then in favor, and published them with his own comments added here and there. . . . In short, Jacobus collected the deeds of the saints as they were current in his day, arranged them in the order of the calendar, and published them. If there are any fables among them, he is not to be considered their originator.[16]

It is not hard to understand why Echard and the Dominican historians who followed him did not try to defend the *Legenda* as Bolland had. For one thing, they knew that Vives was not the only authority of unquestionable eminence who had found the book seriously flawed. Among the critics whom Echard could identify, in fact, were several Dominican luminaries of greater magnitude than Jacobus.[17] But even if Echard and his successors had been inclined to dismiss the views of such authorities, as they manifestly were not, they had more particular reasons for taking a dim view of the *Legenda*. Because of his exemplary conduct as archbishop of Genoa, Jacobus had acquired a considerable reputation for holiness, and his name was still revered, both in the Order of Preachers and at his birthplace, the town of Varazze near Genoa. Indeed, there are some indications that he had already begun to receive the title and honors due to those officially beatified by the church.[18] The problem, of course, was that the fame—or notoriety—of the *Legenda* overshadowed all the achievements for which Jacobus's admirers wished him to be remembered. These facts are implicit in Echard's own discussion; and Antoine Touron, whose history of famous Dominicans presents the fullest version of the eighteenth-century argument, is quite frank about them. Although he too suggests that certain critics might have overstated the case against the *Legenda,* Touron explicitly characterizes it as the least meritorious of all Jacobus's works.[19] And the only critics whom he actually accuses of unfairness are two who had taken the *Legenda* as the measure of Jacobus's stature. Louis-Ellies Dupin had placed all of Jacobus's writings in the same category, ignoring the relative worth of his supposed Italian translation of the Bible;[20] and Adrien Baillet, who draws much more of Touron's fire, had actually contended that the *Legenda* was too reprehensible to have been written by a man of real sanctity. Hence, Touron argues, "Monsieur Baillet shows himself to be even less equitable, or less scrupulous, than Monsieur Dupin. If the latter has made light of the Works of the Archbishop of Genoa, he has not failed to recognize that the Author was quite worthy of esteem because of the purity of his life, because of his piety, above all because of his great charity. The former, on the contrary, recognizes neither virtue nor integrity nor, in the end, anything praiseworthy in a Prelate who deserved so much praise."[21]

In short, it is clear that Jacobus's eighteenth-century defenders had reason to wish the *Legenda* buried and forgotten—or at least removed from the list of his works. What they could not foresee was that the positions they took, and especially their insistence on its total lack of originality, would actually feed the legend which has drawn readers back to it.

After 1816, when Pope Pius VII finally gave official sanction to the veneration of Jacobus, it became almost inevitable that an aura of blessedness would fall over the *Legenda*. This development seems not to have been encouraged by his fellow Dominicans; indeed, they continued to insist on the distinction between his personal merits and the caliber of his most famous book. Thus, for example, a standard Dominican legendary from the end of the nineteenth century still relegates the *Legenda* to a subordinate place among the writings of "le bienheureux Jacques" and closely echoes Echard's unenthusiastic conclusions about its history and general character.[22] Even Filippo Anfossi, whose hagiographical biography of Jacobus was published at Genoa in the first flush of excitement surrounding the beatification, could not quite bring himself to portray the *Legenda* as a creditable achievement. Anfossi goes much further than other spokesmen for the order in praising the excellence of Jacobus's intentions and his dedicated labor as a compiler, and also in casting aspersions on the motives of the book's best-known critics;[23] but whenever he confronts the question of its actual worth, he betrays his essential agreement with Touron and Echard. Most telling is his concluding statement, which cites a series of extenuating factors that serve, in effect, to condemn the *Legenda* even as they excuse Jacobus:

Consequently, if one adds to what has already been said that the aim of Blessed Jacopo da Varagine was not to study the Acts of the Saints and to distinguish the true from the false, but solely to unite in one corpus whatever he had found in other Writers that could be a guide to devotion and to piety; and if to this are added the prejudices of his time and the inclinations of the People for whom he was writing; and if one observes finally that, in the midst of very important business which he had to discharge and which oppressed him from every side, he did not have leisure or liberty enough to weigh everything on the balance of a more rigorous criticism, anyone sees how unjust and unreasonable is the censure which they—these excessively harsh Critics—direct against him and his *Legenda*.[24]

So far as I have been able to discover, the completed legend about the *Legenda* and its critics did not appear in print until the beginning of our own century. Bits of it, of course, were abroad much earlier: Jacobus had been treated unfairly by later scholars; he was a man of saintly character; he followed his sources with utter faithfulness; his work was perfectly in tune with the popular taste of his own era. Once Anfossi had added dramatic coloration to the story, the only missing ingredient was the kind of Romantic value system which could draw the conclusion that popular instinct, and especially medieval popular instinct, was more valid than scholarship. The first hint of this new perspective on the

Legenda was given in 1843, when Gustave Brunet published a modern French translation—the first edition in any language for over 150 years—with a preface that recommended the book as "l'expression la plus naïve et la plus sincère" of a faith almost lost in his own skeptical age.[25] But the real milestone seems to have been passed in 1898, with a prominent and wonderfully misleading tribute to the *Legenda* in Emile Mâle's *L'art religieux du XIIIe siècle en France*.[26]

A careful reading of Mâle's chapter on hagiographical sources reveals that he used *Légende dorée* almost as a generic term. Although Mâle repeatedly suggests that the particular book by Jacobus de Voragine provides all the background an art historian needs in order to understand "nearly all the bas-reliefs and [cathedral] windows which deal with legends," a strikingly large proportion of the legends he uses as examples are not to be found in the *Legenda* at all. This inconsistency is eventually acknowledged in a footnote, with the explanation that "this name *Golden Legend* was for us chiefly a convenient title to denote all the collections of saints' lives in use during the Middle Ages."[27] When Mâle undertakes to defend the *Legenda* against its critics, then, he is really defending medieval hagiography as a whole; indeed, he insists that the two are inseparable: "The attack made on Jacobus de Voragine by scholars of the seventeenth century misses its mark. The *Golden Legend,* which they accused of being a 'legend of lead,' was not the work of a man but of the whole of Christendom. . . . To condemn Jacobus de Voragine is to condemn all the ancient lectionaries, and with them the clergy who read them and the faithful who listened."

Here we see what a Romantic imagination could make of the old Dominican argument about Jacobus's total lack of originality. Indeed, the *Legenda,* as Mâle portrays it, is supremely a book "of the people." When he sets out to explain its popular appeal, he begins by democratizing its very contents: "In that great company deemed worthy to sit at the right hand of God there were shepherds, cattle-drovers, carters, serving men of all kinds, and the lives of these humble Christians showed the seriousness and the depth of which all human life is capable. For the student in the Middle Ages it was a rich storehouse of wisdom. To the simplest it offered a model after which to fashion his life." In truth, of course, there is a noticeable dearth of saintly shepherds, serving men, and the like in the whole body of ancient and medieval hagiography, except perhaps among the martyrs. And one would be hard pressed to find even a single example of each occupation in the *Legenda* itself. Despite such sentimental excesses, however—or perhaps because of them—Mâle's account of the *Legenda* seems to have provided much of the impetus for the rehabilitation of this book in our own century.

Within five years of Mâle's first edition, there was a sudden upsurge of sympathetic interest in the *Legenda,* especially in France. The phenomenon is evident in the nearly simultaneous publication, in 1902-3, of five major tributes to Jacobus and his book: a hagiographical biography of Jacobus, lengthy and appreciative articles on the *Legenda* by André Baudrillart and J.-C. Broussolle, and new French translations by J.-B. M. Roze and Teodor de Wyzewa.[28] These tributes all have recourse, in varying degrees, to the same legend whose prehistory we have been tracing, a legend which now beatifies the book and discredits all the scholars who found it wanting. These writers attempt, moreover, as Mâle did not, to distinguish Jacobus's book from all the books that preceded it, demonstrating its unique merits. Perhaps the fullest expression of the completed legend, and certainly the most influential, is that found in Wyzewa's preface.

As Wyzewa presents it, the *Legenda*'s descent toward oblivion during the Renaissance is a historical tragedy with a very simple explanation. Wyzewa characterizes the book as a pioneering attempt to make religious knowledge directly accessible to the laity: "Its aim is to bring forth from monastic libraries the treasures of sacred truth which centuries of study and discussion had amassed there, and to give these treasures the simplest and clearest form possible, and at the same time the most engaging—in order to make them accessible to simple and ardent souls, who immediately endeavored in a thousand ways to show the surpassing joy with which they received them" (p. 18).[29] In short, the *Legenda* was designed for "the people" (a concept to which Wyzewa, like Mâle, gives the full Romantic coloration), and the people not only cherished it for centuries but underwent a profound spiritual awakening under its influence:

From the thirteenth to the sixteenth century, the *Legenda aurea* remained, above all, the people's book.

And I should add that there is perhaps no other book which has had a more profound, or a more beneficial, effect on the people. For the "small" book by the blessed Jacobus de Voragine . . . was during these three centuries an inexhaustible wellspring of the Christian ideal. By making religion more artless, more popular, and more vivid, he very nearly invested it with a new power. (P. 19)[30]

The Renaissance scholars who attacked the *Legenda* can enter this scenario only as villains or, at best, as sadly misguided men; they took the *Legenda* away from the people, Wyzewa suggests, because they themselves were incapable of appreciating it. Here Bolland's response to the followers of Erasmus becomes the central piece of evidence. Arguing that Jacobus is not to be held responsible for historical inaccuracies in his work, Wyzewa attributes to Bolland a rather more sweeping testimonial on this point than Bolland actually gave: "As Bolland very wisely says, nothing is more unjust than to consider Jacobus de Voragine responsible for assertions which he borrowed in every case from earlier works, doing his best to verify them whenever he could or announcing to us the doubts they raised in him" (p. 20).[31]

For Wyzewa, however, the key statement by Bolland was obviously the little riposte that Erasmus often criticized things he did not understand. Thus Wyzewa suggests that the Renaissance humanists who poked fun at Jacobus's simple Latin had failed to understand its purposes.[32] As for scholars who blamed Jacobus because his accounts were at variance with the sources they had, Wyzewa uses Bolland's riposte explicitly to condemn them all of ignorance.[33] Finally, and most dramatically, Wyzewa charges that scholars like Vives criticized the *Legenda* because they had lost the ability to understand the true spirit of Catholicism: Vives and his successors "did not understand, indeed, that errors like those which they pointed out in the *Legenda aurea* had by no means the same importance for a Catholic reader as for that Calvinist clergyman who haunted their own dreams" (p. 21).[34] Wyzewa goes on to assert that the Renaissance attacks on the *Legenda* are to be understood, in large part, as attacks on certain tenets of the Catholic faith: the presence of the Holy Spirit with the church (p. 21), the ability of God to work miracles through even the humblest of images and the least authentic of relics (pp. 21-22), the compassion of God and his saints toward the sinful human race (pp. 22-23). As for its long neglect even by good Catholics, Wyzewa explains that Jacobus's book fell victim to a general movement, in the seventeenth century, toward a less positive and reassuring version of Christianity:

Given the influence of Protestantism and Jansenism, many excellent Catholics at that time considered it unwise to teach the people too much about the goodness of God. . . . The philosophers insisted on the fundamental difference between divine and human goodness. And in a general way they all strove more to frighten people than to reassure them. Under these circumstances, would the *Legenda aurea* perhaps have seemed to them too comforting—that is, designed to give us too imprecise an idea of eternal justice? (P. 23)[35]

Wyzewa's account of the rise and fall of the *Legenda* is obviously calculated to win the sympathetic attention of a general audience, and it has been highly successful in that regard. In fact, there seem to have been almost as many editions of the *Legenda* in French during the twentieth century as in all other modern languages put together;[36] and the most popular French version, by a wide margin, has been Wyzewa's own. The competing French translations by Brunet and Roze, each prefaced by comments of a more restrained and scholarly character, were reissued at least three times and once, respectively, between 1902 and 1970. Wyzewa's version, on the other hand, was reprinted at least twelve times—in 1905, 1909, 1910, 1911, 1913, 1917, 1923, 1925, 1929, 1935, 1942, and 1960. Far more surprising is the extent to which Wyzewa's undocumented and obviously romanticized conclusions about the *Legenda* have won acceptance in the scholarly world. Ernest C. Richardson, a prolific American bibliographer who in 1888 had published a rather specialized and dispassionate article on the *Legenda* as the possible source of certain motifs in later literature,[37] seems to have been among the first converts. Richardson's second article, in 1903, which cites Wyzewa among its sources, characterizes the *Legenda* as a book admirably designed to promote faith and charity in its readers, and exhibits a new fascination with Jacobus's career as a teacher of the people[38]—a topic Richardson would pursue, devoting his spare time to historical research on Jacobus, for more than three decades thereafter. But Richardson, for all his enthusiasm, was too obviously an amateur in the field to confer real intellectual respectability on the new legend. The scholar whose verdict mattered was Hippolyte Delehaye, the principal spokesman for the Bollandists in the earlier twentieth century and an immensely respected authority on hagiography.

Delehaye's initial reactions to the work of Wyzewa and Richardson and the other new admirers of the *Legenda,* as preserved in two review articles in the *Analecta Bollandiana* in 1903 and 1904, are somewhat puzzling at first sight. Delehaye takes Wyzewa to task on a few minor points, gently chiding him for overestimating Jacobus's knowledge and for taking some of his stories on faith rather than inquiring into the reliability of his sources.[39] But the only severe judgments in these review articles are directed against the two authors who had actually attempted such an inquiry. Abbé Roze's "recherches sur les sources" are dismissed as laughable;[40] and Delehaye shows even less patience with the ignorance of an anonymous writer for an Anglican periodical who had attempted to evaluate the *Legenda* by comparing it with sober biographies of the saints and with the Bible, and had concluded that it could only have been beloved in an age of chaos and superstition.[41] Delehaye's relatively indulgent response to Wyzewa can be understood in part as the fatherly reaction of a specialist to a naive but enthusiastic amateur in his field. But other factors were involved as well.

To Delehaye, the line of argument summed up in Wyzewa's preface seems to have presented itself as a fine solution to an old problem. If the public was rediscovering the *Legenda,* the book—and with it, medieval hagiography in general—would almost inevitably become a target of ridicule again in some circles. Indeed, the process was already underway, as indicated by the Anglican critique in 1903.[42] Although Delehaye indicated more than once that he himself considered the *Legenda* a bit comical, he clearly shared the view of his predecessor Bolland that less well-informed readers ought not to laugh at Jacobus's work.[43] Delehaye himself, however, had weightier problems on his mind than the public reputation of the *Legenda.* The nature and magnitude of his scholarly activity during this period is suggested by the contents of the *Analecta* itself. For the 1903 volume alone he prepared editions of three substantial Greek hagiographical texts; an article evaluating the credibility of another one (the verdict was negative); a note on a fragmentary text found at Jerusalem; and reviews of fully 120 books and articles on topics including early church history, the cult of the Virgin, Christian art, archeology, and ecclesiastical history in various Italian cities, as well as hagiography per se. His contributions to the 1904 volume are similarly massive, and his principal research is still focused on Greek texts.

Under the circumstances, it is not surprising that Delehaye should welcome the assistance of the amateurs who had arisen to defend the *Legenda*—even if he embraced their all-purpose answer to critics without a great deal of analysis. And this, apparently, is just what he did. In the 1903 review article he so warms to Wyzewa's point of view that he actually gives voice to the dictum that the *Legenda* can be understood only by those who suspend their critical faculties:

Those who approach the *Legenda aurea* with the biases of a historian and critic will find themselves disconcerted from the start and will be liable to vent their ill humor in the same way as Vives, Melchior Cano, Launoy, and many others who have undertaken to judge it from a false vantage point.

This is what Monsieur de Wyzewa seems to have understood perfectly. (P. 81)[44]

He seems not to have noticed that such a rule contradicts both the explicit advice of Bolland and the general principles on which his own life's work is based. In the 1904 article he goes further yet, declaring in effect that an enthusiastic response to the *Legenda* proves that one has read it properly; an unfavorable one, the reverse.[45] And, casting aside his own customary reserve, Delehaye proceeds warmly to endorse almost everything Richardson, Baudrillart, and Broussolle (and Wyzewa before them) had said about the excellence of the *Legenda* as a popular devotional book, designed to foster piety and virtue in its readers.

Delehaye's final and best-known contribution to the debate over the *Legenda* appeared the next year, in a sort of postscript to his famous introduction to the study of saints' legends, *Les légendes hagiographiques*. In the last few pages of a book which has emphasized the preponderance of fiction—and rather crude fiction, at that—in the genre as a whole, and which has carefully demonstrated the kind of rigorous criticism to which the historian must subject the documents, Delehaye suddenly adopts a more indulgent perspective. Despite all their defects, he argues, the legends and their authors ought not to be despised. When he introduces the *Legenda aurea* as the classic case in point, both the general strategy and the focus on Vives suggest that he is recalling Bolland's treatment of the matter: "The *Golden Legend* accurately sums up the hagiographical work of the Middle Ages; yet for a long time it was treated with high disdain, and scholars were very hard on the good James of Voragine. 'The man who wrote the Legend,' declared Luis Vivès, 'had an iron mouth and a heart of lead.'"[46] In this final defense Delehaye leaves no doubt that for him, as for Bolland long before, the primary importance of the *Legenda* is symbolic. In fact, Jacobus's book itself disappears as the argument proceeds, becoming incorporated into a larger entity called "legend." Delehaye's account of the *Legenda's* own merits also represents a noticeable retreat from the enthusiastic stand he had taken in the review article of the previous year: "I confess that, when reading it, it is often difficult to refrain from smiling. But it is a sympathetic and friendly smile, which does not at all disturb the religious response aroused by the picture of the goodness and heroic deeds of the saints." But the works he had reviewed so recently seem to have left their mark. Bolland used the criterion of historical accuracy and defended the *Legenda* against critics who had not adequately studied the sources; Delehaye insists instead on the new criterion of "spirit": "Certainly it is difficult to speak of this book severely enough if it be held that popular works must be judged by the standards of historical criticism. But people are beginning to see that this is an injudicious proceeding, and those who have discerned the spirit of the *Golden Legend* are careful not to speak of it disparagingly." And in the first excerpt quoted above, Delehaye offers a far more sweeping testimonial to the accord between the *Legenda* and the rest of medieval hagiography than Bolland gave. On whose research is it based? None of the new admirers of Jacobus pretended to have the necessary expertise, and there is no indication that Delehaye and his fellow Bollandists ever found the necessary time. Although Delehaye's argument leaves the impression that experts have found the *Legenda* to sum up perfectly the inspirational value, as well as the historical content, of "l'oeuvre hagiographique du moyen âge," the major authority behind this verdict seems in fact to be Wyzewa, who simply gave an imaginative interpretation to the old statements by Bolland and Echard.

Despite the relatively casual and impressionistic appearance Delehaye's statements on the *Legenda* give, when they are read in context, they have probably exerted as wide an influence as anything he ever wrote. The entry on Jacobus in the authoritative *Dictionnaire de théologie catholique,* published in 1924, echoes Delehaye's 1904 review article in its concluding paragraph on recent criticism of the *Legenda,* cites Wyzewa's preface as if it were a respectable piece of scholarship, and explicitly endorses the new view of the *Legenda:* "The book's purpose is to supply the people with lessons and models directly inspired by the gospel of Jesus Christ. If the history is not always quite exact, certainly one finds there the most authentic legacy bequeathed by twelve centuries of Christianity."[47] In the updated version of Butler's *Lives of the Saints* published a few years later, the *Legenda* is characterized as a masterpiece of inspirational literature, comparable with the King James Bible and the *Imitation of Christ,* and the whole concluding passage from *Les légendes hagiographiques* is quoted to demonstrate the errors of its critics.[48] Even the relatively recent account in the *Bibliotheca sanctorum,* which does not mention that the *Legenda* was ever attacked and gives no overt indication of familiarity with Delehaye's defense, links the book with the ideal set forth in the final lines of *Les légendes hagiographiques*—using phrases by now so commonly associated with the *Legenda* that the author may not have realized where they came from.[49]

Delehaye's position on criticism of the *Legenda* appears, moreover, to have remained the position of the Society of Bollandists.[50] In a 1943 review of J.J.A. Zuidweg's study of the *Legenda* and its sources, Delehaye's great successor Baudouin de Gaiffier explicitly reaffirmed his final answer to critics of this book:

In *Les légendes hagiographiques* Father Delehaye, hardly a man to suspect of rejecting critical judgment, . . . reproached the humanist Vives with having been too harsh concerning Jacobus de Voragine and concluded with these words, "Legend, like all poetry, can claim a higher degree of truth than history." Monsieur Zuidweg does not accept this assessment. Nonetheless, it is that of the historians who have most perceptively studied the spirit of the Middle Ages, of which the *Legenda aurea* is one of the most characteristic products.[51]

As recently as 1965, a French writer who had ventured an adverse comment on the *Legenda,* under the misapprehension that the Bollandists were on his side, was prominently chastised in the *Analecta*

Bollandiana; and the climactic piece of evidence cited against him was Delehaye's pronouncement on "the spirit of the *Golden Legend.*"[52]

More important than its dampening effect on criticism is the way Delehaye's defense of the *Legenda* has helped to discourage scholarly attention to the book and its history. Several generations of scholars, whether beginning their study of saints' legends with *Les légendes hagiographiques* or consulting the *Analecta* for more recent discoveries, have imbibed the lesson that there is nothing original or distinctive about Jacobus's book, nothing mysterious about the widely divergent reactions it has aroused—nothing, in short, to make it a worthwhile subject for investigation. It is not surprising, then, that for this most prominent late-medieval work about the saints we still have no modern edition based on the manuscripts, nothing resembling a definitive history, and very few careful studies of any kind.[53] While substantial research has been done on other hagiographical texts, even including some of the *Legenda*'s vernacular offshoots, the *Legenda* itself has largely been abandoned to general readers and to scholars in other fields who want to use a typical representative of the genre. And the legend surrounding it has gone unchallenged, uncorrected. In some quarters, indeed, the legend has become even more sentimentalized, or even more tendentious, than it was in Wyzewa's version. As it happens, some of the most striking examples are to be found in the handful of English-language books on the subject.

Readers in this country are most likely to encounter the *Legenda* in the translation by Granger Ryan and Helmut Ripperger, first published in 1941 and reprinted several times since then.[54] Even Ryan and Ripperger's text is rather misleading, since they mistranslate some passages and neglect to inform the reader when they are omitting material found in the Latin version; and their preface is a wonderful pastiche of sentimental commonplaces. Thus they characterize the *Legenda* as a work ultimately "fashioned by the mind and soul of the people" (p. x) and credit it with expressing "the wordless yearnings of our medieval forbears" (pp. xiii-xiv) while contending almost simultaneously, and with no apparent sense of contradiction, that it enlightened the medieval masses about the ideals of the New Testament (p. xiii). Jacobus is portrayed as the graciously unassuming teacher of "the humble folk, the *sancta plebs Dei*" (p. ix), and the villains of the piece are of course scholars—this time, the Erasmians who coined the "ferrei oris et plumbei cordis" jest: "The unkind witticism was repeated from generation to generation, and the result was that the *Legend* fell into disrepute, and apparently into oblivion" (p. vii). Ryan and Ripperger even quote Mâle's account of the *Legenda*'s contents, as if they had managed to translate the book without noticing any scarcity of shepherds and cattle-drovers.

The more tendentious developments of the legend tend to be less amusing. One notable example is the historical overview in the preface to a collection of excerpts from Caxton's version, published in 1914 by George V. O'Neill, a professor of English at University College, Dublin. Although O'Neill derived a large proportion of his information from Wyzewa, whose work he cites with great approbation, he omits the role of Catholic scholars like Vives and presents the decline of the *Legenda* as a simple case of religious prejudice:

Under the two-fold influence of the Renaissance and of Protestantism the vogue and influence of the *Legenda,* in all its forms, rapidly passed away. The Reformers of the sixteenth century, who destroyed the shrines of the Saints, burnt also by thousands the books and manuscripts which glorified them. During the seventeenth and eighteenth centuries the *Legenda* died quite out of general remembrance in England. Elsewhere, if it was mentioned at all by writers of the prevalent modes of thought, it was sneered at by rationalists of the 'Encyclopédie' school as a relic of folly and barbarism, while the Jansenist party in the Church were scandalized by its frequent exemplification of the Divine mercy towards sinners.[55]

Richardson's summation of his long research on Jacobus, published in 1935, presents a more moderate version of the same general thesis. Portraying the *Legenda* as "the quintessence of prereformation Catholicism," Richardson attributes its fall (though not all the attacks) to reformers whose real target was the veneration of the saints and suggests that the notoriously anti-Catholic *Faustbook* of 1587 perhaps delivered the "coup-de-grace" by making fun of the famous story of Theophilus, who was saved by the Virgin Mary despite his bargain with the devil.[56]

Once stripped of its more sentimental trappings, the prevailing modern view of the *Legenda* and its history is not implausible; it could hardly have flourished so long, or earned even tacit assent from scholars like Delehaye and Gaiffier, if it were. The problem is that it is legend— compounded in large part of the repetition, from one generation to the next, of supposed truths which no one has quite bothered to verify. The obvious irony is that parts of Bolland's answer to Witzel and Vives have loomed so large in later memory while the heart of his message has been ignored. The principles of historical scholarship do not cease to be valid when the document in question is a collection of saints' legends, or when its author is beatified. Jacobus's recent defenders have insisted that he should be judged as an educator of the laity rather than as a historian—and rightly so, I believe. But whether the issue is historical accuracy or moral and spiritual teaching, Bolland's rule still applies: the only fair and accurate way of evaluating a derivative work like the *Legenda* is actually to compare it with the sources.

When one examines the actual records bearing on the decline of the *Legenda,* as we will do in the next two chapters, another large irony emerges. For all the supposed enlightenment of our own era, the major Renaissance critics of the book seem to have been more knowledgeable on the subject, and probably less biased, than most of the modern writers who have decried—and misunderstood—the position of those earlier critics. The *Legenda* did not fall victim to Protestant influence, as has so often been asserted, but to a broadly based movement among Catholics that reached its height shortly before the Reformation. Nor were the scholarly attacks on this book dictated by an elitist disdain for works of popular edification; its leading opponents were educators who cared about such works precisely because they played—or should play—a significant role in the instruction of the faithful. It is true that these educators knew less about the development of medieval hagiography than the Bollandists would know, but they were far from being so ill-informed about the sources as one might infer from Bolland's scornful treatment of Georg Witzel. And most of them were even better placed than the Bollandists to judge the practical importance of the way those sources were handled in the *Legenda.* In short, the early opponents of Jacobus's book deserve a much more attentive hearing than they have received in recent times. If we would recognize the actual character of the *Legenda*—and thus, whether as students of medieval culture or admirers of the saints, begin to grasp the larger issues bound up with its phenomenal success in the late Middle Ages—we cannot afford to misunderstand either the explicit testimony of these witnesses or the principles for which they stood.

2
The Fall of the *Legenda* Reexamined

The *Golden Legend* . . . was not the work of a man but of the
whole of Christendom. . . . To condemn Jacobus de Voragine
is to condemn all the ancient lectionaries, and with them the
clergy who read them and the faithful who listened.

Emile Mâle, 1898

The greatest obstacle to understanding the actual import of the reaction
against the *Legenda* is the tendency, even among some early observers, to
entangle it with the great confessional struggles of the sixteenth and
seventeenth centuries. The demise of the *Legenda* is not wholly
unconnected with the emergence of Protestantism, as we shall see; but
the two events occurred so independently that the fate of the book was
virtually sealed by the time Luther posted his famous theses on the door
of the castle church in Wittenberg. As it happens, the early editions
themselves testify rather eloquently on this point.

We can ascertain from Seybolt's list of editions that the Latin text of
the *Legenda* was published in at least fifteen different cities between 1470
and 1489.[1] The data obviously reflect a large international demand for
this book among the clergy or educated laity or both. There were ten or
more editions in both Strasbourg and Cologne; at least five each in
Nuremberg, Venice, Lyons, and Basel; at least three each in Ulm and
Paris; two each in Deventer and Reutlingen; and single editions in
Augsburg, Toulouse, Geneva, Brussels, and Louvain. Since there is no
list comparable to Seybolt's for the period after 1500, it is worth pausing
to note that the vast majority of these editions are also attested by our
supplementary sources, the combined catalogs for the British Library,
the Bibliothèque Nationale, and the research libraries of the United

States. Relying solely on the catalogs, we would have thirteen cities (all of Seybolt's except Geneva and Brussels) and an omission of no more than one verified edition at any of them.

By the 1490s, the demand for the Latin *Legenda* seems already to have been falling off sharply. Seybolt lists only twenty-three editions between 1491 and 1500, as compared with forty-one in the previous decade, and the number of cities represented declines to seven: Strasbourg, Nuremberg, Venice, Lyons, Basel, Louvain, and Hagenau. Only at Strasbourg, Basel, and Lyons, moreover, does business appear to have been brisk enough to warrant as many as four or five new imprints. Our supplementary sources show one major omission, the libraries they represent having all failed for some reason to acquire any exemplar of the four editions from this decade at Basel; otherwise, however, they continue the pattern previously established, falling short of Seybolt's figures by no more than one verified edition per city. The striking development during this period, reflected in both lists, is the sudden decline of activity in the previously flourishing markets of the Empire. After 1488 no further Latin editions are attested from Ulm; after 1490, none from Cologne; after 1496, none from Nuremberg.[2] Early in the next decade Strasbourg too disappears from the picture. Even taking into account the fact that the catalogs supply only a rough indication of the editions actually published, there is no mistaking the general trend. From 1503 to 1517 the only imperial city attested as having published the Latin *Legenda* is Hagenau, with three editions; the remaining editions come, in a diminishing stream, from Venice and the French cities of Lyons, Rouen, and Caen. And after 1517 the only manifestation of continuing interest in the Latin text is the activity of one printer in Rouen and several in Lyons, who went on issuing about two new editions per decade until 1555.

If the *Legenda*'s reputation in the international community of clerics and scholars steadily declined after about 1490, as the publication data suggest, its fortunes among less-educated Christians seem to have varied significantly from country to country. The history of Caxton's version in England, which was published about twice a decade until 1527 and not at all thereafter until the nineteenth century, is perhaps consistent with the theory that the *Legenda* fell victim to the Reformation. But this is not the case anywhere else. There is no indication that the translations published in Spain and Bohemia ever enjoyed much popularity.[3] In the German- and Dutch-speaking regions of the Empire, on the other hand, there seems to have been considerable demand for vernacular translations and adaptations of the *Legenda* until the end of the fifteenth century, when the number of editions falls off sharply.[4] Although these vernacular versions continued to be issued sporadically in Strasbourg, Basel, and Antwerp until at least 1516-17, their relative infrequency after about 1500 suggests that in Germany and the Low Countries general readers began to turn away from the *Legenda* almost as soon as scholars and clerics did. The reaction against the *Legenda* obviously made headway much more slowly in France, where both Latin and vernacular editions continued to appear until 1554-55 or later; but here too its effects can be seen as early as 1500. Just after this date there is a noticeable hiatus in the publication of French versions, and the new Latin editions start bearing lengthy and defensive-sounding titles.[5] Almost as interesting are the publication data from Italy, where the Counter-Reformation seems to have inspired a revival of the *Legenda*—but only in the vernacular. Italian vernacular editions are attested at frequent intervals before 1520, become very rare for the next thirty-five years, and then, a few years after the Council of Trent, start appearing again on a regular basis.[6] This second life of the *Legenda* in Italian, which apparently began after the last editions in every other vernacular language, would last for nearly sixty years.

In the context of the publication data, the celebrated attacks on the *Legenda* during the sixteenth and seventeenth centuries present a significantly different appearance than historians have tended to realize. For one thing, they belong to a very late stage in the decline of Jacobus's book. The first negative verdicts actually published appear to have been those of Juan Luis Vives in 1531 and Georg Witzel a decade later. Both scholars refer to the *Legenda* as if its defects were already notorious among their readers—as, indeed, they must have been. The popularity of the book could hardly have declined so greatly in the preceding decades unless the case against it had become common knowledge. The second important point is that scholarly disapproval of the *Legenda* seems to have been nearly unanimous in the first half of the sixteenth century. There are almost no traces of dissenting opinion, save from the diminishing circle of publishers who continued to issue the book. In short, when Vives and Witzel and their successors condemned the *Legenda,* they were not taking a position that knowledgeable contemporaries would have found unusual, much less radical and dangerous. Since Jacobus's defenders from Echard on have consistently obscured this point, it is worth pausing to examine the few *causes célèbres* they have brought forward.

The only oral attack on the *Legenda* that ever aroused enough controversy to be remembered as a historic event occurred in 1543. During Lent of that year Claude d'Espence or d'Espense (1511-71), a prominent young theologian and professor at the University of Paris, delivered a series of public sermons which focused in part on excesses in the popular cult of the saints; in the process, the *Legenda* came in for strong criticism. These sermons aroused enough furor to occasion a hearing by the theological faculty of the university. Espence countered the accusations against him; but by the advice or compulsion of the tribunal, he returned to the same pulpit twice that summer and retracted certain statements, among them the verdict that the *Legenda* was a book of iron and full of nonsense.[7] This story has been variously interpreted. Some historians have made a good deal of the apparent clash between Espence and other members of the theological faculty, ignoring the references to the *Legenda* and concluding that the authorities of the Sorbonne harbored serious doubts about Espence's orthodoxy; one nineteenth-century source even went so far as to claim Espence for the Protestant side, largely on the basis of statements he is said to have retracted in 1543.[8] Defenders of Jacobus, on the other hand, have tended to present the story as a proof that the Sorbonne theologians cared deeply about the *Legenda;* some add the claim that Espence's unfortunate error in criticizing it ruined his subsequent chances of advancement within the church.[9] The truth, however, would seem to have been more complex and less dramatic than either of these theories.

It is clear, to begin with, that not even the conservative theologians at the Sorbonne can have regarded Espence's views on the *Legenda* as errors against the faith. Hagiographical works did not enjoy that kind of status, either in the sixteenth century or in the preceding epoch. For centuries, in fact, the guardians of orthodoxy had drawn a firm line between the realm of piety, to which was assigned nearly every aspect of the cult of the saints, and the more important realm of doctrine. Although developments in piety did not go completely unregulated, as some historians have supposed, only matters of doctrine were ordinarily assumed to require more than the local bishop's blessing.[10] Hence books like the *Legenda* were full of material which the authorities in Rome and in the theological schools had never scrutinized, much less formally sanctioned. Most of the saints celebrated in these books owed their standing to tradition, not formal inquiry; papal canonization, with its elaborate system of safeguards, was instituted only late in the Middle Ages, and there was no attempt to purge the calendars of saints who had prevously crept in on the basis of pious fiction or fraud or simple error.[11] As for the narratives written about the saints and their miracles, their content was so far from being fixed that it was quite possible for the advocates of a given saint to keep revising and improving his or her legend until its original lineaments had vanished.[12]

If Catholic scholars had no obligation to accept all the old traditions about the saints, however, they might well be reminded of the Pauline injunction against causing unnecessary scandal to the faithful. As Delehaye has testified, the early Bollandists were careful to observe this rule, forbearing for pastoral reasons to thrust the results of their research on less knowledgeable Christians who might have been shocked by them.[13] In Espence's own time Vives, Witzel, and Melchior Cano all condemned the *Legenda* in much the same terms Espence is reported to have used, apparently without arousing any adverse reaction. The obvious difference is that they were content to disseminate their views to that fraction of the church which read learned works in Latin. For Espence to use the forum of public sermons was to risk offending conservative French laymen who still cherished the *Legenda* and encouraging those who were inclined to find fault with the whole cult of the saints. What made the subject so sensitive, of course, was the emphasis contemporary Protestants tended to place on it.[14] And the authorities of the Sorbonne, who had managed just the previous year to have Calvin's *Institutes* officially banned by the French Parliament, were distinctly not inclined to meet the Protestants halfway on any issue. In the wake of some questionable Advent preaching, in fact, all the theologians at the University of Paris had been convoked early in 1543 to take a kind of loyalty oath, pledging to uphold every aspect of Catholic teaching that was under attack—including the power of the saints as intercessors and the legitimacy of praying to them and venerating their images.[15] Hence it is easy to understand why Espence would be questioned, a few months later, about sermons which had criticized certain traditions instead of defending them. Since the authorities are reported to have found his explanations acceptable and there is no indication of a formal censure, the case is best explained as one of indiscretion, not unorthodoxy.[16] And the retraction should presumably be seen as a gesture designed to clarify his loyalties and soothe public feeling.[17]

Defenders of Jacobus have also made a good deal of the notoriety associated with two later critics of the *Legenda,* the French scholars Jean de Launoy (1603-78) and Adrien Baillet (1649-1706). The contemporary outcries against these scholars actually had little to do with Jacobus's book, which had ceased decades earlier to be published even in Italy and was rarely mentioned by their opponents;[18] but these outcries shed a good deal of additional light on the thorny issues bound up with medieval hagiography. By the time Launoy and Baillet declared their distrust of the *Legenda* and many of the stories it had helped to popularize, historical criticism of the old legends was no longer in its infancy. Thanks in part to the great debates between Catholicism and its Protestant adversaries, scholars of all parties had taken a serious interest in the history of the church, searching out relevant but long-neglected documents and subjecting them to critical analysis.[19] A number of legends inherited from the Middle Ages were giving way before more accurate information about the early church and its saints—but not without some surprisingly virulent resistance. Launoy—a priest and doctor of theology whose major offense was to demonstrate the absurdity of such famous medieval legends as those casting Dionysius the Areopagite as the first bishop of Paris and crediting the foundation of the church in Provence to Lazarus, Martha, and Mary Magdalene— aroused such passionate opposition among his countrymen that he gained a lasting reputation as an impious enemy of the saints.[20] Baillet, another priest of exceptional learning, made a more generalized attempt to separate the authentic traditions about the saints from the fables and outright falsifications that had become entangled with them,[21] and he was repeatedly denounced to the authorities as a perpetrator of sacrilege or even heresy, to some effect. Baillet's work on the cult of the Virgin was found blameless by both the faculty of the Sorbonne and the archbishop of Paris, but it was placed on the Index of prohibited books in Rome, *donec corrigatur*. And the volumes containing the major fruits of his research on hagiography, although regarded as erudite and useful by later scholars, were officially forbidden by the Holy Office shortly after their initial publication.[22]

The actual case against Launoy and Baillet appears to have been much like the case against Espence: some reputable authorities deemed them to have taken too critical a stance toward stories and usages that had long enjoyed at least the tacit approval of the church. Even where such traditions were manifestly apocryphal, there was still some feeling that Catholic scholars ought not publicly to reject them, lest they raise doubts in the popular mind about the inerrancy of church teaching on more important matters. And both Launoy and Baillet had added fuel to the fire by adopting a more contentious tone than necessary.[23] By the later seventeenth century, however, the issue was not just indiscreet publication. Where it impinged on the legends of the saints, the whole validity of historical scholarship became open to question. The argument put forth by one of Launoy's more sober opponents, the Dominican Vincent Baron (1604-74), is quite instructive in this regard. Wise scholars like Thomas Aquinas, Baron suggests, had always found better things to do than to meddle with the harmless errors of the faithful: "[St. Thomas] had better things to write about; even if he did scent something doubtful or less convincing, he would (according to the physicians' precept) have been unwilling to be the first to stir up an inactive disease. He would have thought that to bring into dispute beliefs approved and confirmed by long tradition, which do no harm to faith and even promote piety, savors of those inquiries condemned by the Apostle which breed quarrels rather than enlightenment.''[24] Baron was obviously not alone in feeling that the welfare of the church was best served by leaving certain errors uncorrected. In the preface to his *Traité historique du chef de S. Jean Baptiste* (1665), Charles Du Cange argues that the benefits of discovering the truth outweigh the dangers; but he also makes it clear that such research was widely regarded as a threat to the peace of the church: ''I well know that most people who love the peace and unity of the Church disapprove of these controversies and believe it is more advisable to leave the multitudes in their pious errors than to disturb them with unprofitable doubts, which [the scholar] tries to instill in their minds.''[25]

What Du Cange does not quite say is that it was precisely the habit of tolerating ''pious errors'' which had made the old legends so explosive to deal with. The traditional indulgence extended to presumably unimportant matters of piety had allowed particular constituencies within the medieval church to modify the legends for their own advantage, incorporating apocryphal material which enhanced the prestige of local churches and shrines and monastic foundations by exaggerating the antiquity of their origins or the importance of their relics or the stature of their special patrons among the saints.[26] And these traditions had gone unquestioned for so many centuries that the institutions concerned had come to regard them as sacrosanct. Almost inevitably, then, research on the origins of legendary material raised the specter of public scandal. Even where the benefits derived from a spurious tradition were wholly intangible, a historian could not discredit it without damaging the morale and prestige of some segment of the church. And no matter how discreetly he might disseminate his findings, he could hardly avoid arousing the ire of interested members of the clergy. The furor surrounding Launoy himself seems to have been occasioned primarily by such opponents, who became too enraged to confine the debate to scholarly Latin publications, where it had begun, and thus disturbed Frenchmen at large with issues that would not ordinarily have come to their attention.[27] But the pattern is illustrated yet more clearly and dramatically by the storm that broke around the cautious, painstaking work of the Bollandists before the century was over.[28]

In this instance there seems to have been just one crucial offense. The Carmelites had for centuries asserted that their order was founded in remote antiquity by the prophet Elijah himself, a patently absurd claim on which the editors of the *Acta Sanctorum* refrained from commenting as long as they could. In 1675, however, Daniel Papebroch finally yielded to pressure from the Carmelites and gave his opinion, showing in the first volume for the saints of April that their claim seemed to have no historical foundation. The order's response was a barrage of furious pamphlets that continued for twenty years, reaching its climax in 1695 with a violent and comprehensive indictment of Papebroch and the Bollandists, written by a Carmelite provincial called Sebastian de Saint-Paul and specifically designed to persuade the highest authorities of the church to take action. Father Sebastian's accusations, published under the title *Exhibitio errorum quos P. Daniel Papebrochius Societatis Jesu suis in notis ad Acta Sanctorum commisit,* are so far-reaching that they defy any attempt at brief summary.[29] But their general tenor is reflected quite clearly in the decree issued a few months later by the Inquisition at Toledo. The work of Papebroch and his colleague Godfrey Henschenius was condemned on the grounds that it contained "propositions which are erroneous, heretical, savoring of schism, perilous in matters of faith, scandalous, offensive to pious ears, seditious, rash, audacious, presumptuous, gravely offensive to several of the Popes and the Holy See, to the Sacred Congregation of Rites, to the breviary and to the Roman martyrology, minimizing the virtues of several saints and of many writers, and containing as well many disrespectful statements regarding several of the Fathers of the Church and weighty ecclesiastical theologians."[30] Although the sentence of condemnation eventually mentioned the Bollandists' offenses against the Carmelites in particular, the central message was that Papebroch and Henschenius had betrayed the church itself, allying themselves with heretics and infidels in a bold assault on its most sacred traditions. Under penalty of excommunication and fines, Catholics in Spain were forbidden to read or sell all fourteen volumes of the *Acta Sanctorum* for March, April, and May. The reputation of Papebroch was not quite destroyed by these blows, since the authorities in Rome proceeded much more cautiously. After a delay of five years, in fact, they were content to place on the Index only the volume in which he had ventured to trace the history of papal canonization, specifying that the ban would be lifted when a few passages were corrected. But despite the anxious efforts of Papebroch and his friends, the Spanish decree of condemnation was not revoked until January 1715, several months after his death.

The sixteenth-century case of James Lacop, prominently cited by Echard and his successors as an instance of heretical assault on the *Legenda,* is far more ambiguous than those we have been considering, but there are suggestive similarities. James Lacop himself was a young Premonstratensian canon in the Netherlands who was martyred by the

Calvinists at Gorcum in 1572, along with eighteen other Catholics. In 1566 the same man had written a pamphlet entitled *Defloratio aureae Legendae,* which was so controversial that he was compelled to burn it and transferred from Middelburg, where the furor had occurred, to another abbey.[31] The question, of course, is what the pamphlet can have said. William Estius (1542-1613), whose history of the Gorcum martyrs provides the earliest and most authoritative account of Lacop's life, characterizes the pamphlet as a heretical attack on the church which he produced in the course of a temporary apostasy to the Calvinist side:

When the storm of the iconoclastic controversy swept over a number of the leading parts of Belgium, Lacop too, along with many others elsewhere, was by the will of God, who brings all things to good in his elect, wretchedly seduced and evilly persuaded by the heretics. First among the brothers in the monastery he spoke out childishly and impudently, not to say impiously, against the sacred dogmas of the Catholic Church. Soon, deserting the monastery, he undertook the office of preacher among the heretics and wrote a heretical pamphlet in a provocative style, entitled *The Golden Legend Culled.*[32]

Estius was an eminent scholar, and he was in an uncommonly good position to reconstruct the history of this particular group of martyrs, since his uncle, the Franciscan Nicholas Piecke, was among them, and he was himself a native of Gorcum.[33] It may be that he also found witnesses from Middelburg who accurately remembered the nature of the breach between James Lacop and his fellow canons. But the story even as Estius tells it raises some questions. For one thing, he seems to have had no opportunity actually to see the notorious pamphlet. The original had been burned more than thirty years before he compiled his account, and as a later source notes piously, "God granted that the pamphlet not be published."[34] Moreover, Estius's whole account of James Lacop is quite brief and undetailed, in comparison with the biographies he presents for other martyrs in the group; and it is so neatly symmetrical, with its theme of an early fall reversed in the ultimate test of fortitude against the same Protestant adversaries, that it sounds suspiciously like legend. What one can conclude with some certainty is that Echard and Touron and their successors made too much of the apparent conjunction of apostasy and opposition to the *Legenda.* If Lacop briefly forsook his church to join the Calvinists, he is most unlikely to have climaxed this rebellion with an attack on a single Catholic book—especially one which had not been popular in the Netherlands for some fifty years. One might more logically assume that the pamphlet was directed against the whole habit of venerating and invoking the saints, its title reflecting only the special fame—or infamy—of the *Legenda* as a symbol of the old order.

Or, remembering the explosions that greeted Espence, Launoy, Baillet, and Papebroch, when they ventured to criticize certain venerable traditions, one might reopen the very question of Lacop's apostasy. Significantly enough, Estius characterizes him as a promising young scholar of humanistic inclinations[35]—the sort of man who could well have attempted, as a loyal Catholic, to defend earlier and more authentic traditions about the saints by distinguishing them from the apocryphal material in the *Legenda.*

Whatever one makes of the case of James Lacop, there is no question about the general character of the reaction against the *Legenda.* It was not part of the Protestant crusade against the cult of the saints, except perhaps locally and incidentally; in fact, it arose from within the mainstream of contemporary Catholicism. The publication data suggest as much, with their testimony to a generalized movement away from Jacobus's book, beginning among scholars and clerics and gradually spreading to the whole church. The defenders of Jacobus in following centuries inadvertently confirm and strengthen this conclusion; for every important attack they mention turns out, when one examines the facts, to have come from a respected Catholic scholar.[36] As a group, indeed, the early critics of the book represent a rather formidable sample of educated Catholic opinion. Launoy and Baillet, whatever their lapses from discretion, were among the most learned men of their day. The credentials of our four major sixteenth-century witnesses demand to be considered in more detail; the particular stands they took in the religious controversies of the time are at least as important, for our purposes, as their scholarly eminence.

Three of these four scholars were associated with the Erasmian *via media,* a movement whose scope and significance as a forerunner of modern ecumenism has been recognized only in recent times. The German Georg Witzel (1501-73) has the most questionable record as a Catholic, for he left the church a few years after his ordination in 1521, going so far as to marry and accept a series of posts as a Lutheran pastor.[37] Within less than a decade, however, Witzel had become disillusioned with the new movement and returned to Catholicism, taking Erasmus as his exemplar. Thenceforth he served the cause of Christian unity, laboring to persuade Catholics and Protestants alike to return to the model of the early church, whose faith and practice he illustrated in a great outpouring of books; his work on saints' legends was part of this program. Witzel's knowledge, although called into question by Bolland, was quite exceptional for a priest of his time. He had studied at the universities of Erfurt and Wittenberg, where his teachers included Luther and Melanchthon, was sufficiently fluent in languages to master Greek patristic texts as well as Latin ones, and achieved some renown as an authority on the ancient liturgies of the church.

The second Erasmian moderate in the group is Espence, like Launoy a doctor of theology and a fellow of the humanistic College of Navarre at Paris.[38] Espence, whose abilities are suggested by his youthful election as rector of the university, played a leading role in the effort to heal the split in the church by means of negotiation. He visited Geneva to talk with Calvin, met with Peter Martyr Vermigli and Martin Bucer in Strasbourg, and held repeated debates, both orally and in writing, with the French Calvinist leader Theodore Beza. Thanks in part to the influence of his old friend and admirer Charles of Lorraine, Espence was also a prominent participant in the formal colloquies that represented the final, rather desperate attempts to establish some common ground on which the French church might be reunified. As it happened, the last and most forlorn of these conferences, convened by Queen Catherine at Saint-Germain-en-Laye at the end of January 1562, found itself deadlocked over images, the first item on the agenda. Espence and a few other Catholic representatives showed a willingness to compromise, submitting a proposal that would have banished from altars all images except the Cross and forbidden such public ceremonies and gestures in their honor as would be most offensive to Protestants.[39] But the hope of conciliation was futile. The compromise proposal, which did not go far enough to satisfy the real iconoclasts on the Protestant side, was nullified by the opposition of more conservative Catholics. In August Espence's fellow theologians at the Sorbonne would demand both a private recantation and a public gesture, "if only for the sake of weak believers who are easily scandalized."[40] Meanwhile, on March 1, some sixty French Protestants were slaughtered at Vassy, and the long civil wars began.

The most distinguished of the Erasmian critics of the *Legenda* was the Spanish humanist Juan Luis Vives (1492-1540), a respected friend of both Erasmus and Thomas More, and one of the great Renaissance spokesmen for educational and social reform.[41] Vives attained an international reputation as an educator—filling such posts as professor of humanities at the University of Louvain, lecturer in philosophy at Oxford, tutor to the young cardinal-archbishop of Toledo, and educational adviser to the English royal family—while remaining a layman and even choosing to marry. This break with the centuries-old tradition that reserved scholarship and teaching to celibate clerics was both a sign of the times and a telling reflection of Vives' own philosophy. For he did not just reject the established method of education, as many humanists did, on the grounds that it debated trivial questions in bad Scholastic Latin. At a more basic level Vives found a pernicious narrowness in the whole system because it denied any meaningful education to women, encouraged intellectual tyranny on the part of the clergy, and left Christian men so unwise as to accept war and poverty as natural conditions of life.[42] It is hardly necessary to point out the connection between these ideas and the educational goals of More and Erasmus and their older colleague John Colet. As the sixteenth century wore on, it became increasingly evident that neither Catholics nor Protestants were prepared to embrace a reform which declared points of dogma less certain, and less binding on Christians, than the biblical injunctions to unity and social justice. Before his death Vives had seen the execution of More and the abuse heaped on Erasmus by partisans from both sides; but not even in his final and most pessimistic writings did he abandon the ideal of a united Christian society, built on a reformed system of moral and intellectual education.[43] Witzel and Espence lived long enough to witness the victory of more intransigent Catholics at Trent—and to incur a good deal of suspicion for their own refusal to endorse every aspect of the new partisan orthodoxy.[44]

The Spanish Dominican Melchior Cano (1509-60), our final sixteenth-century witness, was an academic and controversialist of a different stripe.[45] Whereas Espence, Vives, and Witzel all dedicated themselves to the ideal of Christian unity, Cano advised Philip II in his disputes with the papacy, endeavored to block the initial establishment of the Jesuits in Spain, and assisted the Inquisition in the persecution of his fellow Dominican and long-time rival Bartholomew de Carranza; although the authorities in Rome found Carranza's work rather harmless, he was imprisoned for nearly seventeen years—largely on the basis of the supposedly heretical propositions Cano had found in his vernacular catechism. The same modern reevaluation which has elevated the reputation of more irenic figures has inevitably lowered that of Cano; but in his own time he was greatly esteemed. At one point he was named to a bishopric, a post he declined to assume. Toward the end of his life the Dominicans of Spain insisted on electing him provincial prior, despite vehement opposition from the pope and from the friends of the imprisoned Carranza. Cano's credentials as a scholar were also impressive. A disciple of the famous Francis de Victoria, who inaugurated the revival of patristic learning in Spain, he climaxed a brilliant academic career by succeeding Victoria in the principal chair of theology at the University of Salamanca. As for *De locis theologicis,* the long treatise on theological method which contains Cano's comments on the *Legenda,* its status as a classic of the period is evident in the capsule description by Pierre Mandonnet: "It is the *De locis theologicis* which has made the theological reputation of Melchior Cano and placed him in the first rank of classical theologians. Indeed, this work is not only outstanding because of its literary form, which makes it comparable to the finest productions of the Renaissance, or because of its author's unfettered intelligence, acute judgment, critical sense, and erudition; it is above all an original achievement [*une création*], and in this respect a landmark in the history of theology."[46]

When one turns from the middle sixteenth century to the earlier period when the fate of the *Legenda* was still in doubt, individual critics of the book become much harder to identify. Part of the reason, of course, is that there are fewer published records of all kinds. And in the simpler and more peaceful religious climate of the fourteenth and fifteenth centuries, Catholics could express their reservations about various traditions without attracting either the suspicions of their contemporaries or the attention of later historians. But there is sufficient evidence to demonstrate that Jacobus's book had been unpopular in some circles for generations before its fall. By the middle of the fifteenth century, reform-minded humanists seem already to have identified it as a problematical sourcebook about the saints. When Nicholas of Cusa took charge of the diocese of Brixen, or Bressanone, his second round of ordinances to the clergy under his jurisdiction included a prohibition against preaching on the kinds of material found in certain specified chapters of the *Legenda;* the year was 1455.[47] One of the most suggestive facts about the *Legenda,* however, is that Renaissance humanists were by no means the first Catholic scholars to find it wanting. Jacobus's fellow Dominicans were distinctly less enthusiastic about this book, almost from the beginning, than its public reputation would seem to have warranted.

The Dominican estimate of the *Legenda* can be gauged in part from the order's early catalogs of its illustrious members. Both the *Catalogus Stamsensis,* compiled before 1350, and the fifteenth-century *Catalogus Upsalensis* identify Jacobus's most famous work simply as the "legenda lombardica";[48] noticeably absent is the honorific adjective "aurea," which had begun to be attached to the *Legenda* by 1300.[49] The testimony of Lawrence Pignon, whose fuller *Catalogi et Chronica* belongs to the beginning of the fifteenth century, is a bit more revealing. When he lists Jacobus's writings, in the section entitled "Catalogus fratrum qui claruerunt doctrina," Pignon uses the popular name for the *Legenda.*[50] But in the earlier section where he sums up the highlights of Jacobus's career, the only works mentioned as still in use by the order are some sermons.[51] More suggestive still is the catalog of distinguished

Dominicans begun by Stephen de Salanhac in the late thirteenth century and completed in 1311 by Bernard Gui. Jacobus figures in the list of "vires illustres in scriptis et doctrinis," but only among the lesser lights of the order; and the approbation accorded to most of the works mentioned is rather conspicuously withheld from the *Legenda:*

13. Friar Thomas de Lentino wrote good sermons on the saints.

14. Friar Nicholas de Byardo, French: sermons and useful and moral distinctions; also a summa on abstinence.

15. Friar Jacobus de Voragine, Lombard: new lives of the saints and a large body of sermons; also a Mariale.

16. Friar Nicholas de Gorran, French, confessor to King Philip: very apt commentaries on Ecclesiasticus, Matthew, Luke, and the Pauline epistles; also good distinctions and sermon outlines for Sundays and saints' days.[52]

The reservations about the *Legenda* implicit in the early catalogs are manifested more clearly in the efforts of the next generations of Dominicans to produce a better book of the same kind. By 1300 at least one anonymous friar had attempted to improve Jacobus's work by omitting some chapters and inserting new ones drawn from other sources.[53] More drastic was the solution of Berengar of Landorra, then master general of the order: within twenty years of Jacobus's death in 1298, he commissioned Bernard Gui to compile an entirely new legendary.[54] The importance attached to this work is suggested by the selection of Gui, the leading historian in the order and a man already burdened with responsibilities in his position as Inquisitor for Toulouse. By Gui's own account, moreover, Berengar was quite insistent on the matter: "I was urged to undertake this task by the virtue of obedience and bound to it by the authority of my superior and reverend father in Christ, Fr. Berengar, Master of the Order of Preachers. When he yet filled that office in the Order (whence he has since been advanced to the archbishopric of Compostella) he imposed and enjoined this task on me with the solemn utterance of his living voice, and even now that he is elsewhere he has exhorted me often in repeated letters."[55]

Gui's labors eventually resulted in a four-part legendary which he entitled *Speculum sanctorale* and published with some fanfare, sending the pope the first two volumes in 1324 and the remaining ones in 1329. The irony, of course, is that the *Legenda* remained popular for another century and a half, while Gui's legendary was quickly forgotten. When Leopold Delisle did a bibliographical study of Gui's works in the later nineteenth century, he managed to locate eleven manuscript volumes of the *Speculum sanctorale,* none containing more than one or two of the four parts, and all produced well before the end of the fourteenth century.[56] Only a few fragments of this work have ever been printed.

At least four other works that might have been designed to compete with the *Legenda* were compiled before the end of the fourteenth century: the massive legendary of Peter Calo of Clugia, another Dominican; the *Catalogus sanctorum et gestorum eorum ex diversis et multis voluminibus collectus* by the Italian bishop Peter Natal, also known as Peter de Natalibus; the *Sanctilogium* compiled by the Benedictine Guy de Châtres; and the *Narrationes: Gesta sanctorum* compiled, or at least copied, by the English Dominican William Pickworth.[57] None of these works seems to have made the slightest dent in the *Legenda*'s enormous popularity; but the very efforts expended to produce them attest to the belief among scholarly churchmen, and Dominicans in particular, that Jacobus's work on the saints was less definitive than the general public assumed it to be.

Perhaps we shall never know exactly who led the reaction against the *Legenda* in the crucial decades between 1470 and 1520. The circle of Erasmus, of course, provides some obvious candidates for such a role. As Bolland suggested, Erasmus himself is likely to have rejected Jacobus's book at least as vehemently as his followers did. Unfortunately, anything Erasmus, More, or Colet may have said on the matter seems to have gone unrecorded. When we look back over our assemblage of witnesses, however, it becomes quite clear why the *Legenda,* which had long reigned as most Catholics' favorite book about the saints, could fall without arousing much controversy at the time. If Erasmian humanists singled it out as a target, in this instance they were at one with their customary adversaries in the Order of Preachers. In this instance, indeed, informed Catholics seem to have reached much the same conclusion regardless of their political or philosophical outlooks. As it happens, the early examples are the most telling of all. Nicholas of Cusa subscribed to so universalist a philosophy that he hoped for the union of Christianity, Judaism, and Islam on the basis of the fundamental truths on which they agreed; Bernard Gui, at the opposite extreme, gave much of his adult life to the mission of extirpating such perceived threats to the Catholic faith as the Talmud, the dualist heresy of the Albigensians or Cathars, the new manifestations of lay piety represented by Waldenses and Beguines, and the age-old belief in sorcery and divination.[58] But Gui and Nicholas—and Berengar of Landorra as well—had in common a perspective on Jacobus's book that was not yet possible for most of their contemporaries.[59] As scholars, all three men had the opportunity and the inclination to search for the best sources, the most useful and trustworthy books from the past. And, equally important, these men were directly involved in efforts to improve the education of the laity, ensuring that they were instructed in the essentials of the faith and protected against prevalent errors and superstitions. This same perspective, with its dual concern for the study of sources and the reform of Christian education, would of course dominate the intellectual life of the church in the generations after Nicholas, becoming a keynote not only of early Protestantism, but also of the Erasmian understanding of Catholicism, the sixteenth-century movement in Spanish theology represented by Victoria and Cano, and the Counter-Reformation itself. And, as this perspective gained ground, the *Legenda* lost its former credibility and eventually its whole audience.

Even if we had no further evidence, there should be little doubt that the fall of the *Legenda* was a victory for Christian education rather than the setback some of its modern proponents have claimed. Opposed almost from the outset by authorities particularly well situated to judge its merits, Jacobus's work succumbed at last to the broadest and least partisan trends in early Renaissance humanism: the rediscovery and dissemination of classic sources. One could well argue, in fact, that the most potent adversaries the *Legenda* ever had were the editors and printers who, from the 1450s on, made it increasingly easy for literate Christians to study the Bible, the writings of the Greek and Latin fathers, and a variety of other works bearing on the history of the church and its saints. Among the books rescued from oblivion as the *Legenda* declined was the fourteenth-century *Catalogus sanctorum* by Peter Natal, which was first printed at Vicenza in 1493 and attracted enough attention to merit at least ten more Latin editions and a French translation in the first half of the sixteenth century.[60] The most telling mark of the new era in hagiography, however, was the revival of the original sources on which Peter and Jacobus and other late-medieval compilers had drawn. By 1480 Bonino Mombrizio, or Mombritius, had published at Milan a huge legendary that presented the lives and passions of the saints almost exactly as Mombrizio had found them in the best manuscripts at his disposal.[61] This example of faithfulness to the sources was a bit excessive, as Bolland would point out, since Mombrizio refrained from correcting even obvious scribal errors.[62] But in his attempt to make available the original accounts of the saints, with all their nuances intact, Mombrizio clearly belongs to the same movement that would eventually produce the work of the Bollandists and the modern tradition in hagiographical scholarship.

Significantly enough, it was Bernard Gui in 1324 who first suggested the necessity of distinguishing the *Legenda* from the true classics of hagiography. In a rather pointed dissent from popular opinion, Gui begins his preface to the *Speculum sanctorale* by transferring the appellation "golden" to the sources themselves, which Gui proposes to abridge less drastically than Jacobus had: "The golden lives of the saints—which after their glorious lives, their great constancy and strength in faith, and their persistence in good works to the end, were searched out by the great diligence of the holy fathers and diligently committed to books and letters—the moderate compass of the present work will endeavor to set forth."63 Eventually, of course, Gui's judgment was vindicated—or nearly so. The works which apparently came closest to replacing Jacobus's book in public esteem were the cosmetically edited versions of the old sources by Laurence Surius, which began appearing in 1570 and gave rise in their turn to a long series of vernacular translations, adaptations, and new abridgements.64 For scholars there would be the *Acta Sanctorum* and fine critical editions of individual classics dealing with the saints. By the time these developments occurred, however, the medieval tradition in hagiography had lost much of its former status. Many Christians ceased to respect the old legends before the sixteenth century was out, as we shall see, and the biases of later critics tended to magnify the damage. Thus the true golden legends unfortunately did not, and still have not, become as generally known and honored as the *Legenda* once was.

The explicit testimony of the *Legenda*'s early critics tends to be more elliptical and difficult to interpret than the external evidence on which the present chapter has focused, but it is even more important to understand. The point is not of course that these authorities can spare us the labor of evaluating Jacobus's compilation for ourselves: if there is one lesson that reverberates throughout the long history of the *Legenda,* it is the need to make careful, first-hand comparisons between this book and the older sources it supposedly summed up. But we cannot proceed to the comparisons without a clearer notion of what we are looking for. What was the nature of the case against the *Legenda* as our medieval and Renaissance witnesses saw it? And what light can they shed on the larger problem of finding suitable criteria for the evaluation of such works? Modern readers are so unaccustomed to making discriminations among saints' legends that we need to be taught, or at least reminded, about the purposes they once served, the kinds of excellence that can reasonably be sought in them, and the kinds of inferiority that would have mattered while the medieval tradition in hagiography was still alive.

3
Towards a Reasonable Standard
for the Evaluation
of Medieval Hagiography

[The life of the saints] is indeed the concrete manifestation of
the spirit of the Gospel; and, in that it makes this sublime ideal
a reality for us, legend, like all poetry, can claim a higher
degree of truth than history.

Hippolyte Delehaye, 1905

Almost every modern commentator has assumed that the weaknesses of
the *Legenda* are those of medieval hagiography as a whole and that the
central problem is the genre's tendency to mix fictions, or fables, with
factual material about the saints. This verdict can be traced back to the
Enlightenment, but that does not of course guarantee its validity.
Indeed, there have been few periods when the typical man of learning
had less sympathy with hagiography, and knew less about its actual
nature and purposes, than the later seventeenth and eighteenth centuries.
During this period it was commonplace for compilations like the
Legenda to be judged as works of historical scholarship and to be found
comically benighted. Jacobus's Latin style and far-fetched etymologies
naturally came in for some ridicule along the way, but the complaint
most often voiced was that he seemed to have been incapable of
distinguishing history from fiction. Fairly typical is the comment of
Louis-Ellies Dupin, faulting Jacobus for being too credulous and
unscientific in his use of source material: "He is the Author of the
Golden Legend, . . . in which, without critical judgment and discrimina-
tion, he has collected a great number of facts, most of them fictitious."[1]
Some of Dupin's contemporaries showed an awareness that their ideal of
pure historicity was rather a new thing, but even they seem not to have
suspected that this ideal might be a poor gauge of medieval saints'

legends. Thus Claude Fleury attempted to excuse Jacobus for the "Fables" in the *Legenda* by shifting the blame to the poor taste of Jacobus's whole era: "Since critical judgment has revived and the love of truth prevailed, this Legend has fallen into great contempt because of the Fables with which it is filled and the preposterous Etymologies which begin most of the Lives. These faults ought to be blamed less on the Author than on the bad taste of his time, when only the marvellous was valued."[2]

Although scholars have largely outgrown such tendencies to scoff at medieval culture, the Enlightenment ideal of historical truth is so attractive and so useful in other disciplines that it continues to interfere with a just appreciation of most saints' legends. In essence, we have inherited a seventeenth-century definition of excellence which earlier hagiographers rarely satisfy because they were aiming at something else. The magnitude of the problem was demonstrated quite clearly in 1905, when Delehaye summed up the results of the Bollandists' long effort to classify the old legends on the basis of their historical value. As he noted with undisguised regret, the entire body of ancient and medieval hagiography has turned out to contain just a handful of brief texts—transcripts from the trials of early martyrs—that can be considered plain, unvarnished records of fact. Better represented in the tradition are eyewitness reports, all of them colored to some extent by the literary conventions of the genre and the limitations of the witnesses' actual knowledge. And by far the most numerous are the accounts which, in the absence or perceived inadequacy of authentic records, have been filled out with oral traditions, borrowings from other legends, or sheer imagination.[3] A reader who demands pure historicity, then, will significantly jeopardize his ability to see distinctions of value among the old legends. For he will be compelled from the start to regard the vast majority of these works, including all the most typical ones, as grievously flawed.

In the hope of doing more justice to the legends, a number of critics have proposed to assess them as works of Christian literature rather than history. But a realistic alternative to the Enlightenment approach has proved difficult to find—not least because Delehaye's famous introduction to the genre, *Les légendes hagiographiques,* points in the wrong direction. Throughout this book Delehaye dwells on the crudities and extravagances he found characteristic of the fictionalized legends, and on their tendency to reduce historical characters and events to a few simple, predictable patterns. Nor does he just condemn such weaknesses; he explains them by embracing the theory that the typical saint's legend is just a kind of Christian folklore, a popular story shaped—and deformed—by the rather childish imagination of the mass public.[4] Thus, although Delehaye mentions a number of literary and religious criteria that might be applied to the old legends, his central message to would-be critics is that we must simply lower our expectations.

Despite Delehaye's unmistakable disdain for "the popular mind" and its products, his influence has helped to keep the folklore theory alive even among critics who want to read some saints' legends as complex works of art.[5] The practical problem, of course, is that the theory makes no provision for the possibility of real excellence in the genre. If the fictionalized legends were all shaped by the collective imagination of the populace, they ought to show as little individuality as Delehaye himself attributed to them. And consigning them to the realm of mass culture is tantamount to conceding that they cannot—and never could—meet the standards of an educated reader.

The larger objection to the folklore theory is that it is misleading; indeed, it has less to do with the facts about hagiography than with what historians have begun to call the "two-tiered model" of the early church. The model says, in essence, that the religion of the educated elite can be readily distinguished from the "popular religion" which flourished among the masses and was always full of folk beliefs and superstitious practices.[6] As Peter Brown has shown, this concept of a "popular religion," surviving alongside the Christianity of the educated few, is another legacy from the Enlightenment; and it has served primarily to help historians account for developments in church history which they themselves found unfortunate or incomprehensible. Delehaye's anthropological explanation of saints' legends has numerous precedents, in short, and some of them have been far more extreme.[7] For few phenomena have more offended church historians, and more often been dismissed as "popular," than the rituals and legends which encouraged the cult of the saints.

When one reexamines the historical evidence, as Brown and others have done, it becomes apparent that the rituals and the legends are closely connected, and that neither can be categorized as the result of "popular" influence. Perhaps the most important of Brown's own findings is that the main impetus behind the cult of the saints came from the upper reaches of Christian society, not the lower ones. Until late in the fourth century, the cult was largely a private affair, and among its chief sponsors were well-to-do Christians who could obtain the privilege of entombing the saints in close proximity to their own families (Brown, pp. 27, 30-35). What happened thereafter, as Brown reconstructs the story, is that Ambrose and other far-seeing Western bishops took charge of the cult on behalf of their sees, and of the community at large. Under their direction the saints' relics were translated to official, public shrines; and the annual festivals of the saints were transformed into lavish public ceremonials which served at once to enhance the bishop's prestige and to symbolize the oneness of the community under his care (pp. 36-49). The festivals thus had political functions, as Brown explains, but they were also capable of a rather profound social and spiritual meaning: ''The ceremonials . . . could widen the bounds of the Christian urban community by giving a place to each one of the various groups within it. They might do more than that. For the festival of a saint was conceived of as a moment of ideal consensus on a deeper level. It made plain God's acceptance of the community as a whole: his mercy embraced all its disparate members, and could reintegrate all who had stood outside in the previous year'' (pp. 99-100). In this context a miracle which healed an individual's disabilities, restoring him or her to full participation in the festival, was obviously not just a private event but a great sign of God's presence and care for the community. Such cures at the shrines were systematically recorded and publicized; and even Augustine, who had little interest in miracles during most of his career, came in his old age to value the comfort they provided (pp. 77-78).

Brown does not trace these traditions past the sixth century, but their longevity can be seen quite clearly in Benedicta Ward's recent study of medieval shrines and their miracle collections between 1000 and 1215. By this period the shrines had multiplied, of course, and many of them were sponsored by monastic communities instead of urban bishops. But there is no reason to suppose that the cult of the saints had somehow become the expression of ''the popular mind.'' Ward's brief chapter on shrines which failed demonstrates that public opinion was by no means sufficient to establish a new shrine; such incipient cults would be quickly suppressed if the bishop or secular authorities found them objectionable, and would simply vanish if they could not attract able and vigorous sponsorship from the clergy.[8] The rather complex formula for success is perhaps best illustrated by the cult of Saint Frideswide at Oxford, which was revised late in the twelfth century and lasted until the Reformation.[9]

The immediate sponsors of Frideswide's cult were the Augustinian canons who presided over the church she had founded and would become the keepers of her shrine, but they found a good deal of support. When the saint's relics were solemnly translated in 1180, the king gave his approval, the archbishop of Canterbury presided, and the participants included at least four more bishops and a papal legate. The miracles which followed—110 of them, in the ensuing year—were recorded by the prior of the house in a collection that focuses on the translation itself, continually linking the miracles with this great public event, and ends on a climactic note with the resurrection of a child whose mother prayed to Saint Frideswide. Ward comments on the effectiveness of this miracle collection and the careful planning exhibited in the whole revival of the cult, crediting both in large part to the abilities of the prior. The competition among shrines was so acute during this period that successful campaigns needed such leadership. Also worth noting, however, is the evidence that the revival served a number of purposes besides enhancing the prestige of one house of canons and stimulating the economy of the town. A healing shrine was made accessible to the residents of Oxford and the surrounding area, a sacred place where they could—and evidently did—experience the mercy of God. The memory of Saint Frideswide was glorified; and since she was a pre-Conquest saint, associated with what Ward calls "the royal, monastic, English traditions of Oxford," the revival of her cult must have inspired patriotic as well as religious sentiment. And of course the great ceremony of translation itself provided a memorable instance of that "moment of ideal consensus" which Brown has identified as a central element in the cult's meaning for its participants.

The survival of the same traditions in the later Middle Ages is amply documented in a monumental recent study by André Vauchez. Vauchez draws a sharp distinction between the situation in Northern Europe, where both the chief promoters of new cults and the saints who were their objects tended to come from the ruling classes, and the more egalitarian developments seen near the Mediterranean.[10] But even in late-medieval Italy, where cults seem often to have been created almost spontaneously by the populace, they could not last without considerable support from at least the local authorities. One of the best-documented cases is the cult of Henry of Treviso, a poor penitent whose death, in 1315, prompted an immediate outpouring of religious fervor in the city, soon followed by miracles which drew many pilgrims from the surrounding area. In the ensuing days and months, the council of Treviso invested a good deal of money and effort in the development of the cult. Under their direction a tomb was built for the new saint at the commune's expense, guards were hired to protect his relics in the interim, records of his miracles were kept in both the cathedral and the local chancellery, special measures were taken to provide enough food for the multitudes of visitors, and the task of writing the saint's *vita* was entrusted to a four-member commission consisting of the bishop and officials from the local Augustinian, Dominican, and Franciscan chapters (Vauchez, pp. 277-79).

Although the leadership exercised by a council of laymen obviously differentiates this Italian cult from its more traditional counterparts elsewhere, the old motif of "ideal consensus" is readily apparent in the details Vauchez reports. One of the council's first gestures, in fact, was a decree releasing those imprisoned for debt. Later, exiles from the city were permitted to return. When the saint's tomb was completed, the bishop solemnly translated his relics in the presence of the clergy, the civil authorities, and the entire local population. The timeless symbolism inherent in such festivals is underlined by Vauchez's conclusion about their meaning: "The deaths, funerals, and translations of the saints are for the people so many opportunities for direct contact with the supernatural and for rejoicing, in the context of an outburst of collective fervor during which the clashes of factions and clans momentarily die away" (p. 280).[11]

Historical studies like those of Brown, Ward, and Vauchez are invaluable to critics because they restore hagiography to its proper context in the life of the church, exposing the naivete of both the folklore theory and the demand for pure historicity. As they suggest, the purposes of the genre were partly promotional; a legend celebrated the greatness of a particular saint in order to encourage his veneration—in the process typically furthering the interests of those who sponsored his shrine. Like the festivals with which they were connected, however, the legends were expected simultaneously to benefit the larger community by providing comfort and inspiration, instruction, encouragements to virtue and the love of God—in a word, edification. One notes the complexity of these expectations, as well as the implicit tension between private interests and the common good. Nonetheless, hagiography seems to have worked fairly successfully for more than a thousand years, retaining the esteem of Christians at large from late antiquity until the Renaissance, when the long consensus about its value rapidly broke down.

The Catholic educators who attacked the *Legenda aurea* in the fifteenth and sixteenth centuries were not experts on every aspect of hagiography. But their testimony provides an important supplement to the discoveries of recent historians because they speak from the period when the weaknesses within the tradition could most easily be recognized. The medieval presumption in favor of most legends was giving way to a critical perspective on the texts; and this criticism, although it foreshadowed the academic approach of the Enlightenment, was considerably more practical and discriminating than later authorities imagined. The legends were still understood as works of edification, and they were taken quite seriously as an influence on the people who read or heard them. Hence our witnesses from the Renaissance tended when evaluating hagiographical works to emphasize such basic issues as the doctrinal soundness of their content, the extent of their ability to inspire reverence and right conduct, and the degree to which their use actually did credit to the saints and to the church. The reasonableness of these criteria in practice remains to be assessed; but it is worth noting at the outset that they accord fairly well with the purposes that hagiography had traditionally been supposed to serve. And the criteria do not of course condemn the whole genre. They condemn certain excesses which impaired its religious and social usefulness—and which, our major witnesses suggest, were more conspicuous in the *Legenda aurea* than in most other sources.

The simplest and most straightforward testimony is that offered by Nicholas of Cusa in 1455. When he set out to reform the diocese of Brixen, a few years earlier, he had found the laity so ill-informed about the faith that he felt it necessary to order that they be given rudimentary instruction on the Lord's Prayer, the Commandments, and the sacraments of the church.[12] Even if the clergy of the diocese had been well-disciplined and sympathetic to their bishop's goals (and apparently they were neither), it would have been extraordinary if Nicholas had found time to worry about nonsubstantive defects in saints' legends. In fact, his directives with regard to the cult of the saints were all aimed at excesses which blatantly encouraged superstition in the guise of Christian piety. Thus he prohibited the celebration of feasts like that of Saint Valentine, which had served hitherto as a quasi-magical rite to ward off epilepsy and cattle disease, and that of "Johannis et Pauli contra tempestates."[13] And he forbade his clergy to teach the people such "superstitiosa" as were found in the *Legenda aurea* accounts of Saints Blaise, Barbara, Catherine, Dorothea, and Margaret of Antioch.[14] There is not much question about his meaning, for the chapters singled out as examples have one thing in common: they promise in unequivocal terms that acts of devotion to the saints in question will magically guarantee one's deliverance from certain evils, among them illnesses, poverty, and damnation itself.[15]

The position of Claude d'Espence is more difficult to reconstruct, since later reports tend to focus on the single statement that the *Legenda* was "a book of iron, full of absurdities."[16] Espence, however, was not much more likely to take a purely academic interest in saints' legends than Nicholas had been. As we have already seen, the guiding principle in his career was adherence to the *via media,* a course that acknowledged the validity of certain Protestant calls for reform without compromising the essentials of the Catholic faith as handed down by the Fathers and the major councils of the church. And his controversial Lenten sermons in 1543 seem to have been quite consistent with this orientation. Such excerpts from the subsequent retraction as have been published indicate that he must have ventured some strictures against the habit of exaggerating the power of the saints, of believing—or acting as if one believed—that more reliance could be placed on their help than on the promises of God.[17] In this context, of course, Espence might well have mentioned the bad influence of just such stories from the *Legenda* as Nicholas had condemned some ninety years before. At any rate, the logical implication is that the absurdities Espence found in the book were departures from sound Catholic teaching on the saints, as he understood it—absurdities, that is, which would have had some practical importance to the kind of audience he was addressing.

The critiques of the *Legenda* by Vives, Cano, and Witzel sound more like verdicts from the Enlightenment, especially at first reading. These three scholars were certainly not immune to the attractions of a good Latin style.[18] More important, they raise the issue of historical authenticity in saints' legends; indeed, Vives and Cano treat hagiography explicitly as a branch of historical writing, discussing its deficiencies in chapters devoted to the characteristics of unreliable historians, and Witzel assures the readers of his own legendary that he has done his best to verify the authenticity of each story he retells. As we shall see, however, all three of these scholars were more concerned with the spiritual and moral impact of a hagiographical work than with its historicity per se. Their main difference from our other Renaissance witnesses is that they do not warn against the doctrinal influence of Jacobus's book; they were writing for other scholars and educators, and they seem to have taken for granted that such readers were in no danger of placing too much faith in Jacobus's stories. On the contrary, they all suggest that the *Legenda* was so obviously untrustworthy that it posed a danger on the other side, encouraging intelligent Christians to look with scorn or suspicion instead of reverence on all the old works about the saints.

Vives' outburst against Jacobus and his book was quoted in part by Bolland, but it makes considerably more sense when one reads it in the original context. The general subject in this part of *De disciplinis* is the way historical sources have been corrupted by authors who deliberately misrepresented the facts in order to glorify their own nation or cause. The issue, in short, is not just inaccurate history but partisan propaganda masquerading as history. Vives makes it clear that he finds such misrepresentations in many of the old books about the saints, but he singles out the *Legenda* as the most appalling example of all:

Nor has any greater care for truth been shown in recounting the deeds of the saints, in which everything ought to be accurate and complete. Each author wrote according to his feelings toward each of them, so that history was dictated by passion [*animus*] rather than by truth. How unworthy of the saints, and of all Christians, is that history of the saints called the *Golden Legend!* I cannot imagine why they call it *golden,* when it was written by a man with *a mouth of iron* and *a heart of lead.* What could be more abominable [*foedius*] than this book? What a disgrace to us Christians that the preeminent deeds of our saints have not been more truly and accurately preserved, so that we might know or imitate such virtue, when the Greek and Roman authors have written with such care about their generals, philosophers, and sages![19]

As this passage suggests, Vives did not expect saints' legends to satisfy some quasi-scientific definition of truth. Like most scholars of his era, he derived his notion of good historical writing from classical models, models which provided rather an apt standard of comparison because hagiography had inherited so many of their conventions—including the license to supplement the known facts with imaginative reconstructions of important speeches and events. The kind of truth Vives expected from hagiographers, then, had at least as much to do with their artistic and moral judgment as with the caliber of their historical research. He sought works of history which were morally useful, both in encouraging virtue and in making readers wiser about human nature and the passions to which it is subject.[20] His general complaint about saints' legends was that their great potential for such purposes had been lost, or at least compromised, because their authors had been too eager to improve on reality. They tended to offer exaggerated and unbelievable pictures of human conduct instead of edifying ones.[21] Moreover, he asserted, such falsehoods are dangerous; even if piously intended, they can only harm religion by lessening the credibility of what is true.[22]

Melchior Cano's critique of works like the *Legenda* is more circumspect than that of Vives but even more illuminating. When he takes up the problem of falsifications by hagiographers and church historians, in *De locis theologicis* 11.6, Cano forbears to identify any offenders by name, explaining that to do so would be to impugn the morality, and not just the scholarship, of these individuals.[23] But he warmly endorses Vives' complaint against the falsifications themselves, arguing more specifically than Vives did that in the long run such attempts to deceive can only weaken the cult of the saints because they bring even the worthiest hagiographers under suspicion:

Vives' complaint about certain fictitious religious histories is entirely just. Wisely and seriously indeed he blames those who have thought it the part of piety to contrive lies in the interests of religion, a thing which is both extremely dangerous and entirely unnecessary. We do not believe a liar even when he tells the truth; thus those who want to arouse men's minds to revere the saints with false and lying writings seem to me to achieve nothing but this, that faith is withdrawn from what is true, because of what is false, and that the sober accounts of undoubtedly truthful authors are also brought into question. (P. 330)[24]

Cano's only explicit mention of the *Legenda* occurs a few pages later in the same chapter; the context is a second principle for evaluating historical sources, this time on the basis of their authors' critical judgment rather than their integrity (p. 333). Applying this criterion to a number of medieval hagiographers, Cano finds them all flawed to some degree. But he makes some telling distinctions. If such authors as Bede and Gregory the Great were occasionally too credulous, Cano suggests, their works nonetheless deserve the highest respect (p. 334). A second and less authoritative class of authors is represented by Jacobus's near-contemporary Vincent of Beauvais and the fifteenth-century Saint Antoninus, both characterized by Cano as well-intentioned men who simply had no conception of critical principles: "Both of them were not so much concerned that they should recount what was true and certain, as that they should omit nothing which was to be found in any sort of written source. . . . Thus while we may grant that they were good men, and quite innocent of deceit, . . . they are without authority among strict and serious critics" (ibid.).[25] As for the *Legenda,* Cano hints at more than he actually says by relegating it to the lowest category. His argument suggests that the major charge against Jacobus is not a lack of selectivity, as in the cases of Vincent and Antoninus, but an actual preference for miracle stories that no perceptive Christian would believe:

It cannot be denied that sometimes the most serious men, especially in recounting the wonders of the saints, accept widespread rumors and pass them on to posterity in their writings. In this, it seems to me at least, they excessively indulge either themselves or at any rate the mass of the faithful; for they know that the common people not only believe such miracles easily, but eagerly demand them. Thus they have recorded many signs and prodigies of the saints, not because they found them easy to believe, but because they did not want to appear to fall short of the desires of the faithful. . . . I do not here excuse the author of the book called *Speculum exemplorum* or the author of the history called *Legenda aurea.* In the former you will find more freaks than real miracles, and the latter was written by a man of iron mouth, leaden heart, and mind neither critical nor prudent. (P. 333)[26]

The inclusion here of the "iron mouth, leaden heart" jest does not necessarily mean that Cano wanted his readers to recall the rest of Vives' angry denunciation. But this allusion to the contemporary notoriety of Jacobus's book at least reinforces the message that it is the kind of untrustworthy source which brings discredit rather than honor to the saints.

The fullest and most poignant commentary on the state of hagiography from the perspective of the middle sixteenth century is supplied by the liturgical reformer Georg Witzel. In the preface to his own Latin legendary in 1541, Witzel argues with some eloquence for the importance of saints' legends to all Christians. His learned contemporaries, he laments, have consigned the saints to oblivion, considering the old legends less worthy of their attention and respect than the lives of pagan heroes. But in so doing they have cut themselves off from a crucial source of religious knowledge and encouragement: "I grieve to see that [the saints] are most shamefully cast from the minds of modern men and lie hidden as if buried, through whom the Divine Majesty . . . has manifested to mortals knowledge of himself and his will, through whom he has performed countless miracles and plainly shown his omnipotence, through whom he has enlightened the darkness of this decaying world, through whom he has cured the ills of the mind, through whom he has led back to the path peoples miserably lost, through whom, finally, he has undone the complete fall of the earlier Adam."[27]

Witzel knew very well of course that the contemporary resistance to saints' legends arose in part from the doctrinal issues that had been raised by his fellow reformers, especially those on the Protestant side. He meets such criticism directly in the course of his preface, attempting to prove that the tradition of venerating the saints is of ancient origin, that its theological soundness is attested by the New Testament and the Fathers of the church, and that it has irreplaceable moral and spiritual value in the experience of believers.[28] As one might expect from the history of the times, Witzel lays special emphasis on the moral question. He pleads with those who would rely on faith alone to remember the examples of the saints: "We want to be carried up to heaven in the moment of our death, but in the meantime we refuse to do the will of our Father who is in heaven, and think it enough to cry, 'Lord, Lord! I believe, I believe!' Why do we not come to our senses while there is time, while wisdom knocks at our doors? And first, with the archetype Christ our Savior well in mind, why do we not contemplate the exemplars of his flock, that is, the saints, bishops, and martyrs, who form, along with us, the living and eternal body of that same Christ Savior?" (sigs. 4ᵛ-5).[29] As the argument proceeds he reminds all his readers that those examples were meant to inspire a kind of piety which transcends sectarian differences: "Let us praise those glorious men and hymn their good deeds, but especially that He may be glorified, by whose authority all good deeds are done. And let us proceed straightway from praise to imitation of those we praise, lest what Plutarch wrote of Demosthenes be applied to us: 'He could indeed praise the deeds of his predecessors, but he was quite unable to imitate them''' (sig. 5).[30]

The other great problem Witzel had to confront was the trustworthiness of hagiography itself. It is clear from his preface that some critical observers were already inclined to suspect the genre of chronic prevarication, especially where miraculous events were concerned; and Witzel takes great pains to overcome such suspicions. He emphatically defends miracle stories in principle, accusing skeptics of irrational prejudice if they refuse to acknowledge that real wonders must have occurred, in fulfillment of the New Testament promises, during those centuries when the faith of the apostles and martyrs still burned brightly in the church (sig. 3ᵛ). He argues further that it is not just reasonable but spiritually helpful "for every Christian to believe that the church of our best and greatest Savior was wondrously distinguished, in times of manifold and savage persecution, as much by miracles of all sorts as by incomparable greatness of spirit" (sig. 4).[31] As this wording suggests, however, Witzel makes no attempt to justify all the inherited stories about the saints. He takes his stand on the strongest and most authoritative elements in the genre, as he perceived them, assuring his readers that he has carefully weighed the credibility of the various sources and found many of them to be above suspicion. His own legendary, he promises, is confined to traditions which he himself considers true and probable ("vera & verisimilia") (sig. 3ᵛ).

It is within this larger argument, of course, that Witzel's verdicts on particular hagiographical sources are to be understood. Since he was attempting to restore the possibility of a broad consensus around the saints and their legends, he was obliged in effect to separate the unimpeachable sources from those that were open to question on the grounds of either doctrine or general credibility. Predictably enough, then, the contents of his legendary and his list of approved sources are noticeably weighted toward authorities from the first five centuries of the church.[32] Like Cano, however, Witzel also gives his stamp of approval to such early medieval hagiographers as Bede and Gregory the Great, and makes some interesting distinctions among the compilers of the later Middle Ages. Several monastic legendaries, apparently from the twelfth century, are singled out for praise (sigs. 2ᵛ-3). Peter Natal is commended as an author who has won approbation in Witzel's own time because he retold the old legends with an agreeable brevity and avoided "mythologia" where possible.[33] Vincent of Beauvais is adjudged at least preferable to Jacobus, and that "Petrus Lombardus" of whom Bolland made so much is praised for adhering very closely to the old sources; both the personal name and the description of this work would fit the legendary of Peter Calo.[34] If Witzel grants at least a modicum of respectability to these and other late-medieval sources, the obvious implication is that he found them sufficiently trustworthy and edifying to have some potential use in ecumenical efforts like his own.

Thus, when Witzel ranks the *Legenda* at the bottom of all the old books about the saints, there should not be much doubt about his meaning, however cryptically he expresses it:

Later, to come down to more recent authors, was Jacobus de Voragine, archbishop of Genoa, who was active around the year 1290. Even a blind man could see what sort of thing he has produced. . . . He indulges too eagerly in "mythologia," which is why he has come into such contempt among all sensible men. It is just this Lombardic history that the teaching authorities of the church have too much used—or rather abused—to the present day, while scorning or at least neglecting those deeds of the saints which the *Ecclesiastical History* of Eusebius Pamphili provided to be taught to the flock of Christ. The common run of monastic libraries contain no history of the saints but this Lombardic one, which they (I cannot imagine why) call "Golden." (Sig. 3)[35]

Jacobus himself is here accused, much as Cano would accuse him, of having filled his legendary with stories that any sensible reader would reject out of hand. Hence the indignation in Witzel's further charge that preachers, and perhaps bishops and abbots as well, had been teaching their flocks from the *Legenda* in preference to ancient and respectable sources like Eusebius's history. Instead of emphasizing the most essential and broadly acceptable elements in the tradition, as Witzel himself was attempting to do, such teachers are suggested to have chosen a book which was so flagrantly unworthy of trust that its continued use scandalized knowledgeable observers and added quite unnecessarily to the issues that were dividing the Christian community.

In the light of the sixteenth-century discussions of the *Legenda,* the old quarrel between Jacobus's critics and his most authoritative defenders, the Bollandists, begins to look very much like an ironic misunderstanding. On the most fundamental question, there was clearly no quarrel at all. Like Bolland and his fellow workers, Jacobus's early critics believed that the legends of the saints were too important to be consigned to a special realm where critical judgment could not touch them. Vives and Cano expressed the fear that the obvious falsifications in some legends would undermine public confidence even in good hagiography. Espence and Nicholas of Cusa addressed the opposite problem, the acceptance of unworthy and potentially dangerous legends, but they too seem to have taken it for granted that saints' legends could play a constructive role in the education of the faithful.[36] Witzel actually undertook to produce a legendary that would solve both problems, saving the essential core of the tradition—and reviving the ancient consensus around it—by pruning away all the questionable material that had become attached to it over the centuries. Bolland himself would suggest, of course, that these forerunners of his enterprise had been unreasonably harsh on Jacobus and his famous book. But Bolland's vantage point was quite different from theirs—and not necessarily superior, in this instance.

For one thing, Bolland seems not to have realized the kind of notoriety the *Legenda* had acquired by the middle of the sixteenth century. One of the more dramatic testimonies to its contemporary reputation was the appearance in 1529 of a French vernacular edition with the following title: *Le Grant et vraye Légende dorée et la vie des sainctz et des sainctes de paradis* [de Jacques de Voragine], *translatée de latin en françoys* [par Jean du Vignay], *nouvellement imprimée et corrigée des erreurs et choses apocrifes estans en la vie de plusieurs sainctz et sainctes.*[37] That such reassurances to the public had been felt necessary even in conservative France, two years before Vives published his opinion of the *Legenda,* obviously confirms what he and Witzel and Cano would suggest about the book's lack of credibility. The fables—or "erreurs et choses apocrifes"—in this particular legendary were so evidently beyond the pale as to arouse skepticism among literate Christians at large.

No other early edition of the *Legenda* testifies quite so explicitly to its controversial reputation as the 1529 French one does. A later French title page, however, adopts the same defensive tone: *La Légende dorée et vie des sainctz et sainctes qui Jésuchrist aymèrent de pensées non fainctes* [de Jacques de Voragine]. . . .[38] And claims that the book has been improved are prominently featured in so many of the Latin editions from the sixteenth century as to suggest that its publishers were seeking rather desperately to meet the objections of better-educated readers. The title-page descriptions of the editions published at Lyons and Rouen between 1500 and 1514 simply state that the work has undergone careful correction, using wording that might be explained as a conventional reference to the removal of printing errors.[39] In 1516 and 1518, however, there were editions at Lyons and Caen which claimed more impressively to have been newly purged of every possible error by a Dominican scholar named Lambertus Campestrus.[40] Thereafter the work appears to have undergone at least one extensive reworking at the hands of another Dominican, one Claudius de Rota, who is credited in various editions after 1519 with having diligently corrected the text "by the authority of the oldest exemplars,"[41] purged it (yet again) of every possible error,[42] and enlarged it by adding a number of legends from other sources. Most suggestive of all are the final attempts to merchandize Claudius's version. In 1554 one enterprising bookseller at Lyons recommended it—under a new and rather ambiguous title—as the latest and most long-awaited product on the market: *Legends, as they are called, of the saints. Now at last examined with the greatest care and diligence by Fr. Claudius of Rota . . . , and purged of countless faults: with the new addition, besides the Lombardic history, of some lives of male and female saints hitherto unpublished. . . .*[43] The next year one of his compatriots tried a more drastic kind of prevarication, using a title-page advertisement which rendered the book almost unrecognizable: *Legends, as they are called; or, Lives of the male and female saints, very diligently collected from diverse histories and arranged according to the progress of the year by the labor of Claudius of Rota.*[44] The implication is that Jacobus's book had become so identified with untrustworthiness in the public mind that no further promises of revision would serve. Even its last and most loyal promoters despaired of finding readers who would buy it if they knew what book it was.

In 1643, when Bolland first raised the suggestion that critics like Vives and Witzel had treated the *Legenda* unfairly, it was no longer easy to distinguish the reputation of this book from the reputation of hagiography in general. The sort of cloud that had fallen over saints' legends by the end of the sixteenth century is illustrated by the statements of the usually moderate Richard Hooker, who looked back on the whole genre as a regrettable lapse into folly:

Some brainless men have by great labour and travel brought to pass, that the Church is now ashamed of nothing more than of saints. If . . . Pope Gelasius did so long sithence see those defects of judgment, even then, for which the reading of the acts of Martyrs should be and was at that time forborne in the church of Rome; we are not to marvel that afterwards legends being grown in a manner to be nothing else but heaps of frivolous and scandalous vanities, they have been even with disdain thrown out, the very nests which bred them abhorring them.[45]

Hooker spoke from the Protestant side, of course, and not without hyperbole. But the kind of generalized contempt for the old legends that Witzel had warned against, two generations earlier, was now so strong among learned Catholics that the early Bollandists had to contend with the view that their work was not worth doing. In 1607, when Bolland's predecessor Héribert Rosweyde formally proposed the project that would become the *Acta Sanctorum,* Cardinal Bellarmine responded with the warning that such scholarship might do more harm than good. The old legends, he suggested, were likely to be so full of foolish, trifling, and incredible things ("inepta, levia, improbabilia") that to recover and publish them in their entirety would arouse nothing but ridicule.[46] And such opinions cannot have been rare; when the first volume of the *Acta Sanctorum* was finally ready for publication, Bolland felt it necessary to defend the intellectual respectability of the whole enterprise in his preface.[47]

It was quite natural, then, for Bolland to assume that the *Legenda aurea* had been just another victim of the prevailing prejudices against the saints and their legends. To my knowledge only one modern authority, the Abbé A. Sévèstre in the mid-nineteenth century, has proposed a radically different reading of the evidence. Sévèstre, who unfortunately neglected to document his conclusions, contends in effect that the prejudices would have been less virulent—and less enduring— had the *Legenda* been displaced long before it was: "The unfortunate success of [the *Legenda aurea*] has done more than a little to diminish the trustworthiness of more respectable commemorations in certain people's eyes. Modern skepticism has been fonder of decrying all miracles than of trying to grasp the truth about a single one. The Protestants have used this legendary as a pretext for glorying over Catholics—as if we were interested in defending it. It is not to them that we owe the initial criticism of this book."[48] Sévèstre's implied connection between the *Legenda* and modern skepticism is best ignored, given the complexity of the historical trends that have undermined belief in the miraculous. But the available evidence seems to support his conclusions that Jacobus's famous book eventually proved to be an embarrassment to the Catholic church and that it damaged the credibility of more respectable works—just as Vives, Cano, and Witzel had feared.

Sévèstre is quite correct in noting that, although Catholic scholars had condemned it already, the *Legenda* provided too tempting an opportunity for Protestant polemicists to resist. In England, for example, Thomas Becon (1512-70) referred to it frequently in his broadsides against the Catholic church, making capital of its notoriety for what he called "saints' lies" in his own generalized attacks on Catholic preaching; the following passage, first published in 1563, is typical:

Christ commanded his disciples to preach, not men's traditions, but the gospel, that is to say, "repentance and remission of sins in his name" to all creatures.

Antichrist commandeth his praters to set forth to the people his laws and decrees, and to intermeddle them with tales out of *Legenda Aurea,* and narrations out of the Festival, Martyrology, &c. He sendeth forth also his pardoners to publish fables and lies unto the people, and thereto granteth he letters and seals, and many days of pardon, and all for money.[49]

A few years later the Anglican bishop John Jewel (1522-71) was challenged to prove his accusation that things were read in Catholic churches which the clergy themselves knew to be "stark lies and fond fables," and he brought forth the *Legenda* as his prime example.[50]

The surprising thing about such polemical exploitation of the *Legenda* is that the passage of time did not end it or even moderate its tone to any appreciable degree. The Anglican bibliographer William Cave (1637-1713), who touched on the subject at the end of the seventeenth century, was fair enough to admit that discerning Catholics disliked Jacobus's book as much as Protestants did; but he portrays the book itself as a combination of papist propaganda and utter nonsense that still blemishes the reputation of the Catholic church: "Is this work to be numbered among the Christian histories, or is it rather to be relegated to the class of Roman fables? It has even been condemned, we observe, by the more sensible bishops—not without bitter objections. Certainly it is the silliest collection of silly lies, and crammed with the most absurd stories, which cannot be read, much less defended, without great scandal to the Christian religion."[51] As late as 1825, nearly three centuries after the last printing of the *Legenda* in England, the book provided ammunition for yet another partisan attack: a little book entitled *Catholic Miracles* in which George Cruikshank (1792-1878) strengthened his reply to Cobbett's *History of the Protestant Reformation* by holding up for ridicule a long series of supposedly typical miracle stories from the Middle Ages, all but two of them taken from Caxton's translation of the *Legenda*.[52] The dreary list of examples might be extended, but the point is already evident. If the memory of Jacobus's book remained alive during the long period when it went unpublished and little read, a good part of the reason was the satisfaction it gave to anti-Catholic sentiment.

That the *Legenda* contributed significantly to the backlash against saints' legends, as Sévèstre seems to be suggesting, is less easy to prove. Quite clearly, however, the special notoriety of this book lends more weight to the warnings of Vives, Cano, and Witzel—and more logic to their anxiety to distance it from better sources—than Bolland and his followers realized. Significantly enough, the major hagiographers of the later sixteenth century seem to have shared Witzel's view that dissociation from the *Legenda* was a prime requisite for the success of their own works. When Jean Crespin presented the Protestants of Geneva with a new book about the martyrs in 1554, he felt it necessary to explain in his preface that the work was not designed to revive either the cult of relics or "fables de *Légendes dorées.*"[53] John Foxe seems actually to have been accused of producing a new *Legenda,* and his famous *Actes and Monuments,* first published in 1563, includes a preface "Ad doctum Lectorem" which indignantly rejects the suggestion.[54] Catholic hagiographers tended to make the point more subtly, but they made it all the same. The huge legendary by Luigi Lippomano, whose first volume appeared in 1551, bore a title calculated to allay the doubts of the most suspicious reader: *Lives of the Ancient Holy Fathers . . . , Written by the Most Trustworthy and Approved Authors* ("gravissimos et probatissimos auctores"). The collection by Surius in the 1570s was more pointedly entitled *Approved Histories of the Saints (De probatis sanctorum historiis),* and it became customary for subsequent compilations to begin with an identification of the "probatissimi auctores" on whose authority they rested.[55]

The most suggestive indication that Jacobus's work damaged the credibility of the genre, however, is the fate of the very term *legenda.* Formerly in wide use to designate texts to be read (the original sense), and lives of the saints in particular, the old term was so discredited by the time Jacobus's book ceased publication that subsequent hagiographers went to some lengths to avoid it. Such legendaries as were not called collections of *acta* or *vitae* or *historiae* came to bear such titles as *Flos sanctorum* or *Trésor des prédicateurs* or even *Lignum vitae*—but not *Legenda.*[56] And by the middle of the seventeenth century *legenda* and its derivatives had gained a new currency as pejorative terms for stories unworthy of belief. This transformation was not limited to the English language,[57] but the dated citations in the *Oxford English Dictionary* provide the fullest and most illuminating record available. As these citations demonstrate, Jacobus's book itself occupied so special a niche that writers often referred to it simply as "the Legend," a habit that continued well after the book had become notorious for untrustworthiness. Hence, for example, the opening statement in Francis Bacon's essay "On Atheism" in 1612: "I had rather beleeue all the fables in the Legend, and the Alcaron, then that this vniuersall frame is without a minde."[58] In this context it was perfectly natural for John Foxe to coin the adjective "legendlike" as an antonym for "truthlike"[59] and to underline his reservations about certain miracle stories by labeling them "Legendary."[60] Here—and in Henry More's later equation of "Legend-mongers" with "intruders of absurd and impossible doctrines" (1680)—one comes closest to direct proof of the link between the negative reputation of Jacobus's book and the conversion of *legend* to a synonym for "fable," or worse; the *OED* shows a gap of at least a few decades between Foxe's pejorative uses of *legendlike* and *Legendary* and the first citation of the common noun *legend* in its negative modern sense.[61] In short, the evidence suggests that the suspicions aroused by the *Legenda* may have played no small part in creating the insistence on historical truth that would loom so large in subsequent evaluations of hagiography—and would ultimately be recognized by the Bollandists themselves as a rather mixed blessing.

It was not just their conception of this book's history, of course, that separated the Bollandists from the early critics of the *Legenda*. More crucial was the way they approached the book itself. From their own perspective, Bolland and his successors were perfectly correct in denying that there was anything very unusual about Jacobus's work. He seemed to have told no stories and used no significant details which were not paralleled elsewhere, usually in sources he himself identified; only the fanciful etymological prefaces could reasonably be ascribed to his own invention. These historians of the saints did not realize, however, that Jacobus's book could be perceived as quite distinctive—and objectionably so, in the view of various Christian educators—because of its selectivity. What we have here, in effect, is an optical illusion. The Bollandists, who looked for the sources of specific pieces of material in the *Legenda,* saw one pattern; other readers, who focused more generally on the kinds of material that did and did not tend to appear in this book, saw quite another. Hence, of course, the puzzling fact that the elements of "fable" or "mythologia" in the *Legenda* drew much more fire than they seemed to deserve, given their occurrence elsewhere. Witzel had called attention to Jacobus's priorities, condemning his apparent eagerness to present "mythologia" and holding up the contrasting example of Peter Natal, who tended to avoid such dubious material when he compiled his own legendary. Even more suggestive is Cano's distinction between Jacobus and compilers like Vincent of Beauvais, who uncritically transmitted everything they found in the sources; the implication is that Jacobus characteristically shortchanged sounder elements in the tradition in favor of questionable signs and prodigies. It is impossible to tell how many other Renaissance scholars consciously recognized Jacobus's selectivity as the major factor differentiating his work from more respectable sources. For our purposes, however, no further confirmation from this period could be so valuable as the testimony of our earliest and most dispassionate witness against the *Legenda*, Bernard Gui.

Gui's preface to the *Speculum sanctorale* leaves no doubt that the work of his best-known predecessor had been found seriously flawed. If the use of the *Legenda* had not raised substantive issues, Berengar of Landorra would hardly have set so high a priority on the production of a better legendary, and Gui himself would hardly have devoted so much of his valuable time to the project. Unlike the critics from the following centuries, however, Gui does not try to identify the practical consequences of the *Legenda*'s inferiority to the best works about the saints. He focuses entirely on the cause of the problem, and he traces it, not to the use of unreliable sources, as one might expect from the theories of Bolland and some later apologists for Jacobus,[62] but to a deficiency of judgment in abbreviating good ones. When he describes the principles behind his own work, Gui implies that the greatest challenge was to combine and condense the sources wisely: "Nothing is more favorable to understanding than lucid brevity. Rereading the old and new legends of the saints . . . , I have attempted, not by reworking, but rather by choosing from both, to collect into one body what was before to be found dispersed in many, passing over what is apocryphal and trimming what is superfluous, as much as possible, but leaving the truth and coherence of the stories intact."[63] When Gui deals explicitly with the deficiencies of his recent predecessors in the genre, the message is even clearer and less equivocal. The crucial error of such abbreviators, Gui suggests, is that they went too far; besides omitting whole legends that ought to have been included, they made such radical cuts in the others as to leave them mutilated ("detruncata"): "The reason for the labor expended on this work was that in the modern compilations the old legends of the saints and the histories of their achievements have been so condensed in so many places by the compilers themselves, in their desire for brevity, that a considerable part of them appears to be mutilated. Furthermore, there is no mention at all of many saints in whom there is interest at present" (p. 423).[64]

With the careful and understated verdict of Gui we reach the limit of what our early witnesses have to tell us about the *Legenda* itself. They cannot be said to have proved their case against it, or even to have set forth their charges in a fully coherent and unambiguous fashion. But they have made it clear what the basic issues were, and they have also suggested a set of doctrinal and literary criteria for evaluating any work in the genre. These scholars were not, of course, prepared to dispense altogether with historicity, assessing the old legends solely on the basis of their value as parables; a solid core of historical truth was considered indispensable in the Middle Ages, as well as in the Renaissance, lest the faithful be deceived into seeking intercession from saints who had never existed or who had not actually possessed the characters attributed to them. Unlike the academic critics of the Enlightenment, however, our spokesmen from the sixteenth century and before all seem to have understood that the most crucial question about a hagiographical work was whether it offered genuine edification to its readers. This is obviously a more subjective test than historicity, since it depends to some extent on the readers' own predilections. But to assemble the testimony of all our knowledgeable witnesses is to find a surprising degree of unanimity on the components of an edifying saint's legend.

Gui's contribution on the subject is found at the end of his preface to the *Speculum sanctorale,* when he explains his reasons for embracing the task urged on him by Berengar of Landorra: "My mind was attracted to undertaking this labor by the desire to know the renowned struggles and eminent deeds of the saints, their splendid virtues, their exemplary lives, and their pathways to perfection, so that I might progress in the way of God by their example, imitation, and teaching, and also that by the intercession of their merits I might be aided in my pilgrimage to that home where they live eternally and reign with Christ, the crown and glory of all the saints" (p. 424).[65] As an inquisitor Gui had developed a keen awareness of the delicate balances on which sound Christian teaching depends; and his statement here, brief as it is, provides a fine summary of the potentially conflicting elements within hagiography that were supposed to be held together. Thus he describes the content as including both the saints' struggles ("agones") and their glorious victories; he indicates that the inspiration derived from their legends is to foster both an active imitation of their virtues and a humble dependence on their aid; and he suggests, not once but twice, that the focus on the saints must lead the Christian beyond them, toward the Lord who is the real goal of his or her pilgrimage.[66] Few Catholic educators in any century could find fault with such standards, and in fact both our Renaissance witnesses and modern historians tend to confirm them. Disagreements arise over the value of particular stories and conventions used by hagiographers, but not over the genre's basic content and purposes.

The humanist educators of the Renaissance demanded more from hagiography than any other group of critics—and inevitably so. Both their own training and the necessities of their era impelled them to search for the Christian classics, the works of such timeless and unquestionable excellence as to be valid for all segments and generations of the church. Hence they looked for credible and effective presentation, as well as for sound religious content, and deplored certain tendencies to excess and extravagance that had presumably gone unchallenged by medieval readers of the legends. What is important to notice, however, is the substantial area of agreement between these critics and our other experts on the genre.

The pattern is particularly clear with regard to the traditional portrayals of the saints' virtues. When Delehaye pauses to defend the old legends, at the end of *Les légendes hagiographiques,* he suggests that hagiographers typically exaggerated the perfection of the saints and that such idealization served the purposes of moral teaching and inspiration: "The saints show forth every virtue in superhuman fashion—gentleness, mercy, forgiveness of wrongs, self-discipline, renunciation of one's own will: they make virtue attractive and ever invite Christians to seek it. Their life is indeed the concrete manifestation of the spirit of the Gospel."[67] As we have seen, Vives and Cano expressed an opposing view of the convention, protesting that portrayals of perfect and apparently effortless virtue were less morally useful, as well as less believable, than recognizably human saints would have been. It may be that this disagreement reflects a real difference between the psychology of medieval audiences and that of the better-educated readers of the sixteenth century; but it is also possible that the convention had never been as effective in edifying audiences as in promoting the claims of one saint over another. In any event, the disagreement is confined to a relatively minor issue. None of our Renaissance critics quarreled with the old principle that a legend ought to emphasize the exemplary aspects of the saint's conduct in order to inspire later Christians to the acquisition of such virtues. Indeed, this moral function seems, if anything, to have been taken more seriously in the sixteenth century than it had been in the Middle Ages. And of course the educators of this period (as, indeed, of most others) would gladly have embraced Delehaye's suggestion that the most edifying virtues for a saint to exhibit are those which clearly evoke the teachings and example of Jesus.

The miracles attributed to the saints have occasioned much more controversy, but here too it is possible to find a central area on which Catholic tradition has been rather consistent. Evidence of miracles has ordinarily been considered no less indispensable in the dossier of a saint than evidence of virtuous conduct; the two reinforce each other, helping to guarantee that the declaration of sanctity came from God, not just from fallible human opinion. It has also been understood that some of these miracles should be incorporated into the saint's legend, so as to edify the faithful. Again Delehaye's famous passage in defense of the legends comes close to summing up the traditional ideal: "Even in this world [the saints] live on familiar terms with God, and he bestows on them, with his blessings, something also of his power; but they use it only for the benefit of their fellow men, and to them men turn to be freed from the ills of soul and body."[68] Delehaye here suggests that the miracles serve to reinforce the central New Testament lessons about the generosity of God, the blessedness of those who know and serve him, and their role in transmitting his healing love to the world. Less constructive kinds of miracles were also recorded in the legends, of course; but the recent studies by Benedicta Ward and Peter Brown confirm Delehaye's emphasis on acts of mercy, and on healings in particular, as the heart of the tradition. Brown also extends the theory, noting for example that Augustine came to appreciate miraculous healings because they proved God's care for the human body as well as the soul, thus foreshadowing "the unimaginable mercy of the resurrection" (p. 77). Acts of mercy could also take on communal significance, as has already been suggested, by becoming what Brown calls "miracles of reintegration into the community"; the examples he cites come from Gregory of Tours and illustrate the special power of such miracles when they occurred in conjunction with the "moment of ideal consensus" at a saint's festival: "'With all the people looking on,' the crippled walk up to receive the Eucharist. The prisoners in the lockhouse roar in chorus to be allowed to take part in the procession, and the sudden breaking of their chains makes plain the amnesty of the saint. The demons loose the bonds by which they had held the paralyzed and the possessed at a distance from their fellow men . . . : the Christian community had, for a blessed moment, become one again" (p. 100).

Nine centuries later, when Witzel attempted to produce a legendary for Christians at large, it was no longer easy to see how such miracles could promote Christian unity. Witzel's own mentor, Erasmus, had poked fun at the credulity of pilgrims to healing shrines and the pretensions of the shrines' keepers.[69] And Protestants were condemning the whole system of relics, shrines, and festivals of the saints as an idolatrous outrage against the true faith. The breadth of the ideological gulf that was opening is suggested by the publication and swift popular success, in the 1550s and 1560s, of such militant replies to the traditional legendaries as Foxe's *Actes and Monuments* and Crespin's book of martyrs—books which not only portrayed the Catholic clergy as wicked persecutors but pointedly rejected all miracles except those of judgment and retribution.[70] In this sort of climate it seems remarkable that Witzel set himself to defend even a limited selection of the healings and other acts of mercy in the old legends. But he knew more about the ancient and respectable functions of such stories than most of his contemporaries did. Thus, although he severely pruned the miraculous content of the genre when he compiled his ecumenical legendary, both the explicit statements in his preface and the particular miracle stories he chose to retell affirm the value of the same mercy-centered tradition that Augustine, Gregory of Tours, and Delehaye all found edifying.

The best proof that our witnesses have identified the essential criteria for saints' legends is the fact that they do justice to classic works of hagiography which do not happen to resemble soberly factual histories. The most striking example—and the most crucial one, for our purposes—is the *Dialogues* of Gregory the Great. Even for a medieval work in the genre, Gregory's book has an unusual number of fanciful-sounding stories about demons and angels and marvellous events, and some post-Enlightenment authorities have dismissed it as a regrettable lapse into childishness or popular superstition.[71] Medieval scholars like Bernard Gui knew better,[72] and so did the more demanding critics of the Renaissance. Both Cano and Witzel recommend particular works which exemplify the kind of excellence they sought in hagiography, and they agree in ranking the *Dialogues* near the top. Witzel makes room for Bede and some other medieval hagiographers on his list of approved sources, but he clearly preferred Gregory to the rest—and, for that matter, to all but a few of the ancient writers in the genre. Although his usual practice is either to summarize the old legends or to replace them with poems or homilies in praise of the saints, Witzel uses substantial excerpts taken verbatim from Gregory's life of Benedict; and he leaves the impression that he would gladly have included the rest of this legend, which constitutes the whole second book of the *Dialogues,* had space permitted.[73] Cano, who exhibits more impatience with the marvellous than any of our other major witnesses, offers a slightly qualified endorsement of both the *Dialogues* and Bede's *Ecclesiastical History,* noting that he finds their authors occasionally too ready to accept inadequately verified miracles. But he recommends these works nonetheless, suggesting that their defects are quite minor in comparison with their value.[74]

These affirmations of the *Dialogues* are not important simply in demonstrating the reasonableness of the pre-Enlightenment approach to saints' legends. What we need most is a concrete standard to use, a work at least superficially similar to the *Legenda* which actually exemplifies the qualities most valued by our knowledgeable witnesses. And Gregory's book of saints and miracles will serve admirably. Delehaye described the archetypal Christian legend as presenting a "friend of God" whose miraculous powers always benefit his fellow men and whose virtues, although superhuman, deserve and invite imitation. The description does not fit all saints' legends by any means, but it certainly fits Gregory's life of Benedict. Gui and Nicholas of Cusa sought sound Catholic teaching, leading inevitably to the God beyond the saints; Vives and Cano stressed credibility and moral usefulness; Peter Brown emphasizes the reassurance the tradition could provide, especially when it manifested the unexpected breadth of God's care for human beings. As we shall see, the teaching of the *Dialogues* is sufficiently rich and well-balanced to meet all these expectations. Even Georg Witzel's demand for content all Christians could accept was satisfied, insofar as any medieval work in the genre could satisfy it, by Gregory's book. The point is not of course that the validity of the *Dialogues* has been always and everywhere granted. But this book, written to encourage the Catholics of Italy during the Lombard invasions of the late sixth century, has proved sufficiently timeless to provide inspirational reading for religious communities throughout the Middle Ages and beyond, to merit a Greek translation long attributed to Pope Zachary (d. 752) and numerous vernacular ones for the laity of the Western church,[75] and to win the respectful attention of a number of modern scholars. The chief reason, our witnesses suggest, is that it gives expression to the very center of the tradition, offering its readers a synthesis of the best and most universally relevant motifs in medieval hagiography.

The final contribution of our medieval and Renaissance witnesses consists in the way they define the task immediately before us. We should begin, of course, by examining the *Dialogues,* and especially Gregory's life of Benedict. The goal is not to make any startling new discoveries about this famous and much-studied legend, but simply to reach some appreciation of the lessons Gregory was teaching and the methods he used. This standard of comparison established, the logical next steps are to discover how the *Legenda aurea* account of Benedict is different, whether the differences are typical of the *Legenda,* and what they mean. Here the path before us will obviously become a bit thorny. Although nearly 350 years have passed since Bolland chided Witzel for rendering judgment prematurely, little has been done to remove the obstacles to research on Jacobus's book. Scholars have taken so little interest in the abridged legendaries of the later Middle Ages that most of them remain unpublished in any form, and for the *Legenda* itself we still lack such basic amenities as a critical edition of the Latin text or even a definitive listing of its thirteenth-century contents. The immense scholarly efforts needed in this area are unlikely to be made, moreover, unless it can first be demonstrated that compilations like the *Legenda* actually merit such attention.[76] Thus we are compelled to make the best of the texts at our disposal—Theodor Graesse's third edition of the *Legenda* (1890), a typical edition of Jacobus's sermons on the saints, and such editions as we can find of the sources behind them—attempting to use them all with such care as to maximize the probability that our conclusions will be valid. All that can be demonstrated beyond any possibility of error are the objective differences between Graesse's text of the *Legenda* (based on a fifteenth-century printed edition)[77] and the other texts we have, principally scholarly editions of the original lives of the saints. The situation is obviously not ideal. But since we will be dealing almost exclusively with authoritative sources like the *Dialogues,* which were protected against serious deformation in the Middle Ages by the very names of their authors, and with chapters of the *Legenda* that appear in all the standard versions, we can be reasonably sure that our texts approximate those familiar to Gui and our Renaissance witnesses.[78] And small textual variants or even occasional large ones ought not to obscure such habitual patterns of change—or mutilation—as these witnesses urge us to look for.

A more difficult problem, but one that must be confronted if we hope to make sense of the *Legenda,* is that of its authorship. There is no reason to question the traditional assumptions that most, if not quite all, of the first 182 chapters in Graesse's edition can be attributed to Jacobus de Voragine and that their content was not greatly revised or augmented after they left his hand. Rather, the crux of the problem is the impossibility of being sure that it was Jacobus himself, and not some intermediate source, who initiated any given departure from the original version of a legend. As the Bollandists have so often pointed out, we do not know the exact nature of the sources he used. Yet this uncertainty too is rendered a good deal less formidable by the recollection that we are concerned with large and consistent patterns of change, and especially of omission, in such legends as were least likely to have been revised in earlier centuries. If Jacobus's book exhibits scores of significant omissions from these legends, all quite consistent in their implications, the most plausible assumption is that he was responsible for most of them. This assumption has the obvious virtue of convenience, permitting us to use "Jacobus" instead of laborious circumlocutions to designate the mind behind the patterns in the *Legenda.* More important, it provides a real possibility of grasping the logic at work in the book, and thus of reaching a fairer and more enlightened verdict than the Renaissance did. To embrace this opportunity is of course to trust in probabilities and likelihoods instead of solid facts. Jacobus's characteristic omissions might conceivably have arisen from his continual dependence on an earlier abridged legendary or legendaries with just the same set of priorities. Should a source of that description come to light, an attempt to explain the selectivity of the *Legenda* in terms of Jacobus's career and personal temperament may look rather foolish in retrospect. But from the evidence I have seen, the risk seems well worth taking. The two earlier legendaries with which the *Legenda* should presumably have most in common, those of Jean de Mailly and Bartholomew of Trent, resemble it a good deal less than has sometimes been claimed. So do the accounts of the saints in Vincent of Beauvais's *Speculum historiale*.[79] Even in those chapters and parts of chapters where Jacobus seems actually to be following one of these works, most often Jean's *Abbreviatio,* his priorities are recognizably his own, not theirs. And for most major legends—including all of those to be emphasized in this study—he seems to have had access to reasonably complete texts. In fact, his accounts in the *Legenda* are full of passages that are not abridged at all, but taken verbatim from the original lives of the saints, and his sermons use additional borrowings from the same sources. As we shall see, moreover, the sermons tend to bespeak very much the same mentality and value system implicit in the selectivity of the *Legenda*.

II. The *Legenda*
and Gregory's *Dialogues:*
The Differences Examined

4
The Richness
of Gregory's *Dialogues*

In the *Dialogues,* and in the second book especially, . . . Saint
Gregory has given more than was asked. People wanted a
collection of miracle stories; Gregory has provided it lavishly.
But . . . the subject he is going to treat in this second book is
vaster and more difficult. For, if it is understood that sanctity
consists in virtue and not in miracles, the analysis of miracles
can shed light on the qualities which make a saint.

Maximilien Mähler, 1973

Although the *Dialogues* were written nearly seven hundred years before
the *Legenda,* the circumstances surrounding the two works are surprisingly similar. In each case the church in Italy faced a crisis of some
magnitude. At the end of the sixth century, the heretical Lombards had
conquered much of the country, tormenting Catholics at large with
doubts of God's will, if not with actual persecution. In the middle
decades of the thirteenth century, northern Italy had seen both the bitter
warfare between the papacy and Frederick II and the chronic defiance of
church authority by lesser princes and local officials who sheltered
heretics, forcibly expelled inquisitors and even bishops from their
territories, and sometimes—like Frederick—took up arms against the
pope.[1] In each case, then, there was a special need to reach the faithful,
to assure them that God had not abandoned the church, and to draw
those who wavered back into the fold. Both Gregory and Jacobus were
learned men, accustomed to teaching and writing about the faith on a
relatively sophisticated level; but each was also in a position calculated to
draw his attention to such public needs—Gregory, of course, the pope;
Jacobus, a teacher or overseer of young preachers in the religious order
whose central missions were to combat heresy and to spread knowledge
of the true faith.[2] Neither man suddenly produced a book for "the
people," in the romanticized sense of the term. As Adalbert de Vogüé

has recently emphasized, Gregory designed the *Dialogues* primarily for monks and clerics, not peasants and villagers.[3] Even Jacobus, who presumably intended the stories in the *Legenda* to reach a humbler audience, seems to have taken it for granted that the actual users of the book would be clerics.[4] But in these books each man came as close as he ever would to addressing the needs of simple believers, in terms they could understand. And the results, if not "popular" to the extent that has sometimes been claimed, were enough so to merit dozens of vernacular translations in the centuries that followed for audiences who could not read Latin.

If the *Dialogues* and the *Legenda* are similar in such respects as occasion, general purpose, and accessibility to less educated Christians, they are more crucially similar in kind. There is of course a great contrast in form between four loosely structured dialogues and a compilation that works systematically through the liturgical calendar, devoting a separate chapter to each saint and holiday. Nevertheless, the two books can be, and sometimes have been, described in almost identical terms. Each is in essence a work of basic instruction, emphasizing those lessons which its author presumably considered most fundamental.[5] Each contains a good deal of sustained, explicit teaching—most notably in the fourth book of the *Dialogues,* where Gregory discourses at length on such topics as the nature of the soul and the power of the Eucharist, and in the chapters of the *Legenda* devoted to the seasons and major feasts of the church year. But the essential flavor of each work resides in the arresting little stories, the anecdotes describing marvellous occurrences in the lives of the faithful and especially the lives of the saints. Sometimes connected to form a continuous narrative, sometimes brought into an argument to illustrate a point, sometimes just listed one after another, these anecdotes so crowd the pages of the *Dialogues* and the *Legenda* that both works might almost be described as collections of miracle stories interrupted by teaching. But clearly the stories themselves—brief, memorable, easily detached from their contexts—have the potential for great pedagogical effectiveness.

In the remainder of this chapter I will be concerned primarily with the basic messages about God, about the saints, and about the Christian life which Gregory conveys in the *Dialogues,* and with the place of the miracle stories in the larger design. Given the outward parallels between his book and Jacobus's, and the fact that the adjectives "naive," "credulous," and "superstitious" have been liberally applied to them both by critics since the seventeenth century, we could hardly find a more relevant illustration of what excellence means in a medieval work of this kind. For Gregory is among the great Christian teachers, and in the *Dialogues* he handles the conventions of hagiography with a mastery and breadth of vision rarely surpassed in any era.

Although his ostensible purpose in the *Dialogues* was simply to demonstrate that Italy too (like the deserts of the East) had been blessed with wonder-working saints,[6] and thus to encourage his flock in a time of crisis, Gregory was not the man to divorce the consolations of the Christian life from its demands on the individual. His determination to challenge each member of his audience is suggested by the hybrid genre of the *Dialogues,* a loose but functional combination of hagiography and treatise which permits him to teach on several levels at once, leaving some points implicit in the stories of the saints while underlining the most essential lessons in his commentary on them. Subtler but equally important are the instructional functions of the dialogue form itself. The deacon Peter, with his naive delight in the miraculous and his unending questions, serves in effect as a stand-in for the reader—a role made explicit in Book IV, when he asks Gregory's leave to impersonate the weak and make further inquiries on their behalf.[7] The point is not just that Peter elicits the explanations an untutored reader (or hearer) might require. The way he listens to the stories of the saints—his emotions engaged, his memory supplying parallels from Scripture, his mind constantly seeking to grasp and assimilate the underlying lessons—impels the reader to give them the same kind of active attention. As for Gregory himself, he moves closer to his audience by taking on the role of Peter's friend and teacher. In fact, having introduced himself not as an impersonal voice of authority but as a man who has lost the way in his own spiritual life (I.Prol.1-6), the Gregory of the *Dialogues* might most accurately be described as a fellow pupil with Peter and with the reader, seeking instruction from the real teacher, God, through the experiences of the saints.

Gregory's account of Saint Benedict in Book II is not only the most extended narrative in the *Dialogues,* but also the center of the entire work. Here ideals discussed elsewhere are brought together, integrated into the portrayal of a single life of surpassing holiness. And here too Gregory's method of instruction can be seen in its full significance, as part of the larger pattern by which God instructs the world through his saints.

Benedict's early life, as Gregory recounts it, has two major turning points. First the young saint renounces this world—leaving his family, his home, his studies, and finally his old nurse—and withdraws to an isolated cave where he can spend himself entirely in the service of God ("pro Deo laboribus fatigari" [II.1.3]). Gregory makes it clear that Benedict loves the wilderness and would gladly remain there, living alone and undistracted in the presence of God.[8] But God has other plans. Incursions into the saint's solitude begin to occur, Gregory explains, when God "want[s] . . . to display Benedict's life as an example to mankind, so that he might shine out like a lamp on a stand, and illuminate all who are in the house" (ch. 1.6). This second turning point is marked by the local people's discovery of Benedict's hiding place; recognizing his holiness, they are drawn to him, and under his influence many reform their own lives (ch. 1.8). This early sequence of events establishes the basic pattern of Benedict's whole life. Again and again he will withdraw to be alone with God, only to be called back by the needs of others. Thus his sanctity, continually renewed at its source, will touch the lives of a growing circle of people—not only his own disciples, in increasing numbers, but travellers and messengers, other religious living near his monasteries, lay relatives of his monks, the poor of the surrounding countryside. Nor does the outward movement end there. After noting the ways in which Benedict's influence is shed abroad within the narrative, we will see how it is extended to Gregory and Peter, and thence to the reader.

The extension of Benedict's influence is inextricably connected with the miracles he performs. Here of course we confront the issue of Gregory's predilection for the marvellous. It is true that, despite his repeated insistence that inner virtues are more important than outward miracles, Gregory gives us far more of Benedict the prophet and wonder-worker than of Benedict the inner man. It is also true that he seems to attribute every possible event to supernatural causes rather than seek a natural explanation. Thus, for example, a little bell that gets broken or a rock the monks cannot lift becomes a manifestation of the devil's enmity toward Benedict (chs. 1.5 and 9); the saint's ability to perceive the pride in a young monk's heart becomes an instance of his miraculous power of prophecy (ch. 20). But one ought not to conclude that Gregory is feeding his audience on trivial wonders instead of solid instruction. As Pierre Boglioni has shown, Gregory did not just believe—with the early Middle Ages in general—that supernatural forces were constantly at work behind the events of this world; he was also impelled by his sense of pastoral responsibility to look for the ultimate meanings of events, the messages being sent to mankind.[9] For Gregory, then, there is no contradiction whatever in using a collection of miracle stories as a vehicle for serious religious instruction; what makes an event miraculous, in his view, is precisely its pedagogical or moral function, "its concrete meaning for the life of the individual or the community."[10]

Let us see how this functional view of miracle manifests itself in practice.

When one looks at the immediate results of the miraculous events in Gregory's life of Benedict, one discovers that virtually all of them promote the welfare of other human beings. To be sure, Gregory includes a few incidents illustrating the classic motifs of combat against the devil, prophecy of the future, and vision of a soul's departure to heaven; but even such inward-focusing events are frequently given an outward, practical extension in his narrative. For example, Benedict's victory over carnal temptation enables him to take on disciples (ch. 2.3-4). The removal of the devil from the rock permits the monks to proceed with the construction of the abbey and shows them the power of prayer (ch. 9). Benedict's knowledge of the monastery's future destruction impels him to pray for and obtain the deliverance of the monks themselves (ch. 17). Of Benedict's actual miracles (as distinct from prophecies and visions), nearly all are acts of mercy, delivering others from hunger or disease or want or captivity or death. And his miraculous knowledge, as we shall see, serves above all to reform lives. Gregory's account includes no arbitrary demonstrations of power and very few retributive miracles. On the two occasions when enemies attempt to poison Benedict, the poisons—but not the enemies—are miraculously dispatched, and Benedict withdraws to prevent further conflict (chs. 3.4 and 8.2-5); when, after additional provocation, one of these enemies is struck down by God, Benedict grieves and imposes penance on a disciple who shows satisfaction (ch. 8.6-7). As these examples suggest, retribution is not lightly inflicted in this narrative, and the decision to inflict it rests with God. Thus one need not choose, in Gregory's account, between Benedict the wonder-worker and Benedict the human example. The miracles worked through and for him consistently support his generous efforts as an abbot and pastor of souls, healing, protecting, nourishing, and above all teaching.

Within the narrative itself, the lessons Benedict teaches by word and example are frequently driven home by miraculous events. Thus, when the monastery's grain supply is exhausted in a time of famine, Benedict reproves the monks for being downcast and assures them that they will have plenty the next day; when new supplies of flour mysteriously appear, just as predicted, the lesson is complete: the brethren give thanks to God, having learned not to doubt him even when they are in need (ch. 21.2). The provision of the water the monks need on a bare mountaintop becomes the occasion for another explicit lesson on the power and goodness of God (ch. 5.3). And of course the miraculous healings and rescues from danger repeatedly imply the same message.

For the most part, however, Benedict's explicit teaching is moral or disciplinary; the emphasis falls, not on what God gives, but on what he demands from individuals. Even the other miracle whereby God provides food in the midst of famine is used in this way. The focus is the cellarer who, having disobeyed Benedict's orders to give away the last oil in the monastery, is not only rebuked in front of the whole community (ch. 28.2) but also shown his own lack of faith when the saint's ensuing prayer is answered with new oil in abundance. And the lesson is learned: "The brother was ashamed at this wholesome rebuke. The venerable father had shown by miracles the power of almighty God, which he had hinted at in his warning, and it was no longer possible for anyone to doubt the promises of him who had in a moment's time replaced a nearly empty bottle with a cask full of oil" (ch. 29.2).[11]

At least three of Benedict's other miracles involve the same explicit pattern of correction and reform.[12] But it is the series of incidents illustrating his gift of prophecy that provides the most vivid picture of Benedict as moral teacher. Five times he confronts individuals with his knowledge of specific lapses they had thought to conceal. The lapses themselves tend to be minor: a meal taken outside the monastery, against the rules (ch. 12); a layman's broken resolution to fast throughout a journey (ch. 13); a young messenger's attempt to keep a flask of wine for himself instead of delivering it to Benedict (ch. 18); a present of a few handkerchiefs concealed and then forgotten by a monk (ch. 19); a young monk's yielding, in recollection of his family's status, to thoughts of pride (ch. 20). But Benedict's approach—as illustrated, for example, with the monks who have eaten outside the monastery— shows that something more is at stake than a broken rule:

He immediately asked them, "Where did you eat?" and they answered, "Nowhere." He said, "Why are you lying? Did you not go into such and such a woman's house? Did you not have such and such to eat? Did you not drink so many cups?" When the venerable father had recounted to them the woman's hospitality, the varieties of food, and the number of drinks, they recognized all that they had done; terrified, they fell at his feet and confessed their sin. He, however, quickly forgave them, judging that they would sin no more in his absence, when they knew he was present in spirit. (Ch. 12.2)[13]

What we see here is a first stage in the training of conscience. The five incidents of this kind make no mention of punishment; under Benedict's probing questions, the culprits are simply forced to confront the actuality of their fault and the fact that it cannot be hidden from Benedict—or from God. If the shame and remorse which ends each incident is based partly on fear of the power Benedict exhibits, Gregory would assure us—as he does elsewhere in the *Dialogues*[14]—that compunction out of fear is the first step toward that higher compunction based on love.

Within the narrative, as we have seen, the miraculous events serve not only to widen the circle of Benedict's influence, drawing others to him in ever-increasing numbers, but also to deepen his impact on individual lives by reinforcing his teaching. The extension of Benedict's influence beyond his own time and place also depends heavily on the miracles— and not just because, as some of Peter's reactions suggest, the wonders in a story make people want to hear it. Paradoxically enough, it is precisely the miracles, once their implications are understood, which make it impossible to hear or read such a story in a detached, escapist fashion. The exchanges between Gregory and Peter in this book of the *Dialogues* might have been designed to emphasize that very point. The central one is perhaps that which begins with Peter's sudden realization, a little way into the narrative, that he has heard these incidents before: "These stories are wonderful and quite bewildering, for in the water drawn from the rock I see Moses; in the blade which returned from the depths, Eliseus; in the walking on water, Peter; in the obedience of the crow, Elias; and in the grief for the death of an enemy, David. This man, I believe, united in himself the spirits of all the just" (ch. 8.8).[15] As Gregory explains, the parallels between the miraculous events in Benedict's life and those recorded in Scripture are not to be attributed to a direct connection between one holy man of the past and another; they are united at the source: "The man of God Benedict, Peter, had the spirit of the one who fills the hearts of all his elect through the grace of the redemption he promises. It is of him that John says, 'That was the true light, which enlighteneth every man that cometh into this world,' and of whom it is also written, 'And of his fullness we all have received'" (ch. 8.9).[16] The quotations from John's Gospel complete the transformation of an academic issue into an immediate reality. Revealing himself through the timeless patterns of Benedict's miracles is the same Lord who is at work in the reader's own life, the same Lord from whom "we all have received."[17]

As this passage suggests, the commentary on Benedict's miracles serves not only to clarify their theological implications but also to connect them with the experience of the reader. Even when he is teaching doctrine, there is nothing abstract or theoretical about Gregory's approach. Thus he tends to avoid such issues as the nature of God in himself or the relationship between the persons of the Trinity; most of the questions he gives to Peter are specific and practical. How, Peter wants to know, could Benedict pardon souls already judged by God (ch. 23.6)? Did he actually know God's thoughts (ch. 16.4)? Could he perform miracles at will, or did he always obtain them through prayer (ch. 30.2)? These questions and Gregory's careful answers to them serve the obvious purpose of clarifying the relationship between the saint's power and God's. But Gregory, as usual, manages to convey something more personal and immediate than a doctrinally correct view of saints. Although he makes it clear that the powers granted to Benedict are extraordinary, his explanations insistently evoke the analogy between what Benedict has been given and what all men have been promised, between God's love for Benedict and his love for the whole church. Thus Benedict's knowledge of God's intentions, with regard to a cleric aspiring to ordination, becomes a manifestation of the spiritual union between God and all those who faithfully follow him (ch. 16.7). Benedict's ability to lift the excommunication of some sharp-tongued nuns after their deaths testifies not only to the power granted to Saint Peter and all who govern the church, but beyond it, to the astounding generosity of a God who descended into the flesh in order to raise it up with him: "It was in order that earthly man should have such power that the Creator of heaven and earth descended to earth from heaven, and God, made flesh for man's sake, condescended to bestow upon flesh authority even over spirits. Our weakness is exalted above itself because God's strength has stooped below itself" (ch. 23.6).[18] Even the limitations on the saint's power—in this case, the impermanence of the gift of prophecy—manifest God's providential care for the individual soul: "By alternately giving and withdrawing the spirit of prophecy, he raises the minds of his prophets to the sublime and yet preserves them in humility; so that receiving the spirit of prophecy they may know what is from God, and again losing the spirit they may know what they are in themselves" (ch. 21.4).[19]

As Gregory's commentary on the miracles emphasizes God's relationship with his creatures, it also adds another level of meaning to the saint's example. The point is partly that the miraculous powers granted to Benedict serve to proclaim the greatness of his sanctity; it is through them, above all, that God has set the lamp of his example on the lampstand, where it can illuminate men who never met him.[20] But what is the continuing relevance of Benedict's kind of sanctity? Here we touch an issue whose importance to Gregory is suggested by the fact that the *Dialogues* both begin and end with it: how should the Christian live in this world? Again we should remember that Gregory addressed himself primarily to monks (or nuns) and clerics; in fact, as Vogüé notes, he seems to have taken it for granted that most good Christians would belong to one or the other of those classes.[21] But the idea of the

Christian life that emerges from the *Dialogues* is far more flexible and universally applicable than one might expect.

In the prologue to the first book of the *Dialogues,* Gregory introduces himself as a man whose interior life has declined so greatly since he took on the responsibilities of a bishop that he can hardly remember the heavenly joys he once knew in contemplation, and he wistfully suggests that the life of seclusion and contemplative peace is most holy and most pleasing to God: "My grief is often increased when I am reminded of the lives of certain men, who have abandoned this world with all their heart; for when I contemplate their heights, I can see how far I have fallen to the depths. Most of them have given pleasure to their Creator in a rather secluded life; and almighty God has willed that they be untroubled by the cares of this world, lest the innocence of their minds be stained by human society" (I.Prol.6).[22]

That the reader should not accept this initial hypothesis without qualification is suggested almost at once. Gregory's first example of extraordinary holiness turns out to be Honoratus, an abbot with the care of nearly two hundred monks (I.1); his second, Honoratus's disciple Libertinus, is described as performing a miracle while travelling on business for the monastery (I.2.2). But it is of course the example of Benedict, the supreme example of sanctity in the *Dialogues,* which most clearly corrects and completes the definition of the holy life with which Gregory began. For the pattern of Benedict's life is not just withdrawal into seclusion, as we have seen, but also return; not just responsibility to oneself, but also responsibility for others; not just contemplation, but also action. So far is Benedict from fitting the mold of a pure contemplative, in fact, that his life illustrates every element in Gregory's own famous definition of the active life:

The active life is: to give bread to the hungry [see, e.g., ch. 28], to teach the ignorant the word of wisdom [chs. 1, 2, 3, 8, et passim], to correct the erring [chs. 4, 8, 12, 13, et passim], to recall to the path of humility our neighbour when he waxes proud [chs. 15, 20, 23, 31], to tend the sick [chs. 11, 26, 27.3], to dispense to all what they need [ch. 27.1-2 et passim], and to provide those entrusted to us with the means of subsistence [chs. 5, 21, 29]. (*Hom. in Ezech.* II.2.8)[23]

One cannot conclude that Gregory's initial emphasis on seclusion and freedom from worldly cares was merely a rhetorical device. Like other theologians of his era, Gregory valued the contemplative life more highly than the active,[24] and he took for granted that withdrawal from the world was the normal path not only toward contemplation but toward heaven itself. At the end of the *Dialogues,* he summarizes the Christian's essential obligations, the requirements one must fulfill in order to depart this life as a free person ("liberum exire"), in terms of participation in Christ's sacrifice. In this final section God is envisioned above all as the Judge who awaits each soul after death; the Christian life, as a process of working out one's own salvation while there is still time. Gregory emphasizes the great miracle that occurs in the Mass: "This sacrifice, which mystically reenacts for us the death of the only begotten Son, is the unique salvation of the soul from eternal death. . . . Who of the faithful can doubt that at the hour of that sacrifice heaven itself opens at the voice of the priest and choirs of angels attend the mystery of Jesus Christ; that highest and lowest meet, earth and heaven are joined, visible and invisible fused into a single whole?" (*Dial.* IV.60.2-3).[25] But he is equally insistent about the inefficacy of that miracle for those individuals who have not forgiven all their enemies (IV.62.1), wholeheartedly despised this world (IV.60.1), and steadfastly turned their minds toward the next: "Then will our sacrifice to God truly profit us, when it makes us the victim. And we must also take care that even after the time of prayer, inasmuch as by God's grace we are able, we preserve the force and concentration of our mind; lest it be weakened by wandering thoughts or undermined by pointless mirth, and the soul lose the profit of its contrition by being careless about the danger of wandering thoughts" (IV.61.1-2).[26]

Within this context, the assumption of active responsibility for others can be regarded as both unnecessary and dangerous, involving as it does the risk of losing oneself in outward distractions. That risk is very real for Gregory, as can be seen from his practical counsels in the *Pastoral Care* and the *Moralia,*[27] and from his commentary on Benedict's abandonment of the first, incorrigible community of monks he tried to lead: "If the holy man had tried to keep these men restrained under his authority for a long time, when they were all conspiring against him and utterly alien in spirit, he might have passed the limit of his strength and, losing the even tenor of his tranquillity, cast down the eye of his mind from the light of contemplation. Wearied by their daily disobedience, he might have been less careful of his own; and he might have lost himself, and yet not found them" (*Dial.* II.3.5).[28] If the spiritual welfare of a Benedict would have been threatened by perpetual involvement with contentious and worldly men, the warning to ordinary Christians is unmistakable.

But Gregory's understanding of the inner life and of God's dealings with mankind precludes the transformation of general guidelines into hard-and-fast rules. Thus he refuses to rule out the possibility of contemplative experience among any category of Christians, however unpromising their outward state may seem:

> It is not the case that the grace of contemplation is given to the highest and not given to the lowest; but often the highest, and often the most lowly, and very often those who have renounced,[29] and sometimes also those who are married, receive it. If therefore there is no state of life (officium) of the faithful, from which the grace of contemplation can be excluded, any one who keeps his heart within him (cor intus habet) may also be illumined by the light of contemplation; so that no one can glory in this grace as if it were singular. (*Hom. in Ezech.* II.5.19)[30]

As for the possibility of actually uniting contemplation with active service to others, Gregory makes it clear that many individuals—notably pastors—are called to do just this. Theirs, he suggests, is a more demanding vocation than that of pure contemplatives, but it is even more faithful to the example set by Christ:

> Christ set forth in Himself patterns of both lives, that is the active and the contemplative, united together. For the contemplative life differs very much from the active. But our Redeemer by coming incarnate, while He gave a pattern of both, united both in Himself. For when He wrought miracles in the city, and yet continued all night in prayer on the mountain, He gave His faithful ones an example not to neglect, through love of contemplation, the care of their neighbours; nor again to abandon contemplative pursuits through being too immoderately engaged in the care of their neighbours: but so to keep together their mind, in applying it to the two cases, that the love of their neighbour may not interfere with the love of God; nor again the love of God cast out, because it transcends, the love of their neighbours. (*Moral.* XXVIII.33 [Butler, p. 176]).

And at least occasionally Gregory goes further, contending that the love of God and the care of weaker neighbors are not conflicting demands, in the end, but a single dynamic that resembles the mystery of the Incarnation itself:

> Hence the very Truth, manifested to us by taking our human nature, cleaved unto prayer on the mountain, and worked miracles in the cities, laying down a way for imitation by good Rulers of souls; so that even though they already scale the heights by contemplation, by compassion, for all that, they share in the needs of the weak; for love then wonderfully mounts to the heights, when it mercifully draws itself to the lowliness of its neighbours; and in proportion as it kindly descends to what is weak, does it mightily return to the heights. (*Reg. past.* II.5 [Butler, p. 181]).[31]

The exhortations at the end of the *Dialogues* present a much more limited definition of the Christian life, presumably because of the relatively wide audience Gregory was addressing in this book; given his understanding of the soul's progress toward God, the most necessary message for the beginner is to remember the Judgment and attend to one's own spiritual welfare. But in the stories of the saints, and above all in the life of Benedict, the reader of the *Dialogues* encounters the full breadth of Gregory's vision. Again and again the content of the stories demonstrates what is implicit in their very transmission and in the dramatized relationship between Gregory and Peter: that to live in spiritual union with God is to participate in the outpouring of his love to mankind. Indeed, at its summit, Gregory suggests, the Christian life is not only an imitation of Christ's earthly life but also its mystical continuation; insofar as the saint's will becomes one with God's, the divine nature shines forth again in the flesh, revealing itself to a new generation. It is here that I would derive the final lesson from Gregory's account of Benedict. For Benedict's preeminence among the saints of the *Dialogues* is not just due to his role in establishing Western monasticism or his ascent to the heights of contemplation, important as those aspects of his life are to Gregory. What matters even more is the way in which Benedict's life of pastoral care bridges the gap between the desert (or mountain) and the city, flight from the world and ministry to its inhabitants, by demonstrating anew that the mercy of God transcends human expectations.

5
The Impoverishment
of Gregory's Narrative
in the *Legenda aurea*

To know the lives of the saints was to know life from many
sides, for in them every age and every condition could be
studied. Modern novels or French *comédies humaines* are less
varied and less rich in their presentation of life than the
immense collection of the *Acta Sanctorum,* and of this great
storehouse the *Golden Legend* gives us the essential part.

Emile Mâle, 1898

To compare Gregory's life of Benedict with Jacobus's abridged version is
to discover the accuracy of Bernard Gui's diagnosis: the root of the
problem is not what the *Legenda* includes, but what it leaves out. Of
course no abridgement can be expected to do complete justice to
Gregory's account; so complex a work must inevitably be simplified as it
is shortened, some of its implications sacrificed in favor of others. The
surprising thing about the *Legenda* is the consistency with which it
sacrifices what most serious readers, in most eras, would consider "the
essential part." Many concrete details from the narrative are carefully
preserved; in fact, Jacobus retells the great majority of Gregory's
anecdotes about Benedict and frequently uses verbatim borrowings from
the *Dialogues,* instead of mere summaries, to convey the saint's words
and actions. At the same time, however, the *Legenda* shows a
remarkable tendency to discard the lessons, both explicit and implicit,
that Gregory attached to these events. In effect, the rind of Gregory's
account is retained while most of the fruit is cast away.

Jacobus's presentation of stories without explicit lessons and interpretations is the most obvious pattern differentiating his book from the
Dialogues, and it is also the easiest to explain. In some ways the
narratives in the *Legenda* are vastly more elementary than the sources
from which they descend. But the romantic image of Jacobus as the

85

great popularizer, the creator of a legendary for the unlearned, is of course an oversimplification. For one thing, he issued the book in Latin, a language incomprehensible to the average thirteenth-century layman, and even to many parish priests. Side by side with the little stories, moreover, the *Legenda* presents a good deal of material that is distinctly not geared to the unlearned: scholastic disquisitions on various doctrinal points, brief essays on the history of particular elements in the liturgy, critical notes on the conflicts between one source and another, and so on.[1] The implication, in short, is that the readers Jacobus envisioned were reasonably well-educated members of the clergy. Such men could be expected to appreciate all the information he packed into the *Legenda,* especially if they had few other books at their disposal. And when they read the little stories or used them in sermons, they would presumably have been quite capable of supplying the appropriate lessons.

There is nothing very revolutionary about the conclusion that the *Legenda* was produced as a sourcebook for clerics.[2] Scholars have long been aware of the prefaces by Jean de Mailly and Bartholomew of Trent, Jacobus's major forerunners and apparent models in the new genre of the abridged legendary. Jean's preface announces explicitly that his *Abbreviatio in gestis et miraculis sanctorum* was compiled for parish priests who did not have enough information on the lives and passions of the saints to teach their flocks about them;[3] Bartholomew's preface, that his *Epilogus in gesta sanctorum* was for Dominican and other preachers who wanted a handy compilation of reliable and edifying material about the saints to relate to their audiences.[4] The special problem in the case of the *Legenda aurea* is that it seems to have been issued without any such explanatory preface and repeatedly mistaken for something other than what it is. Even its standard title is a misnomer, insofar as the term *legenda sanctorum* implies a collection of texts suitable for public reading. As for its translation into the vernacular, one wonders what the translators thought they were doing when they made it possible for relatively unsophisticated readers to peruse this particular book by themselves. For the *Legenda*'s characteristic preservation of narrative detail, at the expense of commentary, would be anything but an advantage in such circumstances. The point is unusually clear in the case of the Benedict legend because Gregory's commentary was so pervasive and so well adapted to the needs of a general audience. In the *Legenda* it simply vanishes—not just Peter's interruptions and Gregory's answers, but with them virtually all of the transitional statements and conclusions within the narrative proper. Since Gregory typically used these statements to complete and explain the stories, as well as to provide some narrative continuity, their omission is a real detriment in terms of both readability and ease of comprehension. What remains in the *Legenda* is not a finished narrative at all, but a disconnected and often cryptic set of anecdotes about Benedict that must have fostered some peculiar ideas when it circulated as it stands.

The incompleteness of Jacobus's book, in the sense we have been considering, presumably had something to do with the kind of backlash it eventually aroused. Had its accounts of the saints remained in the hands of clerics, and had those clerics consistently used them as Jacobus seems to have intended—not just relating the stories to their audiences, but spelling out the implicit lessons and placing them in suitable contexts—Renaissance educators would surely not have found its influence quite so pernicious. The more one studies the *Legenda,* however, the more clearly one sees the logic of the early case against it. For this book is nearly incapable of yielding most of the moral and theological lessons which Gregory emphasized in the *Dialogues*—and which all our witnesses expected from hagiography. Even when the *Legenda* is retelling Gregory's own stories about Benedict and borrowing a good deal of Gregory's wording to do so, it tends to obscure or destroy all but a few of the original implications. And among the prime casualties are Gregory's central, unmistakable themes of charity and pastoral care.

A good introduction to the differences between Gregory's account of Benedict and Jacobus's is provided by the relatively complex story of the monk who could not attend to his prayers until the saint corrected him. This is the first real illustration of Benedict's success as an abbot, after his abortive attempt to reform an undisciplined community of monks, and in the *Dialogues* it clearly demonstrated his exemplary care for souls. The theme of pastoral guidance was brought out from the start by the details in Gregory's description of the saint's first monastic foundations: "He built twelve monasteries . . . , to each of which he assigned twelve monks under the authority of an appointed abbot. A few, however, he kept with himself because he thought they still ought to be educated under his own care" (II.3.13).[5] Once this particular monk's fault had been identified, the *Dialogues* laid some emphasis on the unsuccessful efforts made to correct him, both by his own abbot and by Benedict:

There was a certain monk who could not remain still at prayer; rather, as soon as the brethren had knelt down and applied themselves to prayer, he would go outside with wandering thoughts and busy himself with earthly and transitory things. After frequent warnings from his abbot, he was brought to Benedict [literally, "the man of God"], who also upbraided him severely for his folly. On returning to his monastery he took Benedict's warning to heart for a day or two, but on the third day he returned to his old habits and began to wander off during the time of prayer. (II.4.1)[6]

Only after giving these rather mundane details did Gregory introduce the element of the marvellous: Benedict's ability, when he himself came to the monastery, to see the demon who was tempting the monk; his disciple Maurus's ability to see it too after he and Benedict and the abbot had prayed together for a long time; and the blow from Benedict which cured the monk so completely that he was never again bothered by the tempter.

Jacobus's retelling changes this story at three points. The introductory statements from the *Dialogues* are predictably discarded; instead of setting the story in the context of Benedict's pastoral responsibilities, as Gregory did, Jacobus preserves just enough detail about the new monasteries to introduce the action that follows: "[Benedict] built twelve monasteries for the many who flocked to him. Now in one of these there was a certain monk . . ." (p. 206).[7] The early part of the story is also abridged quite noticeably. The unsuccessful efforts to correct the monk had some importance, as we shall see, but Jacobus's version omits them and hurries on toward the climax: " . . . there was a certain monk who could not remain long at prayer, but when the others prayed would soon go outside and busy himself with earthly and transitory things. When the abbot of his monastery reported this to the blessed Benedict, he came there . . ."[8] Only the marvellous part of the story survives intact, or nearly intact, in the *Legenda*. Here the one significant change is that the prayer, which went on for two days in the *Dialogues* ("Cumque per biduum esset oratum, Maurus monachus uidit"), now seems to accomplish its end immediately ("Orantibus illis Maurus vidit").

The most obvious effect of the omissions in Jacobus's version is to make the saint's success seem easier and more wondrous. Instead of working patiently with the local abbot and the monk himself, over a period of time, the Benedict of the *Legenda* needs only to arrive on the scene, miraculously perceive the demon, and miraculously overcome its influence. Later readers like Vives and Cano would deplore this sort of exaggeration in saints' legends, objecting that it robbed the genre of credibility and moral usefulness; and one can easily understand what they meant. For Jacobus's saint is less recognizably human than Gregory's was and less likely to be perceived as a model for imitation. Even his recourse to prayer is so described in the *Legenda* as to call attention to the power that sets him apart from other men, not the example of faith and effort that might be imitated. The really noteworthy change in Jacobus's account, however, has to do with the qualities for which the saint stands. As Delehaye has reminded us, much can be forgiven medieval hagiography when the deeds it celebrates are shining examples of kindness, self-sacrifice, and generosity to those in need. But to my knowledge no authority on the genre has endorsed the kind of hagiography which ignores those ideals and celebrates power in their place. The story before us exemplifies just such a narrowing of focus.

Both the *Dialogues* and the *Legenda* suggest that the blow Benedict inflicted on the monk can be seen in retrospect as an efficacious blow against the devil himself.[9] But the action was obviously directed against the man. Hence the importance of those repeated attempts at verbal correction, which made it clear in Gregory's version that Benedict was well acquainted with this anonymous follower and that gentler measures had failed; the monk was obstinately refusing to resist temptation, and the saint was morally justified in resorting at last to physical punishment.[10] In short, the story in the *Dialogues* was quite consistent with Gregory's portrayal of Benedict as a just and merciful father. In the *Legenda,* on the other hand, there is no suggestion that anyone has even spoken to the monk himself about his failing, and the blow seems wholly arbitrary: "The next day, then, the man of God found the monk outside after prayer and struck him with a rod because of his blindness; from then on he remained still [*immobilis*] in prayer" (p. 206).[11] If any virtue is exemplified here, it would seem to be the swift and effective use of force.

This first illustration of the *Legenda*'s selectivity would raise no great problems if it were just an isolated instance. Even the most careful redactor can inadvertently falsify the implications of a source from time to time. And even a conscientious preacher might occasionally welcome the opportunity to illustrate a saint's power over the devil—or his impatience with human frailty—without mentioning his larger example of charity and compassion. But it is not easy to explain either the compilation or the massive success of a sourcebook that retells story after story in essentially the same, reductive fashion. The omissions are not always striking in themselves. In the case of the Benedict legend it is helpful to divide the miraculous events into three categories: those whose immediate function in the *Dialogues* was to save or strengthen Benedict himself, those whose immediate function was to reinforce his moral authority, and those whose immediate function was to heal, protect, or nourish other individuals. Each group of miracle stories reveals distinct patterns of change in the *Legenda,* as we shall see. And the same peculiar set of priorities continually emerges. Demonstrations of love and compassion toward other human beings are almost systematically discarded from the legend. Comprehensible justice does not fare much better. Although the saint still manifests certain virtues, the most emphatic messages of the *Legenda* account have to do with his powers and prerogatives.

The group of miracles directed to Benedict's own welfare undergoes the smallest alteration in the *Legenda*. Nearly all these stories are retold with just one notable change: Benedict's experiences are severed from the life of the community. Thus, for example, when Jacobus presents the story in which a priest is sent to feed Benedict in the wilderness (*Dial.* II.1.6-7), he omits Gregory's prefatory explanation that God wished to relieve Romanus, who had hitherto labored alone to provide for the saint, and to reveal Benedict's example of holiness to other men.[12] The story in the *Legenda* suggests only that Benedict himself enjoys the favor of God: "After this the Lord appeared in a vision to a certain priest, who was preparing himself food for the Easter feast, and said, 'You prepare delicacies for yourself while my servant out there is tortured with hunger.' And he quickly arose . . .'' (p. 205).[13] Similarly, when Jacobus retells the famous episode wherein Benedict is inspired to conquer carnal temptation by stripping himself and rolling in the thorns (*Dial.* II.2), he leaves out the explanation that this victory enables Benedict to take on the guidance of other souls; the story in the *Legenda* suggests only the saint's private victory over the flesh and the devil.[14] Even the visions from the latter period of Benedict's life become private experiences in the *Legenda,* rather than manifestations of the bonds between Benedict and other saints. When he sees Scholastica's soul ascending to heaven, he no longer shows any emotion;[15] nor does the *Legenda* retain Gregory's comment on the burial arrangements as symbolizing Benedict's oneness with her (*Dial.* II.34.2)—or, indeed, any indication that Scholastica herself is important to Benedict.[16] All that seems to matter in Jacobus's account is the vision itself, the saint's privilege of seeing what other mortals cannot see. Benedict's great vision on the occasion of Germanus's death (*Dial.* II.35) is privatized in a more striking fashion. Benedict no longer calls his friend Servandus to share the vision; in fact, the *Legenda* leaves no trace of Servandus, whose visit and conversation with Benedict, each revealing his hopes about eternity, had established the whole context for the vision in the *Dialogues*.[17] Again, all that seems to matter in Jacobus's version is Benedict's private knowledge, the proof of his own privileged status before God.

Miraculous events of the second kind, those which served to reinforce Benedict's moral authority, were quite numerous in the *Dialogues,* and

Jacobus's abridgement retells all but two of them.[18] Virtually none of these stories, however, survives with its original implications intact. The most striking example of selective abridgement is the incident involving Totila and his sword-bearer. In the *Legenda* this is a simple story about the testing and vindication of Benedict's power of prophecy: "Totila, king of the Goths, wanting to learn whether the man of God had the spirit of prophecy, gave the royal vestments to his sword-bearer and sent him to the monastery with the whole royal retinue. When [Benedict] saw him coming, he called, 'Take it off, my son, take it off; what you are wearing is not your own.' The sword-bearer immediately fell to the ground, terrified because he had dared to mock such a man" (p. 208).[19] Setting it next to the corresponding passage in the *Dialogues* (II.14), one discovers that the *Legenda* has given a brief but accurate summary of the test Totila devised and an almost verbatim account of Benedict's response and the sword-bearer's terrified submission. In short, the miraculous core of the story is fully intact. But originally this demonstration of Benedict's prophetic gifts—like all such demonstrations in the *Dialogues*—served a practical purpose which has entirely disappeared from Jacobus's version.

In the *Dialogues* Totila was not just a name, but the central figure in this story: an invader whose power and cruelty made him feared throughout Italy. He did not devise the test out of idle curiosity; he was coming to visit the monastery and wished to confirm what he had heard about Benedict's ability as a prophet before consulting the saint on his own behalf.[20] And of course the humbling of his sword-bearer was not the point; it merely laid the foundation for Totila's own encounter with Benedict, a scene which the *Legenda* has omitted without a trace. Having been told how easily Benedict saw through the trick, Totila approached the saint with great awe and humility—and submitted to his rebukes, sought his blessing, and from that time on behaved less wickedly (*Dial.* II.15.1-2). The story in the *Dialogues,* then, was a variation on one of Gregory's favorite themes: Benedict's moral impact on other men. In Gregory's version one could see the way in which the gift of prophecy reinforced the saint's authority as a teacher, suggesting God's instruction of others through the saint. One could see Benedict's care—and, implicitly, God's care—for the spiritual welfare of even such a villain as Totila and for the welfare of those he threatened. In Jacobus's version, on the other hand, the gift of prophecy has no apparent function except the vindication of Benedict himself and the humbling of the relatively innocent sword-bearer. The only lesson remaining, so far as I can see, is that the saint is powerful and must not be mocked.

As in the Totila incident, so throughout this second group of miracle stories: Benedict's miraculous power is exhibited with great thoroughness and care, but the constructive purposes originally served by that power tend to vanish. Even when the *Legenda* retells the simpler stories about moral training, it characteristically deemphasizes the training itself. Benedict still confronts individuals with his knowledge of their secret faults; but the point seems to be simply that he knows, rather than that they learn and change. Thus, for example, the story of the boy who has stolen the wine flask (*Dial.* II.18) stops short when the boy finds Benedict's prophecy fulfilled: "A certain man sent [Benedict] two bottles of wine by a certain boy, but he hid one along the way and delivered the other. The man of God accepted it with thanks and warned the boy as he left, saying, 'My son, don't drink out of the bottle you hid; tip it carefully and see what is in it.' The boy parted from him in great confusion and went back, wanting to test what he had been told. As soon as he tipped up the bottle, a serpent crawled out" (pp. 208-9).[21] Omitting the final and originally crucial step of the boy's remorse ("Tunc praedictus Exhilaratus puer, per hoc quod in uino repperit, expauit malum quod fecit") and the fact that he grew up to become a monk, the *Legenda* transforms him from a beneficiary of Benedict's influence to another adversary confounded, much as the sword-bearer was confounded, by the revelation of the saint's knowledge.

In other stories about Benedict as teacher and disciplinarian, the selective omissions in Jacobus's book give rise to odder and more disturbing messages about the saint's power. Consider, for example, the story of the nuns inadvertently excommunicated by Benedict shortly before their deaths (*Dial.* II.23). The *Legenda* focuses on the marvellous sequence of events after the nuns' burial, emphasizing the way their bodies are compelled to leave the church during each Mass until Benedict intervenes. As usual, the human aspects of the problem and of Benedict's response are minimized, so that the compassion behind his intervention becomes less evident than it was in the *Dialogues*.[22] In this instance, however, the crucial change has to do with the nature of the nuns' offense. Gregory outlined the circumstances carefully, explaining that these nuns manifested a pride and discourtesy quite out of keeping with the religious life; in fact, they continually insulted the very person, a devout layman who looked after their needs, who enabled them to live as religious. After long sufferance the poor man complained to Benedict, who was sufficiently moved to threaten them with excommunication unless they changed their ways.[23] In the *Legenda,* on the other hand, the man in the story has apparently become the nuns' clerical superior,[24] and it is no longer clear that their conduct has violated anything more than his sense of propriety: "Not far from [Benedict's] monastery lived two nuns of noble birth, who did not restrain their tongues, but often exasperated the man set over them with their thoughtless speech. When he reported this to the man of God, Benedict sent them this message: 'Restrain your tongues, or I will excommunicate you'" (pp. 210-11).[25] To be sure, Benedict will still lift the excommunication when it is brought to his attention. But there is so little apparent provocation in the *Legenda* that even the threat of this penalty seems capricious—and so, of course, does the sort of divine justice that proceeds to impose it when the nuns die.

Perhaps the strangest and most disturbing of the disciplinary stories in the *Legenda* account of Benedict is that of the clerk warned against taking holy orders (*Dial.* II.16). In Gregory's version there was no doubt about the beneficence of Benedict's role with regard to this man: by fervent prayer the saint exorcised the evil spirit which had long tormented the clerk, and he sent him home with the warning that the evil spirit would return if he ever presented himself for ordination. Gregory's commentary at the end of the story underlined the point that the warning was a prophecy: Benedict realized that God had permitted the possession in order to prevent the clerk from aspiring too high.[26] Jacobus's account, on the other hand, reduces the exorcism to a very minor event, omitting the long series of earlier efforts to obtain the man's cure and (as usual) the saint's own reliance on prayer, and retains no trace of Gregory's commentary; all the emphasis falls on the cautionary aspects of the story: the warning, the clerk's later decision to disregard it, and his immediate seizure by the devil, who torments him until he dies.[27] The increase in harshness is obvious. And since there is no longer anything to suggest otherwise, the warning seems to be an arbitrary prohibition imposed by Benedict; the clerk's unhappy end, a punishment for disobeying the saint. Once again Gregory's more complex teaching is replaced by the message we have seen repeatedly in the *Legenda:* the saint is powerful and must not be mocked.

If the disciplinary miracles in the *Legenda* identify Benedict with a stern and sometimes incomprehensible kind of justice, the miracles whereby he helps those in need ought, one would think, to provide a countervailing emphasis on the traditional theme of mercy. Significantly enough, however, miracles of this last and most reassuring kind are considerably less numerous in Jacobus's account than they were in Gregory's. The miracles of healing, in particular, show a remarkable tendency to vanish. Of the five exorcisms and cures recounted by Gregory, the *Legenda* retains only the brief story of the boy healed from leprosy or "elefantiosus" (*Dial.* II.26)[28] and a mention of the exorcism that precedes Benedict's warning to the clerk aspiring to ordination. As for the two resurrection stories, the *Legenda* entirely omits the longer and more powerful one (*Dial.* II.32) and reduces the other to a single sentence.

The stories in which lesser human needs are relieved through Benedict's intercession do not receive such consistent treatment—or nontreatment—as the healings. Two of them are omitted altogether.[29] Another one, the provision of flour for the monastery in a time of famine, is actually borrowed in its entirety from the *Dialogues,* with the *Legenda* retaining even Gregory's explicit lesson about the generosity of God (*Dial.* II.21.1-2; *Legenda,* p. 210). For the most part, however, these pastoral stories are presented in abridged forms which markedly deemphasize the theme of mercy. Fairly typical is the story in which Benedict retrieves the blade of a scythe from the lake into which it has fallen by accident (*Dial.* II.6). Gregory placed this little incident in a context which demonstrated its personal and pastoral significance. The man involved was identified as a simple and well-meaning Goth whom Benedict had recently welcomed into the community at Subiaco.[30] He was clearing land for a garden at the saint's behest when the accident occurred; in his dismay the poor man ran trembling to Benedict's assistant, Maurus, blaming himself for carelessness.[31] Hence Benedict's intervention showed his fatherly care and understanding—a point Gregory underlined when he ended the story with the saint's words of reassurance to his new follower: "Here it is; now work and don't be unhappy" ("Ecce, labora, et noli contristari"). In the *Legenda,* however, so much of this human context is omitted that the story is reduced to an impersonal demonstration of the saint's power: "One time when a certain man was using a scythe to clear brambles near the monastery of the man of God, the blade flew off the handle and fell into a deep lake. He was very upset about this, but the man of God put the handle in the lake and the blade immediately floated up to rejoin it" (p. 206).[32]

One sees here both the lessening of the hardship relieved by the miracle and an even more familiar pattern: the distancing of Benedict from the other characters in the legend. In the *Legenda* even the saint's followers typically cease to have individual characteristics, names, or personal relationships with him. They are simply his foils, anonymous characters whose weaknesses supply the occasions for demonstrating his strength. This change from Gregory's practice is partly explainable, of course, in terms of the use Jacobus envisioned for the *Legenda.* The development of minor characters is a feature of connected narratives, not of collections of exempla for preaching. Nonetheless, it is worth noting how rarely Jacobus provides exempla which could be used to illustrate the spiritual fathership of the saint or the ideal solidarity of the community he heads. The pattern he seems to prefer is illustrated in an unusually suggestive way in the story about the water provided on the mountain for three monasteries Benedict had recently founded there.

Like many of Benedict's miracles, the story of water on the mountain has antecedents in the Old Testament; in fact, a subsequent comment in Gregory's account explicitly urged the reader to connect it with Moses' miraculous ability to produce water from a rock (Exod. 17:1-7; Num. 20:2-13),[33] when the people of Israel were complaining of thirst in the desert. The human context in which Gregory placed the miracle, however, was very far from recalling the conflict between Moses and his intransigent flock. There was no question about the seriousness of the problem to which these monks were reacting when they all came to Benedict, urging him to relocate their monasteries, and the saint's response was entirely sympathetic:

[These monasteries] were high among the rocks of the mountain, and it was a real hardship for the monks to be always climbing down to the lake to draw water, especially because it was a very dangerous trip for those who fearfully descended the steep mountainside. Therefore the monks from these three monasteries came together to the servant of God, Benedict, and said, "It is a hardship for us to climb all the way down to the lake every day for water, and therefore we must move the monasteries from that place."

He consoled them kindly and sent them away, and that night he climbed the cliffs of that mountain with a little boy named Placidus . . . , and there he prayed for a long time. (*Dial.* II.5.1-2)[34]

In short, Gregory's story was differentiated from its Old Testament counterpart by the spirit of harmony and mutual concern that informed it. The omissions in Jacobus's version cancel out precisely that difference. First, the *Legenda* fails to mention the danger involved in the monks' daily descent, and even suggests that their protests go on for some time before Benedict takes action; thus the impression is created that there is more grumbling than substance in the monks' appeal: "Three of these monasteries were high among the rocks of the mountain, and they drew their water from far below with great labor. And when these monks had often begged the man of God to move their monasteries, he climbed the mountain one night with a certain boy, and there he prayed for a long time" (p. 206).[35] Nor does the *Legenda* indicate Benedict's sympathy with the monks as the *Dialogues* did. The reference to his consoling manner is omitted; and he is not shown as sending them back to the spot where he has prayed with reassuring words about God's mercy ("For almighty God has the power to produce water

even on that mountaintop, so that by his goodness he may free you from
the labor of such a trip''), as in Gregory's version, but only with a rather
cold lesson about God's ability to give them water on that mountain:
"For the Lord has the power to produce water for you thence."[36] In
effect, then, the links between miracle and need, and between Benedict
and the monks, are severed in Jacobus's account. This miracle can still
be interpreted as a proof of God's desire, seconding Benedict's, to
improve the monks' daily lot. But, given the obvious parallels with the
story about Moses and the Israelites, it might more logically be taken as a
vindication of Benedict against the monks' complaints.

The story just examined is particularly important, it seems to me, for
the light it sheds on the logic behind the *Legenda* account of Benedict.
Although the *Legenda* retells some stories in which human needs are met
because of Benedict's power, it is quite clear that the value attached to
the miracles no longer depends on this consideration. Gregory of course
used the stories to show how individuals were reformed, taught, and
strengthened, and the community built up, under the care of God and his
saint; but Jacobus seems intent primarily on piling up the demonstrations that Benedict is more powerful and more favored than other men.
In effect the saint's miracles are reduced to signs, or proofs, of his own
greatness—and signs with rather combative overtones. The new focus on
the humbling of Benedict's adversaries, already seen in a number of the
disciplinary miracles and more unexpectedly in the water on the
mountain story, is manifested most tellingly of all by the material which
Jacobus keeps in preference to the two resurrections.

The second and longer resurrection story was paired in the *Dialogues*
with the story in which Benedict humbles the cruel heretic Zalla by
loosing the bonds of his prisoner with a mere glance (*Dial.* II.31.1-3).
Gregory used this story to illustrate the marvellous powers entrusted to
the saint and used the resurrection to illustrate what Benedict could
accomplish only through fervent prayer. Resurrections are of course the
greatest of miracles, by all the traditional criteria; and this particular
story has a special resonance because it illustrates the extension of the
saint's care to an unimportant stranger, a farmer who has no claims on
Benedict's attention except his grief over his dead son and his stubborn
faith that Benedict can restore the child to life. In terms of the value
system governing the *Legenda,* however, the indispensable miracle is the
victory over Zalla, where the saint's power is dramatically challenged
and vindicated. While the resurrection vanishes, this story is given
almost in its entirety, despite its unusual length.[37]

The earlier resurrection (*Dial.* II.11.1-2) had two meanings in
Gregory's version: it was both a victory over the devil, who in mockery

of Benedict had caused the sudden death of a young monk, and a manifestation of the saint's compassionate care for his followers. The priorities of the *Legenda* are demonstrated again when it ignores the pastoral motif, omitting all the indications of grief and solemnity that originally surrounded the resurrection, to focus on the saint's victory:

When the monks were raising the wall a little higher, the ancient enemy appeared to the man of God and indicated that he was going to visit the monks who were working. Benedict immediately sent a messenger to tell them, "Brothers, be careful, for an evil spirit is coming to you." The messenger had hardly uttered these words when the ancient enemy pushed over the wall and crushed a certain young monk in the ruins. But the man of God had the boy, dead and mangled, brought to him in a sack, and, reviving him with his prayers, sent him back to the aforementioned work. (Pp. 207-8)[38]

The patterns we have been tracing—the separation of the saint from the community, the willingness to identify him with a rather harsh kind of justice, the insistence on his privileges and powers but not on his ability to teach or reform or heal other human beings, the prominence of confrontations—are found in nearly every chapter of the *Legenda* I have examined.[39] The special importance of the chapter on Benedict is that it so clearly demonstrates the narrow selectivity which differentiates Jacobus's work from the real classics of hagiography. Part of the problem, at least for sober-minded readers in later centuries, is the *Legenda's* tendency to emphasize the saint's miraculous deeds at the expense of his human efforts and decisions. Far more surprising and important, however, is the narrowing of the miracle stories themselves. Despite all the surface details preserved from the *Dialogues,* the whole spirit of these stories has changed in the *Legenda*—and so, quite obviously, has their meaning. Instead of manifesting God's generosity toward the community, and toward mankind at large, supernatural power is put forth above all to ensure Benedict's own triumphs—over the devil, over the enemies who tried to poison him, over the sword-bearer who tried to deceive him, over the clerk and the nuns who disregarded his orders, over the monks who grumbled or disobeyed. In short, whereas the central motifs in Gregory's account were large, inclusive ideals of healing, reintegration, and fruitfulness, the central motif in Jacobus's is just the vindication of the saint against his adversaries.

Since the experts summoned earlier in this study unanimously affirmed the central importance to the tradition of inclusive motifs like Gregory's, there is no need to belabor the point that Jacobus's account of Benedict is much less suitable than its source for the general purposes of instruction, inspiration, and reassurance. The large question before us, then, is what other purpose or purposes Jacobus can have had in mind when he compiled the *Legenda*. By itself his account of Benedict does not supply the answer, but it certainly narrows the range of possibilities.

Jacobus's emphasis on vindications against adversaries is not of course unprecedented in hagiography. The most famous adversarial works in the tradition are the conventionalized passions that were composed, some time after the great persecutions, to celebrate the martyrs' triumphs. For our purposes, the noteworthy thing about these passions is their fondness for a pattern which Charles F. Altman has identified as diametrical opposition; typically they recognize just two degrees of value, two alternatives, and the plot consists in the separation of the righteous characters from the unrighteous ones.[40] Those who oppose the martyrs tend to be identified as enemies of God; the martyrs' chief role is to resist and vanquish them; and some of the miracles which accompany the struggle serve no evident purpose except to prove God's favor toward the martyrs and to ridicule the blindness of their enemies.[41] The analogy between these passions and Jacobus's chapter on Benedict ought not to be pressed too far; for one thing, the passions nearly always incorporate miracles of healing into their climactic scenes, emphasizing the divine mercy which upholds the martyrs during their ordeal, reintegrates their broken bodies after death, and is extended to all the faithful at their tombs.[42] But the resemblances are very interesting because the passions tend to occupy a disproportionate amount of space in late-medieval legendaries, given the centuries that had passed since the last of the great persecutions,[43] and Jacobus's book is distinctly not an exception. In fact, the major saint or saints celebrated in nearly two-thirds of the legends he retells can be classified as martyrs,[44] and in many cases their persecution, intrepid resistance, death, and burial (no longer accompanied by the inclusive motif of healings) constitute the whole plot. Some fruitful confessors—teachers, builders, and peacemakers whose work actually made a difference in this world— might have provided late-medieval audiences with a more relevant model of the Christian life, as well as a richer one; but Jacobus rarely takes this opportunity. Instead, he so abridges even a source like Gregory's life of Benedict as to produce yet more exempla about confrontations with adversaries, yet more miraculous proofs that God is on the saints' side, yet more emphasis on the martyrs' code of uncompromising resistance to evil. His collection thus becomes all too predictable, but it also takes on an unusual note of urgency.

Earlier hagiographical literature provides one other suggestive set of precedents for the emphases of Jacobus's chapter on Benedict. Acts of mercy were the miracles most valued in ordinary circumstances, as we have seen, but some of the miracle collections surveyed by Benedicta Ward exhibit a remarkable emphasis on acts of power against the saints' enemies. In the records at Monte Cassino and at Fleury, the French monastery which also claimed to have his relics, Benedict himself was for several centuries less typically credited with cures than with rather fierce defenses of his shrines and their keepers. Among the examples mentioned by Ward are the miraculous punishments inflicted on thieves who broke into the monastery at Monte Cassino (p. 44), a Norman who harassed a fisherman from the monastery (p. 44), numerous local knights who on various occasions attacked lands and properties belonging to Fleury (p. 47), and at least seventeen landholders around Fleury "who in some way offended the saint by attacks, trespass, mockery, or harm to the saint's dependents" (p. 49). Other interventions by Benedict persuaded a runaway serf to return to Fleury, helped the monks there win lawsuits and actual battles against their enemies, and punished laborers who neglected to observe the saint's feast days (p. 49). Such stories obviously violate the traditional expectation that the miracles attributed to a saint would be edifying to the public as well as politically useful to the sponsors of his cult; in effect, the saint's power is appropriated by the sponsors as a source of consolation for themselves and a threat to their enemies and rivals. It is also important to recognize, however, that this sort of polemical hagiography did not tend to flourish when the sponsors' position was secure. As Ward notes (esp. pp. 45-47), a much greater volume of it was produced at Fleury, where the monks needed to prove that they actually possessed Benedict's relics, than at Monte Cassino, whose claims to the saint's special patronage had been established for centuries. And the acts of power recorded at these and other shrines also reflected the genuine insecurity of such institutions in a period of barbarian invasions, political chaos, and general lawlessness. As the position of a shrine became less precarious, miracles of healing characteristically multiplied again in the records, and miracles of power and vengeance diminished markedly (Ward, pp. 50-51, 62, 65, et passim).

The evidence considered thus far seems to be telling us that the *Legenda* was not compiled to provide edification and reassurance to Christians at large, but to arm preachers for battles against some current enemy or enemies of the saints and their sponsors. This hypothesis makes perfectly good sense in the context of thirteenth-century ecclesiastical politics, as we shall see. But it so clearly contradicts the modern image of Jacobus de Voragine as a gentle, nonpartisan teacher and peacemaker that there is good reason to pause and make sure we have

not drawn the wrong inferences from the patterns of omission in the
Legenda. The best way of establishing whether those patterns actually
mean what they seem to mean, and of determining whether Jacobus
himself can plausibly be held responsible for them, is to examine his own
sermons on Benedict and other saints.

6
Jacobus as a Teacher: Supplementary Evidence from the Sermons

The *Legenda aurea* is, in essence, an attempt at popularization, at "laicization," of religious knowledge. Many other
theologians before Jacobus de Voragine had written not only
saints' lives, but commentaries on all the festivals of the year.
. . . But all those works were addressed to theologians, to
clerics, and the *Legenda aurea* is addressed to laymen. Its aim
is to bring forth from monastic libraries the treasures of
sacred truth which centuries of study and discussion had
amassed there, and to give these treasures the simplest,
clearest, and at the same time most engaging form possible.

Teodor de Wyzewa, 1902

Jacobus has often been depicted in modern times as a champion of the
humble masses—a thirteenth-century proponent of ecclesiastical democ-
racy, in effect. The actual contents of the *Legenda* point in rather a
different direction, as we have seen. The book was not of course
intended as a legendary for the laity but as a sourcebook for clerics, who
would retell the stories on such occasions and with the addition of such
lessons as they deemed proper. And there is nothing very egalitarian
about the lessons that come to mind when one reads stories about a
saint's privileges and his power to overcome his adversaries. Jacobus's
sermons abut the saints are significantly different in some respects from
the *Legenda* chapter on Benedict. But their characteristic emphases tend
to reinforce and clarify the implications of that chapter, not contradict
them.

Although Jacobus's surviving sermons were apparently published as
models for other preachers to follow, they cannot have been designed to
accompany the *Legenda* and demonstrate its use directly, as Ernest
Richardson once claimed.[1] In fact, the sermons tend both to draw their
quotations from the older accounts of the saints, instead of the
abridgements in the *Legenda,* and to treat the sources more ambitiously
than the *Legenda* does. Consider, for example, what is made in each
case of Benedict's first miracle, the restoration of a mortar (*capisterium*)

101

for his nurse, who had borrowed and broken it. Gregory's account of the miracle, the source for both *Legenda* and sermon, is worth quoting for purposes of comparison:

> Benedict was a devout and dutiful boy, and when he saw his nurse crying he felt sorry for her. Taking the two pieces of the mortar with him, he gave himself up to tearful prayer; and when he arose from his prayer he found the vessel beside him, perfectly sound, without any sign of the break. At once he returned to his nurse, reassured her gently, and handed her, in one piece, the mortar which he had taken away broken. (*Dial.* II.1.2)[2]

Jacobus's first sermon on Benedict (no. 389 S26) abstracts the moral content from this incident and incorporates it into a rather elaborate logical design:

> He began with compassion: as Gregory says, "Benedict was a devout and dutiful boy, and when he saw his nurse crying he felt sorry for her." And so he merited divine mercy: *Blessed are the merciful, for they shall obtain mercy* [Matt. 5:7]. He began with devout prayer, for he mended a broken mortar by his devout prayer. And so he merited great confidence and security from God: *The prayer of him that humbleth himself shall pierce the clouds . . . and he will not depart until the most High behold* [Ecclus. 35:21].[3]

Within the sermon as a whole, these are two of the five examples of Benedict's early virtue, each neatly supported with a reference to Gregory and another to Scripture, which constitute just the first of three subdivisions ("He was beloved by God because he began devoutly, lived more devoutly, and ended most devoutly") demonstrating the first of three major points ("He was . . . beloved by God, dear to men, and worthy of all fame"). And the three major points themselves are obtained, not from Gregory's account at all, but from a verse of Scripture related to Benedict by word association: *"Dilectus Deo, & hominibus, cujus memoria in benedictione est"* (Ecclus. 45:1).

When Jacobus treats the same incident in the *Legenda,* all the abstractions disappear. Indeed, the emphasis falls so completely on the visible events that the story is reduced in effect to a sequence of two pictures: "When Benedict saw [his nurse] crying, he took the pieces of the mortar, and when he arose from his prayer he found them firmly reunited" (*Legenda,* p. 204).[4] Besides the great stylistic simplification, one notes Jacobus's lack of attention here to the exemplary aspects of the saint's conduct. Gregory's explicit statement about Benedict's compassion, quoted in the sermon, has vanished, and so have the visible manifestations of that compassion: the saint's tears and the way he hurried back to comfort his nurse after the miracle. Nor would a preacher relying on the *Legenda* be very likely to see here a lesson about the devoutness of Benedict's prayer. Omitting "he gave himself up to tearful prayer" in favor of "when he arose . . . ," this abridgement transfers attention from the virtue emphasized in Jacobus's own sermon to the miracle which the sermon just mentioned in passing.

The differences between the *Legenda* and Jacobus's model sermons are rarely quite so sharply defined as they appear in this instance. But the basic contrasts in style and emphasis deserve attention at the outset because they alert us to two important points which might otherwise go unnoticed. First, and most obviously, the fact that Jacobus's own sermons are built from intricate structures of abstract ideas, instead of from such anecdotes and pictures as he supplied for other preachers' use in the *Legenda,* tells us that he envisioned two different groups of listeners. Both would of course be comprised primarily of laymen, but one group is credited in effect with far more knowledge and intellectual sophistication than the other.[5] The departure from Gregory's example is worth noting, for Gregory made the *Dialogues* popular in an inclusive sense; although they are accessible to readers with relatively little education, they are also designed to challenge and delight the learned. The stories in the *Legenda,* on the other hand, seem to have been produced specifically, even exclusively, for use with an unsophisticated segment of the public, an audience quite distinct from both the clergy who would teach them and the educated laity assumed by Jacobus's model sermons.

The disappearance from the *Legenda* of the very details Jacobus emphasizes in his sermons, and vice versa, is a more striking phenomenon, and one which occurs with some regularity in the case of Benedict; but it demands to be interpreted with caution. One does not always find so neat a division between Jacobus's two works—virtues for the sermons, miracles for the *Legenda.* What one does find rather consistently is evidence that, unlike Gregory and all our commentators on saints' legends, Jacobus saw some reason to separate these two aspects of the saints' experience. And for ordinary purposes of instruction he preferred the virtues. His concentration on the miraculous when he compiled the *Legenda* was thus a deliberate choice, reflecting the particular audience and occasion for which that book was intended. His sermons dwell by preference on the moral lessons to be derived from the saints' exemplary conduct—but not, as we shall see, on the same kinds of lessons that were central for teachers like Gregory.

The most fundamental similarity between the model sermons and the *Legenda* is Jacobus's tendency to reshape the old legends, bringing out different and less inclusive lessons than the original authors emphasized. Here the sermons on Benedict are rather typical. One might naively suppose that a thirteenth-century friar would naturally seize on the ways in which Benedict's example of faithfulness and charity applies to the laity or to their pastors or to both. What Jacobus's sermons present, however, is an interpretation of Benedict's life that is much narrower and less encouraging to uncloistered Christians than the one in the *Dialogues*. A handful of lessons seem directed to believers at large. Adding his own interpretations to the details Gregory gave, Jacobus explains that Benedict received the sacrament just before death "to arm himself against the malice of the devils who lie in wait for souls,"[6] that he had himself carried into the church in order to express his gratitude for God's grace, and that the way he had his tomb prepared shows his exemplary eagerness to die (no. 389 S26, p. 108; cf. *Dial.* II.37.2). The posture in which Benedict died becomes the occasion for a little commentary suggesting more strongly that all Christians should prepare for death as he did: "Some die on their backs because they are barren of good works; some on their faces, who have been tripped up by sin; some lame, who had faith without works; some cured of their weakness, who have returned from sin to penitence; some standing like the saints, who are free of sin, full of good works, and of upright intention" (ibid.).[7] At the beginning of the same sermon Jacobus gives a list of the young saint's virtues which, as we have seen, includes compassion and prayer. But the lessons that receive the most emphasis in the three sermons on Benedict are lessons about the special demands and rewards of the religious state.

Jacobus's tendency to portray Benedict as an exemplar of the religious state, rather than of the Christian life in general, is especially clear in the third sermon (no. 391 S26). Here Jacobus's text is the famous call to Abraham in the twelfth chapter of Genesis, the beginning of God's covenant with Israel: "Go forth out of thy country, and from thy kindred, and out of thy father's house, and come into the land which I shall show thee. And I will make of thee a great nation, and I will bless thee, and magnify thy name, and thou shalt be blessed [*benedictus*]" (Gen. 12:1-2). Jacobus proceeds of course to relate the text to Benedict, and thence to other Christians—but only to those who are prepared to embrace the special calling of the *religiosus:*

These words, which the Lord spoke to Abraham, can be applied to the blessed Benedict and to all religious men. In them the Lord urges each of us to three things.
First, to contempt of the world . . .
Second, the Lord urges us to make a beginning in religion . . .
Third, he announces the fruit of religion . . . (Pp. 110-11)[8]

As its major headings suggest, the entire sermon is devoted to showing how God's call is answered, and his promises fulfilled, in the religious life. If he sees any way for a layman or a woman to emulate the faith of Abraham and Benedict, Jacobus does not mention it.

Jacobus does not neglect to suggest that some varieties of the religious life are preferable to others. In the first sermon he uses an analogy between the *Rule* bequeathed by Benedict and the moon, illumined by the sun after its setting, as the occasion for a slap at worldly monks: "The moon, however, does not shine when the earth is interposed; likewise the monastic state is darkly shadowed when it is spattered with earthly greed" (p. 108).9 In the second sermon (no. 390 S26) the criticism is harsher and more sweeping. All of Benedict's own sons, it seems, have deserted him: "[It is written,] *Let [him] be blessed with children* [Deut. 33:24] . . . but now he can complain, *I have brought up children and exalted them, but they have despised me* [Isa. 1:2]. His sons have fallen away from his example, for they scorn the observance of his rule, and they are eager for prelacies and abbotships. They use temporal things unduly, and they do not attend to the honor of God, but to their own advancement" (p. 109).10 The contrast between such behavior and that of the new mendicant orders, still rigorously emulating the poverty of their founders, would presumably not have escaped a thirteenth-century audience. And when Jacobus describes the basic thrusts of Benedict's career, he assimilates him rather noticeably to the ideals of study and preaching that characterized the Dominicans in particular: "He lived more devoutly, for his whole life was passed in prayer, so that he deserved to be heard . . . ; and in reading,11 so that he deserved to be imbued with divine wisdom . . . ; and in contemplation, so that he deserved to be filled with celestial revelations . . . ; and in profitable speech, so that he deserved to be heard by his audience; as Gregory says, 'When they brought him food for the body, they took from his mouth the food of life' [*Dial.* II.1.8]" (no. 389 S26, p. 108).12

But if the Benedict of Jacobus's sermons can serve as a model for preaching friars as well as for monks, the reason has almost nothing to do with the active-life motifs in the *Dialogues*. In fact, Jacobus ignores Gregory's whole emphasis on the way Benedict reconciled the ideals of the desert with the demands of the city, preferring to dwell on the conventionally monastic—even eremitical—aspects of the saint's life. Thus he comes very close to reducing Benedict to the model of a pure contemplative. The pattern is evident in the passage just quoted, and it is even clearer when Jacobus sums up the saint's journey toward perfection: "Saint Benedict came from the dark world to the desert of penitence, and from the desert of penitence he attained the taste of heavenly grace, and from the taste of grace he reached the contemplation of the divine vision" (no. 390 S26, p. 109).[13] Nor does Jacobus make much room in his sermons for the charity, and especially the care for weaker neighbors, that figured so prominently in Gregory's account of Benedict. Instead, the sermons keep returning to a small group of virtues and decisions from the first and most reclusive stage of the saint's career: his renunciation of worldly goods,[14] his detachment from earthly pleasures, his flight from the praise of men, his complete conquest of carnal temptation.[15] Thus the essential element in Benedict's example, as Jacobus presents it, seems to be withdrawal from the world—precisely the element that sets him apart from Christians with secular responsibilities and distractions. The recurrent message is that his life has no practical relevance to laymen, or even to secular clergy, unless they are prepared to exchange their own vocations for the higher and more austere calling of the *religiosus*.

Oddly enough, when Jacobus praises another famous preacher (Ambrose) for adapting his teaching to the needs of different audiences, it is Gregory whom he cites as the great authority recommending this procedure: "We should not use one and the same method of teaching for everyone, but adapt it according to the nature of the audience, as Gregory indicates in the *Moralia*,[16] when he says, 'Often what is a help to some is a hindrance to others. For often plants that are nourishing to some animals are fatal to others; quiet whistling calms horses but rouses dogs; the medicine which cures disease in one man aggravates it in another; the bread which gives strength to strong men kills little children'" (no. 423 S4, p. 154).[17] But Gregory clearly had not envisioned quite so literal a separation between the nourishments appropriate to different groups, or between the groups themselves, as Jacobus did. With regard to moral instruction, it is worth recalling that the *Dialogues* offered teaching for "strong men" alongside the lessons especially necessary for "little children" and repeatedly suggested the relevance of the saints' experience to the life of every Christian. Jacobus, on the other hand, characteristically finds lessons for the faithful at large only in the way a saint dies. Elsewhere, he seems almost automatically to divide Christians into classes—male and female, celibates and noncelibates, *religiosi* and seculars, and so on. And his sermons emphasize the distinctions, not the continuities, between one class and another. One important consequence of his approach is the devaluing of those virtues which all Christians are supposed to practice. He places so much emphasis on the higher callings of monks and regular clergy and bishops, and so insistently defines the perfection of those states in terms of the special virtues they require, as to suggest that the basic New Testament ideals of faith, humility, charity, and hope are rather poor things by comparison. Another consequence, of course, is the continual suggestion that the church is necessarily a hierarchical institution, not a democratic one.

The conservative thrust of Jacobus's sermons is most strikingly illustrated by the way he reinterprets those legends which seem to contradict the established late-medieval order. One prominent example is Martin of Tours, a fourth-century bishop whose personal witness to the Gospel included a life-long refusal to assume privileges and dignities that would distinguish him from the humblest members of his society. In an earlier study I have shown in some detail how Jacobus manages to reverse the social and political implications of the *Vita S. Martini* so that even Martin becomes, in effect, a pillar of the thirteenth-century establishment.[18] His career is used to exemplify the orderly steps in the hierarchy from layman to monk to bishop; and as bishop, Martin's principal characteristics are dignity and power, not the poverty and humility which set him against the worldlier bishops of his own day—and of Jacobus's.[19] The legend of Catherine of Alexandria seems to have posed a more complicated challenge, from Jacobus's point of view. He credits her with the special merit of preaching, placing some emphasis on her consequent superiority to other virgin martyrs, but he also takes pains to prove that her example provides no occasion for supposing that other women and laymen should have the right to preach. In one sermon (no. 591 S85) he argues that Catherine actually upheld the standard rules instead of violating them. Thus, he asserts, she did not venture to preach without permission; indeed, she and a few other holy women were authorized to do so by the Holy Spirit: "Although the office of preaching is prohibited to women, nevertheless the Holy Spirit has granted to certain holy virgins the office of preaching, as a privilege of singular grace" (p. 366).[20] But neither did Catherine preach without the requisite knowledge. With an eye perhaps on the spiritual claims of the Waldenses and other lay preachers of his time, Jacobus insists on the social and educational status of Catherine's converts[21] and on the excellence of her own education. In fact, he suggests—reversing the priorities of the legend itself—that the special efficacy of her preaching was due, not to the wisdom infused by God, but to her background in all the liberal arts.[22]

At times Jacobus uses the examples of the saints to suggest broader lessons about the order established by God. Thus Martin's virtues as a layman, as defined in two sermons, include obedience to his superiors in society, kindness to his inferiors, and amiability to his equals.[23] When Jacobus deals explicitly with the virtue of justice, in one sermon on Thomas of Canterbury, he sketches in the outline of a whole Christian ethic based on due order: "Now, justice is defined as the virtue which renders to each his due: that is, to God, obedience; to a superior, reverence; to an equal, harmony; to an inferior, instruction [or discipline]; to enemies, patience; to the wretched and suffering, active compassion; and to oneself, sanctity" (no. 339 S12, p. 46).[24] In practice, however, he focuses more attention on the interactions of superiors and inferiors than on the other kinds of human relationships, reinforcing the message that inequalities of rank are part of the divine plan, and must be recognized and respected. One interesting example occurs in the second sermon on Benedict (no. 390 S26), when Jacobus sets out to show why Benedict's *Rule* is pleasing to God and to men. The Biblical text he has chosen presents three images of mutual harmony: "With three things my spirit is pleased, which are approved before God and men: The concord of brethren, and the love of neighbours, and man and wife that agree well together" (Ecclus. 25:1-2). But Jacobus's explanation invokes an allegorical interpretation of the third image which adapts it to the monastic life and brings out a more general lesson on authority and obedience: "By that rule monks are taught . . . how much obedience is owed to superiors [*Praelatos*], and so it is said *man and wife that agree well together;* for the superior, as we are to interpret *man,* and the inferior, as we are to interpret *wife,* agree well together when the superior rules wisely and the inferior obeys humbly" (p. 109).[25]

That women are naturally inferior was a truism in the Middle Ages, of course, but Jacobus repeatedly goes out of his way to drive home this lesson. The most dramatic example occurs in the *Legenda* chapter on the Purification of the Virgin, which makes room for a lengthy and apparently gratuitous discussion of why Leviticus 12 prescribes a longer period for purification after a daughter's birth than after a son's. The purification period is identified with the length of time between conception and the completion of the fetal body (40 days for a male child, 80 for a female), and this supposed biological difference is given three allegorical explanations which conclude in so many words that women are greater sinners and that God prefers men.[26] There is nothing quite so blunt in Jacobus's sermons, but there the achievements of female saints tend rather paradoxically to elicit long comments on the moral frailty of their sex. Ignoring the wedding night Cecilia spent alone with her pagan bridegroom, for example, Jacobus derives from her legend the lesson that women can preserve their chastity only by avoiding dangerous relationships with men:

Fourth, [Cecilia preserved her virgin loveliness] by avoiding suspect intimacy. She had no intimate relationshps except with holy people like Bishop Urban and with the poor whom she fed. For according to Chrysostom, it is very dangerous for dedicated women to be on intimate terms with men, for two reasons. One is that women are incautious and weak. . . . But even greater is the danger to virgins, as the same authority tells us, because they are incautious, and because they are weak, and because they are inexperienced. . . . But the greatest danger is to widows. . . . (No. 586 S83, p. 360)[27]

Similarly, Catherine's triumphs over temptation become the occasions for lessons about the corruptibility of women in general;[28] her independence of action, for a reminder that women need strict governance and supervision.[29]

If Jacobus firmly sets women in their traditional place at the bottom of Christian society, he reminds his audience even more frequently that the highest positions of authority belong to bishops and other prelates. In the sermons his most characteristic method is simply to emphasize the special power and perfection attained by saints who held such offices. Occasionally, however, he uses some rather strong polemic to prove that the authority of the higher clergy is sacred and unchallengeable, especially by laymen. Thus, for example, two of his sermons on Pope Sylvester give more prominence to the Donation of Constantine than to any point about Sylvester himself. And in the second one Constantine's humble withdrawal from Rome, lest an earthly ruler presume to compete with the pope, is just the beginning; as the climactic point Jacobus adds Constantine's reported tribute to the assembled bishops at Nicaea as gods, set over all men as judges who cannot themselves be judged except by God:

We read in the *Ecclesiastical History* that when, at the Council of Nicaea, the various bishops presented Constantine with memoranda so that he could decide among them, he threw all the documents in the fire, saying, "God has given you the power of judging us, and so it is right that we be judged by you; but you cannot be judged by men. For God has given you to us as gods, and it is not right that gods be judged by men, but by him of whom it is said, *God hath stood in the congregation of gods* [Ps. 81(82):1]. (No. 343 S13, p. 52)[30]

Also worth noting is a passage from the second sermon on Thomas of Canterbury; here Jacobus dwells on the unworthiness of the assassins— and, by implication, any layman—to touch something so holy as the body of the martyred bishop:

Now the body of Saint Thomas was an instrument of the Holy Spirit, God's pearl, Christ's sacrifice [*hostia*]; but his persecutors were dogs, and so they ought not to have touched the instrument of the Holy Spirit; and because they were swine, they ought not to have trodden upon God's pearl . . . ; and because they were profane, they ought not to have handled Christ's sacrifice. Thus the body of Saint Thomas, after it had been offered up like the sacred Host, ought to have been touched only by God's ministers, for even in the old law the victims that had been sacrificed to God might not be touched except by the hands of priests. (No. 340 S12, p. 48)[31]

Given the general tenor of Jacobus's social teaching in the sermons, it seems to be no great anomaly that the *Legenda* emphasizes the privileges and powers of a saint like Benedict instead of his imitable virtues. Even when the lay audience Jacobus envisioned was serious and well-educated, its members capable of forgoing colorful anecdotes in favor of intricately structured arguments about the ways in which the saints pleased God and fulfilled the allegorical meanings of Scripture, he could give them only the most limited encouragement to follow the saints' examples. Sometimes, as in the third sermon on Benedict, he seems to be inviting properly qualified laymen to embrace the religious life—preferably as Dominicans. More commonly, however, his sermons urge their auditors to remember their ordained place within the hierarchy, and to honor and obey those set above them. For due order, as Jacobus understood it, was the crucial thing. The traditional rules had to be reinforced and defended; and he uses the examples of the saints to serve that purpose, whether the original legends were conducive to it or not.

If the adversarial motifs in the *Legenda* begin to seem less puzzling in view of the assumptions revealed in Jacobus's model sermons, so does the *Legenda*'s tendency to reduce miracles to signs. For one thing, Jacobus devotes little attention in the sermons to miracles per se; to indicate the magnitude of the saints' virtues and favor with God, he prefers such supernatural events as visions and visits from angels. Thus, for example, in the six sermons on Dominic (nos. 491-96 S54) he virtually ignores all the wondrous events in the legend except the visions surrounding the saint's birth and those confirming the divine origins of his order. The three sermons on Ambrose (nos. 421-23 S4) give more space to the visions and revelations vouchsafed to others about the saint, but show a similar lack of interest in the miracles he performed.

Even more interesting are the lessons Jacobus draws—and does not draw—on the rarer occasions when he deals explicitly with miracles. In the sermons on Martin of Tours he presents a large number of the saint's miracles in neatly classified lists. The systems of classification vary: one list demonstrates how the saint manifested his power over the various categories of creatures—the elements, plants, animals, and men, both living and dead; two others use miracles simply as signs that he had pleased God; yet another connects his miraculous powers over the devil with specific virtues he possessed.[32] But all the lists share the same tendency to privatize the miracles, deemphasizing the practical benefits many of them conferred on other human beings. The same priorities are exhibited yet more strikingly in the first sermon on Benedict (no. 389 S26). This time the statement preceding the list seems to promise a concentration on the merciful aspect of the saint's miracles: "Second, he was dear to men. This was because of the many favors [beneficia] and miracles he performed among them" (p. 108).[33] But Jacobus does not proceed, as one might expect, to deal with such categories as healings, exorcisms, and rescues from danger. Rather, he divides the miracles according to whether Benedict performed them "in reference to himself" ("quantum ad semetipsum"), "in reference to the microcosm" ("quantum ad mundum minorem"), or "in the world at large" ("in majori mundo")—a classification system in which the practical effects are subordinated once again to the miraculous means. Thus the first miracle cited, the rescue of a hostage, is used to illustrate the power coming forth from Benedict's eyes; and the next three—a deliverance of Benedict himself, his excommunication of the sharp-tongued nuns, and his gift of prophecy (the practical functions of which are not suggested)—show how far Jacobus actually is from equating miracles with beneficia toward other men.[34] Only the second category, that of miracles in reference to the microcosm, or man, is limited to acts of mercy; and even there Jacobus's focus on the saint, rather than on the beneficiaries, is revealed by the way he defines the resurrection of the second monk primarily as a victory over the devil: "Some he preserved in life from demonic temptation, like the monk who could not remain in prayer; others, however, [he preserved] at death from demonic violence, like the monk whom the devil crushed in the ruins of a wall; others [he preserved] after death" (p. 108).[35] The Legenda, of course, has just the same focus.

The sermons are more illuminating than the Legenda, however, for they repeatedly suggest that there is nothing accidental about Jacobus's tendency to downplay the more attractive aspects of miracles. When one section of sermon 389 S26 is devoted to the material we have just seen, supporting the assertion that men loved Benedict for his miracles, it is prefaced by a longer and more substantial argument that God loved him for his virtues; and, lest any member of the audience doubt which value system he is being invited to share, the sermon concludes with another section emphasizing the lasting influence of the saint's virtues. When Jacobus describes Sylvester's triumph over his Jewish adversaries by rational arguments reinforced with a miracle, he pauses to suggest in the present tense that wise men do not need miraculous proofs: "The wise are convinced by arguments, the simple by miracles" ("sapientes acquiescunt rationibus, simplices miraculis" [no. 343 S13, p. 51]). When he describes Dominic's preaching he uses a different system of classification, but again he implies that the usefulness of miracles consists in their ability to reach a certain fraction of the people who stand outside the normal (and preferable) channels of communication: "[Dominic] used doctrine, examples, and even miracles. For some were ignorant and unlearned, and in their case he made use of good and profitable doctrines, to instruct them; others were indifferent and undevout, and in their case he made use of examples and the graces of his character, to attract [them]; some, however, were hard-hearted and stubborn, and in their case he made use of miracles, to convert them" (no. 492 S54, p. 235).[36]

In short, both Jacobus's explicit statements and his practice in the sermons indicate more than a little ambivalence toward miracles. Although he uses certain kinds of miraculous events (especially visions) in his sermons and grants an instructional value to miracles in general, he clearly does not share Gregory's conception of their importance. Instead of essential communications addressed by God to all his people, miracles serve primarily, Jacobus suggests, as vehicles whereby the "simple" or the "hard-hearted and stubborn" can be persuaded to accept what the rest of the church already knows. The implication is that well-instructed Christians like Jacobus himself, and even the kind of laity implicit in his model sermons, have nothing to learn from the bulk of the material brought together in a book like the *Legenda*. But some of them may use it to teach others. Thus the instructional model of the *Dialogues,* in which God taught Gregory as well as Peter and the audience through the miracles of the saints, gives way to a model in which the spokesman for the church uses accounts of miracles simply as exempla, illustrating truths he himself has learned through different channels.

Besides the palpable shift in the teacher's relationship to his audience, this change has one practical ramification worth mentioning. Since miraculous events now serve the teacher, rather than the other way around, he can freely ignore or revise the details surrounding a miracle to make it fit the lesson he wants to teach. Jacobus does precisely this in his own sermons; sometimes he even reuses the same miracle in entirely different ways, as dictated by his immediate needs. A nice example occurs in the sermons on Martin of Tours. The fact that Martin performed two resurrections while he was a monk and only one in all the later years had led his original biographer, Sulpicius Severus, to conclude that the saint's miraculous powers declined once he was burdened with the cares and distractions of a bishop.[37] Jacobus, who takes a more positive view of the episcopacy than Severus did, reverses the original message when he composes a sermon on Martin's virtues; by assigning every miracle—including all three resurrections—to the final stage of Martin's life, he demonstrates the saint's steadily increasing perfection and the great powers befitting a bishop.[38] When his theme is the graces vouchsafed to Martin, on the other hand, the resurrections answer a different need; Jacobus takes them as a third sign of divine approval, balancing Christ's appearance to Martin while he was a layman and the globe of fire seen over his head as a bishop, and assigns them all—as symmetry dictates—to the monastic years.[39]

Given all the unanswered and perhaps unanswerable questions about the sources he used, there is no way of proving that Jacobus de Voragine originated all the salient patterns of omission in the *Legenda*. His model sermons reveal only that he could have done so—and that those patterns actually make sense, in terms of his basic assumptions and concerns as a preacher. For most practical purposes, surely that is confirmation enough. Having observed Jacobus's own practice in the sermons, one need harbor no lingering doubts as to the intention behind a collection of miracle stories without interpretations. The preachers using the *Legenda* were not expected to recall the lessons originally attached to the stories, but to supply new ones as current needs dictated. Nor is it very surprising, in the light of Jacobus's sermons, that the *Legenda* tends to preserve such a narrow selection of the motifs originally inherent in the stories. For Jacobus apparently did not feel that the major themes in the old legends were suitable for the kind of public preaching that was needed in his time. Even when he addressed himself to a relatively promising segment of the laity, he did not urge them to try emulating the saints' virtues, much less to set a great value on their miracles; he encouraged them instead to respect and obey the authorities who had been placed above them. The *Legenda* of course focuses yet more narrowly on a few key themes. But that difference seems simply to confirm what is implicit in the book's pictorial style and heavy reliance on miracle stories—and in the combativeness of its tone, another characteristic that distinguishes it from most of the sermons: it was compiled to meet the special needs of preachers who faced audiences far less well-educated, and more intractable, than those assumed by Jacobus's model sermons.

The *Legenda* chapters on Ambrose, Augustine, and Dominic do not depart very radically from the patterns we have already seen, but they complement the chapter and sermons on Benedict in some exceptionally illuminating ways. For these are not just ordinary chapters of the *Legenda*. All three of these saints seem to have had considerable importance in Jacobus's own life. Dominic of course was the founder of his own order; Augustine, his favorite theologian; Ambrose, the great fourth-century bishop of Milan whose memory still had a special resonance in North Italy. The abridged accounts of their lives in the *Legenda* are considerably more ambitious and interesting than the accounts of Benedict and most other saints, and they also exhibit unusually clear parallels with Jacobus's model sermons. Instead of just abbreviating the standard biographies, these chapters of the *Legenda* incorporate material from a number of additional sources, most of it reinforcing exactly the same themes that are central in the corresponding sets of sermons: the heroic role of Ambrose in defending the church against its enemies, the famous conversion of Augustine and his subsequent greatness as a teacher, the significance of the new preaching order founded by Dominic, the special virtues exemplified by each of these saints. The majority of the themes chosen would seem to demand an emphasis on motifs that were minimized in Jacobus's treatment of the Benedict legend. So would the explicitly pastoral vocations of these three saints and Jacobus's evident desire to prove their special greatness. As we shall see, however, even these exceptional chapters of the *Legenda* continually manifest the same fundamental tendencies as the chapter on Benedict. Inclusive patterns give way to adversarial ones, acts of mercy to miracles that simply vindicate the saints, examples of pastoral care and fruitfulness to examples of lonely fortitude. One could hardly wish for a clearer demonstration of the uniformity of outlook that pervades Jacobus's famous book.

Even more important than the confirmations they provide is the light these legends shed on the mentality behind the *Legenda*. Thus far, following the lead of Bernard Gui, we have focused primarily on the negative significance of the book: the kinds of material characteristically excluded from its abridged accounts of the saints, the major themes—and potential sermon topics—thus obscured or destroyed, the kinds of theological and ethical teaching not preserved. Such omissions surely played a part in the collapse of the *Legenda*'s reputation in the later fifteenth century and thereafter. But it is equally important to understand what purposes the book can have served in the late-medieval church—and why so many Renaissance spokesmen accused it of promoting "saints' lies," or propaganda and silly superstitions. As one studies the chapters on Ambrose and Augustine and Dominic, and compares them with Jacobus's sermons, the answers to these questions become increasingly apparent. But one also learns enough about Jacobus and the particular historical dilemmas to which he was responding, by way of the *Legenda,* to gain a more sympathetic perspective on the book than its Renaissance critics had.

III. Jacobus's Work
in Its Historical Context

7
Saint Ambrose
and the Enemies of the Church

How unworthy of the saints, and of all Christians, is that history of the saints called the *Golden Legend*. . . . What could be more abominable than this book?

Juan Luis Vives, 1531

Later, to come down to more recent authors, was Jacobus de Voragine. . . . Even a blind man could see what sort of thing he has produced.

Georg Witzel, 1541

Even in a book full of confrontations with adversaries, the *Legenda* chapter on Ambrose stands out for its militancy of tone. Unlike Gregory's life of Benedict, Jacobus's major source for this chapter—the *Vita S. Ambrosii* by the saint's pupil and secretary Paulinus—was rather harsh and combative from the start.[1] But in Jacobus's retelling it has become noticeably more so. Paulinus had found room for numerous suggestions of the saint's role as healer, teacher, and peacemaker. There were acts of mercy during Ambrose's lifetime: the resurrection of a child (*Vita* 8.28), numerous exorcisms (9.43), and the healings of a paralyzed woman and a crippled man (3.10, 9.44). There were indications of Ambrose's pastoral care for a wide range of individuals: the sons of the emperor, received into the church and entrusted to him (8.32); the barbarian queen for whom he wrote a catechism (8.36); the resurrected child, for whom he wrote a little book of instruction (8.28); the deacons and future bishops identified as his pupils (10.46); and even sometime adversaries like the emperor Theodosius himself (esp. 7.24). There were stories of reconciliation and conversion—most memorably, that of the soldiers who quietly rebelled against the Arians' orders to close the Portian Basilica, permitting Catholics to enter (though not to leave) and even joining the assembled congregation in the affirmation of the Catholic faith (4.13). And among the posthumous miracles described by

Paulinus were appearances by Ambrose to reassure the faithful (10.49), to encourage a city and an army faced with powerful enemies (10.50, 10.51), and to give a blind man the instructions whereby he was healed (10.52).

In Jacobus's version of the legend every one of these inclusive motifs has vanished. The only posthumous miracles he relates are a sign that confirms the saint's stature and two cautionary tales in which churchmen are suddenly and fatally struck down for daring to disparage him.[2] One brief conversion story remains from Ambrose's lifetime, that of an obdurate heretic won over to the Catholic side by a vision: "When one heretic, a very subtle disputant who was stubborn and could not be converted to the faith, heard Ambrose preaching, he saw an angel speaking into his ears the words he was preaching to the people; and after this vision the man began to defend the faith which he used to attack" (*Legenda,* p. 252).[3] Even here the theme of reconciliation is clearly overshadowed by the vindication of the saint's authority. But the heretic's vision of the angel is worth citing because it is the only event in Jacobus's whole chapter on Ambrose which recalls the traditional ideals of healing and reintegration into the community. Against that single suggestion of divine mercy, the miracle stories with harsher implications loom very large. For in this chapter of the *Legenda* the saint's human adversaries are not usually just humbled; they are subjected to punishments ranging from exile to maiming and torture to violent death.[4]

Although there is nothing very edifying about Jacobus's account of Ambrose, it has considerable value for our purposes because it should persuade even the most sentimental reader to lay aside the romantic image of the *Legenda* and attend to the thirteenth-century realities that are actually reflected in the book. One of those realities, as we shall see, was an ecclesiastical hierarchy that had begun to lose its moral authority and was trying to compensate by using its powers to intimidate and coerce. Another is the character of the early Dominicans themselves. In a very real sense these men were reformers of the church—a new breed of clerics who circulated in the cities but maintained a stricter discipline than most cloistered monks, lived in true poverty and abstinence, and devoted themselves to study and teaching. But they were also an important part of what one historian has called the "papal militia" of the period.[5] Founded to promulgate the faith and to defend it against its enemies, the early generations of Dominicans bore no small resemblance to a military order—an army of preachers, missionaries, and, when need dictated, inquisitors, in the service of the pope. Some unusually pertinent illustrations of their spirit are provided by the modern

Dominican historian William A. Hinnebusch, in his account of the friars' special emphasis on books.[6] One directive by Humbert of Romans, master general of the order from 1254 to 1263, emphasizes the importance of accumulating books for use against unbelievers: "Whosoever are zealous defenders of the faith should seek and collect books that can be used against the unbelievers among whom they live, whether Jews, Saracens, or heretics, so that they can debate at the opportune time against them, if there be need, creditably, for the defense of the faith" (p. 192). Another of Humbert's directives recommends the copying of useful books in explicitly military terms: "The authorities drawn from books are like weapons whereby we defend ourselves and attack the foe . . . [T]he arms of preachers are the authorities taken from books" (p. 231). That such metaphors were a commonplace in the order is suggested by the wording used when the provincial chapter of Florence issued a decree, in 1257, against the unauthorized sale of Dominican books: "Lest the brethren, by casting the weapons of our warfare aside through scattering them outside the Order, be found unarmed, we strictly forbid the books of the friars to be sold outside the Order without special permission of the prior provincial" (p. 194). Hinnebusch himself sums up the friars' main literary activity in this period—the compilation of summas, handbooks, collections of sermons and exempla and saints' legends, and the like—as "stocking a vast arsenal for every kind of battle" (p. 232). That, surely, is the right context in which to place the *Legenda*.[7] But for what particular kind or kinds of battle was it designed?

The confrontations in the *Legenda* account of Ambrose are particularly suggestive because of the issues chosen—and not chosen—for defense by the saint. Ambrose's famous role in the controversy over the Altar of Victory occupied some space in Paulinus's account (*Vita* 8.26-27); but Jacobus makes no reference to it, presumably because he did not expect his own readers to have much interest in the problem of paganism.[8] Although some followers of Dominic were already turning their attention to the Moslems and actual pagans who dwelt on the outskirts of Christendom, Jacobus seems to have been arming the users of the *Legenda* to face challenges nearer home. More noteworthy is the omission from the *Legenda* of Ambrose's dramatic and victorious stand against the order given by Theodosius, after an Eastern synagogue was destroyed by zealous monks, that the church pay reparations to the Jews (*Vita* 7.22-23). Throughout the chapter on Ambrose, in fact, Jacobus ignores the theme of enmity between Christians and Jews that was so prominent in Paulinus's account. Jacobus may be presenting an adversarial picture of the Christian life in the *Legenda,* but anti-Semitism is not usually part of that picture.[9] In his version of Ambrose's life there are just three major enemies to be overcome: demons, heretics, and temporal rulers who challenge the authority of the church.[10]

Ambrose's role as a defender of the church is given special emphasis when Jacobus sums up his virtues. Oddly enough, there are two lists of virtues in this chapter of the *Legenda*—the first based on that given by Paulinus; the second and far longer one, drawn from additional sources and placed at the end. Jacobus simplifies and abbreviates Paulinus's list and adds to it constancy and fortitude, virtues here equated with a refusal to tolerate the faults of rulers ("imperatoris vel principum vitia" [p. 253]) and illustrated with the story—to which we will return—of a malefactor handed over to Satan. In the second list *fortis constantia* against powerful secular rulers occupies a dominant position both explicitly and implicitly. One of the other seven virtues in this list, Ambrose's reliance on prayer, is illustrated with a reference to the way he withstood the enmity of the empress Justina: "Fifth, [he was praiseworthy] for his persistent prayer. Thus it is said, in the eleventh book of the *Ecclesiastical History,* 'Ambrose defended himself against the queen's fury not by hand or weapon, but by fasts and constant vigils; kneeling at the altar he made God, by his entreaties, the defender of himself and of the church'" (*Legenda,* p. 256).[11] No fewer than four of the other virtues—Ambrose's liberality to the poor, his steadfast faith, his desire for martyrdom, and his tears of compassion over injustice—are demonstrated by citing statements he made while resisting the emperor Valentinian's command to hand over the Portian Basilica. And, as the first two instances suggest, the virtue most evident in these illustrations is Ambrose's heroic defense of church property:

It should be observed that the blessed Ambrose was praiseworthy in many respects. First in generosity, since all that he had belonged to the poor. Thus he tells us that, when the emperor demanded the basilica, he said (as reported in *Decretum* 23, quest. 8): . . . "If he asked for what was mine—my estate, my money, or other similar possessions—I would not refuse, even though all I own belongs to the poor. . . . Third, [he was praiseworthy] for the steadfastness of his faith. Thus when the emperor demanded the basilica, he said (as reported in the same chapter), "Better he should take my life than my see." (P. 255)[12]

It is worth noting that the source from which Jacobus derived these statements was a work of canon law, not hagiography; the thrust of the chapter in question is accurately summed up by the heading in Migne's edition: "That churches are not subject to emperors" ("Ecclesiae imperatoribus non sint obnoxiae").

The other enemies of Ambrose, demons and heretics, do not go completely unmentioned in this part of the *Legenda* account. The extended discussion of his *fortis constantia* itself comprises three sections, the first of which demonstrates the saint's constancy "in defense of Catholic truth" ("in defensione catholicae veritatis"); here Jacobus summarizes Justina's offenses against the church, linking her explicitly with the Arians she protected, and uses a liturgical quotation that celebrates Ambrose's victories over all three classes of enemies: "In that war she battered Ambrose, who was a wall and mighty tower of the church. Thus it is sung of him in his own preface, 'You strengthened him with such virtue, adorned him with such a heavenly gift of constancy, that by him demons were cast out and tortured, the Arian heresy was driven out and dissolved, and the necks of secular princes were bent under your yoke and made humble'" (p. 256).[13] But the next section, on the saint's exemplary constancy "in watching over the liberty of the church" ("in tuitione ecclesiasticae libertatis"), returns yet again to the confrontation over the basilica, neglecting as before to mention the heretics for whom Valentinian intended the building. Thus the problem is defined as a simple struggle between the church and the state; and the supporting material is a long pastiche of quotations from the *Decretum,* all directed at a single point: Ambrose's insistence that an emperor can have no authority over the things of God.[14]

Equally suggestive is the material used to illustrate Ambrose's constancy "in rebuking sin and all unrighteousness" ("in objurgatione vitii et omnis iniquitatis"), the third and last subdivision of *fortis constantia.* Here the *Legenda* presents a very long story about another confrontation with an emperor: Ambrose's demand that Theodosius perform public penance after the emperor, wreaking vengeance on the city of Thessalonica for a minor uprising, unleashed a massacre in which many innocent citizens were slain. Jacobus appears to have told this story twice for the *Legenda.* The first version, based on Paulinus's relatively brief account (*Vita* 7.24; cf. *Legenda,* p. 252), he presumably considered inadequate; for instead of moving it to this section he draws from the *Tripartite History* of Cassiodorus a much more detailed version. Despite the rubric under which Jacobus introduces it, this retelling of the story does not emphasize the nature of the emperor's guilt or the appropriateness of the penalties imposed by Ambrose; in fact, Theodosius's sin and repentance are almost side issues. Virtually all the new material consists of confrontations in which the holy bishop asserts the primacy of divine law over imperial power; Theodosius and his lieutenant Rufinus, serving as representatives of the latter, are dramatically chastised and humiliated until they accept the fact that Ambrose has all the authority in such matters.[15] One prominent motif in the story is the idea that the emperor would profane the temple of God if he were allowed to enter it before performing the necessary penance.[16] But, in a telling little coda, Theodosius is taught that even an emperor who has done his penance is still just a layman, and thus barred from the sacred precincts reserved for the clergy:

When, however, after his reconciliation [Theodosius] entered the church and stood within the chancel, Ambrose asked him what he was looking for. When he answered that he wanted a view of the holy ceremonies, Ambrose said, "Emperor, the inner area is meant only for priests. Leave, then, and trim your expectation to the common level; for the purple makes emperors, not priests." The emperor immediately obeyed him. When he returned to Constantinople, he therefore stood outside the chancel; and, on being asked to enter by a bishop, he replied, "I have only just learned the difference between an emperor and a priest, for I have only just found a teacher of the truth; indeed, Ambrose is the only one I know who deserves to be called a pontiff." (P. 258)[17]

Given all the new material identifying Ambrose with the defense of church property and clerical prerogatives, it is not unreasonable to attach a special significance to the numerous miracles of retribution against his enemies. One lesson, driven home by the fates of the posthumous detractors, is the danger of scoffing at the saint's memory. But a surprisingly large proportion of the remaining stories in the *Legenda* recount the punishments inflicted on heretics or worldly laymen, or both, who presume to treat the holy bishop as if he were just another man. This lesson was already quite explicit in one of Paulinus's stories, that of the Arian girl who lays violent hands on Ambrose in the church where he has gone to consecrate a Catholic bishop (*Vita* 3.11); the story is transferred to the *Legenda* with relatively minor changes. In both versions Ambrose chides the girl for showing so little respect for the office he holds, and warns her to fear God's judgment: "Ambrose said to her, 'Even though I am unworthy of such a priesthood, nevertheless it is unfitting for you to lay hands on any priest; wherefore you should fear the judgment of God, lest something befall you'" (*Legenda,* p. 251).[18] And, both versions assert, that judgment falls on her almost immediately. She dies the next day, and the saint—apparently more merciful in this instance than his God—is said to render kindness for insult ("gratiam pro contumelia") by conducting her burial. Jacobus's only significant departure from his source comes at the end of the story, where he omits the larger function that Paulinus ascribed to these events. Whereas the girl's death, so swiftly fulfilling Ambrose's prophecy, served in the *Vita* to bring great peace to the church for the bishop's consecration ("Sed hoc factum non levem adversariis incussit metum pacemque magnam ecclesiae catholicae in ordinando episcopo tribuit''), in the *Legenda* it is said only to have terrified everyone (''Quod factum omnes perterruit'').

The *Legenda* also gives a reasonably faithful rendering of Paulinus's story about Macedonius, a government official whose doors were closed to Ambrose when the holy bishop sought his aid in a case. When, later, Macedonius flees to the church, seeking refuge from his enemies, he finds himself miraculously prevented from entering although the doors are open. The official's punishment—noticeably greater than the crime of insufficient respect for Ambrose, despite the neat parallel in circumstances—evokes the same sort of awe as the sudden death of the Arian girl; and this time there is no separation between the will of Ambrose and the power that takes vengeance on his opponents. For he speaks prophetic words at Macedonius's door which sound much less like a general warning than a specific threat of the punishment to come: ''Even thus you will come to the church and not find a way in, though the doors will be open'' (*Vita* 8.37).[19]

More suggestive than the stories Jacobus repeats from the *Vita,* of course, are those he alters in some substantive way. Four stories about punishment stand out in this respect. The simplest case is that of the hired would-be assassin who finds his arm suddenly paralyzed when he raises his sword against Ambrose. In Paulinus's version this story illustrated both the divine protection of Ambrose and the mercy extended to a man not yet far gone in crime: ''Another man got as far as his bedroom with a sword to kill the priest, but when he drew his sword and raised his right hand, it was struck immovable. After he confessed that he had been sent by Justina, however, the arm—which was paralyzed when he extended it unrighteously—was cured by his confession'' (*Vita* 6.20).[20] In the *Legenda,* however, there is no hint of a moral distinction between the hapless assassin and the great enemy of Ambrose who employed him. Omitting both the man's confession and the physical healing that symbolized his regeneration, Jacobus's version reduces the story to another object lesson about the folly of attacking one whom God has set apart: ''Another man, induced by the requests and promises of Justina, came to his bedroom at night to kill him with a sword; but when he raised the sword to strike him, his hand was instantly withered'' (*Legenda,* p. 252).[21]

The distinction between Justina and those she hired is obscured again when the *Legenda* retells the story about the foolish layman who plotted the abduction of Ambrose (*Vita* 4.12). The unfortunate plotter finds himself taken into exile in the same vehicle—and, in the *Legenda,* on the very same day[22]—he had chosen for the removal of the holy man. What disappear from Jacobus's account are the details that originally mitigated both the crime and the punishment. In the *Vita* the man was identified as one of the weak led astray by Justina; the *Legenda* suggests only that he was driven by a furious greed for the rewards she promised.[23] Nor does Jacobus's version retain the original indications that the man's eyes were opened to the sinfulness of his intention, once he found the tables turned on him, and that Ambrose understood and forgave him.[24] The story still ends with a generous gesture on the part of Ambrose, but the lesson driven home is the swiftness of God's retribution on his enemies: "But by the judgment of God, [the man] was himself driven into exile on the very same day on which he had thought to seize [Ambrose], in the same chariot, from the same house. Nevertheless Ambrose, returning good for evil, supplied him with provisions and other necessities" (*Legenda,* pp. 251-52).[25]

The third story in this category, that of the soothsayer who tried using black magic against Ambrose (*Vita* 6.20), is altered in a more thoroughgoing way. The *Legenda* describes this enemy's second futile attempt, when the demons sent to kill Ambrose find that a miraculous fire prevents their even approaching the saint's house.[26] Again the divine protection of the saint is clear. But the larger meaning of this protection has vanished. In Paulinus's account the magician attempted Ambrose's life only after being thwarted in his original design to destroy the people's love for the holy bishop and for the faith he represented.[27] By omitting this part of the story, the *Legenda* sacrifices a strong testimony to the bonds between the bishop and his flock—and to love as the basis of his influence on others. Even the Ambrose of the *Legenda* occasionally shows some kindness, as we have seen; but Jacobus seems more intent on evoking wonder and fear at the power that surrounds him. A subtler change in this same story reinforces the point. In the *Vita* the soothsayer confessed his attempts to harm Ambrose while being tortured for other crimes; the saint's angelic protector, he cried, was torturing him more severely than the human judge did: "When a certain soothsayer named—though in fact not—Innocent was being tortured by a judge on a charge of sorcery, he began to confess something different from what he was being questioned about; he cried out that he suffered greater torments from the angel that protected Ambrose" (6.20).[28] But in the *Legenda,* where there is no mention of a confession, the invisible torture seems to have only a punitive function—and the torturer has become Ambrose himself: "When the aforementioned soothsayer was being tortured by a judge because of certain crimes, he cried out that he was tortured more severely by Ambrose" (p. 252).[29]

The new message—that retribution belongs not only to God, but also to the holy man who acts in his name—is not conveyed very frequently by the *Legenda* chapter on Ambrose; but it is suggested by the story of Macedonius, as we have seen, and it figures quite prominently in the last of the punitive miracles borrowed from the *Vita*. Paulinus had outlined the circumstances rather carefully. The culprit, a trusted servant of Count Stilicho, was staying in the basilica at his master's recommendation after being cured of demonic possession. During this time reports came that he was forging official documents. Apparently both Stilicho and Ambrose disbelieved the accusations at first; but the count, although reluctant to punish his servant himself, became dissatisfied enough to complain to Ambrose. The bishop, after questioning the man and ascertaining his guilt, determined that one who had so flagrantly betrayed the trust of his master, and misused his earlier cure, should be handed over to the devil as a warning to other malefactors (*Vita* 9.43). That the man was seized on the spot by an evil spirit, which began to tear his body to pieces, lent considerable horror to the story even in the *Vita*. But, given the circumstances, there was clearly some appropriateness in the verdict pronounced by the saint.

When Jacobus retells the story, on the other hand, he omits all those crucial circumstances. The man becomes wholly anonymous and the nature of his crime is left to the imagination; all the emphasis falls on the terrible punishment itself and on Ambrose's role in inflicting it: "When a certain man had committed some crime and had been brought before him, Ambrose said, 'He should be given over to Satan for the destruction of the flesh, that he may never again dare to do such things.' That very moment, while the words were still in his mouth, an unclean spirit began to tear the man apart" (*Legenda*, p. 253).[30] This portrait of the holy bishop as judge, or executioner, with his harshness no longer explained in any way, is by far the most chilling passage in the *Legenda* account of Ambrose. But it clearly satisfied Jacobus's notion of the qualities for which the saint should be remembered, at least by the audience of the *Legenda*. For he does not just present it; this is the story he attaches to Paulinus's list of Ambrose's virtues, as an illustration of exemplary "constancy and fortitude" in refusing to tolerate the crimes of the mighty.

The particular lessons brought to the fore in Jacobus's account of Ambrose permit more specific conclusions than one could draw from his account of Benedict. If the Benedict of the *Legenda* recalled the image of biblical figures like Moses, leaders upheld by God against a stubborn and rebellious people, the chapter on Ambrose leaves little doubt about the significance of that image. One major thrust of the book is the defense of bishops and other prelates, the contemporary leaders of the church, against those who challenged their authority. The way in which

Jacobus tends to conduct this defense, insisting on the special prerogatives (but not the special responsibilities) of the clergy with regard to such
matters as the control of church property and the administration of
justice, is manifestly inimical to most later notions of church reform—
and so, of course, is Jacobus's repeated suggestion that no punishment is
too dire for God to inflict on those who fail to respect and obey their
clerical superiors. One need hardly look further for an explanation of
the angry impatience with which Vives and Witzel dismissed Jacobus's
famous book. To Erasmus and his sixteenth-century followers, few
human tendencies seemed more dangerous than the readiness to identify
violence and coercion with the will of God. And it would be hard to
imagine anything better calculated to outrage Vives, in particular, than
saints' legends which could be—and presumably had been—used by
members of a clerical elite to justify their own privileges and powers, and
to intimidate potential critics.[31]

This polemical aspect of the *Legenda* is no more attractive in the late
twentieth century than it was in the sixteenth, but there is good reason to
withhold any final judgment until one has tried to see its purpose from
Jacobus's point of view. Here again the chapter on Ambrose is
unusually instructive.

Both the identities of Ambrose's major enemies and the issues given
prominence, in the *Legenda* account, irresistibly recall the situation in
Italy during Jacobus's own lifetime. Not long before the book was
compiled, the protracted struggle between Frederick II and the papacy
had climaxed in the emperor's deposition, or attempted deposition, by
Innocent IV; in fact, the little history of the Lombards that Jacobus
inserts into the *Legenda* chapter on Saint Pelagius ends with the reign of
Frederick, in a passage that stresses his assaults on the clergy and the
popes' response:

After the deposition of Otto, Frederick, son of Henry, was elected, and crowned
by [Pope] Honorius. He promulgated excellent laws in support of the freedom
of the church and against the heretics. He surpassed all others in wealth and
glory, but he abused these gifts with pride, for he tyrannized over the church. He
threw two cardinals into chains and had prelates seized whom Gregory IX had
summoned to a council; therefore, he was excommunicated by him. Then
Gregory, oppressed by many tribulations, died; and Innocent IV, a native of
Genoa, convoked a council at Lyons and deposed the emperor himself. From his
deposition and death to this day the imperial throne has remained empty.
(P. 844)[32]

That the history breaks off with the death of Frederick in 1250 is
presumably a tribute to his stature as an adversary, as well as yet another
testimony to Jacobus's fondness for stories of vindication; he can hardly

have issued the *Legenda* before another decade or so had passed.[33] During those years the inconclusiveness of the papal victory became all too evident. For one thing, the policies adopted by Gregory and especially Innocent, in their long warfare against the emperor, had made it easier rather than more difficult for other rulers to challenge the authority of the church. As one modern historian has put it, the Hohenstaufen dynasty had been destroyed, but only at a great cost to the credibility of the papacy as a spiritual institution:

Innocent himself became bitterly, obdurately convinced that a victory for the emperor would mean the enslavement of the Roman see, and he may well have been right in that assumption. But to contemporaries it seemed that the pope was using every spiritual resource at his command for the sole purpose of advancing his interests as a temporal ruler in Italy. Certainly Innocent used every power inherent in the papacy that was meant for the good governance of the church and the defence of Christian society—excommunication, interdict, ecclesiastical taxes, episcopal appointments, crusading privileges—for the one end of coaxing or coercing reluctant supporters all over Europe to join in the struggle against Frederick.[34]

A related issue, raised even more unmistakably during the struggle with Frederick, was that of the material wealth controlled by the clergy. The emperor's radical proposal in 1246 that Christian kings should unite against the greed and oppression of clerics, reforming the church at one stroke by confiscating its property, was a desperate response to the decree of deposition, and it seems to have shocked rather than persuaded most responsible contemporaries. But that such a proposal was even put forth, by a mid-thirteenth-century ruler, suggests the extent to which the church was already perceived as vulnerable to attacks on its property rights.[35]

Thus it is not very surprising that Innocent and his successors found it no easier to consolidate their control over the territories Frederick had claimed than it had been to defeat the emperor himself. The political and religious situation was particularly explosive in Jacobus's own Lombardy, where the heretical sects of the Waldenses and especially the Cathars had put down deep roots, despite the draconian "excellent laws" Frederick had issued against them in the 1220s. As Dondaine has shown, the Cathars at the height of their influence rivalled the Catholic church even in the complexity of their ecclesiastical organization, with hierarchical structures headed by bishops; and no fewer than six such hierarchies had been established in Italy, four of them in Lombardy itself—at Concorezzo near Milan, Bagnolo near Mantua, Vicenza, and Verona.[36] The number of "perfect" who actually undertook to live out the Cathar definition of purity may never have surpassed a few thousand; but Dondaine estimates that the number of simple "believers" and "friends" of the sect, in Lombardy alone, reached into the hundreds of thousands in the middle thirteenth century.[37] If the heretics flourished in Lombardy, of course, a large part of the reason was the protection afforded them by local nobles and communes who cared less about religious orthodoxy, as Rome defined it, than about their own political and economic interests. For generations, in fact, the Lombards had been preoccupied with the rivalries between papal and imperial factions, between nobles and *popolani,* and between one city-state and another. Faced with the prospect of domination by the foreigner Frederick, much of Lombardy came together in an alliance against his armies; but once the threat from the Empire was removed, these prosperous and fiercely independent cities returned to their customary feuds, finding fewer reasons than ever for cooperating with the papacy.[38]

Although Dominic had headed a preaching mission against the heretics of Lombardy as early as 1220 and both Frederick and the popes had attempted at least sporadically to mount an effective inquisition in this region, the concerted campaign was launched by Innocent IV shortly after Frederick's death.[39] His chosen instruments were friars from Dominic's—and Jacobus's—order, and it is well worth noting the *Legenda's* own description of the challenge that confronted them: "When the plague of heresy broke out in the province of Lombardy, and the terrible pestilence had already infected many cities, the pope sent a number of inquisitors from the Order of Preachers to various parts of Lombardy to stamp out this demonic plague. But the heretics who occupied Milan were great not only in number but also in secular power, acute in deceitful eloquence, and full of devilish learning" (p. 280).[40]

Here one sees the heretics, demons, and secular rulers that were Ambrose's enemies brought together into a single menace, controlling Ambrose's city of Milan until the pope dispatches against them another heroic defender of the church—Peter Martyr, the first follower of Dominic to be canonized and the first Dominican to die in the line of duty as an inquisitor:

Therefore the pope, knowing and understanding that the blessed Peter was a courageous man, who would not fear the number of the enemy—and noticing also his steadfast virtue, which would not allow him to make even the smallest concessions to the power of his adversaries; and recognizing also his eloquence, with which he might easily expose the fallacies of the heretics; and, finally, not unaware that he was thoroughly learned in divine wisdom, so that he might refute the frivolous arguments of the heretics with reason—decided to send this vigorous champion of the faith and indefatigable warrior of the Lord to Milan and its county, and appointed him his inquisitor with plenary power. (Ibid.)[41]

As the *Legenda* presents the story, the pope's confidence in Peter is vindicated in a predictably swift and dramatic way. Powerless to answer the saint's arguments, his adversaries are forced to murder him, and the city is cleansed of heresy through his merits and posthumous miracles as a martyr.[42] In reality, of course, neither Milan nor the rest of Lombardy was so easily restored to the fold. The Catholic manpower assigned to the campaign had repeatedly to be increased in the ensuing years,[43] and new measures taken to ensure the inquisitors' protection and enable their work to proceed. Groups of laymen were organized as a special police to defend and assist them. Threats were made, and actual crusades set in motion, against secular rulers who openly defied the pope and banned the Inquisition from their domains. The inquisitors themselves were given more powers—including, from 1256 on, the right to have suspects tortured without depending on "the secular arm" to do it.[44] Even so, violent resistance continued at least sporadically, at Milan and elsewhere, for several more decades.[45] The costs to the Dominicans of this long and frustrating campaign are reflected most clearly in the thirteenth-century lives of Dominic himself (see Chapter 9, below), but even Jacobus's chapter on Peter Martyr contains one significant admission. For among the fruits of Peter's martyrdom is the conversion of new friars who are "even now" ("usque nunc") continuing the battle in which he fell: "Indeed, from [the converts in Milan] many great and renowned preachers entered the order, who even now pursue all heretics and favorers of heresy with an amazing zeal" (p. 282).[46]

Given all the historical coincidences, it was almost inevitable that Jacobus would see the relevance of the Ambrose legend to the embattled inquisitors of his order and the popes they served. What is important to recognize is the way he has selected and revised positions actually taken by Ambrose in order more fully to identify him with these successors in the old struggle against worldly rulers and heretics. As we have seen, the story of the penance imposed on Theodosius looks like a thoroughly political story in the *Legenda*. The emperor is reduced from a fallible but well-meaning member of the saint's flock to a representative of temporal power; Ambrose, from the emperor's pastor to a spokesman for clerical privilege. The original moral and spiritual issues are similarly ignored, in favor of the political ones, in the way the *Legenda* presents the struggle over the basilica and the supernatural punishments visited on those who attempt to harm Ambrose himself. Even the recourse to coercive methods that compromised the moral standing of Innocent IV and of contemporary inquisitors, transforming their *constantia et fortitudo* from the ability to endure persecution to the ability to inflict it in their turn, is wrapped in the mantle of Ambrose. To the stories in the *Legenda* that celebrate his ability to punish malefactors, one of Jacobus's sermons adds the explicit claim that he combatted heresy not only with sound teaching and miracles but also—as inquisitors did in Jacobus's time, when the secular authorities would cooperate—with the coercive power of the state: "Second, he defended [the church] from the deceit of heretics, and he did this in three ways. First by judicial action, coercing them through the secular arm. *If thy brother would persuade thee [secretly, saying: Let us go and serve strange gods, . . . consent not to him, hear him not], neither let thy eye spare him [to pity and conceal him], but thou shalt presently put him to death* [Deut. 13:6-9]" (sermon 422 S4, p. 152).[47]

As a sample of Jacobus's polemic, the case of Ambrose is unusually clear and consistent—but not, I think, so unrepresentative as to mislead us about the kind of warfare for which the *Legenda* was designed. Occasionally, as in the first sermons on Pope Sylvester and Peter Martyr, and the *Legenda* chapters on All Souls Day and the Nativity of John the Baptist, one sees Jacobus going out of his way to counter specific doctrinal errors associated with the heretics of his time.[48] But for the most part he seems bent rather on supplying ammunition for the political battles that were raging about the Dominicans and about the whole contemporary leadership of the church. The major unbelievers implicit in his work are not actual heretics but skeptical or disaffected Catholics, potential favorers (*fautores*) of heresy who might tolerate or even applaud such challenges to clerical authority as the maltreatment of the pope's representatives and the seizure of church property by laymen. And the major tactic he uses against them is to identify the order they were questioning with the will of God, as manifested time and again in the lives of the saints.

In the sermons Jacobus's most characteristic method is to show the conformity between the examples of the saints, who pleased God, and the political theory of their current successors—sometimes bending the historical record noticeably, as we have seen, to associate prestigious earlier saints with a thirteenth-century conception of due order. The preachers who would use the *Legenda* are supplied with some material for such arguments; hence, for example, the long passages illustrating Ambrose's refusal to surrender the basilica. But the mission of these preachers, as Jacobus apparently perceived it, required simpler and more potent weapons against skepticism and disloyalty. And of course he provides them in abundance: stories about the power that upholds God's servants and humiliates or destroys their enemies.

The message to Jacobus's contemporaries is most obvious in those chapters of the *Legenda* whose heroes are prelates, wielding a sacred authority that puts kings and emperors to shame. Thus, for example, the major events in the account of Saint Fabian (*Legenda,* p. 108) are the miraculous sign that procures his election as pope and a scene in which, like Ambrose, he faces down an emperor who tried to enter the church before doing penance for his sins. Another bishop, Saint Germain of Auxerre, deposes a king who has refused him hospitality and gives his throne to a swineherd who was generous to the holy man and his companions (p. 450). Sent to Aquitaine as a legate, Saint Bernard conquers the rebellious duke with the power of a consecrated Host and his own fiery eloquence (pp. 536-37).[49] Attila the Hun falls at the feet of Pope Leo and complies with his request to stop ravaging Italy, later explaining to his own incredulous followers that even such a conqueror as he was inevitably overcome by that priest ("sacerdos") because of Leo's supernatural protector (p. 368).

In dozens of additional chapters, the church is represented by martyrs who fearlessly defy secular rulers, from emperors on down, because they serve a higher authority. Such stories were, of course, a staple in late-medieval legendaries, but it is hard not to see a connection between Jacobus's versions and the contemporary battles over the rights of the church. For one thing, Jacobus lays great emphasis on greed and ambition as the motives of those who persecuted the saints; and he returns with exceptional frequency and vigor to the wickedness of Julian the Apostate, who (like Frederick II) had seemed during his youth to be a pious Christian.[50] Moreover, Jacobus characteristically minimizes the sufferings of the martyrs, preferring to dwell on the miraculous events which frustrate the persecutors' efforts to break their bodies and their resolve. Saint Primus swallows boiling lead as if it were cool water, and the lions and bears that are unleashed to maul him and his fellow martyr stretch out at their feet like gentle lambs (p. 345). Saint George thwarts three attempts to kill him—two by poison, and one by immersion in molten lead—simply by making the sign of the cross (pp. 262-63). The boy-martyr Saint Vitus is delivered from chains, preserved in quick succession from a fiery oven and a raging lion, and finally rescued from torture by a great earthquake which destroys the temples of the idols and kills many people; at this point the persecuting emperor flees, lamenting that he has been defeated by a child (p. 351).

The idea of a contest with the saints, which the persecutors cannot win, is not always made so explicit; but in chapter after chapter Jacobus drives home the essential point by describing the dire punishments visited on the persecutors themselves. The assassins of Saint Thomas of Canterbury, for example, are afflicted with a variety of horrible maladies (p. 69). Aegeas, the persecutor of Saint Andrew, is seized by a demon and dies in the street on his way home from the saint's execution (p. 19). As soon as Saint George has been executed by Dacian, a fire falls from heaven and consumes Dacian and his assistants (p. 264). The prefect who executes Saint Juliana is drowned soon thereafter, along with a number of companions, and the sea casts up their bodies to be devoured by beasts and birds of prey (p. 178). While Saint Agatha is being tortured on the orders of Quintianus, an earthquake destroys his palace and kills two of his advisers; later, Quintianus sets out for the martyr's house, to look for riches he can confiscate, and dies violently on the road (pp. 172-73).

Although the actual slayers of the saints are most often the targets of such retribution, the *Legenda* is very far from leaving the impression that lesser acts of persecution go unpunished. One Ballachius, an Egyptian official with Arian sympathies who has been mistreating Catholic monks and virgins, makes light of Saint Antony's warning to beware the wrath of God and even dares to threaten Antony himself; a few days later Ballachius is struck down—thrown and mortally injured by his horse (p. 107). The prefect Tarquin threatens Saint Sylvester with torture and death, threats never implemented because he himself chokes to death that same night, fulfilling the saint's prophecy (p. 70). The prefect who attempts (and of course fails) to rape Saint Anastasia is struck blind on the spot, dies soon thereafter, and is explicitly sentenced to hell (pp. 48-49). After a warning vision the emperor Mauritius repents his acts of persecution against Gregory the Great and begs God to punish him in this life rather than in the life to come; in response to his plea, God decrees that he and his whole family are to be slain by the soldier Phocas, who will take the imperial throne (p. 196). Even the property rights of the church are reasserted with a few stories which closely resemble those found by Ward in the old shrine collections at Fleury and elsewhere:[51] a prefect suffers illnesses and a premature death because he repeatedly seizes a field which belongs to a church of Saint Andrew (pp. 21-22); a deacon is miraculously struck dead for trying to steal sheep from a church of Saint Julian (p. 141); a greedy judge is barely saved from damnation after he unjustly takes possession of real estate belonging to churches of Saint Lawrence and Saint Agnes (pp. 494-95).

Jacobus's emphasis on such lessons does not, of course, mean that his book was aimed directly at the thirteenth-century rulers, large and small, who were combatting the papacy on various fronts. Rather, the strategy implicit in the *Legenda* is a continuation of the strategy devised two generations earlier, when Honorius III first sent Dominic and a few companions on a preaching mission to Lombardy. As Hinnebusch explains, so little reliance could be placed on the men at the top of the social order in this region that the pope's emissaries were compelled to begin at the bottom: "It would be no use to solve the problems from above unless the ground were prepared from below. The preachers would seek to reawaken the Catholic conscience of the people, who in turn would influence their leaders and their governments."[52] What the *Legenda* suggests is that "reawakening the Catholic conscience of the people" turned out to be an enormously difficult challenge. Jacobus did not fill the book with miracle stories as a mere concession to the tastes of "the simple," but as the best means he knew of persuading them to turn their backs once and for all on the heretics and especially the secular leaders who were competing with the church for their loyalty. In this context the emotional force of the stories is obvious. Those who support the heirs of the saints are invited to rejoice in the proofs that theirs is the side God favors; those so foolhardy as to join the opposition, to tremble at the vengeance awaiting them. Even the chapter on Benedict repeatedly suggests that dire consequences befall those who underestimate the power of a saint. And the chapter on Ambrose, with its distribution of harsh punishments even to rather insignificant followers of the saint's real enemies, clearly reinforces the lesson that it is a dangerous thing to enlist even temporarily on the wrong side.

It would not be fair to leave the impression that ecclesiastical politics are always uppermost in the *Legenda*. The book contains a good deal of political propaganda, some of it more blatant than the samples examined thus far; but Jacobus is also intent on demonstrating the superiority of the sacred to the secular, the way of the saints to the ways of this world. From a wider perspective his book can thus be seen as an effort to reverse the drift toward modern, secular values that had already become evident in urban Italy. In effect he would rebuild the authority of the church by reviving in the untutored laity some of the old wonder and awe before the supernatural. Perhaps a Gregory the Great could have done it, even in the thirteenth century. But unless the psychology of late-medieval audiences was vastly different from the psychology of modern ones, Jacobus's weapons against secularism cannot have been very effective. The punishments inflicted on the saints' opponents have great emotional force, once their purpose is understood. But Jacobus's adversarial selectivity tends to undercut the rest of his case, greatly diminishing the apparent validity of the ideals put forth as alternatives to the secular. The legends already studied provide some obvious examples. When Jacobus reduces Benedict to a solitary warrior against evil, he sacrifices splendid opportunities to demonstrate the value and fruitfulness of religious communities. In the Ambrose chapter he empties the bishop's role of positive content, affirming neither the holy man's functions as a pastor and peacemaker nor his ability to pardon sins; indeed, the Ambrose of the *Legenda* seems to have no mission but to assert his own prerogatives and those of the church.

The more one ponders Jacobus's work, the more clearly one sees both the cost of his adherence to adversarial patterns at the expense of inclusive ones and the evidence that it was not just an oversight in the heat of battle. The phenomenon recurs even where one would least expect it, in the all-important chapters on Augustine and Dominic. And in the context of those chapters it takes on a kind of logic which brings us closer to understanding Jacobus's own outlook and the factors that shaped it.

8
Saint Augustine
and the Holy Life

Is [the *Legenda aurea*] to be numbered among the Christian
histories, or is it rather to be relegated to the class of Roman
fables? . . . Certainly it is the silliest collection of silly lies, and
crammed with the most absurd stories, which cannot be read,
much less defended, without great scandal to the Christian
religion.

William Cave, 1698

If there is any chapter of the *Legenda* which demands to be taken
seriously as an expression of Jacobus's religious values, it is the lengthy
and ambitious chapter on Augustine. Jacobus's fondness for this
particular Father of the Church is reflected not only in the traditional
(and absurdly implausible) claim that he knew all of Augustine's writings
by heart, but also in the existence of a *Tractatus de libris a beato
Augustino editis* that has been ascribed to him at least since the
fourteenth century[1] and in the unusual tributes to Augustine in his
better-known works. The *Legenda* account itself contains a long series
of testimonials to Augustine's profundity and importance as a theologian (pp. 560-61); and for his life Jacobus supplements the standard *vita*
by Possidius with dozens of quotations from Augustine's own writings.
In this chapter, moreover, the special priorities that ordinarily distinguish the *Legenda* from Jacobus's sermons almost vanish. Jacobus
includes relatively few miraculous events, most of them posthumous and
none vengeful or threatening, and hardly mentions the heretics and
worldly leaders whom Augustine found himself opposing at various
points in his career as bishop. The emphasis falls instead on Augustine's
personal experience and on his virtues. The implication may be that this
particular narrative, like the learned disquisitions in other chapters, was
meant for the edification of the clerics who used the *Legenda* directly; in

135

any event, it was sufficiently sober and scholarly to make an unusual impression on Bernard Gui, whose own account of Augustine ends with several pages of material borrowed from Jacobus's.[2]

Thanks to all these exceptional circumstances, the *Legenda* chapter on Augustine provides an unusual opportunity to discover the religious logic behind Jacobus's selectivity—a subtler and more elusive matter than the political logic. As Cave's verdict suggests, it is all too easy to overlook or misunderstand the religious teaching in the *Legenda*. Even the Catholic critics of the sixteenth century tended to dismiss the book, obvious propaganda aside, as a collection of trivial and ridiculous stories.[3] What the chapter on Augustine brings to the fore is the seriousness, even severity, of Jacobus's intentions. His favorite moral and spiritual themes are uncompromisingly idealistic—so much so, indeed, that some of them can almost be mistaken for the teachings of later Puritan reformers, or for the views of the dualist heretics who were challenging the church in his own time. And Jacobus seems to have applied the same principles with some rigor elsewhere in the *Legenda*. As we shall see, in fact, his characteristic avoidance of healings follows almost inevitably from the ideal put forth in the Augustine chapter. And so does his predilection for the strange and pointless-looking anecdotes which have led many readers to take his book lightly.

Although the *Legenda* account of Augustine begins with a reference to the *Vita* by Possidius and a few lines which echo the opening of Possidius's narrative, Jacobus clearly found that *vita* inadequate for his own purposes.[4] The story he wanted to retell was the one just briefly outlined in Possidius's first two chapters: the story of Augustine's conversion, its causes, and its transforming effect on his life. Here the great source is of course the *Confessions,* and it is to this work that Jacobus turns for most of the particulars in his narrative and a good deal of the wording. What is important to note from the outset is that Augustine's conversion means something rather different in the *Legenda* than it meant in the *Confessions*.

The first change in the *Legenda*—and the most puzzling one, at first sight—has to do with Augustine's state before conversion. Jacobus clearly wanted to show the seriousness of his spiritual plight, for he retells a substantial fraction of the long, emotional history in the *Confessions:* Monica's prayers and tears, her patient journeys after her errant son, Augustine's search for guidance from various teachers, his bitter lamentations in the garden. Since Jacobus frequently emphasizes the importance of the sacraments,[5] one might assume that he retained all the suggestions of urgency here in order to underline Augustine's peril until he consents to be baptized. But it is no longer readily apparent what this decision means in Augustine's case, or why he finds it so difficult to make.

As Augustine himself told the story, the major impediments to his conversion were of course sins. It was intellectual pride, above all, that caused him to reject the simple faith of his mother and the apparent crudity of the Bible in search of a religion befitting his superior abilities; the habit of sensuality, that held him back from baptism even after his intellectual errors had been overcome. In Jacobus's retelling, however, these sins have nearly vanished. At one point Jacobus retains a phrase in which Augustine refers to himself as a habitual sinner, but the context directs one's attention to the excellence of his education rather than to his moral frailty: "He was so well educated in the liberal arts that he was considered a supreme philosopher and most brilliant orator. Indeed, he learned and understood on his own the works of Aristotle and all the books of the liberal arts that he could get to read, as he testifies in his *Confessions,* saying, 'I, who was then a most wicked slave of evil desires, read and understood all the books which are called "liberal" [i.e., appropriate to free men] that I could get to read'" (*Legenda,* p. 549).[6] Adeodatus, who is mentioned as receiving baptism with the saint, is explained as the gifted son "whom Augustine begot during his youth, when he was still a pagan and a philosopher" (p. 552).[7] The narrative itself retains no other trace of Augustine's mistresses and the problem they symbolized, although there is another allusion to once-felt lusts in a series of quotations which Jacobus adds, at the very end of the chapter, to emphasize Augustine's virtues after conversion (p. 566). As for pride, there is only a second quotation on Augustine's education, this one mentioning that he did not pay tribute to God as the source of his intellectual gifts and accompanied by the mild little moral, "wisdom without charity does not build up, but puffs up" (p. 549).[8] How far Jacobus is from identifying the young Augustine as a sinner of any magnitude is shown vividly a few pages later, when he compiles a list of the boyhood sins recounted in the *Confessions* and uses them to illustrate the great purity and humility of a soul that would bother to confess such trivial flaws (p. 555).

If Augustine's sins tend to fade from the story as Jacobus retells it, so do the intellectual errors and doubts recorded in the *Confessions.* Only his adherence to the Manichaean heresy is mentioned, and Jacobus does not present even Manichaeanism as a very great problem. In fact, he trivializes its philosophical implications, characterizing it simply as a denial of Christ's literal incarnation and of bodily resurrection, and retaining from all its effects on Augustine only a foolish bit of superstition about a fig tree's sorrow when its leaves or fruit are plucked.[9] Had Jacobus intended this heresy to be the issue at stake in Augustine's conversion, moreover, he would surely have revised the sequence of events. In his account, as in the *Confessions,* Augustine is freed from heresy long before he is enabled to take the step symbolized by his baptism.

Since the Augustine one sees in the *Legenda* seems not to be very seriously entangled in either error or sin, whence all the delays and suggestions of difficulty about his baptism? One might be tempted to conclude that Jacobus had no coherent plan in mind when he abridged the narrative from the *Confessions.* But there is an alternative explanation which would have occurred to serious-minded medieval readers, and which actually makes good sense of the story as Jacobus presents it: that Augustine has hitherto served the world, and that his conversion means renouncing and withdrawing from the world to become a man of God. The ideal of withdrawal from the world becomes increasingly evident as Jacobus's account proceeds, and once one has identified this theme, the apparent oddities in the initial section of the chapter also begin to fall into place. It is worth pausing to note the resemblance between the Augustine of the *Legenda*—characterized from the outset as a brilliant scholar, with his exceptional learning and intelligence far outweighing his sins—and the kind of distinguished convert most prized by the early Dominicans.[10] Several other unexpected emphases in the narrative reinforce the impression that Jacobus is presenting Augustine as a sort of advertisement for the religious life, and especially for the Order of Preachers—a natural enough connection, since it was the *Rule* of Saint Augustine which Dominic and his first followers had adopted as the foundation of their own constitutions. What demands our attention in this chapter of the *Legenda,* however, is not the polemical purpose Jacobus may have intended it to serve, but the extent to which his narrative is colored by contempt for this world.

As Jacobus relates the series of events by which Augustine was led to conversion, he greatly alters their implications by removing God from the scene. One explicit instance of divine guidance remains in the saint's early life: once he has abandoned the Manichaean heresy and begun to seek a genuinely Christian way of life, God gives him the idea of going to Simplicianus for advice.[11] But almost every other suggestion of God's providential care for Augustine has been deleted from the narrative. Possidius, who covered this period of the saint's life in much less detail than Jacobus does, paused to emphasize and reemphasize the point that Ambrose instructed Augustine by the prompting and assistance of God's mercy. Jacobus characterizes Ambrose's role much as Possidius did, but entirely omits God's.[12] Even more striking is what happens in the *Legenda* to the communications between God and Monica. In the *Confessions* there was never any doubt that God heard her constant prayers on behalf of her son. All three of the anecdotes which Jacobus retells, in fact, illustrated specific ways in which God answered her: consoling her with a prophetic dream (*Conf.* III.11.19-20), providing another reassuring message through the unlikely agency of a bishop's impatience with her pleas (III.12.21), refusing the letter of one request so that her deeper desire might eventually be fulfilled (V.8.15). And the next passage on which Jacobus draws is an eloquent summary of God's compassionate presence and help to Monica during her whole ordeal.[13] In the *Legenda,* however, God vanishes even from these stories. Monica's grief and dedication are met with anonymous signs—or with silence.[14] Since Augustine is eventually converted, and that result attributed partly to the merits of Monica,[15] the logical inference is that her devoted prayers were noticed in heaven. But the consolation of a direct, personal relationship with God is no longer a part of her experience, as Jacobus relates it.

Jacobus's tendency to increase the apparent remoteness of God, and the apparent autonomy of the saints, can be seen in other chapters of the *Legenda,*[16] but this pattern stands out in the case of Augustine because it involves so fundamental a departure from the saint's own teaching on grace. Although Augustine was obviously influenced by the Greek conception of God as Unmoved Mover, even the most casual reading of the *Confessions* reveals his countervailing emphasis on the personal, loving, actively redemptive side of the divine nature. Throughout this work, indeed, he offers praise and thanks to God precisely because God does not hold himself aloof, making his servants responsible for their own salvation and that of others. For, Augustine insists, they are utterly incapable of fulfilling such a demand. Augustine's experience testifies not only that God is the real teacher, whose grace supplies the lessons one needs to hear and the ears with which to hear them, but that such enlightenment is no more than the first step in the process of redemption. The will remains to be converted, turned from the love of lesser goods to the love of God, and it is too weak to make this ascent. But God, merciful beyond hope, actually descends to lift it up. One does not greatly oversimplify the *Confessions* by asserting that the remedies for all of Augustine's doubts and sins—and those of the human race he represents—are found in the Incarnation. Man's intellectual pride is vanquished by the humility of a Lord who embraced the condition of his creatures, flesh and all; man's fear of commitment, by the magnitude of the love that reaches down to him; the bondage of his habitual sins, by the liberty conferred on his will when he simply surrenders to Christ, confessing his total dependence on him and participating in his saving humility.

Given the centrality of this incarnational pattern in the *Confessions,* its disappearance from the abridgement in the *Legenda* suggests a good deal abut Jacobus's own brand of religious idealism. The point is not just his familiar deemphasis of God's mercy but his apparent reluctance even to identify God with the pattern of humble descent. Besides having Monica pray to a deity who apparently remains enthroned in a distant heaven, Jacobus omits the discovery of Christ's humility from his account of Augustine's spiritual education. He describes Augustine's reservation about Cicero, who teaches contempt for the world but never mentions the name of Christ;[17] but he leaves no trace of the saint's more important criticism of the Neoplatonists, whose doctrines, otherwise so similar to Christianity, Augustine finds to foster ingratitude and foolish pride because they insist on the loftiness of the Lord they seek and take no account of the Incarnation (see esp. *Conf.* VII.9.13-15 and 19.25-21.27). And of course he never sets the Incarnation against the Manichaean version of pride and folly, as Augustine did in earlier books of the *Confessions* (esp. V.3.3-5). Most suggestive of all is the way he alters the implications of Augustine's first mystical experience. In the *Confessions* this was another manifestation of divine help and guidance. In effect, Augustine was given a brief glimpse of the light he was still incapable of seeing for himself:

When first I knew you, you took me up, so that I might see that there was something to see, but that I was not yet one able to see it. You beat back my feeble sight, sending down your beams most powerfully upon me, and I trembled with love and awe. I found myself to be far from you in a region of unlikeness, as though I heard your voice from on high: "I am the food of grown men. Grow, and you shall feed upon me. You will not change me into yourself, as you change food into your flesh, but you will be changed into me." (*Conf.* VII.10.16)[18]

This foretaste of joy in God kindled Augustine's desire, spurring him on toward the discovery of the humble Mediator through whom that desire might be satisfied. Jacobus not only omits that sequel to the vision but removes the suggestion of God's loving condescension ("you took me up, so that I might see that there was something to see, but that I was not yet one able to see it") when he describes the visionary experience itself (p. 551). Since the rest of Augustine's reflection on this experience is repeated word for word in the *Legenda,* the omission stands out; and its effect is rather dramatic. Instead of experiencing the generosity of a God who stoops to lift him up, a foreshadowing of the pattern of redemption as the *Confessions* present it, the Augustine of the *Legenda* finds his efforts repulsed by a God who dwells far above him. Since the next incident retold is Augustine's visit to Simplicianus, who urges him to enlist among God's servants,[19] the apparent lesson is that the gulf separating him from God is not to be bridged unless he himself takes the initiative.

The way Jacobus has altered the psychology behind Augustine's conversion is clearly exemplified in the ensuing scenes. The plot is quite simple. From Simplicianus and his own friend Ponticianus, Augustine hears of others who have preceded him in conversion, and his heart is inflamed to follow them; he rushes out into the garden, where he bitterly laments his own slowness to enter God's service and is brought at last to the decision. Although every detail in this part of the *Legenda* account comes directly from the *Confessions,* the material has been so selected as to exclude the pattern of humble descent in favor of the idea that conversion raises one's status. The change is particularly striking in the story about the great scholar Victorinus, who became a convert late in life and eventually mustered enough courage to come to church for baptism and a profession of his faith. In the *Confessions* (VIII.2.3-5) this was a story about Christian humility; but Jacobus retells it without mentioning either the cost involved in Victorinus' public gesture, which meant repudiating both his former beliefs and his influential friends, or the understanding of Christ's humility which gave him the strength to go through with it. In the *Legenda* (p. 551) the emphasis falls instead on the acclamation with which the church welcomes such a convert. Jacobus's fondness for motifs that identify conversion with raising one's own condition, rather than with humility and gratitude to God, is clearly manifested again in the single passage he retains to convey Augustine's reaction to the human examples that have been held up before him: "Augustine was so much inflamed by their examples that he turned on his companion Alypius, his face reflecting the turmoil of his mind, and exclaimed violently, 'What is the trouble with us? What do we hear? The unlearned rise up and take heaven by storm, and we with all our erudition sink into hell! Are we ashamed to follow, because they have gone ahead of us? Is it no shame to us not even to follow them?'" (pp. 551-52).[20] Given the new context Jacobus has established, the suggestions of competitiveness here loom much larger than they did in the *Confessions,* and so does the image of raising oneself from earth to heaven.

Half a page earlier, when he describes the frame of mind in which Augustine went to see Simplicianus, Jacobus provides one more bit of evidence on the saint's motives for conversion: "All that he did in the world [*in saeculo*] displeased him, in comparison with the sweetness of God and the beauty of God's house, which he loved" (p. 551).[21] One clear implication here is that Augustine's love for the church has made him recognize the inferiority of his life in the world. But how is one to interpret that "sweetness of God" when Jacobus has removed from the narrative nearly every suggestion of God's generosity and of the humility by which he makes himself known to his creatures? There would seem to be just one possible answer: what Jacobus designates sweet is the very otherness of God, the grandeur and mystery that separate the divine from the lowliness of the human condition.

Jacobus does not quite simplify the conversion process to a matter of human aspiration, reaching up toward the divine. The actual conversion of Augustine is marked in the *Legenda* by three sudden and apparently miraculous changes. At the end of the scene in the garden, Augustine opens Paul's epistle to the Romans, reads the crucial exhortation,[22] and finds that all his doubts have vanished. The next incident is his cure from a severe toothache, as soon as he and his companions kneel to pray.[23] But the great miracle, as the *Legenda* presents it, is the inner transformation that takes place with his baptism: "At once he was wonderfully confirmed in the Catholic faith, and abandoned all the hope that he had in the world. . . . How much delight he thenceforth experienced in divine love, he himself reveals in this book of his *Confessions*" (p. 553).[24] The implicit lessons about grace are so evident that one almost expects a large turn toward the incarnational themes of the *Confessions*. But Jacobus is consistent. The grace conferred on Augustine at baptism initiates his release from this world, not his empowerment to assist in its redemption. In fact, despite the space devoted to the remainder of the saint's life in the *Legenda,* virtually the whole argument is foreshadowed in the passage just quoted. Ignoring most of the themes in the later chapters of the *Vita* and the *Confessions,* Jacobus proceeds to show Augustine's holiness after conversion by associating him with a "divine love" which is as otherworldly as possible and by insisting on his indifference to all earthly pleasures and rewards. Significantly enough, moreover, he makes the love sound less important than the indifference.

Even when his theme is the sweetness of Augustine's spiritual experience after conversion, Jacobus does little to modify his earlier suggestions about God's distance from his servants on earth. He presents a pastiche of quotations from Book IX of the *Confessions;* but nearly all the passages chosen actually describe Augustine's state of mind while he was awaiting baptism, and the dominant note is unsatisfied longing. From the second chapter, for example, Jacobus repeats the metaphors of being pierced and set on fire with God's love and of ascending from the vale of tears while singing a gradual psalm; from the sixth, Augustine's description of the way he wept as he listened to the hymns and canticles sung in church; from the fourth, expressions of Augustine's desire for the peace and changelessness of God, and of his regret for the period when he was a perverse enemy of Scripture (p. 553). When one sets these excerpts against the *Confessions,* one discovers that Jacobus has skipped over a number of more joyful-sounding motifs, including praise and thanksgiving for the generosity God has already shown to Augustine and his friends (e.g., *Conf.* IX.3.5-6 and 4.7,9). More noteworthy, however, is the way Jacobus has broken the original connections between the natural and supernatural dimensions of the saint's life. No longer does Augustine's experience of divine love serve, as it did in Book IX of the *Confessions,* to illuminate his studies, to clarify the practical decisions before him, to strengthen the bonds that tie him to Alypius and Monica and other Christians, or even to inflame him to teach others.[25] In the *Legenda* the "sweetness of divine love" is associated with nothing more earthly than psalms, church services, and pious tears.

Thus it is quite fitting that Jacobus reorders his excerpts to present the following passage as the climactic illustration of Augustine's new relationship with God:

O Christ Jesus, my helper, how sweet did it suddenly become to me to be free of the sweets of folly: things that I once feared to lose it was now joy to put away. You cast them forth from me, you the true and highest sweetness, you cast them forth, and in their stead you entered in, sweeter than every pleasure, but not to flesh and blood, brighter than every light, but deeper within me than any secret retreat, higher than every honor, but not to those who exalt themselves. (P. 553)[26]

In the *Confessions* Augustine's sudden joy in renouncing his former pleasures and desires was just the first manifestation of his liberty as an adopted son of God. But in the *Legenda,* where the issues have been redefined, one can almost say that Augustine's earthly existence ends with conversion. Instead of releasing him from the bondage of sin, supernatural love releases him in effect from the bondage of nature, the lowly state of "flesh and blood." If not much closer to his Lord in terms of intimacy, henceforth at least he resembles him, sharing in the sublime detachment from this world that has replaced the more complex ideal of the *Confessions.*

Far less subtle than the passage on divine love are the ensuing demonstrations of Augustine's marvellous indifference to the pleasures and rewards of this life. Here the *contemptus mundi* that underlies Jacobus's whole account receives its fullest expression, and it is no longer possible to misinterpret the stance he has adopted. One can hardly help seeing the resemblances between the conversion narrative, with its evident rejection of the flesh, and the teaching of the dualist sects that Augustine had condemned and Jacobus's own order was combatting.[27] But the particular kind of dualism or near-dualism manifested in the *Legenda* can best be understood as a puritanical response to the evil of worldliness, not a symptom of actual heterodoxy on Jacobus's part. The issues are shown most clearly in the way he uses Augustine's *Soliloquies.*

Augustine wrote the *Soliloquies* during the period when he had renounced his former life but was still awaiting baptism, and this brief work reflects his plan to devote himself to study and contemplation in a small community, detached from the world and its preoccupations. The particular section on which Jacobus draws has Ratio (Reason) questioning Augustine about his attitude toward the worldly rewards and pleasures he once desired. Augustine replies that he ceased long since to seek wealth, has recently lost his former desire for honors, and finds it easy to be temperate with regard to such necessities as food.[28] When Ratio inquires into his attitude toward marriage, trying to tempt him with the prospect of a wife endowed with every charm and virtue, Augustine answers much more vehemently: "No matter how much you choose to portray and endow her with all good qualities, I have decided that there is nothing I should avoid so much as marriage" (*Solil.* I.10.17).[29] After he has explained his reasons for shunning marriage, Ratio presses the matter further and elicits an outburst against sexual desire:

> R.   I am not at present interested in what you have decided, but I want to know whether you are still struggling or whether you have by this time overcome lust itself. For this concerns the health of your eyes.
> A.   I do not seek nor do I desire anything of this kind, and it is with dread and distaste that I even recall it.[30]

But even in this early work, colored as it is both by Neoplatonic ideas and by the convert's revulsion against the way he has lived heretofore, the thrust of Augustine's thought is inclusive rather than adversarial, and practical rather than doctrinaire. If he spurns the desirable objects of this world, it is primarily because they would interfere with his dedication to the higher goal of learning about God and the human soul. The very passage just quoted continues with an affirmation of the divine beauty that has captured his heart: "What more do you want? And this boon grows on me day by day, for the more my hope increases of seeing that Beauty which I so long for, the more is all my love and delight turned toward Him." And as the discussion goes on he acknowledges, under Ratio's prodding, that it would in fact be legitimate to accept earthly wealth or honors—or even, conceivably, a wife—if this acceptance would significantly assist him and his companions in the pursuit of wisdom (*Solil.* I.11.18). Thus the moral issue is redefined, with the realization that what must be excluded from Augustine's new life is not so much worldly things per se as the tendency to desire them for their own sakes:

A.   . . . when I used to desire riches, I desired them that I might be rich; I wanted those honors, the craving for which I said I have only recently overcome, because I was dazzled by a certain indescribable glitter about them. Always, when I craved a wife, I craved only that she might, in good repute, bring me sensual satisfaction. At that time there used to be in me a real desire for such things, but now I spurn them all. If, however, it is only through such things as these that I may pass to the things which I now desire, I do not seek them as something to be cherished, but I submit to them as something to be tolerated.

R.   Very good indeed: for I do not think that we should call it desire [*cupiditas*] with regard to things which are sought for the sake of something else. (*Solil.* I.11.19)

The actual moderation of Augustine's stance, with his suggestions even in the *Soliloquies* that objects of worldly desire could be converted to the service of God, was frequently forgotten in the Middle Ages, of course. The sterner moralists of the period preferred to portray him as an uncompromising foe of the world and its gifts. Nonetheless, Jacobus's handling of the subject is unexpectedly dramatic. For he does not just cite the most negative statements from the *Soliloquies,* ignoring the original qualifications. He actually presents these statements as his climactic examples of Augustine's sanctity, as if there were nothing more splendid in the saint's whole career than his prebaptismal renunciation of wealth, honors, and the rest. The pattern occurs at least three times. As the culminating proof of Augustine's moral perfection in one sermon, Jacobus asserts that the saint had so entirely conquered disorderly inclinations ("inordinatas affectiones") as to look back on them with horror or contempt, when he remembered them at all; the supporting material is Ratio's two questions about marriage and the more vehement parts of Augustine's replies.[31] In a second sermon, whose first two sections deal in some detail with Augustine's conversion, the third and final section proves his piety thereafter by quoting portions of the answers to Ratio which show the saint rejecting riches, honors, and pleasures.[32] Not a word is said about the higher goals that Augustine was pursuing instead. In the *Legenda* itself a very similar selection of material from the *Soliloquies* composes a sort of appendix to the chapter on Augustine,[33] following both the testimonies to the excellence of his writings and the posthumous miracles, several of which show his exceptionally high status in heaven. Thus Jacobus seems to be providing one more great tribute to Augustine's stature as a saint, and this time the introductory wording leaves no doubt whatever about the standard being invoked. Instead of proving the saint's greatness by recalling the magnitude of his love for God or his dedication to learning or his service to the church, Jacobus celebrates the magnitude of his contempt for what worldly people value: "We should observe that there are three things which worldly men desire: riches, pleasures, and honors. But this holy man reached such a degree of perfection that he despised riches, spurned honors, abhorred pleasures" (*Legenda,* pp. 565-66).[34]

Jacobus's tremendous emphasis on separation from the world, at the expense of the more positive themes in the life of Augustine, is a bit more perplexing than his tendency to portray saints like Ambrose as fierce champions of the church against the state. In this instance too, however, an explanation begins to emerge when one considers the religious climate of the time and the particular situation in which the early Dominicans found themselves.

The ideal of separation from the world has a long history, most of which need not detain us. The tradition was alive in the church well before the end of antiquity, manifesting itself most dramatically in the lives of the early monks who retreated far into the desert to avoid the corrupting influence of secular society. The idea that it was imperative to separate oneself from the *saeculum,* and to do so quite literally, became much more widespread during the early Middle Ages; and it was still very influential in Jacobus's time—as witnessed for example by the prevailing assumptions that enclosed religious were more certain of salvation than their counterparts in the secular clergy, and that a layman could improve his chances by taking refuge in a monastery as death approached. In theory, of course, the new mendicant orders of the thirteenth century affirmed the possibility of sanctification for Christians who remained in the world. But old ways of thinking do not change overnight. Although the mendicants did not physically withdraw, one should not forget the extent to which they were identified in the early years with a compensating ideal: a more thoroughgoing break with secular values than monasticism itself had managed. On the great issues of wealth and worldly privilege, no monastic reformer had proposed so radical a solution as that of Saint Francis, who cast off every kind of possession—including his family name, his social respectability, and even the humblest forms of physical comfort and security—in order to fulfill the Gospel imperatives as he understood them. Francis's example of utter poverty quickly proved incompatible with the needs of the institution that grew up around him, but it so captured the imagination of contemporary idealists that its influence reached very far indeed. Best known is the stand of the Franciscan "Spirituals," who for several generations subjected themselves to persecution, and brought scandal and near-disaster on their order, by refusing to compromise with the world—and the rest of the church—on the question of possessions.[35]

The Order of Preachers had been founded by a more practical man, who gave their mission the highest priority and emphasized poverty as a means to that end, not an absolute value. But if the Dominicans thus escaped the internal quarrels that plagued the disciples of Saint Francis, they were not immune to the appeal of an uncompromising stance against worldliness. For one thing, as Marie-Humbert Vicaire has shown, many of the early friars visualized their conversion in the traditional terms of flight from a world full of sin and danger.[36] Such converts seem to have been drawn to the order by a variety of more or less penitential motives, including the fear of death and judgment, revulsion against the vain pleasures and "pomps" of secular society, a desire to expiate particular sins, and the general notion that those who lived too comfortably on earth would have to suffer hereafter. The most revealing story mentioned by Vicaire is that of the dream which helped to impel Henry of Cologne to renounce the world. Since he had always lived virtuously, Henry at first felt no fear when transported in his dream to the Last Judgment. But the accuser who singled him out did not inquire about actual sins. Instead he demanded to hear what, if anything, Henry had ever given up for the sake of Christ. With this warning in mind, the young man awoke, dedicated himself to the ideal of sacrificial poverty, and eventually became a Dominican.[37]

If converts like Henry had strong incentives to emphasize renunciation of the world and its gifts, so did men who joined the Order of Preachers in the hope of saving others. For Dominic's altruistic ideal of a mission to the world evidently seemed quite new to religious men in the thirteenth century, and much more hazardous than the familiar pattern of withdrawal to save oneself. Even Humbert of Romans, whose treatise on preaching is full of encouragements to undertake this mission, betrays more than a little uneasiness about the spiritual dangers that confront the preacher when he leaves the cloister: opportunities for better food and more frivolous conversation than he would find in a Dominican setting, the temptation to visit his family often, possible entanglements in worldly affairs, the general dangers that arise from associating too much with seculars.[38] Since Dominican preachers could not be insulated against such dangers by the traditional barriers of stone or geographical distance, Humbert suggests that they must rely on their own vigilance and on the continual recollection that they have renounced the world for a superior way of life. Under the circumstances it is not surprising that Humbert continually appeals to his readers' pride in their vocation, dwelling on such themes as the special glory and merit of the preacher's office and the way both glory and merit are lessened if the preacher involves himself with worldly things.[39] Like Jacobus in the Augustine chapter, Humbert thus tends to suggest that separation from the world is not a sacrifice at all, but an enhancement of one's status.

Probably least among the early Dominicans' reasons for emphasizing world renunciation, but still worth mentioning, was the inevitable rivalry with other religious bodies of the period. Humbert, who presents preaching as the most meritorious work a Christian can do, ordinarily emphasizes its usefulness to others rather than the sacrifices it entails; but in one striking passage he seizes the opportunity to assert that the itinerant preacher's life is unparalleled in hardship, and to cite the testimonial of a former Cistercian as proof:

Who could adequately describe all the pains that a preacher, poor and zealous for the good of souls, endures in the care he expends in their behalf, in the fatigues of travel, in numerous privations, in anxiety concerning his success, and so many other similar causes, so that he has been compared to a woman in the pains of childbirth, exposed to sufferings truly inexpressible? . . . [A] religious of the order of Citeaux, who became a Friar Preacher, said that he suffered in his new life, in a few days, much more than in the whole time spent in his first vocation.[40]

Subtler but even more revealing are the hints of rivalry with the Franciscans. Although Dominican poverty had from the beginning been conceived in terms of a more thorough renunciation of the world's gifts than was customary among the monastic orders,[41] the brethren could hardly ignore the fact that the Franciscan stance was more radical yet. Here the most interesting bit of evidence is Bernard Gui's record of a proposal, apparently made by Stephen of Salanhac at a provincial chapter in 1254, that the order seek permission to improve the official prayer to Saint Dominic by deleting the petition for temporal assistance;

the contrast with the Franciscans' prayer, which asked instead for help in despising earthly things, is mentioned as if it were an embarrassment.[42]

The proposal cited by Gui obviously brings us close to Jacobus's recurrent suggestion that using worldly things in God's service is less admirable than shunning them altogether. Since the Dominicans did not in fact proceed to delete the reference to *temporalia* from the official prayer, one can infer that the majority of Jacobus's contemporaries within the order were not ready to go so far. But now that we have seen what separation from the world meant to some of those contemporaries, the general logic of his own position is not hard to grasp. If contempt for earthly things was a great mark of perfection, it should be manifested to an unparalleled degree by his favorite saints.[43] And if the same virtue was also the surest remedy against the dangerous influence of the world, he should encourage it by every means possible. And so he does. A substantial fraction of the little sermons built into the *Legenda* are devoted to just this theme. In the chapter on All Saints' Day, for example, Jacobus sums up the essential content of the saints' example in a single lesson: we should despise earthly things ("terrena") and desire heavenly things instead.[44] The etymological prefaces to a number of chapters make the same point in a more emphatic way. Thus, to cite just one striking example, Jacobus so interprets Vincent's name as to condemn the world and suggest the necessity of conquering it completely:

"Vincent" means *vitium incendens* (burning up vice) or *vincens incendia* (conquering fires) or *victoriam tenens* (maintaining victory). For he burned up—that is, consumed—vices by mortification of the flesh; he conquered the fires of punishment by the resolute endurance of tortures (or penances); he maintained victory over the world by despising it. For he conquered three things that exist in the world, namely deceitful errors, impure loves, and earthly fears; and he conquered them by wisdom, cleanness, and constancy. Of these things Augustine says, "The martyrdoms of the saints teach and have taught how this world, with all its errors, loves, and fears, may be conquered." (*Legenda*, p. 117)[45]

Although it is possible to miss the implicit connections in this passage between penitential suffering, "the fires of punishment," and the martyr's example of purity, there is no such ambiguity in the chapter on All Souls Day. There Jacobus gives a lengthy and rather daunting account of Purgatory, describing the pains to be suffered by all Christians who have done insufficient penance for their sins in this life, whether because of an untimely death or the erroneous leniency of a priest; the principle is that no sin may go unpunished. Moreover, Jacobus explains, those who have not freed themselves from the love of such earthly "riches" as material possessions or a spouse must have those loves burned away by the same terrible fire:

The third group who descend into Purgatory are those who carry wood, hay, and straw—that is, those who are held by a fleshly attachment to their riches, although they put nothing before God. For the fleshly attachments to which they were devoted—houses, spouses, possessions—are signified by those three things; and they will burn, according to the measure of their love, either for a long time, like wood, or less long, like hay, or very briefly, like straw. And this fire, as Augustine says, though it is not eternal, yet it is exceedingly severe, for it surpasses any pain that anyone has ever suffered in this life. Never has such pain been felt in the flesh, despite the fact that the martyrs suffered astonishing torments. (Pp. 729-30)[46]

Less dramatic than such warnings but even more noteworthy is the way Jacobus broadens the class of impure earthly things that are evidently to be despised and cast away. The pattern and its major consequences can most easily be seen by returning to his chapter on Augustine and invoking Gregory's *Dialogues* again as a standard of comparison. To recall Gregory at this point is not to forget about Augustine, whose influence pervades the *Dialogues* as it pervades the *Legenda,* but simply to notice the aspects of Augustine's thought that Gregory preserves and Jacobus tends to discard. This procedure has some logic because Gregory was the most influential medieval interpreter and popularizer of Augustine, and rather a stern moralist himself. And it will help us to avoid belaboring the obvious point that Jacobus's position lacks the philosophical subtlety of Augustine's. Jacobus's significant departures from both Gregory and Augustine on the issue of *terrena* are summed up in their respective answers to three practical questions: the relative claims of contemplation and active service, the worth of human relationships, and the proper attitude toward the lesser goods of human life.

As has already been suggested, the *Legenda* account of Augustine's life after conversion has one dominant theme: the saint's detachment from earthly things in favor of heavenly ones. And most of Augustine's work as a bishop appears, oddly enough, to have impressed Jacobus as belonging to the former class. Although he uses a good deal of material from the *Vita* in this portion of his narrative, he shows no interest whatever in Possidius's portrayal of Augustine as a dynamic leader of the church. The saint's involvement in the ecclesiastical affairs of his day—attending councils, helping to formulate policies on important issues, working tirelessly to combat heresies and to reconcile their adherents to the church—goes almost unmentioned in the *Legenda.*[47] Nor does Jacobus preserve many glimpses of Augustine's care for his own flock. Near the end of the chapter he makes room for numerous tributes to the excellence of Augustine's writings, but only a few general statements and one quasi-miraculous anecdote remain to connect the saint with the actual business of teaching his neighbors.[48] Even more telling is what happens to Augustine's involvement with the temporal affairs of his see. Where Possidius emphasized the disinterested wisdom with which the saint oversaw such matters as legacies and offerings, making the point that he cared more about principles than possessions (*Vita Aug.,* ch. 24), Jacobus simplifies the lesson by mentioning only such gestures of renunciation as the properties Augustine did not wish to buy and the legacies he refused to accept (*Legenda,* p. 557). And where Possidius indicated the saint's willingness to spend some of his time on the irksome duties of administration,[49] Jacobus so revises the account as to associate him wholly with spiritual pursuits: "Moreover, he was not fondly attentive to or entangled in property that he possessed in the church, but day and night he contemplated Scripture and the things of God. And he never had a desire for new buildings, avoiding the entanglement of his soul in them because he wanted it always free from all outward annoyance, so that he could freely engage in uninterrupted meditation and constant reading" (*Legenda,* p. 557).[50] It is Possidius who draws an explicit parallel at this point between Augustine's way of life and that of the church hereafter, when Martha's labors will be ended and only the better part chosen by Mary will remain;[51] but clearly it is Jacobus who has carried the motif to its logical conclusion. Abandoning the defense of episcopal prerogatives that marks less personal chapters of the *Legenda,* he suggests that the holiest bishop is the one who pays least attention to the mundane responsibilities of his office.

Augustine's own stance on the question of contemplation and action is clearly set forth in a well-known chapter of the *City of God.* Although he affirms the desirability of a life wholly intent on God, Augustine suggests that so blessed an existence is a privilege ordinarily reserved for heaven. For every Christian way of life is subject to the double imperative of the New Testament commandments: "No man has a right to lead such a life of contemplation as to forget in his own ease the service due to his neighbor; nor has any man a right to be so immersed in active life as to neglect the contemplation of God."[52] A bit later in the chapter Augustine defines the life of a bishop as one of work for the welfare of others, and he adds that such work cannot in conscience be refused: "Holy leisure is longed for by the love of truth; but it is the necessity of love to undertake requisite business. If no one imposes this burden upon us, we are free to sift and contemplate truth; but if it be laid upon us, we are necessitated for love's sake to undertake it." On this issue Gregory of course went further, venturing the idea that the contemplative life might actually be enriched and made more Christlike by the admixture of active service, and illustrating the ideal with the example of Benedict, who reached the summit of contemplative perfection without ceasing to attend to the earthly needs of his neighbors.[53]

The lasting influence of this ideal can be seen in the writings of some of Jacobus's great Dominican contemporaries. Thomas Aquinas, for example, concludes that the episcopal state is superior to the monastic because of the bishop's commitment to service; and he explains, citing Gregory, that one shows more love for God by feeding his flock than by serving him alone.[54] The treatise on preaching by Humbert of Romans occasionally suggests, as the *Legenda* does, that only the highest and most spiritual things are fit for the attention of a spiritual man. But Humbert's dedication to the ideal of service emerges unmistakably when he argues not only for preaching itself, but for concern with the listeners' temporal welfare. He reminds would-be preachers of the example set by Jesus when he fed the multitudes who had come to hear him, and he also cites Gregory on the practical necessity of thus condescending to the flesh: "Many, says St. Gregory, are wholly taken up with the spiritual side of the care of souls and completely neglect anything having to do with the temporal. By thus neglecting what belongs to the life of the body, they will not be able to do a great deal for those confided to their care."[55]

Since Jacobus himself frequently asserts the superiority of bishops and preachers to Christians in other states of life, one cannot conclude that he stood so far from Gregory, Thomas, and Humbert as to see no value in service to others. Rather, what his account of Augustine calls to our attention is the way this ideal is overshadowed, and impoverished, by his insistence on contempt for *terrena*. His chapter on Gregory predictably emphasizes the perfection the saint had attained in the monastery (p. 189) and his sorrow at being compelled to assume the cares of the papacy, and thus to let his soul be defiled by the dust of earthly business (p. 191). Elsewhere in the *Legenda* Jacobus omits most of the details that originally associated Benedict, Ambrose, Martin, and Dominic with pastoral care and teaching.[56] Although the titles remain to identify these and other saints with the vocations of abbot, bishop, and preacher, Jacobus's selectivity continually cancels out the image of a dynamic holiness that descends to involvement with the nonholy, for love's sake. In fact, the only work of mercy that receives much emphasis in the *Legenda* is selling one's property and giving the money to the poor, a gesture that usually symbolizes the saint's separation from the world.[57]

In the sermons Jacobus gives some attention to preaching as well as to the giving of alms, but there too he exhibits a marked preference for a monastic or even eremitical definition of the holy life. We have seen the pattern already in the sermons on Benedict,[58] and it turns up regularly and with surprisingly few modifications in Jacobus's sermons on saints who were not monks at all. How far he is from offering an alternative based on service to others is demonstrated rather neatly by the stratagems he adopts in one sermon on Ambrose; here he deals explicitly with the *vita contemplativa, vita actuosa,* and *vita composita,* citing the *City of God* as the source behind the terms and attempting to show how they are all illustrated in Ambrose's life. As one would expect, his definition of the contemplative life is focused on the saint's relationship with God: "The first life, the contemplative, is comprised of faithful prayer, the revelation of divine things, and the praise of God" (sermon 423 S4, p. 154).[59] But the *vita actuosa* is not focused on the saint's obligation to his neighbor. Ignoring both Gregory's standard definition, which consisted wholly of works of mercy, and Augustine's own message that the active life is one of public service, Jacobus defines it in terms barely differentiated from the contemplative pattern of individual purification and spiritual experience: "The second life, the active, is comprised of mortification of the flesh, generosity in almsgiving, and useful employment. . . . [Ambrose] had [useful employment], for he was always either preaching or writing or praying."[60] Since he might easily have broadened the picture by recalling Ambrose's work as a statesman, church administrator, spiritual counsellor to princes, or healer of the sick, the implication is that such forms of activity are insufficiently holy to deserve mention. As for the *vita composita,* Jacobus proceeds to define it quite inappropriately as observance of the counsels to poverty, chastity, and humility, as if the crucial mark of the "mixed" life were not service at all, but the renunciations that set religious and especially mendicants apart from the world.[61]

On the second question, the worth of human relationships, the general trend of Jacobus's teaching is already quite clear. One recalls the ways in which he removed the traces of Benedict's friendship with Servandus and other holy men, and separated both Benedict and Ambrose from their followers. Where Gregory and even Paulinus seemed automatically to visualize the Christian life in the context of a community, Jacobus depicts the saints as solitary individuals. Again his account of Augustine sheds additional light on the problem.

Unlike the saints in the *Legenda* who seem to have been born holy, Augustine begins as a fallible human being, and Jacobus leaves no doubt about his debts to Monica, Ambrose, and other members of the Christian community; indeed, as we have seen, his conversion is credited almost entirely to the efforts of these people, rather than to the grace of God. It is only after the conversion that Jacobus distances Augustine from the community. The timing confirms that he is identifying solitude with the special condition of the saints, rather than with the common lot of mankind. And his point is not just that saints need no further assistance from men. The sequence of events initiating Augustine's new life, in the *Legenda,* clearly suggests that all human attachments are left at the threshold of the holy life. Augustine receives baptism with his son Adeodatus and his friend Alypius, neither of whom is mentioned again in the *Legenda.* During the ceremony Ambrose and Augustine collaborate, in antiphonal fashion, to compose the *Te Deum* (p. 553);[62] with this illustration of the harmony between the two saints, their relationship apparently comes to an end. Then follow Augustine's renunciation of "all the hope that he had in the world" and the quotations on his experience of divine love, quotations in which Alypius and Augustine's other friends no longer play any part. Immediately after Augustine's expression of his new ability to do without the joys he used to fear losing, Jacobus recounts his return to Africa, referring almost parenthetically to the death of Monica on the way: "Then, taking Nebridius and Evodius and his mother, he journeyed back to Africa, but when they were at Ostia Tiberina his devout mother died. After her death Augustine returned to his own estate where, along with his followers, he devoted himself to fasting and prayer to God, wrote books, and instructed the untaught" (p. 553).[63] The community has not yet vanished entirely, although Nebridius, Evodius, and "the untaught" will fade from the narrative as abruptly as they appeared. But the message is clear. Even Monica, whose piety and love for Augustine received so much attention earlier in Jacobus's account, ceases to matter once he has begun to love God. There is no room in the *Legenda* for the blessing of the old bonds between them, or for the great vision they shared at Ostia, or for his grief at her death (*Conf.* IX.8.17-13.37). True holiness, Jacobus suggests, means detachment not only from mundane affairs but from all earthly loves.

It is hardly necessary to point out that neither Augustine nor Gregory presented an ideal of emotional detachment from other human beings. The deepening love between Augustine and Monica in the *Confessions* is just the most memorable instance of Augustine's teaching on human relationships. As for Gregory's position, perhaps the climactic bit of evidence is the story in which Scholastica's last visit with Benedict is prolonged by divine intervention; Gregory explains that God answered her prayers, overruling her brother's wish to return to his monastery, because hers was the greater love.[64] Jacobus's tendency to exclude such lessons from the *Legenda* can be related of course to the general shift from corporate to individual emphases that has often been noticed in the spirituality of the later Middle Ages. And his refusal to endorse familial love in particular reminds one that Humbert mentioned frequent visits to relatives as one of the temptations to which travelling preachers might yield unless they were well armed against it.[65] But the larger issues raised by Jacobus's selectivity become quite evident when one considers the principles bound up with Augustine's affirmation of human fellowship.

Augustine takes a very strict line on the obligation to love God with all one's heart and soul and mind, insisting that nothing else is to be loved for its own sake, but only as a means to the ultimate end of fruition in God. From one perspective this teaching seems to encourage just such a dismissal of human relationships as one sees in the *Legenda*. As we have seen, however, Augustine's emphasis on the ultimate end precludes any absolute rejection even of equivocal earthly goods like wealth and honors. And he is very far indeed from classifying human companionship as an equivocal good. In fact, he seems to have taken for granted—much as Gregory did—that communion with other human beings is part of the end for which mankind was created. At one point in the *City of God* he expresses agreement with the classical philosophers who made social intercourse an essential part of the ideal life; "For how," he asks rhetorically, "could the city of God . . . either take a beginning or be developed, or attain its proper destiny, if the life of the saints were not a social life?" (*City of God* XIX.5). In a richer and more eloquent passage from another chapter of the same book, Augustine describes the whole dispensation in which human affections play their part:

God, then, the most wise Creator and most just Ordainer of all natures, who placed the human race upon earth as its greatest ornament, imparted to men some good things adapted to this life, to wit, temporal peace, such as we can enjoy in this life from health and safety and human fellowship, and all things needful for the preservation and recovery of this peace, such as the objects which are accommodated to our outward senses, light, night, the air, and waters suitable for us, and everything the body requires to sustain, shelter, heal, or beautify it: and all under this most equitable condition, that every man who made a good use of these advantages suited to the peace of this mortal condition, should receive ampler and better blessings, namely, the peace of immortality, accompanied by glory and honor in an endless life made fit for the enjoyment of

God and of one another in God; but that he who used the present blessings badly should both lose them and should not receive the others. (Ibid., ch. 13).

Perhaps the most crucial point here is the suggestion that man's natural desires for health, safety, and human fellowship were created to be fulfilled. Besides the implication that these goals are worthy of desire, one notes the larger premise of continuity, rather than contradiction, between what God wills for his creatures and what the laws of their nature impel them to seek. Augustine is not asserting, of course, that the fallen human will is incapable of bestowing its love in the wrong places. But here and elsewhere he clearly suggests, foreshadowing the famous teaching of Thomas Aquinas, that it is the work of grace to perfect nature, not destroy it. The result of redirecting the will toward God is not the abolition of human emotions and desires but their liberation and renewal. Hence, instead of urging his readers to love their fellow creatures less, Augustine can put forth an ideal of charity that incorporates the natural loves and lifts them too towards God:

When He said, "With thy whole heart, and with thy whole soul, and with thy whole mind," He did not leave any part of life which should be free and find itself room to desire the enjoyment of something else. But whatever else appeals to the mind as being lovable should be directed into that channel into which the whole current of love flows. Whoever, therefore, justly loves his neighbor should so act toward him that he also loves God with his whole heart, with his whole soul, and with his whole mind. Thus, loving his neighbor as himself, he refers the love of both to that love of God which suffers no stream to be led away from it by which it might be diminished.[66]

As the preceding discussion suggests, the divine love Jacobus praises in the *Legenda* is a frail and attenuated version of what Augustine—and Gregory and Humbert, for that matter—meant by charity. Characteristically excluding the themes of friendship and familial love from his accounts of the saints,[67] and greatly weakening the theme of active service, Jacobus reduces charity from a powerful, transforming virtue to a private state that seems almost irrelevant to the rest of human life. Again one sees the cost of his refusal to present an ideal that embraces the lowliness of the human condition in order to raise it up. What the case of human fellowship brings into relief is the extent to which he reverses the Augustinian stance on natural law, implying that whatever comes naturally to man is suspect, if not absolutely inimical to holiness.

If human fellowship cannot be reconciled with sanctity as Jacobus depicts it, neither of course can the enjoyment of lesser earthly goods. On this issue the most vivid evidence in the Augustine chapter is the last block of illustrative material from the *Confessions,* this one inserted among the borrowings from Possidius which describe the saint's personal habits and virtues. Jacobus introduces it under a rubric which conveys the interesting dual message that Augustine blamed himself for very minor faults and that he is to be highly commended for doing so: "Such were his purity and humility that in his *Confessions* he acknowledges and humbly accuses himself before God of even the smallest sins, sins which among us are considered as nothing or very little" (*Legenda,* p. 555).[68] After briefly listing half a dozen of Augustine's boyhood transgressions, Jacobus comes to the substantive examples: a long series of quotations from the portion of Book X in which Augustine confesses his continuing vulnerability to the temptations posed by earthly pleasures, and pleasures of the senses in particular. It is worth pausing to note that Jacobus passes over all the affirmations of the natural order in Books X to XIII of the *Confessions.* In fact, he never cites Augustine on the way the mind can be led toward God by the splendor of his creation. Instead, Jacobus singles out discussions like this one, where earthly things appear in their most problematical guise, and he presents them in a way that magnifies their negative implications.

In this instance the original issue was unfaithfulness to God. The problem, as Augustine explained it, was the fact that man is surrounded by earthly sources of delight which tempt him to cherish them for their own sake.[69] And Augustine's solution was not of course to reject them out of hand; he was too sensitive to the errors of the Manichaeans to deny the intrinsic goodness of created things, and too practical to ignore the potential usefulness of lesser goods in assisting himself or his neighbors on the pilgrimage towards God. Jacobus evidently felt no such constraints. As the introductory rubric suggests, he was intent on showing Augustine's great purity. The first set of quotations is prefaced by a statement which defines the moral issue as pleasure itself: "In the same book, the *Confessions,* [Augustine] accuses himself of that moderate pleasure which he sometimes took in eating, saying . . ." (pp. 555-56).[70] The apparent lesson is that Augustine manifested his virtue by deriving little pleasure from food and by blaming himself for being even that susceptible to an earthly love. Here Jacobus obviously comes close to expressing the principle that holiness means the abolition of natural sensations and desires, rather than their subordination to a higher end. The selective quotations that follow reinforce this new message. Omitting the more positive emphases in Augustine's own discussion, Jacobus reduces the saint's reflections on food and drink, sweet odors, and the beauty of church music to a series of demonstrations that he deeply distrusted sensory pleasure.[71] And Jacobus skips the whole chapter on the pleasures of the eyes, with its powerful illustrations of the saint's delight in the magnificence of the visible world (*Conf.* X.34). What takes its place under the rubric about sight ("Accusat etiam se de visu") is a listing of the more trivial examples from Augustine's chapter on vain curiosity: occasions on which, the saint confessed, his attention had been drawn to such mundane phenomena as a running dog or a spider catching flies, when he should have been concentrating on his prayers and meditations (*Legenda,* p. 556; cf. *Conf.* X.35.57). Thus Augustine's ideal of loving only God, despite the delightfulness of the world he has made, gives way in the *Legenda* to a negative ideal of ceasing to appreciate—or even notice—the beauties and pleasures of earthly life.

It is not hard to see the coherence of the patterns we have been considering. Jacobus's whole account of Augustine's life as a Christian seems designed to demonstrate the saint's triumphant purity—a purity which overcomes the world by scorning everything the world labels good, from riches and marriage to public activity, human companionship, and all the delights of the senses. The logical corollary that the saint scorns life itself is contradicted by one detail in this chapter. When Jacobus retells the story from the *Vita* about the invalid miraculously healed by Augustine while the saint was on his own deathbed, he lets Augustine respond to the man's plea in a way that suggests he himself would like to be healed: "What is this you say, my son? Do you think that if I could do any such thing, I would not already have done it for myself?" (*Legenda,* p. 559).[72] The inconsistency is remedied, however, in one of Jacobus's sermons on Augustine, which retells the same story as a proof of Augustine's generosity to others and then undercuts that lesson by observing that the saint himself wished to die: "Behold how great his charity was, when he preferred to expend his charity on the sick man who came to him rather than on himself. Nor is this surprising, since he desired to pass to God" (no. 524 S63, p. 282).[73] Elsewhere in the *Legenda* chapter Jacobus uses selective retellings of several anecdotes from the *Vita* to prove that Augustine praised the desire for death as a great virtue in others[74] and fervently exhibited this desire in his own case.[75]

I have not found another chapter of the *Legenda* that does such a systematic job of dissociating a saint both from worldly values in the usual sense and from what human beings naturally desire. But Jacobus consistently goes so far in condemning the love of this world that his teaching merits the label "puritanical" in a sense that Augustine's and even Gregory's do not. In a number of his sermons, including one of those on Augustine, the uncompromising positions he attributes to the saints are explicitly set against the conduct of worldly churchmen.[76] But it is more characteristic of Jacobus, especially in the *Legenda,* to suggest that earthly existence itself is so corrupt and so perilous that Christian wisdom can almost be summed up as a matter of rejecting the gifts of this life, lest one lose those of heaven. In one particularly dramatic instance, he adds to the chapter on Ambrose a story Paulinus had not told about the saint's visit to a prosperous Tuscan landowner.[77] When his host informs him that he has been favored with great riches and a large household of servants, and has never suffered the least adversity, Ambrose immediately summons his companions to flee from the place: "Come, let us escape from here as fast as possible, for the Lord is not in this place. Hurry, my sons, hurry! Don't hesitate in your flight, lest divine vengeance overcome us and involve us in their sins" (*Legenda,* p. 254).[78] The predicted vengeance strikes a few moments later, when the earth opens up to swallow the landowner and his household. And Ambrose's explanation drives home the lesson that earthly prosperity is a curse, not a blessing: "Behold, brothers, how mercifully God disposes when he gives adversity here, and how very angry he is when he grants continuous prosperity."[79]

Elsewhere, Jacobus rather frequently discourages the desire for comfort in this life by emphasizing the relative brevity and lightness of earthly suffering in comparison with the pains of Purgatory or Hell; the implication is that no one is permitted to escape both. Thus, in the *Legenda,* Saint Sebastian exhorts others to endure martyrdom by condemning the life they will relinquish as a begetter of nothing but evils and by reminding them of the eternal pains of Hell (pp. 109-10). Saint Eustace is explicitly given the alternatives of enduring the necessary tribulations at once or deferring them to the end of his life; of course he chooses the former (pp. 713-14). Saint Peter the Exorcist explains to his jailer that God does not intend his servants to reach eternal glory except by the route of transitory suffering (pp. 343-44). In one sermon on Saint Sebastian, Jacobus goes so far as to differentiate the sufferings of the martyrs from those in store for the wicked solely in terms of degree; God, he suggests, is responsible for both: "If therefore God so punishes those whose life is holy, how severely will he punish those whose life is unrighteous? *If the just man receive evil in the earth, how much more the wicked and the sinner* [Prov. 11:31]. If [God] so punishes those in whom he is blessed, how severely will he punish those in whom he is blasphemed?" (no. 357 S17, p. 66).[80]

It is particularly instructive to recall the teaching of the *Dialogues* at this point because Gregory has so often been characterized as a stern and legalistic descendant of Augustine. Although there is certainly some

truth in the common idea that Gregory depicts God as a fear-inspiring
Judge, even the fourth and grimmest book of the *Dialogues* is full of
reassurances about God's fatherly care for individuals. Thus, for
example, when Gregory describes the scourge of blindness endured by an
abbot named Spes, he emphasizes the inner strength and consolations
which God conferred together with the punishment, lest it prove too
heavy for the old man to bear, and he relates the eventual cure which
reassured the abbot of God's love (*Dial.* IV.11). As this story suggests,
Gregory preserves at least something of Augustine's teaching about the
continuity between nature and grace. It may well be that he had no such
appreciation of the natural world as appears in the *Confessions,*[81] and
there is no denying his insistence on flight from the corruptions of the
saeculum. But Gregory did not so distrust human nature and its loves as
to portray the lesser goods of this life as anything but blessings. The
miracle stories he tells, especially in the life of Benedict, repeatedly
affirm the validity of desiring such things as health, safety, food,
companionship, even money. For they are all provided by the Father
who recognizes each man's needs and, repeating the pattern of the
Incarnation, bends to the level of human nature in order to raise it up.

The question that remains to be answered is why the *Legenda* came to be
associated with "silly lies" and popular superstitions instead of with
stern religious teaching. Reform-minded readers in the fifteenth and
sixteenth centuries ought in theory to have appreciated the severity of
Jacobus's emphases. Where other medieval hagiographers tend to
promote the cult of the saints with the promise of earthly rewards as well
as heavenly ones, Jacobus rather consistently purifies the old legends of
such concessions to the flesh. Here it is instructive to recall the scattered
examples of "superstitiosa" found in the *Legenda* by Nicholas of
Cusa.[82] By far the most extravagant ones are the promises in the
chapters on Saints Barbara and Dorothea, chapters relegated to a sort of
appendix in Graesse's edition because they were almost certainly added
to the *Legenda* by a later author or authors. One can hardly imagine
Jacobus himself promising, as the chapter on Barbara does (p. 901), that
devotion to the saint will ensure the remission of all one's sins at the
Judgment. Instead he insists on the necessity of penance, illustrating the
greatest mercy of the Virgin and other intercessors with stories in which
an unhappy malefactor is restored to life long enough to fulfill this
requirement.[83] Even more incompatible with Jacobus's principles is the
Dorothea chapter (p. 911), which promises those who honor this saint
both remission of their sins at death and deliverance from all earthly
tribulations. Jacobus, of course, insists that earthly tribulations are

more desirable than earthly well-being, and his selectivity with regard to miracles continually reinforces the point. Significantly enough, the one healing he retains from Gregory's life of Benedict is supplemented—and justified, in effect—with the claim that the boy who was healed went on to lead so good a life that he died blessedly.[84] In one sermon, as we have seen, Jacobus finds a more ingenious solution, crediting Augustine simultaneously with the power to heal and the virtue of preferring sickness and death for himself. Among the resurrections and cures he admits to the *Legenda,* a strikingly large number conform to at least one of these patterns: it is made clear that the beneficiary dedicates the remainder of his or her life (often quite brief) to spiritual matters, or the desire for life and health is shown to conflict with the value system of the saints.[85] In short, Jacobus goes to some lengths to discourage the notion that the supernatural might be used as the means to an earthly end. The great problem is that he does too thorough a job. Indeed, the very zeal with which he dissociates the supernatural from impure earthly things goes some way towards explaining why so many Renaissance critics found it impossible to take his book seriously. A small sample of the prodigies held up for admiration in the *Legenda* will suffice to illustrate this paradox.

If one of the central virtues celebrated in the *Legenda* is fortitude against the world, the other is transcendence of the earthly code of values that labels life preferable to death, health to suffering, sensory pleasure to insensibility, and so on. The chapter on Augustine makes the point clearly enough, but wherever possible Jacobus gives more spectacular demonstrations. Saint Bernard, for example, is credited with so despising the needs of the body as to condemn overly sound sleep as a symptom of worldliness and go to meals as if to torture (p. 530), and with achieving a level of physical insensibility that permits him to drink oil by mistake, consume raw blood without noticing that it is not butter (p. 531), and journey for hours beside a large lake without even seeing it (p. 533). On the death of Saint Vaast (Vedastus), an old man named Audomatus is cured of blindness so that he may see the saint's remains and then rendered blind again at his own request (p. 174).[86] Saint Giles (Aegidius), severely wounded by an arrow, refuses medical attention and beseeches God never to restore him to health, since he knows that virtue is perfected in infirmity (p. 583). Saint Hilary goes considerably further, using his prayers to obtain an early death for his daughter, lest she weaken in her resolve to remain a virgin, and performing the same favor for the daughter of a pious friend (pp. 98-99). And the chapter on Saint Petronilla celebrates both the virtue of a father who miraculously inflicts a debilitating illness on his daughter, in the interests of her soul, and the virtue of the girl herself when she chooses—and obtains—death instead of marriage (p. 343). These are admittedly among the more extreme displays of supernatural—or antinatural—virtue in the *Legenda,* but they are far from being isolated instances. A number of the martyrs are so eager for torture and death that they present themselves before the persecutors instead of waiting to be arrested;[87] and at least one of them, Saint Apollonia, actually commits suicide, leaping into the fire that her tormenters have kindled to frighten her (p. 294). The beautiful young wife of Saint Adrian rejoices at his arrest for the faith, enthusiastically oversees every detail of his torture and execution, and is preparing to throw herself into the fire that is burning the martyrs' bodies when it is quenched by a sudden storm (pp. 598-600). Quite apart from the ethical issues raised by these and all the similar stories in the *Legenda,* one can hardly ignore the psychological effect produced by Jacobus's continual recourse to such prodigies. Some readers of the *Legenda* presumably perceived his real message and were inspired to despise this world and all its gifts; but by glorifying immunity to natural human instincts rather than, say, mundane care for one's neighbor, Jacobus has made it all too easy to find the same sort of entertainment in the saints' achievements that modern children find in cartoons about superheroes and in books of world records.

Cautionary punishments aside, the miracles in the *Legenda* are at least as open to misunderstanding and misuse as are its portrayals of saintly virtue—and for the same reason. Here too Jacobus tends to exhibit the supernatural in its purest possible form, purging away so much of the human context that the marvels sound like ends in themselves. The chapter on Dominic, which contains an unwontedly large and beneficent collection of posthumous miracles, provides several good illustrations. There is, for example, the story of a devout nobleman whose young son dies during the family's visit to a shrine of Dominic in Hungary; the grieving father returns to the holy place with the child's body, beseeching the saint to restore him to life. Although he retains the father's emotion, Jacobus omits the original ending, in which the reunited family joyfully returned to their home, and leaves his readers with the wondrous and rather eerie image of the child's body, suddenly reanimated, moving about the dark church.[88] The cure of a crippled scholar named Nicholas is an even stranger story, as Jacobus presents it. Detaching the marvellous sequence of events from the original explanations, the version in the *Legenda* conveys the impression that Nicholas is healed, not by his exemplary faith in Christ and Saint Dominic, but by the quasi-magical expedient of winding a thread around his body while invoking their names.[89] Most purely supernatural of all—and most pointless, in human terms—is the story, just preceding that of Nicholas, about a woman whose piety is rewarded with the sight of candles that light themselves and burn inside a towel:

> . . . a certain matron, who had arranged for a mass to be said in honor of Saint Dominic, did not find the priest at the appointed hour; so she wrapped the three candles she had brought for the mass in a clean towel and put them in a receptacle. Then she went away for a short time, and when she returned she saw the candles burning with a bright flame. Everyone ran to see this amazing sight, and stood trembling and praying until the candles—without damaging the towel—had completely burned out. (P. 480)[90]

Given the assumptions revealed in Jacobus's treatment of Augustine, it is perfectly understandable that he should fill the *Legenda* with such marvels. In effect he would encourage his audience to value the supernatural for its strangeness, its very lack of connection with the rest of human life. The Renaissance concluded, and with some justification, that his stories fostered superstition. But poor Jacobus might more aptly be accused of having so impoverished the idea of the supernatural, in his attempts to keep it pure, as to hasten the victory of the secularism he detested.

9
The Legacy of the Founder

In short, Jacobus collected the deeds of the saints as they were
current in his day, arranged them in the order of the calendar,
and published them. If there are any fables among them, he is
not to be considered their originator.

Jacques Echard, 1719

Thus far we have focused on Jacobus's treatment of very old sources,
leaving aside the thorny question of his similarity, or lack of similarity,
to other hagiographers of his own era. Although no definitive answers
can be reached while so many hagiographical texts of the later Middle
Ages remain to be published and studied, one "modern" legend retold
by Jacobus provides an illuminating introduction to the subject. The
legend is that of Dominic, the saint who, above all others, occupied the
attention of Jacobus's contemporaries and immediate predecessors in the
Order of Preachers. In this instance there is no standard,
long-established *vita* of the saint to set against the version in the
Legenda. Indeed, the Dominic legend underwent so much revision and
augmentation in the middle decades of the thirteenth century that it is
not always possible to be sure whether Jacobus is depending on earlier
written versions or on oral traditions that would be incorporated into
later ones.[1] For our purposes, however, the important issue is not
Jacobus's source for particular stories about Dominic but the larger
relationship between the way this legend developed, during the first half
of Jacobus's lifetime, and the priorities that govern the *Legenda*.

Although Dominic died in 1221, the first written account of his
life—in the *Libellus de principiis Ordinis Praedicatorum* by Jordan of
Saxony, who had succeeded him as master general of the order—did not

164

appear until twelve years later.[2] If that initial delay suggests a certain indifference to the way the founder was remembered, however, the friars' literary output in the next generation vividly demonstrates that their attitude had changed.[3] Within a quarter-century of Dominic's canonization in 1234, not one but three revisions of the legend had been produced and authorized, in turn, for liturgical use during the Octave of the saint: the version of Peter Ferrandus between 1235 and 1239; that of Constantine of Orvieto, compiled at the request of Master General John of Wildeshausen in 1247-48; and the definitive version, overseen and perhaps personally compiled by Master General Humbert of Romans between 1256 and 1260.[4] Jacobus would not have witnessed the beginning of this process, since he was just a young child at the time of the canonization,[5] but he entered the order in 1244, before Peter's version had given way to Constantine's. During the next fifteen years at least two general chapters called on the brethren to search out and report additional testimonies to the sanctity of Dominic and the early history of the order;[6] such edifying anecdotes as did not find their way into the liturgical lives were collected elsewhere—most notably in the *Vitae fratrum,* compiled by Gerard de Frachet and issued with Humbert's blessing about 1260 "for the encouragement and spiritual profit of the brethren" ("ad frat[r]um consolacionem et spiritualem profectum").[7] The *Vitae fratrum* seems to have been intended only for internal use; in fact, Humbert's preface unequivocally commands that its contents not be disseminated outside the order without his express consent.[8] For the larger public a third group of accounts were compiled, two of which certainly predate the *Legenda aurea.* By 1243 the newly recruited friar Jean de Mailly had already incorporated a brief life of Dominic into the second edition of his *Abbreviatio in gestis et miraculis sanctorum* for the use of parish priests.[9] And the legendary of Bartholomew of Trent, issued a few years later for Dominican and other preachers, includes a different abridgement of the legend.[10]

As Vicaire has noted in a valuable article on the subject, this proliferation of early lives does not imply any great internal controversy over the way Dominic was to be remembered.[11] What it reflects instead is the progressive definition and elaboration of an official image of the saint. Jordan's *Libellus,* the most historically informative of all the versions and the main source underlying the rest, was obviously felt to give an inadequate picture of the founder's sanctity and importance. A telling gesture was made in 1242, when the order in general chapter voted to delete from Jordan's account the humorous little admission of human weakness that Dominic had made on his deathbed.[12] A later chapter in 1259 ordered that Dominic's name be substituted for that of Diego of

Osma, his early patron, as founder of the convent at Prouille (Vicaire, p. 289). Much more far-reaching is the revision of Jordan's image of Dominic in the versions of the legend produced between 1235 and 1260. Although the liturgical lives are much alike, each supplements the previous one with additional miracles and omits a little more of the concrete, realistic detail found in the *Libellus* and in the eyewitness testimonies of the *Acta canonizationis*. The complexities and ambiguities of Dominic's experience are progressively smoothed away, the proofs of his wisdom and moral perfection made increasingly numerous and emphatic. The same kind of development is manifested, in magnified form, in the sequence of popular abridgements.

Given the close involvement of at least three of Dominic's first four successors as master general in the writing and rewriting of his life, one can feel rather certain that the increasing elevation of the founder is not just a reflection of individual friars' piety. Clearly the idealized accounts serve to encourage the veneration of Dominic—and thus to strengthen the institution with which he is associated—as the more complex and circumstantial historical records do not. The institutional character of the legend, thus revised, is particularly evident in the major themes selected for emphasis: the divine initiative behind the foundation of the order, Dominic's role as father and patron of the order, and his example as model preacher (Vicaire, pp. 296ff.). These themes have much less to do with Dominic's personal experience than with the needs of the order in the early years; among their major functions are the definition of its mission and character, the assertion of its importance within the divine plan, the encouragement of the brethren—and the discouragement of their enemies and detractors—with assurances of powerful protection from heaven. The polemical element is noticeable in nearly all the versions of the legend, but it tends to become increasingly prominent in the later ones, suggesting a growing sensitivity to the charges against the order and a growing resolve to counter them.

The general development of the Dominic legend during Jacobus's youth, with its increasing elevation of the saint and its increasingly marked polemicism, bears a marked resemblance to certain tendencies we have seen in the *Legenda*—and logically so. Jacobus's conception of the purposes of hagiography must have been shaped at least in part by the uses to which his order was adapting the legend of Dominic. As we shall see, however, Jacobus's work seems to represent an extreme development of a few strands within the tradition, at the expense of the rest. His relationship with his Dominican predecessors can most efficiently be shown by setting his own version of the Dominic legend against the three earlier versions with which it seems to have most in common. Jacobus's departures from his principal source, the liturgical life by Constantine of Orvieto, are always worth noting—especially when he supplements it with more extreme material paralleled only in the *Vitae fratrum* or in the definitive liturgical life ascribed to Humbert. Equally instructive is the relationship between the *Legenda* account of Dominic and the corresponding chapters in the earlier legendaries by Jean de Mailly and Bartholomew of Trent. All three are selective abridgements, drawing from the growing body of source material the incidents and lessons their authors presumably considered most important for the public outside the order. In sequence, they rather neatly reflect the increasing subordination of Dominic's historical experience to later polemical needs. But the crucial difference is that Jean and Bartholomew simultaneously promote the interests of the order and teach broader lessons that resemble those in Gregory's *Dialogues;* Jacobus, as usual, does not.

The most obviously polemical feature in the early lives of Dominic is the multiplication of proofs that his new order was blessed from the beginning with special aid and encouragement from heaven. Even the account in the *Abbreviatio,* the earliest and by far the least tendentious of the abridged lives, devotes a substantial proportion of its length to such material. Retold in detail are the famous story about the appearances of the Virgin to Reginald of Orleans, healing him of the grave malady that threatened his life and encouraging his resolve to join the Order of Preachers (*Abrégé,* pp. 309-10),[13] and two stories in which the foundation and growth of the order are identified more directly with the will of God. In the first of these a priest's hesitations about joining the order are overcome when someone providentially comes to sell him the New Testament he needs and when the first passage he reads, after praying for guidance, is the Spirit's command to Peter in Acts 10:20: "Arise, therefore, get thee down and go with them, doubting nothing: for I have sent them" (pp. 310-11).[14] In the second story, a papal legate explicitly raises the question of whether this new kind of religious order is an invention of men or a work of God; he finds his answer by invoking the Lord and then opening the missal on the altar, where his eyes light on the motto of the Order of Preachers—"Laudare, benedicere et praedicare"—and he is converted into a wholehearted supporter of the brethren (p. 311; cf. Peter Ferrandus, sec. 43). The polemical purpose of these stories is obvious; but neither Jean de Mailly nor Peter Ferrandus, whose recension he is following, can be described as a mere apologist for the order. Their concern with sound teaching is manifested even here; lest ignorant members of the audience be misled by the way the priest and the legate used the sacred books, both writers pause after the second story to explain the difference between hoping for an answer to prayer and trusting in sorcery.[15]

The abridged life of Dominic by Bartholomew of Trent, designed for practical use by preachers, also seems to have been based primarily on the liturgical life by Peter Ferrandus; but it is noticeably different from Jean's abridgement for parish priests. Instead of selecting a few anecdotes for detailed presentation, as Jean did, Bartholomew provides rapid summaries of a large number of incidents, conveniently ordered by topic rather than chronology and shown to illustrate specific points about Dominic and the order. The result, whatever it lacks in narrative interest, is a highly efficient resource for preaching. And it also represents a relatively advanced stage in the polemical development of the legend. Thus, to demonstrate heavenly approval of the order, Bartholomew does not just retain the three stories retold by Jean. The story of Reginald's visions is improved a bit by the implication, apparently original with Bartholomew, that the Virgin actually chose the distinctive habit worn by the brethren, rather than showing the existing habit to Reginald.[16] And Bartholomew uses additional miracle stories to fill out the demonstration that the Order of Preachers enjoys the special favor of both God and the Virgin. The papal confirmation of the order is not attributed to divine intervention, as it would be in later versions of the legend; but Bartholomew's introduction of miracles at this point serves in effect to identify Honorius's approval with the will of God: "And so [Pope] Honorius confirmed the order; and God, lest the feeble flock be shaken with fear, began to encourage them with revelations and miracles. For instance, a certain brother called simply Dominic, who was tempted most seductively by a certain woman, cast himself between two bonfires burning close together; he emerged unharmed and converted the unhappy woman" (sec. 10).[17] Bartholomew adds a new vision story which vividly illustrates the Virgin's love and protection of the brethren:

[Two brothers] visited a woman imprisoned for the Lord. When she saw their youthful grace, she began to doubt whether such men could be kept unsullied by this world. She was troubled about them; and as she prayed devoutly the Virgin Mary—queen, consoler of the grieving, protectress of her own—stood beside her and, spreading before the troubled woman the indescribable cloak she wore, showed her those about whom she was troubled standing beside her. And the Virgin said, "Be not troubled for these men or their like, for they are mine and I shall protect them for myself." Trusting in this great hope, as well they might, they cried out continuously, "Hail to thee, who art our life, our delight, our hope!" (Sec. 18)[18]

It is worth pausing to note the character of the miracle and vision stories touched on thus far. Their polemical function is apparently to defend the new order against the common charge that it represented an unjustifiable departure from the laws and traditions of the church; the emphasis on chastity in Bartholomew's group of stories perhaps represents a more specific response to critics who questioned the friars' ability to maintain this virtue while working so closely with women. Despite the implicit awareness of conflicts involving the order, however, none of the stories is very militant in tone. The interventions attributed to God and the Virgin are uniformly merciful and reassuring. No enemies are struck down or confounded, no signs given which do not testify to the generosity of God as well as to the credentials of the Dominicans.

When one turns to the *Legenda* chapter on Dominic, one finds miraculous justifications of the order beside which those used by Jean and Bartholomew appear very small and rudimentary indeed. The crucial decisions on which the order was built are firmly buttressed now, dramatically demonstrated to have fulfilled God's will, not just man's. Thus, for example, Jacobus need not rely, as Bartholomew did, on indirect suggestions that the papal confirmation was divinely inspired. Both Constantine's revision of the legend, Jacobus's principal source, and the definitive version by Humbert include a new miracle story that neatly manages to transform Dominic's inconclusive meeting with Innocent III from a potential source of embarrassment into a striking vindication of the founder and his plans; that Innocent withheld official confirmation ceases to matter, for according to Constantine's and later accounts he was wholly won over, before Dominic left Rome, by a vision of the saint holding up the crumbling walls of the Lateran church.[19] Dominic's dispersal of the first group of friars to preach and found new houses throughout Europe, implying as it does a vast broadening of the order's original mission, is clearly another decision which called for miraculous justification in the view of later apologists. Jean was content to supply a human reason: Dominic realized that seeds bear more fruit when sowed abroad, and he acted accordingly (*Abrégé,* p. 308). Bartholomew suggested the supernatural basis of this decision much as Jordan and Peter Ferrandus had done, tying it to a little symbolic vision about the death of the Count of Montfort.[20] But again Constantine provides Jacobus with a much stronger polemical weapon: a vision in which Peter and Paul appear to Dominic and commission him in effect as their successor, an apostle to the whole world: "And so when he was in Rome in the church of Saint Peter, praying for the growth of his order, he saw the glorious apostles Peter and Paul approaching him; and first Peter seemed to give him a staff, and then Paul a book, and then they said, 'Go and preach, for God has chosen you for this ministry.' And suddenly it seemed that for an instant he saw his sons scattered throughout the world, walking two by two" (*Legenda,* p. 469).[21]

Since Constantine's account also includes the older justifications involving Reginald, the priest, and the legate, together with literally dozens of miracles that might be used to demonstrate God's favor toward Dominic and his followers, Jacobus might have armed his preachers rather effectively just by transmitting the relevant miracle stories from Constantine. But in fact he goes considerably further, omitting the story of the legate and inserting instead, after the vision of Peter and Paul, a series of three extraordinary visions apparently drawn from the opening chapter of the *Vitae fratrum.* In each of these stories an anonymous informant from outside the order reports having witnessed a scene in heaven, just before the institution of the Dominicans, in which the Virgin was begging an angry Christ to have mercy on the human race. The first two stories (*Legenda,* pp. 469-70) are much alike. Christ resists the initial entreaties of his mother, protesting that he has already done everything possible for mankind: "He said thus [in the words of the first story], 'Mother, what more can I or should I do for them? I sent patriarchs and prophets, and they hardly changed. I came to them myself, and then I sent apostles; and they killed both me and them. I sent martyrs and confessors and teachers, and they did not listen to them.'"[22] Eventually he yields, in response to her pleas, and consents to give the human race one more chance by sending them the Order of Preachers. But each vision ends by underlining the message that Christ's patience is running out:

"Since it is not right for me to deny you anything, I will give them my preachers, through whom they may be able to be enlightened and purified; but if not, I will come against them." [First vision]

"At your request I will have this much mercy on them, that I will send them my preachers to warn and teach them; and if they do not correct themselves, I will spare them no longer." [Second vision][23]

The threat in the third vision (p. 470) is even more vivid. In this story, attributed to a Franciscan informant, Dominic himself, while waiting in Rome for the pope's decision to confirm the new order, sees Christ already brandishing three spears over the world—preparing to destroy it because of its vices of pride, concupiscence, and avarice. The Virgin runs to intercede, kneeling before him with a plea for mercy; this time it is she who proposes sending Dominic as man's last chance: "She said to him, 'Moderate your wrath, my son, and wait a little; for I have a faithful servant and vigorous champion who will run through the world, conquering and subduing it to your rule.'''[24] This time, too, there is an additional theme. Dominic is not to go alone; the Virgin proposes also to send Francis—in a subordinate role, to be sure: '''I will also give him another servant as a helper, who will fight faithfully at his side''' ("Alium quoque servum sibi in adjutorium dabo, qui secum fideliter decertabit"). After Christ has seen the two saints and commended Mary's choice of such strong and dedicated warriors, the vision itself ends. But the story continues: when the saints happen to meet the next day in church, Dominic recognizes and embraces Francis as his companion, declaring his confidence that no enemy will be able to stand against their united strength.[25] And the two founders, having henceforth "one heart and one soul in the Lord" ("cor unum et anima una in domino"), enjoin their followers always to live in harmony.

The extreme tendentiousness of these three stories presumably reflects the occurrence of some exceptional crisis in the life of the young order. One possibility is not far to seek: the uncharacteristic linking of Dominic with Francis in the third vision reminds one that the attacks on both mendicant orders, led most notoriously by William of Saint-Amour, were at their most virulent during the decade or so that separated Constantine's account from the *Vitae fratrum*.[26] But, however strong the provocation, it is rather ironic to find even an internal publication of the Order of Preachers—the order specially founded to combat ignorance and errors about the faith—giving its sanction to stories which portray Christ as a figure of wrath and terror and which set Mary in his place as the principal intercessor for mankind.[27] And it becomes more ironic, of course, when such stories are included among the likely ingredients for public sermons in a sourcebook like Jacobus's. There is good reason to pursue the issue, however, asking how far such aberrations should be attributed to individuals and how far to the general climate within the order in the mid-thirteenth century.

The official tradition summed up in the liturgical lives sets at least a partial precedent for the threatening polemic in the *Legenda*. As Vicaire has pointed out, the official depictions of Dominic in the thirteenth century frequently identify him as a precursor of Judgment—the Vesperus, or evening star, sent to herald the second coming of Christ as John the Baptist heralded the first. The theme is found fully developed in the first of the liturgical lives, that by Peter Ferrandus: "Blessed Dominic, leader and renowned father of the Preachers, who shone out like a new star at the approach of the end of the world, was born in Spain in a village called Calaroga, in the diocese of Osma. It was indeed appropriate that [the Lord] who had once brought forth the morning star in his time should now, at the approach of evening, cause the evening star to rise in the west over the sons of the earth" (sec. 2).[28] This arresting image of the saint, shining above the darkness which is about to engulf the world, is incorporated into Humbert's definitive legend with only minor variants in wording; its currency within the order in the thirteenth century is further illustrated by the echoes in the early liturgies for the feast of Dominic (Vicaire, pp. 302-3) and the placement of a star in a number of the official portraits (Vicaire, pp. 291-92).

The eschatological character of the Vesperus image conforms, of course, to the temper of the times. The tendency to interpret the upheavals of the early thirteenth century as signs that the last days had begun and that the biblical prophecies were at last being fulfilled was by no means restricted to the new orders of friars. But it is also clear that the Dominicans, like the Franciscans, found eschatological prophecy to be a very effective controversial weapon. If the final age of the world had arrived and Dominic (or Francis) was its divinely appointed precursor, what force remained in the standard charge that he had violated ecclesiastical tradition by founding a new kind of order? The friars did not rest their case on the founder's credentials alone, however. Even more prominent than the Vesperus image in the liturgical lives of Dominic is the eschatological function ascribed to the order as a whole. Significantly, each version begins, not with Dominic, but with an allegorical interpretation of Christian history which casts the order as the servant of Luke 14:17ff., sent out at the last moment to summon mankind to the Lord's feast: "In many and various ways has God invited the chosen to the eternal feast, and at last in these days—that is, the eleventh hour—he has sent his servant to tell the guests to come, for all is ready. Gregory explained that this servant, the Order of Preachers, was to be sent out in the last days to warn the minds of men of the near-approaching judgment. For Scripture foretold [this]" (Peter Ferrandus, sec. 1).[29] Constantine, who omits the Vesperus passage, turns after this one to a summary of the founder's virtues and then launches into the legend proper. But Peter Ferrandus apparently felt the need for a more elaborate justification of the order, and Humbert follows him. After a few lines which counter the charge of novelty directly,[30] they go on to find references to the order elsewhere in Scripture, identifying the friars first with the laborers added at the eleventh hour in the parable of the vineyard (another explicitly eschatological interpretation) and then, more briefly, with the witnesses to the Lord's righteousness in Psalm 91(92):15-16, with the bells at the hem of the priestly garment prescribed in Exodus 28:33, and with the strong horses drawing the fourth chariot in the vision of Zacharius (Zach. 6:3ff.).[31]

Clearly the eschatological justifications of the order bear a close kinship to the threatening visions used in the *Vitae fratrum* and the *Legenda*. In each case the end of the world is imminent, the sending of Dominic and his followers represents a last warning from heaven, and their mission is to awaken and reform mankind before it is too late. The urgent summons to heed the Dominicans is always unmistakable and so is the appeal to fear, rooted in the emphasis on Christ's Advent as Judge. But there are also two far-reaching differences. First, the visions glorify the order—and Mary, its special patron—at the expense of Christ, where the more official biblical justifications do not. In the Vesperus and summoning servant and vineyard passages, the sending of Dominic and his followers is implicitly a sign of divine mercy; Christ approaches in Judgment but sends ahead a warning, a final expression of his desire to save mankind. Second, the visions are not really eschatological; rather than being precursors of an inexorably approaching judgment, Dominic and the brethren represent a chance to postpone it. Vicaire has suggested (pp. 303-4) that this substitute for the standard claim might have arisen in response to the attacks of William of Saint-Amour and his adherents, who bitterly agreed that the advent of the mendicants was a sign of the end, but identified them as the false apostles of the last days, precursors of Antichrist.[32] Whatever the rationale behind it, the change has an unfortunate effect. Along with their lesson on the order's behalf, the biblical justifications present a moral summons of rather universal validity: repent now, for time is short. In the visions, on the other hand, the only message driven home is the crude partisan threat: honor and obey the Dominicans, or Christ will destroy the world.

It is important to remember that Humbert himself gave his blessing to the internal use of the *Vitae fratrum,* questionable visions and all, and that his prohibition against disseminating its contents outside the order was not invoked to prevent Jacobus from drawing on them. Clearly Jacobus was not the only influential member of his order who saw a place for such materials within the preachers' arsenal. But the limited and equivocal nature of their acceptance is confirmed in a very interesting way in one of Jacobus's own model sermons on Dominic. The bulk of the sermon (no. 492 S54) consists of proofs for the assertion that the order was not founded by chance or by human initiative, but was ordained by God (p. 235); a combative posture is indicated both by the sheer number of proofs and by their tone. But the proofs selected are considerably more restrained than those used in the *Legenda*. Like the liturgical lives, Jacobus here begins with the summoning servant of Luke 14 and the eschatological application to the order. The second proof text is Zacharius's vision of the four teams of horses—also mentioned by Peter Ferrandus and Humbert, but here explicitly interpreted as the successive orders of martyrs, confessors, virgins, and doctors and preachers, and reinforced with the significant little assertion that the preachers are called strong because "they know how to fight and defend themselves strongly" ("fortiter sciunt pugnare & se defendere"). Most of the remaining proofs are miraculous signs; and they too are paralleled, with a single important exception, in the liturgical lives: Reginald's vision, showing the Virgin's activity on behalf of the order;[33] the commissioning vision of Peter and Paul; the pope's vision of Dominic holding up the church. In short, Jacobus found within the official traditions of the order almost enough ammunition for the battle he was waging in this the most tendentious of his sermons on the founder. The one addition is even more telling, for it is an edited version of the first vision from the *Vitae fratrum* which greatly reduces the emphasis on Christ's anger, removes the dramatic gestures and pleas that set Mary against him as the sole representative of mercy, and omits the final ultimatum:

Thirdly, this Order was requested by the Mother of God. . . . For when, before the founding of this Order, a certain holy man was praying earnestly, he saw the blessed Virgin Mary interceding for the human race. And Christ said to her, "What more can I do? I sent patriarchs and prophets, and they hardly changed. I came to them myself, and then I sent apostles; and they killed both me and them. I even sent martyrs and confessors and teachers, and they did not listen to them. But, since it is not right for me to deny you anything, I will give them my preachers." (*Sermones,* p. 235)[34]

That Jacobus removes the harshest and most questionable features of the story when he retells it in the sermon does not necessarily prove that he recognized them as excessive and deliberately let them stand when he compiled the *Legenda.* But it provides a final and rather conclusive demonstration that the kind of threatening polemic used in the *Legenda* was a bit extreme even by the standards that prevailed in the order during a difficult and contentious period.

The *Legenda*'s position at the fringe of Dominican tradition, rather than near the center, becomes yet more evident when one considers the remaining themes chosen for emphasis by the order: Dominic's role as father and patron and his example as model preacher. Here the earlier abridgements by Jean de Mailly and Bartholomew of Trent deserve special attention. As examples of Dominican hagiography designed for use with relatively unsophisticated audiences, issued a mere generation before the *Legenda* and almost certainly familiar to Jacobus himself,[35] these two accounts provide exceptionally valuable testimony to the possibilities residing in the genre as he inherited it. As we shall see, neither account deserves to be ranked with a great classic like Gregory's life of Benedict. In effect, they offer partial and simplified versions of Gregory's teaching, with Jean emphasizing the call to righteousness implicit in the saint's human example and Bartholomew, the divine love manifested in the miracles. The progression from one to the other reveals again the increasing polemicism of the Dominic legend as it developed. In their different ways, however, both Jean and Bartholomew demonstrate the continuing vitality of the traditions exemplified in the *Dialogues*.

Beginning again with Jean's account, one finds the motif of Dominic as father and patron in an early and undeveloped form. The events and decisions leading up to the foundation of the order are recounted in detail, with Diego of Osma playing the central role. Dominic accompanies him on the journey during which they become aware of the heretics' influence, and Dominic's promise as a preacher is suggested at several points in the subsequent account of their work in southern France. But it is Diego who takes the crucial steps, renouncing his see for the Cistercian habit in order to devote himself to the conversion of the region and realizing the importance of apostolic poverty in countering the apparent virtue of the Cathar leaders (*Abrégé*, p. 306; cf. Peter Ferrandus, secs. 12-14). Diego is credited also with founding the convent at Prouille to receive girls previously entrusted to the heretics for upbringing, and even with deciding to seek papal permission for a special body of clerics dedicated to preaching (p. 307; cf. Peter Ferrandus, secs. 16-17). Only with Diego's untimely death does Dominic step forward as the leader, carrying on the preaching mission itself and eventually building the Order of Preachers on the foundation laid by Diego.

Thus the creation of the order is depicted, in this earliest and most nearly historical of the abridged lives, as a mutual achievement. The ideal is transmitted from Diego to Dominic—and thence to Dominic's own spiritual sons, who will carry it abroad in wider and wider circles. What is most noteworthy, in view of the legend's later development— and of Jacobus's characteristic portrayal of the saints—is the extent to which Jean incorporates Dominic into this pattern of continuing human effort and faith, instead of elevating him to a special level. As has been mentioned, he presents Dominic's decision to scatter his first group of followers without reference to any great revelation; Dominic simply decides what should be done and calls his friars together to tell them. Jean does not mention their dismayed reaction, a nice human touch found in previous accounts (Jordan, sec. 47; Peter Ferrandus, sec. 31), but that dismay is implicit in the matter-of-fact details of the scene as Jean presents it, lending additional weight to the lesson Dominic is teaching the brethren. For Dominic does not ask them to risk more than he is prepared to risk; the uncertainty of his own future is quietly underlined when he has them elect a new leader to govern them: "He called them all together and told them his resolve to scatter them in various lands, although they were so few. He had them elect an abbot, Brother Matthew, who would rule over them all since he himself intended to go preach the faith to the pagans" (*Abrégé,* p. 308).[36] And his faith, thus communicated to them, enables them to persevere and win others: "Some of the brethren departed for Spain, others for Paris, still others for Bologna, where in the nakedness of an extreme poverty and by the power of God they greatly increased their numbers" (pp. 308-9).[37]

Throughout Jean's account there is more emphasis on the ideals Dominic transmits to his sons than on the miraculous powers that set him apart from them. It is their joint example of dedication to preaching, in apostolic poverty, that inspires the priest's desire to join them and first brings Reginald to meet the saint (pp. 311 and 309). Only four miracles are attributed to Dominic between the foundation of the order and his death, and two of these—the resurrection of Cardinal Stephen's nephew and an odd little incident in which the saint stays dry in a rainstorm by making the sign of the cross—are just mentioned in passing. The cure of Reginald is linked with Dominic's urgent prayers on his behalf; but on the morning after the Virgin's first healing visit, the saint is so unaware of what has transpired that he does not at first understand what Reginald is trying to tell him: "In the morning blessed Dominic came seeking news of the sick man, and the latter told him that he was in good health. Since the man of God thought he was referring to the state of his soul, Reginald emphasized that he meant bodily health and minutely recounted the supernatural visit that had been granted him" (pp. 309-10).[38] In the remaining miracle story Dominic's role as intercessor for the brethren is more prominent. He has a prophetic dream in which the dragon of temptation devours his followers, but his warnings to them are efficacious in only a few cases; his perseverance in prayer, however, brings better results: "Although he had warned them and exhorted them to stand resolutely against the devil, Saint Dominic nonetheless saw all but three of them abandon him. But the holy man was not disheartened in his prayers for them, and after a short time nearly all of them returned, prompted by the Holy Spirit" (p. 310).[39] Even here one notes the emphasis on Dominic's example and the realistic limitation of his powers; his prayer can accomplish a great deal, but not quite everything.

Jean's account of the saint's death and its aftermath is similarly restrained. Realizing his death is imminent, Dominic calls together the local brethren, urges them to maintain their chastity as he has done, and bestows on them a fatherly legacy of good counsel—with a special curse directed to preserving the poverty so crucial to their imitation of the first apostles: "As his patrimony he left the brethren no earthly wealth, but rather the treasures of heavenly grace. That is, he ordered them to live in charity, to maintain humility, and to possess voluntary poverty; with the utmost vigor he forbade the introduction of temporal possessions into the order, threatening that both God's curse and his own would fall on anyone who defiled the order's poverty with the dust of riches" (p. 312).[40] After describing the saint's funeral, conducted by the future Pope Gregory IX, Jean contents himself with recounting a single revelation of Dominic's ascent to heaven and referring in a general way to the posthumous miracles which the brethren, "par l'humilité indiscrète," initially tried to conceal (p. 313). His account ends with the translation of Dominic's remains in 1233 and the miraculous fragrance that flowed from them, providing a further testimony to Dominic's eternal beatitude.[41] Although he asserts that the saint was more admirable than imitable (p. 312), the whole tenor of his account invites the reader to embrace Dominic's ideals and follow him.

The ideals of the founder do not lose their importance in the account by Bartholomew of Trent; indeed, Bartholomew places more emphasis than Jean did on the example of active charity that Dominic presents, the dedication to saving others that defines his identity as a preacher. But Bartholomew's account encourages imitation of Dominic a good deal less than it encourages dependence on him as father and patron. In a significant addition to Jean's account of the final legacy, the saint promises to be even more useful to the order after death than he has been in life.[42] And the contributions made during his lifetime are noticeably larger and more numerous in Bartholomew's account than in Jean's. For example, more is attributed to Dominic—and less to Diego—when Bartholomew describes their original mission in southern France. Although Diego is still identified as founder of the convent at Prouille, he is no longer portrayed as Dominic's leader and courageous model in the actual preaching against the heretics—or as the real originator of the ideas behind the order. The plans cut short by his death are not mentioned, and when apostolic poverty is brought forward as a strategy for countering the heretics' influence, Dominic receives equal credit for the idea.[43] Dominic's importance to the order is similarly emphasized when Bartholomew describes his relationship with Bishop Fulk of Toulouse. Jean's account mentioned only the personal bond between

Dominic and Fulk, "qui l'aimait tendrement" (*Abrégé*, p. 308). What Bartholomew shows, however, is the way Fulk's love for Dominic is translated into material support for the saint and his little band of followers: "Fulk, bishop of Toulouse, who loved Saint Dominic, granted property to him and his followers, and gave in addition, with the consent of the chapter, one-sixth of all the tithes of his diocese" (sec. 7).[44] When he retells the stories of Reginald and the priest, Bartholomew does not mention the impact of the joint example set by Dominic and the brethren. Instead, he adds another incident in which Dominic personally wins for the order a powerful friend and supporter in the church hierarchy.[45]

If Dominic's ability to attract human support to the order is emphasized in Bartholomew's account, so is the efficacy of his prayers. Jean's strongest illustration of this theme, the story in which Dominic sees the dragon devouring the brethren, is improved a bit; in Bartholomew's version the prayer of the saint appears to have brought back all the deserting friars, and to have done so with relative ease.[46] Bartholomew also summarizes a number of new stories which extend the demonstration of Dominic's power as guardian of his followers: a novice's temptation to return to the world is miraculously vanquished; a disobedient lay brother is freed from demonic possession; in response to the saint's prayers, bread is miraculously provided for the community (secs. 14 and 15). When the brethren are sent forth, moreover, Dominic no longer arms them only with the encouragement of his example and the knowledge that practical arrangements have been made to assure continuity of leadership. Omitting that relatively indirect demonstration of Dominic's fatherly care, Bartholomew chooses instead to emphasize the tireless prayers with which the saint aids those who have gone out to preach.[47] The new vision of Mary as their protector is presented as just one evidence of the fruit borne by these intercessions.

Bartholomew's stress on the power of Dominic's prayers and example mirrors, on a smaller scale, a development already noted in the official thirteenth-century sources: as the justifications of the order are strengthened, so are the demonstrations of Dominic's own sanctity and importance. This development also was probably designed in part to silence enemies and detractors. That the order had allowed twelve years to pass before seeking Dominic's canonization raised embarrassing questions in retrospect, especially when the inevitable comparisons were made with Francis, whose sanctity had been widely hailed even before his death in 1226 and officially confirmed a mere two years later. Given the rivalry between the two mendicant orders, Franciscan polemicists could not be expected to ignore such an opening. Even the most charitable interpretation of the facts suggested the superiority of their own founder; an uncharitable one could undermine the whole reputation of Dominic and his order, as Salimbene's malicious gossip illustrates:

And when [John of Vicenza, O.P.] was rebuked by the Brethren for the many follies which he did, then he answered and spake unto them: 'I it was who exalted your Dominic, whom ye kept twelve years hidden in the earth, and, unless ye hold your peace, I will make your saint to stink in men's nostrils and will publish your doings abroad.' For [at the time of the Great Alleluia in 1233] the blessed Dominic was not yet canonized, but lay hidden in the earth, nor was there any whisper of his canonization; but, by the travail of this aforesaid Brother John, who had the grace of preaching in Bologna at the time of that devotion, his canonization was brought about. To this canonization the Bishop of Modena gave his help; for he, being a friend of the Friars Preachers, importuned them, saying, 'Since the Brethren Minor have a saint of their own, ye too must so work as to get yourselves another, even though ye should be compelled to make him of straw.'[48]

The order's growing emphasis on Dominic's role as father and patron clearly provides a strong defense against such charges. The message is not just that he was indeed a great saint, but also that the brethren benefited from his sanctity long before the events of 1233-34. In the liturgical lives, and even more clearly in Bartholomew's brief account for preachers, any suggestion of discontinuity is thus laid to rest. The importance granted to Dominic as the order's heavenly patron is but the logical culmination of his role in life as guide, inspiration, and intercessor for the brethren.

If the portrayal of Dominic as father and patron was useful in warding off attacks on the order, it must have served even more significantly to reassure the brethren and their supporters. Post-Renaissance readers are apt to prefer an account like Jean's, with its historical complexities and its portrayal of the founder and the brethren as vulnerable human beings upheld by faith; but the very subtlety of this ideal might well have worked against it in the Middle Ages.[49] Convention demanded numerous miraculous proofs of a saint's power and favor with God; and these proofs, when well chosen and presented, could serve the purpose of edification and effectively promote the saint's cult at the same time. Most of the later accounts of Dominic conform reasonably well to these traditional expectations, but again Bartholomew's account provides the clearest example of all. One new vision introduced in connection with the founder's death vividly suggests Christ's love for Dominic himself: "The illustrious father . . . knew that the dissolution of his body was near, for he saw a very handsome young man who called him with these words, 'Come, my beloved; come to joy, come"'' (sec. 19).[50] And virtually all the other miraculous events Bartholomew relates show the extension of this love to others. Even the little miracle of the averted rain reaches a bit further in his account than it did in Jean's; this time Dominic has a companion, Brother Bertrand, who is also kept dry, and the placement of the anecdote suggests that it provides further testimony to God's encouragement of the brethren in the early years (sec. 11).

Although Bartholomew includes demonstration after demonstration of Dominic's love—and God's love—for members of the new Order of Preachers, there is nothing exclusive about the messages in his account. In a significant addition to the more official lives of Dominic, he praises Francis in his parallel role as a founder and patron: "Saint Francis, who founded the Order of the Friars Minor, was renowned during the same period, and Saint Dominic was bound to him with such love that their opinions were the same on all topics. Thus the two orders grew under identical fathers" (sec. 13).[51] This assertion of the two saints' unanimity is worth comparing with the third vision in the *Legenda,* which makes the same point. Here Dominic and Francis are not warriors but fathers, presiding over a growing body of disciples. And the mission of those disciples, as Bartholomew defines it, is not to threaten members of the larger community with divine vengeance but to attract them with the evidence of divine love. The pattern is shown clearly in the story of Reginald, whose cure by the Virgin, at Dominic's entreaty, transforms him into a powerful preacher who spends the remainder of his life winning others to Christ.[52] Even more striking, however, is the way in which Bartholomew himself fulfills the role of such a disciple. For the whole structure of his account embodies the idea—already encountered in Gregory's *Dialogues*—that the divine love reaches out, through the saint, to touch a steadily widening circle of believers. During Dominic's lifetime this extension is manifested primarily in the definition and growth of the order, a new body of preachers inspired by the saint's example of charity and empowered by his intercessions. But Dominic's death and canonization mark the opening of an additional channel for the transmission of Christ's love to the world. In Bartholomew's account the posthumous miracles are all healings—a great outpouring of beneficent miracles serving not only to prove Dominic's sanctity but also to suggest the boundless mercy of his Lord:

Nicholas the Englishman, as I saw myself, was cured of a severe multiple paralysis as we stood about him, and sprang up like a stag, happy and rejoicing. It is confirmed further that many others suffering from various sorts of paralysis were cured in various ways. . . . By praying to Dominic, many who suffered from chronic fevers were cured by Jesus Christ because of the merits of Christ's servant. Many suffering from intestinal maladies were restored by Jesus Christ because of his merits. Three who had been given up and abandoned to death, as was confirmed and certified, he restored to life and health. A boy who was taken for dead by everyone for several days Christ returned to this life because of a prayer made to Saint Dominic. He loosed the tongues of many, including four certified to have been mute. He restored sight to the blind and hearing to the deaf. (Sec. 24)[53]

The portrayals of Dominic by Jean and Bartholomew weigh heavily against the notion that the priorities of the *Legenda* might have been dictated by some fundamental change in the conventions of hagiography, when the old monastic-type legendaries gave way in the thirteenth century to abridged ones, or by some special Dominican definition of the teaching most needful for the laity. Although their works are so similar to the *Legenda* in terms of provenance, genre, and presumed audience, Jean and Bartholomew show none of Jacobus's inclination to deemphasize the mercy of God, or to present fortitude and *contemptus mundi* as the central Christian virtues, or to set the saint in diametrical opposition to his weaker neighbors. They seem in fact to have taken for granted, as Gregory did, that all the important patterns in the life of an influential confessor would be inclusive. Thus is the saint's greatness manifested, in the continuing communities he shapes and inspires. And thus is the larger audience brought within the circle of his influence, shown the analogies as well as the differences between his life and their own. Jean continually suggests the capacity of lesser Christians to imitate Dominic's efforts and embrace his ideals, and thus to grow in his likeness. Even Bartholomew, who tends, like Jacobus, to emphasize the inimitable powers of the saint, invites the audience, whatever their state of life, to experience the same divine love that inspired Dominic and transformed his first disciples. In short, the two predecessors whom one might expect Jacobus most closely to resemble seem to have operated on very different premises from those characteristic of the *Legenda*. It does not follow, however, that Jacobus's adversarial portrayals of the saints represent something entirely new in Dominican hagiograpy. Again the more official versions of the Dominic legend itself foreshadow the emphases of the *Legenda* in a rather illuminating way.

The first official image of Dominic was that of a loving, fruitful apostle and father. Gregory IX summed it up quite clearly in the bull of canonization:

Drawing from his intense love for souls unutterable joy, he dedicated himself to spreading God's word. Becoming through Christ's Gospel the father of many children, in the conversion of a multitude . . . , he has deserved to attain upon earth the glory and achievement of the great patriarchs of old. Made a shepherd and celebrated leader among the people of God, he founded the new Order of Preachers by his holy labors, adorned it by his exemplary life, and has not ceased to support it by manifest and authenticated miracles.[54]

The same positive themes—charity, joyfulness, dedication to spreading the faith, spiritual fatherhood of many children—are central in the first of the liturgical lives, compiled by Peter Ferrandus a few years after the canonization, and they also dominate the abridged accounts by Jean and Bartholomew, as we have seen. They are not abandoned thereafter; in fact, the later recensions of the official legend retain most of Peter's anecdotes intact, or very nearly so, and supply many additional illustrations of Dominic's compassion and fatherly care for those in need. But these later recensions sound some new and rather discordant notes as well. For one thing, retribution is admitted into the legend—making its first appearance, so far as I have been able to determine, in the authorized version compiled by Constantine of Orvieto in 1247-48. In Peter's recension all the posthumous miracles were healings; the abridged account by Bartholomew, quoted above, omits most of the details but preserves the essential logic and spirit of this series of anecdotes. Among the posthumous miracles related in Constantine's recension, on the other hand, is the illness inflicted on a certain Franciscan who said blasphemous things about Dominic and who is not cured until he vows never to do so again (sec. 119). In the next section Constantine presents a similar but more vivid cautionary tale about the loathsome malady that strikes a laywoman when she refuses to celebrate the feast of Dominic's translation and impugns the morals of those who do:

Some women who had attended the ceremony of the mass in a church of the brothers were returning home when they found a certain woman sitting outside her door, spinning. When they reproved her with charitable words, asking why she did not desist from servile work on the feast of such a saint, she immediately said to them with indignant heart and angry face, "Celebrate the feasts of your saint, you who are the whores of his friars!" At once her eyes were changed to itching swellings, and worms began to swarm out of them, so that a neighbor whom she summoned in her terror plucked eighteen worms from her eyes in an instant. And so her spirit was humbled, and she ran wailing to the church of Saint Dominic. . . (Sec. 120)[55]

Both stories are repeated, a decade later, in Humbert's definitive version of the legend.[56] The effect of these additions is not very dramatic, given the length of the liturgical lives and the continuing preponderance of stories about Dominic's beneficence as father and patron.[57] But their very inclusion in the official legend bespeaks a defensive posture, an anxiety to discourage detraction by every means possible, which is noticeably at odds with the spirit of the earlier accounts by Peter, Jean, and Bartholomew.

A second and apparently simultaneous change in the legend is the multiplication of minor wonders. Again it is Constantine's recension in which the crucial additions are made; Humbert's recension simply reproduces them. Besides the marvel of the candles that light themselves,[58] introduced without explanation after the greater post-humous miracles of resurrection and healing, these accounts make room for such material as a long exorcism story whose whole point seems to be Dominic's power to elicit answers from demons,[59] the report of a strict Lenten fast that left his body stronger and plumper than it had been before,[60] and a series of small miracles which alleviate the hardships he endured during his travels.[61] Several of these stories clearly have the function of encouraging the brethren to emulate the founder's example of apostolic poverty, trusting God to supply their daily needs. Since Constantine presents most of them in the context of Dominic's experience on the road ("in via") during his journeys as a preacher (sec. 40), one can even infer that the little mercies bestowed on the founder are meant to illustrate God's help and encouragement to those who share Dominic's dedication to preaching. Nonetheless, this set of stories suggests a little retreat from the original emphasis on fruitfulness, in response to the newly felt needs of the brethren themselves.

The last and most dramatic change in the official legend is a new emphasis on Dominic's involvement in the ongoing warfare against heresy. In the liturgical life by Peter Ferrandus, as in the abridged accounts by Jean and Bartholomew, the founder's preaching against the Cathars was treated merely as a period of training and preparation for the universal apostolate he envisioned. Shortly after the founding of the order Dominic announced his own plan for a preaching mission to the Saracens and dispersed his little group of followers to apply his principles in other settings.[62] Thenceforth, in these early versions, the focus shifts to the growth and apostolic work of the order; the initial mission against heresy seems to have been transcended. In the liturgical lives compiled around mid-century, on the other hand, the struggle against heresy is restored to prominence in later chapters. And these accounts exhibit a certain eagerness to identify Dominic with developments in that struggle which actually took place well after his death. Introduced among the final anecdotes from his lifetime, in the recension by Constantine, is a story which casts the founder as an actual inquisitor.[63] Although the historical Dominic's measures against heresy seem to have been limited to preaching, debate, and his personal example of apostolic poverty, this story credits him with having convicted a group of heretics, handed them over to the secular arm for punishment, and then intervened to spare the life of one of them, whose conversion and reform he can foresee; the rest are executed. The story is unbelievable on a number of grounds, as Vicaire has shown; but the crucial point for our purposes is the way it contradicts the earlier image of Dominic as model preacher, the apostle so full of pity for perishing souls that he would make any sacrifice to rescue them. The definitive liturgical life by Humbert reproduces this story, just as one has come to expect. Even more interesting, however, is one of the few innovations in Humbert's recension: a new account of the very first miracle in Dominic's career as a preacher.

Jordan, Peter Ferrandus, Jean, Bartholomew, and Constantine all give essentially the same version of this story. At a public disputation with the heretics in Toulouse, a little book written by the young Dominic is selected as the best presentation of the Catholic position and eventually submitted to a test by fire against a similar document from the heretic side. The heretics' book is consumed by the fire, but Dominic's is miraculously ejected, unharmed, on each of three attempts to burn it. The obvious point of the story, explicitly underlined by each narrator, is the public vindication of the saint and the orthodoxy he represents.[64] No immediate fruit is mentioned; but the story, standing as it does at the beginning of Dominic's career, is full of promise. The mission of the gifted young saint, upheld and reinforced by manifest signs of divine approval, cannot fail.

Although Humbert's recension of the liturgical life is dependent on either Peter's or Constantine's for the vast majority of its contents, in this instance their story is just mentioned in passing (end of sec. 18); what Humbert retells in full is a variant with much grimmer implications.[65] Dominic's special gifts as a teacher of the faith are no longer emphasized; indeed, the new version of the story implies that such gifts are irrelevant. The saint writes out his arguments for a heretic he hopes to persuade, but there is no indication that anyone actually reads them before testing them in the fire. Nor is the test conducted at a public gathering, where it can illuminate witnesses of all persuasions and potentially bear fruit in a number of lives. This time only a group of heretics, performing the test in secret, see the fire refuse to burn Dominic's writing. The miracle still vindicates the saint, proving beyond question that his is the side of truth. But its central function now is to demonstrate the utter perversity of his adversaries. The heretics have pledged among themselves to embrace the Catholic faith, should Dominic's arguments in its favor not burn. But when the sign is clearly and repeatedly given to them, they resist and ultimately refuse to heed it:

Those present were astounded [at the first sign]; but one, more stubborn than the rest, said to them, "Throw [the booklet] back into the fire, and then we will know the truth more fully." They threw it in again, and again it sprang out unburned. When that man, stubborn and slow to believe, saw this, he said, "Throw it back a third time, and then we will certainly know the outcome of this matter." They threw it in a third time and it was not consumed this time either, but sprang from the fire untouched and unharmed. But even after seeing so many signs the heretics were not willing to be converted to the faith; rather, persisting in their wickedness, they swore solemnly to one other than none of them would tell about this miracle and allow it to come to our notice. (Humbert, sec. 18)[66]

That this story was introduced at the end of the 1250s—the decade which saw the real beginning of the effort to extirpate heresy from the territories formerly controlled by Frederick II, the murder of Peter Martyr by heretics in Milan, and such unexpectedly stubborn resistance elsewhere that the Dominican commitment to the campaign had to be increased manyfold—lends additional weight to its defensive overtones. Its apparent purpose is to account for the transition, left unexplained by Constantine, from the original ideal of apostolic preaching to the torture and execution of heretics. If such adversaries refused to be converted even when Dominic himself tried to teach them and when God reinforced his efforts with unmistakable signs, who could blame his followers for using coercion against them? At the same time, however, this last revision of the official legend represents the most suggestive retreat of all from the positive polemic of the early versions. Instead of showing the importance of Dominic and the order in terms of their real or potential influence on others, this story of failure supplies an excuse for abandoning that criterion, at least where heretics are concerned. Dominic's goal of saving all mankind with apostolic preaching is conceded in effect to have been unrealistic. Some men, like the heretics of the story, perversely insist on being damned instead.

Jacobus's portrayal of Dominic can almost be predicted, once one has seen the kinds of logic at work in the *Legenda*. Nonetheless, it is instructive to see how much further he goes than his elders did in revising the legend of the founder. Dominic's importance as father and patron still receives a good deal of emphasis. Indeed, Dominic now appears to have laid the groundwork for the order singlehandedly; Diego has shrunk to a very minor figure in the narrative (p. 467), and even less remains to suggest the assistance received from Fulk and other early benefactors. Dominic's image as a father is impaired somewhat by Jacobus's customary focus on supernatural power for its own sake;[67] but enough stories are retold about the founder's care for his followers and for other pious Christians who honor his memory so that this chapter of the *Legenda* conveys an unusually clear invitation to join one of those groups and reap the benefits.[68] The crucial change from earlier accounts is the extent to which Jacobus redefines the purpose of the order, abandoning the once-central ideal of apostolic preaching.

The experience of Dominic's followers, as Jacobus presents it, manifests the change in its simplest form. Bartholomew of Trent had emphasized the way in which Dominic's intercessions empowered the brethren to spread the message of God's love; so did all three recensions of the liturgical life. Jacobus makes no such connections; in fact, he hardly mentions the active, public dimension of the brethren's lives. Toward the end of the *Legenda* account he inserts a very long story in which the devil tours a Dominican priory, explaining how he tempts the brethren in each room and confessing his ultimate defeat by the strict disciplines they undergo;[69] and the chapter also includes four stories, three of them quite lengthy, about supernaturally inspired conversions to the order. But the order is no longer depicted as a company of preachers who actually go forth from their priories and multiply the founder's impact on the world. In Jacobus's retelling even the cure of Reginald leads only to the recruitment of new friars.[70] And the major example of Dominic's efficacious prayer is the story wherein he wins for the order another highly desirable convert, Master Conrad the German—a distinguished scholar remembered above all, Jacobus suggests, for his edifying death:

This man was a very conscientious member of the order and a most beloved lector in the order. When at last he was dying and had already closed his eyes, and the brothers thought he had passed away, he opened his eyes and gazed around at them, saying, "The Lord be with you." When they answered, "And with your spirit," he added, "The spirits of the faithful rest in peace through the remembrance of God." And with that he himself slept in peace. (P. 476)[71]

The inward focus of these stories, with their recurrent suggestion that becoming a preaching friar means improving one's own chance for salvation and little more, obviously undercuts the traditional argument for the special importance of the order. And this change can hardly be written off as mere accident, for the new message is rather consistently reinforced by the way Jacobus depicts Dominic's own experience.

Although Jacobus does not entirely ignore the founder's public mission, he conveys a narrower and less optimistic picture of that mission than any of his predecessors did. The pattern can be seen even in the little miracles which alleviate Dominic's hardships on the road. In the *Legenda* there are six of these stories, three borrowed from

Constantine and the others evidently from the *Vitae fratrum,* and they are very much alike. In each case Dominic is travelling when he encounters an obstacle: the loss of his books in a river as he crosses; a monastery and a church whose doors are locked when he arrives at night; the rainstorm mentioned in the earliest accounts; a boatman who demands to be paid with money, which the saint never carries; an inability to communicate with a foreign churchman who has joined him on the road. Each obstacle is overcome by miraculous means: the books are later retrieved, dry and unharmed, by a fisherman; the saint is mysteriously transported within the locked doors; the rain is averted by the sign of the cross; a coin appears at Dominic's feet so that the surly boatman may have the fare he demands; the saint and his foreign companion suddenly find themselves able to speak each other's language. Just one important thing is missing from these stories, as Jacobus retells them. In his sources four of the miracles were connected in some way with Dominic's apostolic preaching, and Jacobus has severed those connections.[72] Both the omissions and their implications stand out with unusual clarity in the first case, the story of the lost books.

In the *Vitae fratrum* (II.4) this little story provides a nice illustration of a favorite Dominican theme: the model preacher's ability to teach by example. Although the books clearly have some importance to the mission on which he is bound, Dominic cheerfully accepts God's will when they are lost; and he tells the story to an acquaintance who lives nearby: "In the region of Toulouse it also happened that Saint Dominic, who often travelled for the sake of preaching, was fording a stream called the Ariège when his books, which he was carrying in the fold he made by girding up his robe, fell out in midstream. Praising God, he came to the house of a certain good woman and told her about the loss of his books."[73] At this point some manuscripts insert a little dialogue which spells out the lesson implicit in the saint's conduct: when the woman shows sorrow over his loss, he tells her that whatever God sends us ought to be accepted with equanimity.[74] The lesson about trusting God is reinforced when the books are found safe and delivered to the woman, who happily returns them to the saint.

In Jacobus's retelling of the story, on the other hand, it is no longer clear that the miracle has anything at all to do with preaching. The explicit reference to Dominic's mission has vanished, and so have his example of trust and the good woman who was its first beneficiary: "When he crossed a certain river in the region of Toulouse, his books, which had no case, fell into the river. Three days later, however, a certain fisherman cast in his hook and, thinking he had caught a big fish, pulled out the books, as completely unharmed as if they had been carefully kept in some cupboard" (*Legenda*, p. 471).[75] One effect of Jacobus's selectivity here is to increase the apparent solitude of the saint. And since there is no mention of his apostolic purpose, in this or any of the related stories, the references to a Toulousian setting merely heighten the impression that Dominic is journeying through hostile territory, hindered and opposed at every turn. In short, Jacobus tends to make the little road miracles yet more private than they were in the liturgical lives and the *Vitae fratrum,* and also bleaker in their implications. Instead of rewarding the model preacher's trust in God and strengthening his ability to communicate this virtue to others, the miracles are reduced to signs that heaven has not abandoned the preacher himself.

Aside from the road miracles, just two kinds of material remain in the *Legenda* to indicate the nature and efficacy of Dominic's public mission: one story about a cure from moral frailty and half a dozen stories about the saint's encounters with heretics. The conflict with heresy had already been given a new kind of prominence, of course, in the accounts by Constantine and Humbert. But it is only in the *Legenda* that this conflict becomes the dominant motif, crowding out the broader and more positive themes in Dominic's career. His desire to undertake a preaching mission to the Saracens goes unmentioned. So do the pastoral stories with which the liturgical lives had illustrated his patient and fruitful care for Catholics outside the order. Although the moral cure mentioned above might have added this dimension to Jacobus's account, he passes over the version used by Constantine (sec. 59), a story in which Dominic attracts the confession of a dean (*decanus*) too weak to achieve continence, encourages him with a reminder of God's mercy, and obtains his cure through prayer. What Jacobus retells instead is a variant from the *Vitae fratrum* in which a lustful scholar is instantly cured by approaching the saint in church and kissing his hand; the new message, spelled out in the conclusion, is the wondrous power of the saint's own purity.[76]

The other great virtue attributed to Dominic, and the one that looms largest in Jacobus's account of his mission, is fortitude against the heretics. This adversarial emphasis is hardly surprising, given Jacobus's practice elsewhere in the *Legenda,* but it is worth pausing to note its special polemical disadvantages in the case of Dominic. As Jacobus's predecessors seem to have recognized, the image of the founder as an opponent of heresy has less breadth of appeal than the image adumbrated by Gregory IX and developed at length in the liturgical lives, that of the apostle to mankind. Nor does Dominic's work against the Cathars provide a very satisfactory picture of his power and importance. This campaign seems in fact to have been peripheral to his real achievements: the expression of an ideal of apostolic preaching, the attraction of followers and supporters who would share his dedication to this ideal, the impact of his personality and example on Catholics in other states of life. Thus it was logical as well as efficacious for his admirers to downplay the fact that he also devoted years of his life to preaching against the heretics, making only a little headway against their influence. But Jacobus seems to have marched to a different drummer. Whatever the polemical consequences, he reduces the founder's public career to a series of small victories and vindications against these adversaries. And the effect is very suggestive indeed. With the loss of such well-disposed minor characters as the good woman in the story of the lost books and the weaker Catholics cured and counselled by Dominic in the pastoral stories, Jacobus's account suggests that nearly everyone the preacher encounters outside the order's own buildings is an enemy of the faith. Nor are most of them to be converted. In Jacobus's selective retelling of these stories, the central theme is no longer Dominic's desire, mirroring God's desire, to save perishing souls from the consequences of their own sins and errors. The heretics become more recalcitrant. Dominic becomes less compassionate. And the will of God becomes very ambiguous indeed.

The crucial precedent for Jacobus's account of Dominic and the heretics is of course the story, retold in Humbert's version of the liturgical life, of the heretics who refused to be saved. That last, defensive revision of the official record suggests a good deal about the mood of the order within a decade or so of Jacobus's work; but in Humbert's conservative account it is still almost an isolated phenomenon, one of the rare negative notes within a portrayal of Dominic that elsewhere retains the original emphases on his charity, fruitfulness, and joyful trust in God. Like Humbert, Jacobus retells this version of the story (p. 467) instead of the earlier and more positive one. But in Jacobus's account this story of a preacher's frustration, with its heretics who resist ordinary persuasion and its miraculous signs that fail to make any difference, has become the logical center of the legend. In effect the founder is transformed from a fruitful apostle to a lonely prophet, sent to warn of God's judgment on the heretics. One exponent of heresy is converted by his preaching.[77] Some women, deceived by the heretics, are won back to the faith by more drastic means.[78] For the most part, however, the heretics and their supporters seem to be doomed. The large number of miraculous events that vindicate Dominic, without bearing real fruit, seem to signal either God's inability to save the saint's opponents or his verdict that they are not worth saving.

The new tenor of Dominic's mission is particularly clear in the way

Jacobus relates the two dramatic encounters with heretics that had
entered the official legend in Constantine's version. In the first of these
stories some women are converted when the god they have been
following is revealed to them as a huge, hideous cat. As usual, Jacobus
greatly reduces the gentler and more pastoral aspects of the founder's
example as a preacher. He retains the beginning of the women's appeal
for help, wherein they explain that they have heard Dominic's preaching
that day and have come to doubt the validity of their former beliefs.[79]
Excluded from the *Legenda,* however, is virtually all of the remaining
dialogue, which served in Constantine's version to establish a personal
relationship between Dominic and the women and to soften the impact
of the terrible apparition that follows. The women no longer express
their need for a sign from God, begging Dominic to pray on their
behalf.[80] And Dominic no longer offers them reassurance, either before
or after the apparition—or, indeed, gives them any positive lesson about
the nature of the true faith. The only remaining indications of his role as
model preacher are a rather cold exhortation to behold the truth and the
apparition itself—magnified because Jacobus describes it in full detail
while abbreviating everything else in the story, and apparently produced,
in Jacobus's retelling, by Dominic's own power and initiative. Thus the
story becomes a more spectacular demonstration of the single lesson
Jacobus seems to care about: Dominic's ability to reveal the ugliness of
heresy.

Jacobus's version of this story is significant also for what it does not
say about the founder's relationship with God. As noted above, the
Legenda omits the women's request that Dominic pray for the sign. And
Dominic's response to them is revised significantly. In Constantine's
account the saint's hesitation demonstrated his dependence on God; his
words, a total confidence in God's mercy: "Then the man of God stood
still for a while and prayed silently, and after a while he said to them, 'Be
firm and wait confidently. I have faith that the Lord my God, who
wants no one to perish, will soon show you what sort of lord you have
followed hitherto'" (sec. 49).[81] In Jacobus's version, however, there is
nothing to suggest either the presence of God or the extent of his saving
will: "[Dominic] said to them, 'Be firm and wait a little, that you may
see what sort of lord you have followed'" (p. 475).[82]

That Dominic no longer expresses his faith in a God "who wants no
one to perish" lends additional weight both to the ambiguity about
God's will in the story of the obdurate heretics and to the role played by
the saint himself in the story immediately following that of the cat
apparition. This, the final illustration of Dominic's work with the

heretics and the only one that portrays him as an inquisitor, was not very reassuring even in Constantine's version, and Jacobus makes it less so. The apparent point of the story is Dominic's ability to foresee the conversion and reform of one Raymond de Grossi some twenty years before it occurs. The saint intervenes to spare this single individual out of a group of heretics, all "convictos" by his own efforts and now being taken away to be executed; eventually Raymond sees the light and becomes a Dominican. The harsher aspects of the story are mitigated somewhat in Constantine's version, where the legal procedures are clearly spelled out: the heretics have refused to return to the faith and have therefore been handed over to the secular arm, whose sentence is at least theoretically distinguishable from the will of the saint himself; except for questioning the heretics after their arrest, Dominic has no role in the proceedings except that of perceiving God's will as it pertains to Raymond and giving him the first indication of the grace whereby he is to be saved.[83] Jacobus, on the other hand, seems not to have felt it desirable to limit the founder's apparent involvement in the judgment and execution of heretics. In the *Legenda* there is no mention of a preceding arrest or a refused opportunity to recant or, indeed, of any agency other than that of Dominic and some anonymous officers who obey him. The suggestions of God's presence have disappeared again.[84] The whole burden of responsiblity for the heretics' fate thus seems to be borne by the saint himself, who spares the future Dominican among them and sends the rest off to be burned.[85]

At this point one naturally recalls the militant portrayal of Ambrose in the *Legenda*—and Jacobus's approving references to inquisitorial force as a weapon of the saints. What one sees with special clarity in his account of Dominic is the kind of pessimism implicit in this militancy. The founder is no longer visualized as a fruitful apostle whose preaching and example set in motion a great renewal of the church. Indeed, the controlling premise in the *Legenda* account seems to be the impossibility of any such renewal. The message about the perversity of the heretics, admitted into the official legend by Humbert, is pursued to its logical and quasi-allegorical extreme: the world itself perversely resists the founder's influence. And God seems to have withdrawn from the scene. Although Dominic is upheld with miraculous proofs that heaven is on his side, even he no longer appears to enjoy the consolation of God's actual presence[86] or the security of a son who knows his Father's love. The founder's joyful trust in God, a central theme in most earlier versions of the legend, is conspicuously deemphasized in Jacobus's version—vanishing not only from the story of the heretic women and the apparition, but also from a number of stories about Dominic's personal experience and his care for the brethren.[87]

The change in Dominic's own relationship with God is summed up rather nicely in two passages near the end of the *Legenda* account. When Jacobus pauses to generalize about the founder's character and way of life (pp. 476-77), he retains very little of the traditional emphasis on Dominic's joyfulness and the love he inspired in everyone who knew him.[88] What Jacobus dwells on instead are the penitential austerities to which the founder subjected himself: solitary vigils in the church while others slept; lying on the floor with a stone for his pillow when weariness finally overcame him; self-flagellation with an iron chain three times every night; deliberate avoidance of his own diocese, where he had friends and admirers, in favor of a hostile one where everyone attacked him.[89]

The new bleakness of the founder's experience is equally clear in the second passage, the scene immediately preceding Dominic's death. In the *Legenda* the death itself is portrayed as a joyous event; in fact, Christ and Mary personally come forth to welcome the saint to heaven (p. 479). But Jacobus markedly heightens the contrast with the life from which the saint is being released—and in which he leaves his sons. For the famous scene of parting, Jacobus supplements Constantine's account with Humbert's, weaving the two together in a way that suggests complete familiarity with the material. He retains the central image of Dominic as a father, bestowing on his sons a final legacy and comforting them with the promise that he will be more useful to them after death; even the grief of the brethren and the tenderness with which he addresses them are clearly shown. But again Jacobus omits the details suggesting the saint's knowledge of a generous God. Both Constantine and Humbert link Dominic's promise of continuing help with his confident trust in God; Jacobus omits this explanation.[90] When he comes to the legacy, he merely quotes the counsels Dominic gave his sons, following Humbert's wording: "He drew up a will, saying, 'These things I leave to you, as my sons and heirs, to hold by right: have charity, preserve humility, possess voluntary poverty'" (p. 478).[91] What vanishes here is the intervening material suggesting the greatness of this legacy, the spiritual riches with which God rewards those who give up worldly wealth for his sake: "He drew up a will that befitted a pauper of Christ, rich in faith, fellow heir to the kingdom that God has promised to all who love him. A will, I say, not of earthly wealth but of grace, not of material furnishings but of spiritual virtues, not of earthly property but of heavenly fellowship. In short, what he possessed, he bequeathed. 'These things I leave . . .'" (Humbert, secs. 62-63).[92]

Humbert returns to this theme after quoting Dominic's words, and Constantine, from whose account Jacobus draws most of the rest of the scene, also pauses to emphasize the nature and source of the wealth left by the founder.[93] So, for that matter, did Peter Ferrandus and Jean de Mailly.[94] But Jacobus retains no suggestion whatever of spiritual wealth, or of the New Testament promises, or indeed of a God whose love can be experienced in this life. He turns directly from the counsels themselves to the curse that turns the last of them into a commandment, enforced by the wrath of the saint and the power of God: "As strictly as he could, however, he forbade anyone ever to introduce temporal possessions into his order, threatening a horrible curse from almighty God and from himself on anyone who should dare to soil the Order of Preachers with the dust of earthly riches" (p. 478).[95]

This final insistence on poverty is all the more striking in the *Legenda* because Jacobus never connects it with the missionary work for which the order was founded.[96] In fact, the ideal of preaching in imitation of the first apostles has almost vanished from the narrative, as we have seen. Thus the renunciation of property and comfort seems to have become a purely private imperative—the great proof of the brethren's separation from a wicked world and their best hope of satisfying its Judge.

The pessimistic implications of the founder's legend are so pervasive in Jacobus's retelling, and so evidently in keeping with his emphases in other chapters of the *Legenda,* that one could easily construct a new legend of Jacobus himself as a discouraged son of Dominic, an idealist who lost all his faith in human nature and some of his faith in God when apostolic preaching failed to win over the enemies that confronted the order. It would be an appealing story for our times, and it would certainly reflect the tenor of the book more accurately than the prevailing legend has done. But let us resist the temptation. What the facts before us actually warrant are some relatively small and undramatic conclusions which are more likely to approximate the truth about the *Legenda* and its author.

Given the source material it uses and the particular controversies it seems to reflect, Jacobus's account of Dominic can hardly be dated much before 1260. But there is every reason to suppose, with Monleone, that the *Legenda* was essentially completed before 1267[97]—during the period, that is, when Jacobus was still leading a relatively cloistered, bookish life, and probably well before he reached the age of forty. Jacobus's own words on the subject suggest not only that this book predates his sermons on the saints but that it was his first important piece of writing.[98] The earlier the date assigned to the *Legenda,* of course, the easier it is to explain its excesses of zeal as the faults of a rather young and inexperienced follower of Dominic. One notable difference between Jacobus and most of his predecessors is that he thinks like a logician instead of a pastor. The utter consistency with which he works out his favorite ideas, regardless of the human values he is sacrificing, suggests that he was accustomed to teaching theories, not practical applications. Nor does he seem to have an appreciation of other perspectives, other value systems, besides the essentially monastic one he celebrates. The point is most obvious when he tries to justify Dominic and the order on the basis of their separation from—and apparent uselessness to—the very denizens of the world at whom the stories in the *Legenda* were aimed. But his lack of empathy with Christians who must live in the world, and with weaker souls who care about earthly blessings, is everywhere apparent. Even his model sermons, which are less extreme than the *Legenda* in most respects, exhibit a noticeable disregard for the everyday needs and concerns of the laity who would hear them. This characteristic of Jacobus's work becomes more understandable when one recalls that he cannot have seen very much of the world before he renounced it in 1244, at the age of fourteen or thereabouts.[99] And the increasingly militant stance of the order in the ensuing years was hardly calculated to sway a young convert towards open-mindedness.

Jacobus's gloomy account of the founder's public career is obviously colored by the same eagerness to condemn the world that is everywhere manifested in the *Legenda,* but it also sheds a bit of additional light on the premises behind the book itself. For, insofar as Jacobus ever offers an apologia for the book's harshness, he does so here. If he does not rely on the kinds of gentle persuasion his predecessors used, the explanation he offers is that persuasion has failed. Dominic steadfastly bore witness to the truth, and almost no one heeded him. Miracles proved he was right, and still almost nothing changed. The world remains locked in its sin and error, apparently doomed to destruction. Against this scenario it is not surprising that Jacobus should bring out the heavy artillery, arming the preachers who would use the *Legenda* with a polemic considerably more threatening than was characteristic of Dominican hagiography—or of his own model sermons. The interesting point here is the analogy between Jacobus's recourse to such measures and the rationale for physical coercion which the order had incorporated into the official legend of Dominic. In each case rather drastic departures from apostolic preaching are justified by the assumption that the particular human beings confronting the preacher are not only beyond the reach of persuasion, but also beyond the reach of God's mercy. Hence the preacher is obliged to conquer their resistance, for their own good and for the good of the church.

Since Jacobus's selection of themes in both the *Legenda* and the model sermons was evidently dictated in large part by the way he envisioned their auditors, his own perspective on the faith can be reconstructed only conjecturally. But I see no reason to believe that the image of God as a loving, accessible Father played a much larger role in his own spirituality than it does in these works. One need not go to the lengths of concluding that he himself pictured Christ as the wrathful figure of the visions he used for polemical purposes in the chapter on Dominic. Nor is it necessary to infer from his bleak account of the founder's final legacy that his own experience as a Dominican had been devoid of spiritual consolations; his selectivity here can and perhaps should be interpreted as an attempt to magnify the heroic poverty of Dominic and the brethren by dissociating them from as many kinds of comfort as possible. No matter how tortuously one reasons, however, there is no way of making the evidence yield a very optimistic message about God's relationship with his creatures. It may be that Jacobus was more susceptible than his Dominican predecessors had been to the apocalyptic currents of the time, with their despairing view of the present world and their focus on the Judgment ahead. Or he may simply have been less able to reconcile the evils he saw about him with the notion of a Deity who actually loved fallen man and descended to lift him up. In any case, the whole thrust of his theological imagination appears to have been adversarial and puritan rather than inclusive and humanistic. Perhaps the most telling evidence in this regard is his tendency to equate sanctity with isolation, joylessness, virtual sterility, and contempt for the values of lesser men. His predilection for these emphases may well have been less deliberate than instinctive, given the myriad small choices involved and the rather disastrous results on the polemical level. But the continual emergence of such a pattern, especially in the legends of the saints who meant most to him, suggests even more about Jacobus's mental picture of God—and of his own calling—than do his more dramatic images of the saints as representatives of divine justice.

10
On the *Legenda* as a Medieval Best-Seller

The prodigious success of the *Legenda aurea* by the blessed James de Voragine has almost completely blocked out the memory of similar works that were issued during the same centuries. For example, who remembers the *Sanctorale* of Bernard Gui or, indeed, the legendary of Bartholomew of Trent? Nowadays the only people acquainted with them are some specialists and a few antiquarians. The *Abbreviatio in gestis et miraculis sanctorum* by Jean de Mailly is even less known. . . . However, sometimes the favors of Fortune are distributed without perfect justice, and it seems permissible to lodge an appeal against her.

Antoine Dondaine, 1947

Once one has recognized the special biases of the *Legenda,* its singularly privileged position in the late Middle Ages seems odder and more problematical than even Dondaine has suggested. How did it happen that this particular compilation was proclaimed the noblest of all books about the saints and disseminated to massive audiences, both in Latin and in the vernacular, while its rivals were nearly forgotten? What need or needs did it satisfy, during the two centuries when its preeminence went almost unchallenged? And what sort of influence did the book actually have on the life of the late-medieval church? These are of course the great questions in the case of the *Legenda,* and the questions least capable of being answered from the kinds of evidence that have been published hitherto. Just enough pertinent facts have come to light to justify some hypotheses on the meaning of the book's success and to suggest some possibilities for further research.

The obvious inference to be drawn from the hundreds of surviving manuscripts and incunabula of the Latin *Legenda* is that members of the Western European clergy found the book exceptionally useful in the fourteenth and fifteenth centuries. And it can hardly be supposed that the *Legenda*'s selectivity was more of a liability than an asset in their eyes. In addition to its authoritarian and puritanical biases, Jacobus's book had of course the practical advantages of being compact, conveniently arranged, generally simple and concise in its style, and full of information a clergyman might want to know. But in most of these respects it was equalled or even surpassed by the earlier legendaries of Jean de Mailly and Bartholomew of Trent.[1] And one can assume, on the basis of the manuscripts extant, that the clergy of the period preferred the *Legenda* to each of these rivals by a margin of about forty to one.

There is nothing inherently implausible about the hypothesis that the Latin *Legenda* owed some of its success to the biases traced in this study. Indeed, the success of such a book seems to have been part of a large trend in the late-medieval church. As André Vauchez has recently demonstrated, the cult of the saints reached a major turning point around the year 1270.[2] In the preceding eighty years the papacy had responded with unusual sympathy to the religious ideals and aspirations of the various groups within the church. A large and diverse company of new saints had been canonized: monastic reformers and regular canons; bishops from Northern Europe who exemplified the right use of wealth and authority; humbler Southern European representatives of the new mendicant orders, including Dominic, Francis, and Clare; and members of the laity who had worked in the world, ministering to the poor and combatting injustice. Although most of these canonizations reflected the traditional preference for saints of aristocratic or even royal birth, the relatively modest origins of the mendicants and a few of the lay saints affirmed the possibility that Christian perfection could also arise from the humbler reaches of society. Equally significant is the number of these saints who were penitents—former sinners whose conversion and final glorification underlined the lesson that saints are made, not born. In short, the faithful had been permitted, even encouraged, to venerate recent saints who were recognizably like themselves and whose examples they might reasonably hope to emulate. Although the cult of the saints had not quite been democratized, all segments of the church had been told in effect that they were important enough to have appropriate patrons and models of their own. In the final decades of the thirteenth century, however, papal policies on canonization suddenly became much more restrictive. Local cults of recent saints, or *beati,* continued to multiply until the end of the Middle Ages, but the vast majority of them received no recognition whatever from the authorities in Rome. Nearly all the exceptions, the candidates deemed at least potentially worthy of canonization, were sponsored by powerful dynasties and religious orders that were closely allied with the papacy.[3] And the relatively egalitarian ideals of the late twelfth and early thirteenth centuries were rapidly left behind. What took their place were narrower and more exclusive definitions of sanctity which bear more than a passing resemblance to the definitions in the *Legenda*.

As Vauchez notes, the new saints of the later Middle Ages tended to be credited with increasingly spectacular endowments, a phenomenon which must be attributed at least in part to the increasingly demanding criteria used by the papacy. The first great change in the criteria for canonization was signalled by Innocent IV, who declared that sanctity required a life of continuous, uninterrupted virtue.[4] From 1270 on, Innocent's successors implemented this principle by refusing even to consider the canonization of any more penitents. And the official dossiers that were found acceptable in Rome became more and more idealized. Although penitential virtues retained a prominent place in the lives of later saints, noticeable efforts were made to dissociate these saints from any kind of imperfection that might actually have called for repentance.[5] Thus the ideal of redemption was replaced in effect by the loftier ideal of impeccability. Another important milestone was passed in the fourteenth century, when the authorities in Rome began to reserve the honor of canonization for saints who had exhibited extraordinary, or "heroic," degrees of virtue. Again the change can be traced to a papal pronouncement—in this case, a sermon by Boniface VIII in 1297 which described the life of Saint Louis as having transcended the capacities of human nature.[6] Within a few decades, the possession of supernatural gifts had become a key element in the official definition of sanctity. And the gifts that received the most emphasis were much more singular and rarefied than the gift of healing or the theological virtues of faith, hope, and charity. Hence the dossiers of fourteenth- and fifteenth-century saints are full of prodigies and wonders which resemble those in the *Legenda*.[7] Even more striking, however, are the resemblances of character between these saints, as their admirers portrayed them, and the saints of Jacobus's book.

To read Vauchez's account of the individuals who were canonized or seriously considered for canonization between 1270 and about 1450 is to encounter parallel after parallel to Jacobus's devaluation of the active life in favor of private, contemplative virtues. Thus, for example, just one of these later saints was closely identified with the original mendicants' ideal of apostolic preaching; he was Saint Yves Hélory (d. 1303, canon. 1347), who had been educated by the Franciscans and who demonstrated his charity and humility by becoming and remaining a mere parish priest (Vauchez, pp. 358-64).[8] The two mendicant saints of this period, Thomas Aquinas (d. 1274, canon. 1323) and the young Franciscan Louis of Anjou (d. 1297, canon. 1317), were both distinguished scholars, not lowly preachers, and the contemporary witnesses to their sanctity laid great emphasis on their lifelong purity and detachment from the world. Indeed, Saint Louis of Anjou was credited with such virtues as possessing an immense library, showing a great inclination for intellectual and doctrinal *disputatio,* avoiding the company of laymen and women as much as possible, and preserving his baptismal innocence all his life. Vauchez concludes that his spirituality was essentially a return to the old monastic pattern of *contemptus mundi:* flight from the world, abstinence, penitential practices, and aspiration to an "angelic life" (pp. 398-400). The canonization of Thomas Aquinas presumably represented the vindication of a theology that embraces mundane realities instead of fleeing from them; nonetheless, the witnesses on Saint Thomas's behalf were eager to characterize him as a completely spiritual being who never paid any attention to terrestrial things (p. 401).

The growing emphasis on purity and detachment from the world can be seen just as clearly in the domain of episcopal sanctity. In the first two-thirds of the thirteenth century, ten bishops had been canonized; between 1270 and 1450, one can find three if one counts Louis of Anjou, who was bishop of Toulouse for less than a year before his conscience impelled him to renounce the office (pp. 355-56), and Saint Peter of Morrone, or Celestine V (d. 1296, canon. 1313), an Italian hermit who was elected pope at a very advanced age and abdicated within six months (pp. 366, 372-73). The only late-medieval bishop officially recognized as a saint for having exercised his authority successfully, instead of giving it up for the sake of his soul, was Saint Thomas of Cantilupe, bishop of Hereford (d. 1282, canon. 1320), a transitional figure whose dossier is unusually complex and revealing.

In many respects Thomas of Hereford recalls the renowned English bishops of earlier periods. He was a great aristocrat who rebuked the powerful, gave lavishly to the poor, and had churches built at his own expense; and he was also known as a dedicated pastor who visited all his churches and was never too busy to confirm children or hear confessions. His public reputation for sanctity evidently arose in large part from these traditional manifestations of generosity and pastoral zeal (pp. 350-51).[9] By the end of the thirteenth century, however, more unusual gifts were required for canonization. Nearly all the male saints canonized after 1270 were extraordinarily learned, and Thomas of Hereford was no exception to this rule: educated at the Universities of Paris and Orleans, he had taught canon law and then theology at Oxford and twice served as chancellor of the university before he became a bishop (p. 463). Nor is it likely to be mere coincidence that Thomas of Hereford, like most of the bishops who were seriously considered for canonization during this period, shared some of the sterner virtues of the prelates in the

Legenda.[10] He was known as a strict disciplinarian who took unusually vigorous measures against wrongdoers (p. 342). He defended his see with remarkable aggressiveness and tenacity, taking on some of the most powerful laymen in England in order to win back properties and rights which his predecessors had allowed to lapse (p. 339). And if the more sophisticated witnesses to his sanctity are to be believed, his personal virtues were almost indistinguishable from those of a good monk: humility, asceticism, a poverty of spirit which compensated for the outward luxury of his life, and so strong a love of chastity that he never took baths and refused to embrace his own sisters once he had become a bishop (pp. 341-42). As Vauchez points out, no such puritanism had been associated with episcopal saints a few decades earlier.

Most striking of all is the changing image of lay sanctity in the late Middle Ages. At the end of the twelfth century Innocent III had been willing to canonize one Homebon of Cremona (d. 1197, canon. 1199), a widowed merchant who had voluntarily adopted the special garb and disciplines of a penitent; the bull of canonization emphasized Saint Homebon's piety, his obedience to his confessor, his works of mercy on behalf of the poor, and his constructive involvement in the religious politics of the city (pp. 412-13). The possibility of sanctification by such down-to-earth virtues as penitence and practical charity was reaffirmed in the thirteenth century by the examples of Saint Elizabeth of Thuringia (d. 1231, canon. 1235) and Saint Hedwige of Silesia (d. 1243, canon. 1267), both of whom had been influenced by the early Franciscans. Rather than take the traditional step of entering a convent after their husbands died, these pious noblewomen chose to remain in the world leading "mixed" lives of prayer, personal austerity, and active service to the poor and afflicted (pp. 431-35). By canonizing them and Saint Homebon, the medieval papacy obviously went some way toward providing a model of perfection that was specifically designed for lay Christians.

After 1270, however, the monastic ideals of purity and detachment from the world were strongly reasserted even in the realm of lay sanctity, and so was the clerical ideal of exceptional knowledge. The magnitude of the change is suggested by the character of the four laywomen who became serious candidates for canonization in the fourteenth and fifteenth centuries: all four were mystics who had renounced the world to devote themselves to the solitary pursuit of union with God, and the great proofs of their sanctity were the extraordinary signs and revelations they had been granted (pp. 438-46).[11] Even more interesting for our purposes are the gifts attributed to Saint Elzéar of Sabran (d. 1323, canon. 1369), a Provençal count who was the only layman actually canonized in the fourteenth century. Like the female lay saints of the period, Saint Elzéar lived a secluded, contemplative life, intent on spiritual matters rather than temporal ones. He was credited with a remarkable understanding of theology, much of it revealed to him in visions. What stands out most in the case of Saint Elzéar, however, is his identification with an ideal of spotless purity. The great marvel in his life was his virginal marriage to Dauphine of Puimichel, a union which lasted for some twenty-five years without ever being consummated. His biographers explained that Dauphine had persuaded him at the outset to join her in a vow of continence, and his feat of purity was proclaimed even more wondrous than the famous but relatively brief ones of a Saint Joseph or a Saint Alexis. At least one of the biographers went so far as to suggest that Saint Elzéar had been born in a state of perfect innocence and had ensured his salvation simply by avoiding any taint of sin. After reviewing the idyllic details, Vauchez himself observes that Saint Elzéar sounds much less like a representative of the medieval laity than like a character out of the *Legenda* (pp. 418-20).

The obvious question at this point is what caused the late-medieval church to start preferring such an idealized, essentially monastic definition of sanctity to the relatively flexible and inclusive definitions which had prevailed before 1270. The principal theory offered by Vauchez is that the change reflects the influence of a conservative elite among the clergy who wanted to restrain and control the cult of the saints, largely for reasons of church politics. A number of prominent churchmen seem to have been troubled by the sheer number of recent saints who were being venerated, especially at the local level. The influx of new saints was naturally seen as a threat to the status of older and more traditional cults,[12] and it also raised the specter of a fragmented church in which every little community and interest group would be venerating different saints.[13] Vauchez repeatedly suggests, however, that the primary cause of conservative disquiet was the degree to which the cult of the saints had begun to foster a democratic conception of the church instead of a hierarchical one.[14] And he concludes that the official policies on canonization after 1270 were designed in large part to reverse this trend by establishing a very clear distinction between the "eminent, distinguished sanctity" which deserved special honor and the kinds of holiness which ordinary members of the church might hope to attain (p. 607). In effect, these policies confirmed the spiritual superiority of cultured, knowledgeable Christians to uneducated ones, that of recluses and cloistered religious to persons with secular concerns and responsibilities, and that of celibates to noncelibates. The most obvious beneficiaries would have been highly educated members of the regular clergy—persons rather like Jacobus de Voragine, in fact. And the group identified as least holy—and, by implication, least suited to the exercise of any spiritual authority—would have included ignorant and undisciplined secular clergy, along with the vast majority of laypeople.

Although Vauchez barely mentions the *Legenda,* his findings can clearly be extended into an explanation of the book's success. If the official redefinition of sanctity in the late Middle Ages was the work of politically conservative clerics, intent on reinforcing the traditional hierarchy of states within the church, these clerics and their supporters are most unlikely to have confined their attention to the credentials of recent saints. Even more indispensable for their purposes would have been the wide use of a legendary like Jacobus's, which assimilated dozens of earlier saints to the same exclusive patterns and underlined the message with powerful propaganda on behalf of the papacy, the mendicants, and clerical authority in general. When one recalls the sixteenth-century reaction against a tradition of "saints' lies," and against this book in particular, one is inclined to conclude that the *Legenda*'s popularity among the clergy must have been based on political expediency. To adopt this hypothesis is not, of course, to rule out the need for further investigation. Even if the hypothesis turns out to be reasonably accurate, there is good reason for wanting to know which segments of the late-medieval clergy embraced the *Legenda* most enthusiastically, just how they used it, and what particular goals and interests came to be identified with the book in the fourteenth and fifteenth centuries. Since the success of Jacobus's book was not just an isolated phenomenon, the answers to such questions are likely to shed new light on some of the larger issues discussed by historians of the period—including, most obviously, the degree to which a conservative, elitist view of the church prevailed among the clergy at large and how important it was in creating the new preference for idealized definitions of sanctity. If one should discover, for instance, that the clerics who used the *Legenda* were actually less interested in the political ammunition it provided than in its exempla about penance and its uncompromising lessons against earthly wealth and pleasures, one might reasonably assume that many of the changes traced by Vauchez were also expressions of stern moralism, not just of church politics.

Compiling all the necessary information about the use of the *Legenda* will not be a simple task, but at least there is no shortage of potentially useful source material. Many manuscripts of the Latin *Legenda* itself undoubtedly contain clues to the identities, the institutional affiliations, and even the intentions of their original owners and users.[15] There are also medieval indexes to the book, compiled for the convenience of preachers, which ought to be studied for the evidence they can provide about the kinds of lessons that were customarily drawn from Jacobus's stories about the saints.[16] And surviving sermons from the period will surely supply additional evidence, once a systematic effort is made to discover and evaluate their borrowings from the *Legenda*.

The apparent success of Jacobus's book among the laity of the late Middle Ages is as problematical and interesting a matter as its success among the clergy, but not of course for the same reasons. One crucial difference is the fact that most laymen had no opportunity whatever to choose between the *Legenda* and the alternative books in its genre. So far as I have been able to determine, no other abridged legendary was made available in even one vernacular language until 1523-24, when a French translation of Peter Natal's *Catalogus sanctorum* was published in Paris. Translations of Jacobus's book had begun appearing some 225 years earlier,[17] and of course they multiplied enormously during the fourteenth and fifteenth centuries. In view of the *Legenda*'s political content, this long monopoly looks suspicious enough to merit some attention. I have found no reason to suppose that less authoritarian collections were somehow suppressed in favor of Jacobus's. Given the standard assumption that pious literature fell outside the realm of doctrine, and therefore need not be closely regulated, individual teachers and translators would presumably have been allowed to popularize any legendary they liked. Nonetheless, it is an odd and disturbing coincidence that those individuals should unanimously have concluded that the *Legenda,* rather than any of its rivals, was the most suitable collection for laymen to have.

Among the abridged legendaries of the later Middle Ages, at least one—the *Abbreviatio* by Jean de Mailly—was a more natural candidate for vernacular transmission than the *Legenda* was. Gui's *Sanctorale* and the legendary of Peter Calo are essentially works of scholarship, not attempts at popularization, and even the clergy of the period seem to have been unprepared to appreciate their merits. The massive compilation by Peter Natal may also have been too ambitious for the tastes of most medieval readers. At the opposite extreme, Bartholomew of Trent's sourcebook for preachers tends to summarize the old legends so efficiently that most of their narrative interest vanishes—and with it, of course, their ability to attract a general audience.[18] The *Abbreviatio,* designed to be used by parish priests with no great sophistication, has none of these disadvantages. Nor does it share most of the peculiarities which made the *Legenda* itself a dubious choice for transmission to the laity. As Dondaine has noted, it lacks the learned digressions for which Jacobus made room—hardly a major liability where most laymen were concerned. And its content in other respects is distinctly more suitable for general purposes of instruction and inspiration than is that of the *Legenda*. Jacobus had not of course designed his compilation for such purposes at all; envisioning an audience of well-trained preachers, he had supplied some rather dry discussions of theological issues and a host of anecdotes without interpretations, for use in sermons. And most of the anecdotes were calculated to make an impression on a particularly unpromising segment of the laity in a difficult time, rather than to edify Christians in all circumstances. It seems clear from Jacobus's model sermons, in fact, that he himself believed that such extreme, sensational material as he had provided in the *Legenda* was unfit for regular consumption by mature, intelligent believers. Had he been able to foresee the enthusiasm of translators like Jean de Vignay, who presented his version to the queen of France, and William Caxton, who did so much to popularize the *Legenda* among the lay reading public in England, he might well have urged them to consider a more moderate book like Jean's *Abbreviatio*.

Jean's handling of the old legends does not always differ so radically from Jacobus's as the special case of the Dominic legend might suggest. Almost uniformly, however, his abridgements are better balanced than those in the *Legenda*—less apt to substitute political propaganda for religious teaching, more restrained in their use of the marvellous, and more intent on the role of the saints as models for imitation. Thus Jean shows very little of Jacobus's inclination to prove the saints' glory by emphasizing the wondrous ease of their victories. In the *Abbreviatio* even the martyrs, the great heroes of the church, tend to appear as recognizable human beings whose greatness consists in suffering, endurance, and dependence on God. Saint Anastasia, for example, is given no swift, automatic triumph over the greedy prefect who persecutes her; unlike Jacobus, Jean recounts a long ordeal, throughout which the saint is upheld by prayer (*Abrégé*, pp. 53-54; *Legenda*, pp. 48-49). Similarly, the Saint Sebastian of the *Abbreviatio* is vulnerable enough to need help and healing after the first, abortive attempt to execute him; and instead of deliberately seeking out his persecutors thereafter, as he seems to do in the *Legenda*, he consents to flee and encounters them by accident (*Abrégé*, p. 117; *Legenda*, p. 112). The contrast between the two books is even clearer in the case of Saint Eusebius. The *Legenda* predictably minimizes the saint's sufferings at the hands of the Arians, just mentioning the worst of the cells in which he was confined and giving no hint that his own strength was insufficient to the occasion (pp. 453-54). In the *Abbreviatio*, on the other hand, Eusebius is sufficiently human to complain at least once about the cruelties he endures during his long imprisonment, and Jean underlines the point that he could not have survived without divine help: "If the angels had not visited and strengthened him, his poor human body would not have been able to endure such torment for long. But he who kept Jonah alive in the sea-monster's belly sustained Eusebius in his cell" (*Abrégé,* p. 299).[19]

As the preceding examples suggest, both the homiletic content of the *Abbreviatio* and its use of realistic detail serve to point up the universal lessons in the saints' experience; thus every reader is encouraged to identify with the saints and to see the relevance of their virtues to his or her own life. Equally significant is Jean's tendency to place most of his emphasis on fundamental Christian virtues like charity, humility, and trust in God, not the special virtues associated with the monastic ideal. Thus the most obvious theme in his brief account of Saint Augustine is the saint's enormous activity and fruitfulness after conversion (*Abrégé,* pp. 361-63). The motif of world renunciation receives relatively little attention. With regard to earthly pleasures, in fact, Jean's chapter on Augustine holds up moderate use as the ideal, suggesting that excesses of austerity and luxury are equally blameworthy because both are symptoms of pride.[20]

The superiority of the *Abbreviatio* as a guide for the laity, in particular, is perhaps most clearly exemplified by its relative moderation on the issues of virginity and marriage. The *Legenda* contains some rather extreme propaganda for virginity, including legends of questionable orthodoxy which flatly condemn sexual intercourse even within a lawful marriage.[21] And Jacobus frequently goes so far as to suggest that the way one treats other human beings is immaterial, so long as one preserves one's own purity. A vivid but not atypical example can be seen at the beginning of his chapter on Saint Agnes:

The wise virgin Agnes . . . lost her death at the age of thirteen, and found life. She was a child in years, but the maturity of her mind was immeasurable; her body was young, but her spirit hoary; her face was beautiful, but her faith more beautiful. Now as she was returning from school the prefect's son fell in love with her, and offered her jewels and limitless wealth if she would not refuse to marry him. Agnes answered, "Begone from me, tinder of sin, nurse of evil, fodder of death! For I am already engaged to another lover. . . . Him I love, who is far nobler than you and of much higher lineage, whose mother is a virgin, whose father has known no woman, whom the angels serve." (*Legenda,* pp. 113-14)[22]

Jean, however, tends to avoid the sweeping lessons against both women and marriage for which Jacobus would make room,[23] and his virgin martyrs set examples that are noticeably gentler and less intolerant than those in the *Legenda.* Thus his retelling of the Agnes legend conveys the

ideal of virginity without any admixture of invective against the prefect's
son:

> Blessed Agnes was born in Rome, of a rich and noble family. One day when she
> was thirteen years old, she was returning from school when the prefect's son
> noticed her; captivated by her beauty, he wanted her for his wife. Agnes rejected
> all his entreaties and all his gifts. She did not wish, she said, to wrong her fiancé
> by violating her eternal marriage and deserting him who was so powerful, so rich,
> and so handsome. (*Abrégé*, p. 118)[24]

The same pattern can be seen in a number of other chapters on
persecuted virgins.[25] Where the *Legenda* glorifies the saints' fierce
defiance of their enemies, sometimes including members of their own
families, the *Abbreviatio* holds up more positive and charitable models
of conduct.

The basic contrasts between the *Legenda* and the *Abbreviatio*
represent something much larger, of course, than the individual priorities
of Jacobus de Voragine and Jean de Mailly. In a very real sense the two
books are identified with two different movements in the late-medieval
church: the *Abbreviatio,* with the general trend toward liberalization
and inclusiveness that reached its height in the early thirteenth century;
the *Legenda,* with the reassertion of conservative, clerical values that
followed. Since Vauchez has shown how completely the latter movement
displaced the former in the selection of candidates for canonization in
the fourteenth and fifteenth centuries, one should not be very surprised
by the fact that it was the *Legenda* which triumphed, while books like the
Abbreviatio were forgotten. But the *Legenda*'s popularization among
the laity still raises some enormous questions. Most obviously, one
would like to know whether the book's particular biases did not arouse
some strong opposition early on. Was it only in the Renaissance that the
lay reading public became sophisticated enough to start noticing the
social and political implications of Jacobus's narratives? Were the
late-medieval clergy in general so uninterested in the religious instruction
of laymen that they completely overlooked the *Legenda*'s deficiencies for
this purpose? Did even the more progressive, or more radical, segments
of the clergy stand by in silence while Jacobus's narrow, elitist view of
sanctity was disseminated to the Christian public at large? The surviving
documents from the period are likely to provide a good deal of valuable
evidence on these matters, especially if the investigation is extended to all
the vernacular translations and adaptations of the *Legenda*. Should
these versions of the book turn out to have retained every bias of the
original Latin version, and to have been found generally acceptable
nonetheless, one would have to draw some bleak generalizations about

the state of Christian education in the fourteenth and fifteenth centuries. It seems much likelier, however, that the vernacular manuscripts of the *Legenda* will exhibit a considerable variety of reactions to Jacobus's biases. Individual readers may well have left marginalia which show their special admiration for certain aspects of the book and their doubts about others. Some of the book's early translators may have introduced significant changes which reflect their own reservations about the wisdom of Jacobus's emphases. Thus, for example, one would expect to find at least a few vernacular *Legenda*s which attempt to mitigate the severity of Jacobus's teaching, to prune away his most blatant propaganda, and to add explicit lessons or stories designed to edify a lay audience. And it would be naive to deny the possibility that one may also find vernacular versions whose contents are even narrower and more extreme than those of the Latin *Legenda*.

The consequences of the *Legenda*'s wide dissemination in the late Middle Ages can hardly be estimated at this point. There is not much doubt, however, that the choice of Jacobus's book for general use, while more moderate and traditional legendaries were virtually forgotten, was a momentous occurrence in the life of the medieval church. Most members of the clergy still had access to better sources, of course, and they may not have been inordinately influenced by the particular biases of this one. But in a period when even the most literate families possessed a mere handful of books, which were read again and again, and when vernacular Bibles were still relatively rare, the contents of the *Legenda* must have exerted a profound influence on the religious outlook of many laymen and women. The exact nature of that influence will become easier to grasp as we learn more about the lessons which contemporary preachers tended to draw from Jacobus's stories, the book's general reputation among laymen, and the actual tenor of the versions which they could read for themselves. It may be helpful, however, to sum up the apparent implications of the evidence which has already come to light.

When the educators of the Renaissance condemned the *Legenda* as a dangerous influence on the faithful, they charged in essence that the book had two detrimental effects: it aroused skepticism in sophisticated readers and fostered superstition in credulous ones. Since what they evidently meant by "superstition" was doctrinal error, and in particular the error of overestimating the saints' power, one must conclude that they oversimplified the problem. But rather a strong case might be made for the hypothesis that the *Legenda* persuaded susceptible believers to adopt a number of habits and beliefs that were "superstitious" in the sense of being at odds with a rational, well-balanced understanding of the faith. Where more traditional works of hagiography had subordinated wonders to serious teaching, for example, Jacobus's narrow selectivity would inadvertently have made it easy for untrained readers to cherish the marvellous and the sensational for their own sakes. Where traditional hagiography at least sometimes presented ordinary laymen and women with examples they might reasonably be expected to imitate, the *Legenda* effectively told them that they could only revere and obey the saints. And, where hagiography had almost always encouraged the love of socially useful ideals like charity and compassion and reconciliation, the *Legenda* might well have encouraged its readers to value individual purity and intolerance instead. Thus one might reasonably suppose that the wide use of Jacobus's book had something to do with such phenomena as the extraordinary aversion to marriage and sex which seems to have sprung up among pious laywomen in the fourteenth and fifteenth centuries,[26] and the growing tendency among the laity in general to attend as many Eucharists as possible, staying just long enough in each case to witness the miracle of consecration. Vauchez remarks on a number of lesser trends in late-medieval piety which might also have been encouraged by Jacobus's book.[27] His most interesting example for our purposes, however, is the life of Charles of Blois (d. 1364), an immensely devout Breton duke who was considered for papal canonization shortly after his death. According to the witnesses who had known him, the daily devotions of this important nobleman included a remarkable number of prayers, as many as three or four Eucharists, at least one confession of his sins, various penitential exercises, and the reading of saints' lives, most often from the *Legenda*. Since the devaluation of specifically lay forms of sanctity was such a generalized tendency in the fourteenth century, it is not very surprising that Charles of Blois tried to live like a monk and reportedly lamented that he could not actually enter a religious order. More extraordinary, however, was this nobleman's deference to all members of the clergy. Besides rebuilding and lavishly decorating a number of churches, he evidently insisted on bowing before every bishop he encountered, entertaining simple monks and priests as if they had been dignitaries, and upholding the ecclesiastical side in every dispute between local churchmen and his own followers. Although the clergy hailed him as a saint, his retinue and his aristocratic neighbors seem to have considered him a fool and a traitor to his class (pp. 420-24). In fact, one might simply conclude that Charles of Blois took the *Legenda* very seriously.

Notes
Works Cited
Index

Notes

The following abbreviations have been used throughout the notes:

Acta SS	*Acta Sanctorum quotquot toto orbe coluntur* . . . . Brussels [etc.], 1643-.
Anal. Boll.	*Analecta Bollandiana.* Brussels, 1882-.
BN *Cat.*	*Catalogue général des livres imprimés de la Bibliothèque Nationale.* Paris, 1897-.
DTC	*Dictionnaire de théologie catholique.* Paris, 1915-50.
MOPH	*Monumenta Ordinis fratrum Praedicatorum historica.* Rome, 1896-.
NUC	*National Union Catalog: Pre-1956 Imprints.* Washington, D.C. [etc.], 1956-.
PL	*Patrologia latina,* ed. J. P. Migne. Paris, 1844-90.

Preface

1 For reasons explained fully at the end of Chapter 3, I have used Theodor Graesse's 1890 Latin edition of the *Legenda.*

Introduction

1 Albert Poncelet's landmark article "Le légendier de Pierre Calo," *Anal. Boll.* 29 (1910): 5-116, still provides an invaluable introduction to the whole phenomenon of the abridged legendary in the later Middle Ages. On the long-neglected legendaries by Jean de Mailly and Bartholomew of Trent, the most valuable supplements to Poncelet are two articles by Antoine Dondaine: "Le dominicain français Jean de Mailly et la *Légende dorée,*" *Archives d'histoire dominicaine* 1 (1946): 53-102, and "L'*epilogus in gesta sanctorum* de Barthélemy de Trente," in the festschrift for Father Charles Balić entitled *Studia mediaevalia et mariologica* (Rome, 1971), pp. 333-60. A few additional manuscripts of the *Abbreviatio* are enumerated by Guy Philippart in "Le manuscrit 377

213

de Berne et le supplément au légendier de Jean de Mailly," *Anal. Boll.* 92 (1974): 74, n. 2.

2   The best and most recent list in print is that in Thomas Kaeppeli's *Scriptores Ordinis Praedicatorum medii aevi,* 2 (Rome, 1975): 350-59.

3   Paul Meyer believed he had found seven different medieval French translations of the *Legenda*; these are listed in his "Notice du MS. Med.-Pal. 141 de la Laurentienne," *Romania* 33 (1904): 3-5.

4   On the influence of the *Legenda* in England, the major recent authority is Manfred Görlach; see esp. his discussion of the problems involved in establishing the sources of the *South English Legendary,* in *The Textual Tradition of the South English Legendary,* Leeds Texts and Monographs, n.s. 6 (1974), pp. 21-63. Görlach seems to accept the traditional conclusions about the role of the *Legenda* as a major source for Mirk and for the anonymous authors of the *Scottish Legendary* and the Shorter Vernon Collection of saints' legends; see, e.g., his *South English Legendary, Gilte Legende, and Golden Legend* (Braunschweig, 1972), pp. 7-8. As for Chaucer's tale, the most recent study of its dependence on the *Legenda* seems to be my own article "The Sources of Chaucer's 'Second Nun's Tale,'" *Modern Philology* 76 (1978-79): 111-35.

5   The editions are listed in Seybolt's article "Fifteenth-Century Editions of the *Legenda aurea,*" *Speculum* 21 (1946): 327-38. His identification of doubtful cases occurs in the article immediately following, "The *Legenda aurea,* Bible, and *Historia scholastica,*" p. 342.

6   Seybolt, "The *Legenda aurea,* Bible, and *Historia scholastica,*" p. 341.

7   This figure includes the one Spanish edition mentioned in the catalogs used. Since the *British Museum General Catalogue of Printed Books (to 1955)* dates it "1500?" and Seybolt omits it from his list of fifteenth-century editions, I have assumed it belongs to the beginning of the sixteenth century.

8   The single edition attested during this period is a Latin *Legenda* published in Madrid in 1688; for the particulars, see the *NUC Supplement,* 738:64.

9   Sherry L. Reames, "The Cecilia Legend as Chaucer Inherited It and Retold It: The Disappearance of an Augustinian Ideal," *Speculum* 55 (1980): 38-57, and "Saint Martin of Tours in the *Legenda aurea* and Before," *Viator* 12 (1981): 131-64.

Chapter 1: The Modern Legend of the *Legenda aurea*

1   John Bolland, "Praefatio generalis in vitas SS," *Acta SS,* Jan., 1 (1643; rept. Paris, 1863): ix-lxi. My quotations are taken from pp. xix-xx.

2   "Deinde quam illud falsum, nullas in vulgaribus coenobiorum bibliothecis praeter hanc Legendam extare Sanctorum historias! Nullum contra

reperire est antiquum monasterium, quod quidem haereticorum aevi hujus effugerit rabiem, quin aliqui in eo praeclari de Sanctorum rebus gestis codices extent, ac plerique antiqua manu exarati.''

3   "Bellovacensem denique Voraginensi praefert Wicelius. Habebit me in eo suffragatorem, sed non etiam, ut *sub eosdem annos,* quod ipse ait, scripsisse utrumque confitear, cum hic anno 1298 ille 1256 dicatur decessisse.''

4   "Sed addidit alius (ut puto) quispiam vitis nonnullis ineptam et ridiculam nominum interpretationem, indignam sane Jacobi eruditione.''

5   "Omitto cetera non minus absurda; quae cum indocti homines pro pulpitis identidem declamarent, nauseam et risum movebant eruditis, seque ipsos et Sanctorum historias in summam adducebant contemptionem.''

6   Bolland makes the point explicit in the way he links his introduction of Witzel to the passage just quoted: ". . . in summam adducebant contemptionem. Unde illa sunt Georgii Wicelii. . . .''

7   In fact, there are more plausible possibilities, as discussed below in Chapter 3.

8   "An omnia quae de Sanctis dicentur, nisi sint ex Eusebio sumpta, aspernabitur Wicelius? Unde ipse S. Bennonis, S. Clarae, S. Aegidii, S. Augustini, et aliorum plurimorum gesta accepit?''

9   "Ubi vero mythologiae studet Jacobus, bone Wiceli? Ego certe non omnia probo quae ille scribit; quin tamen vetera secutus sit monumenta, non dubito, et plurimas ejus historias reperio cum veteribus et genuinis congruere: non omnes evolvi; nec necesse est, cum fontem reperi, rivos consectari.''

10   "Quam, inquam, breviatoribus aut paraphrastis adjungere fidem par sit, ex veterum statuo cum ipsorum scriptis collatione. Censeo igitur, injuria, ut plurimum, neotericorum judiciis vapulare eam Legendam.''

11   "Ludovicum Vivem semper permaximi feci, singulari eruditione, gravitate, prudentia virum; planeque illi assentior, praestantissimos Divorum actus accuratius debuisse, quam vulgo factum sit, mandari litteris. Sed quod Legendae illius auctori ita maledicit, ut virum sanctum et sapientem *plumbei cordis, oris ferrei* appellet, id sane miror, in homine praesertim gravi et moderato.''

12   "Hauserat id fortassis a Desiderio Erasmo praeceptore suo, severissimo Aristarcho, qui nullum prope scriptorem intactum et non censoria virga notatum praeteriit.''

13   "Fuerit Jacobus stylo minus compto, ut illa erant tempora, at erat non modo doctus et pius, sed prudentia judicioque singulari, ut quam probabilia essent quae scriberet, Vive Erasmoque melius potuerit judicare.''

14   Jacques Echard and Jacques Quétif, *Scriptores Ordinis Praedicatorum,*
      1 (1719; rept. Turin, 1961): 454-59.

15   Thus, e.g., Echard does not deny Jacobus's responsibility for the
      far-fetched etymologies but urges his contemporaries to take a more
      tolerant view of such harmless reflections of medieval taste: "Praefa-
      tiones cuilibet vitae a Jacobo additae, quae fere in nomine sancti lusus
      sunt, palato hujus seculi saniori non placent, sed is erat seculi XIII &
      sequentium gustus; & quid patribus nostris non condonandum, ubi de
      fide non agitur?" (ibid., p. 456).

16   "Justa porro Jacobi defensio est quam ipse innuit, vitas has SS. non a se
      compositas, sed ut ipse ait compilatas tantum, id est jam diu antea a
      variis scriptas, sed & apud varios dispersas a se collectas, in ordinem
      digestas, & ex historicis sacris qui sua aetate in pretio erant locupletatas
      in lucem prodiisse, additis passim suis annotationibus. . . . Itaque ut
      paucis concludam: acta sanctorum qualia sua aetate vulgata erant,
      collegit, juxta ordinem Kalendarii disposuit ac edidit Jacobus, si quae
      sint in iis fabulae, harum auctor censendus non est" (ibid.).

17   The Dominican authorities in question, all mentioned by Echard and
      most of his successors in the order, are Melchior Cano, Berengar of
      Landorra, and Bernard Gui. The nature and importance of their verdicts
      on the *Legenda* will be discussed in Chapters 2 and 3 of this study.

18   In a passage first published in 1725, the Bollandists cite some rather
      compelling evidence for the tendency of Jacobus's admirers, some
      Dominicans among them, to anticipate the Holy See in naming him
      beatus: "Jacobus de Voragine Genuensis archiepiscopus, ex Ordine S.
      Dominici assumptus, satis communiter a suis *Beati* titulo insignitur,
      sicque hoc die refertur in Diario Marchesii: quin et imaginem altari, ejus
      nomini dicato impositam asserit Joannes Michaël Pius, in Dominicana
      progenie pag. 422, appensaque ibidem anathemata etc. Scimus, virum
      multa doctrinae et sanctitatis laude claruisse, mortuum anno 1298;
      verum *Beati* aut *Sancti* honores legitime permissos aut decretos hactenus
      ignoramus" (*Acta SS,* July, 4 [rept. Paris, 1868]: 4).

19   "Mais de tous les Ouvrages de notre Auteur, le plus connu (quoique sans
      doute le moins estimable) est son Recueil des Vies des Saints, qu'il
      apelloit une *Légende*" (Antoine Touron, *Histoire des hommes illustres
      de l'Ordre de saint Dominique,* 1 [Paris, 1743]: 594).
          Touron begins by disputing Baillet's charge that the order pretended
      Jacobus's beatification already to be a reality: "Il y a long-tems, il est
      vrai, qu'on a fait des démarches pour obtenir la Béatification du
      Serviteur de Dieu: le Saint Siége s'expliquera quand il le jugera à propos.
      Nous ne prévenons point son jugement: nous l'atendons" (pp. 593-94).
      Presumably Touron was not aware of the note that had appeared in the
      Acta Sanctorum some eighteen years earlier.

20   The tradition crediting Jacobus with the first Italian translation of the Bible has had a long life, despite the fact that no such achievement is mentioned either in Jacobus's own list of his works or in the early catalogs of Dominican writers. Echard expressed doubt on the subject (*Scriptores Ordinis Praedicatorum,* 1:459), but Touron seems to have taken for granted not only that Sixtus of Siena (1520-69) was correct in attributing such a translation to Jacobus, but that he had actually found it (see, e.g., pp. 585, 594, and 600 of Touron's discussion). A number of Jacobus's later admirers, including Anfossi and Richardson, made even more of the supposed Biblical translation than Touron did. Only in the past forty years have most standard reference works dropped it from the list of writings attributed to Jacobus.

21   "M. Baillet s'est montré encore moins équitable, ou moins scrupuleux que M. Dupin. Si celui-ci a fait peu de cas des Ouvrages de l'Archevêque de Gênes, il n'a pas laissé de reconnoître que l'Auteur étoit très-estimable par la pureté de sa vie, par sa piété, sur-tout par sa grande charité. Celui-là au contraire ne reconnoît ni vertu, ni probité, ni rien enfin de louable, dans un Prélat qui a mérité tant de louanges" (Touron, *Histoire,* 1:600).
     For Baillet's criticism of the *Legenda,* see his *Vies des saints,* 2d ed., vol. 1 (Paris: Louis Roulland, 1704), cols. 35-37.

22   See the anonymous "Le bienheureux Jacques de Voragine," in *L'année dominicaine,* 7 (Paris, 1895): 253-62.

23   Thus, e.g., Anfossi implies that all the Renaissance critics of the *Legenda* were attempting to win glory for themselves by mocking and insulting Jacobus; and he not only accuses Baillet of having presumed to condemn Jacobus without having read his works, a charge apparently originated by Touron, but also raises questions about Baillet's personal character and intellectual credentials as a Catholic (Filippo Anfossi, *Memorie istoriche appartenenti alla vita del Beato Jacopo da Varagine* [Genoa, 1816], pp. 84 and 91).

24   "Che se al fin qui detto si aggiunga, che lo scopo del B. Jacopo da Varagine non era di esaminare gli Atti dei Santi, e distinguere i veri dai falsi, ma solamente di unire in un corpo quanto aveva ritrovato negli altri Scrittori, e poteva essere conducente alla divozione, ed alla pietà; se vi si aggiungano i pregiudizj del suo secolo, ed il genio del Popolo per cui scriveva, e si osservi per ultimo, che in mezzo agli affari importantissimi, che ebbe a trattare, e che l'opprimevano da ogni parte, non aveva ozio abbastanza, nè libertà da esaminare ogni cosa sulle bilancie di una critica più rigorosa; ognun vede quanto ingiusta sia, e irragionevole la censura, che fanno di lui, e della sua Leggenda que' Critici soverchiamente severi" (ibid., p. 94).

25   Gustave Brunet, "Notice préliminaire," *La Légende dorée par Jacques de Voragine,* trans. G[ustave] B[runet] (1843; rept. Paris, 1906), 1:1.

26   The first edition of Mâle's work (Paris, 1898) is rather rare, but the
      critical passages on the *Legenda* are retained with only insignificant
      variants in at least the second and third French editions (Paris, 1902 and
      1910). I quote from the English translation by Dora Nussey (*The Gothic
      Image: Religious Art in France in the Thirteenth Century* [1913; rept.
      New York, 1972]), pp. 273-74.

27   "Ce nom de *Légende dorée* était pour nous surtout un titre commode qui
      désigne tous les recueils de vies de saints en usage au moyen-âge" (Mâle,
      L'art religieux, p. 355). This note is omitted in Nussey's translation.

28   Marguerite de Waresquiel, *Le bienheureux Jacques de Voragine, auteur
      de la Légende dorée* (Paris, 1902); André Baudrillart, "La psychologie
      de la *Légende dorée,"* *Minerva* 5 (1902): 24-43; J.-C. Broussolle, "La
      Légende dorée," *L'université catholique,* n.s., 44 (1903): 321-57; *La
      Légende dorée de Jacques de Voragine,* trans. J.-B. M. Roze (Paris,
      1902); *La Légende dorée,* trans. Teodor de Wyzewa (Paris, 1902). My
      quotations and page references from Wyzewa are taken from vol. 1 of
      the Librairie Académique Perrin edition (Paris, 1960).

29   "Elle a pour objet de faire sortir, des bibliothèques des couvents, les
      trésors de vérité sainte qu'y ont accumulés des siècles de recherches et de
      discussions, et de donner à ces trésors la forme la plus simple, la plus
      claire possible, et en même temps la plus attrayante: afin de les mettre à
      la portée d'âmes naïves et passionnées qui aussitôt s'efforcent, par mille
      moyens, de témoigner la joie extrême qu'elles éprouvent à les
      accueillir."

30   "Du treizième siècle jusqu'au seizième, la *Légende Dorée* reste, par
      excellence, le livre du peuple.
            "Et je dois ajouter qu'il n'y a peut-être pas de livre, non plus, qui ait
      exercé sur le peuple une action plus profonde, ni plus bienfaisante. Car
      le 'petit' livre du bienheureux Jacques de Voragine . .. a été, pendant ces
      trois siècles, une source inépuisable d'idéal pour la chrétienté. En
      rendant la religion plus ingénue, plus populaire et plus pittoresque, il l'a
      presque revêtue d'un pouvoir nouveau."

31   "Ainsi que le dit très sagement Bollandus, rien n'est plus injuste que
      d'attribuer à Jacques de Voragine la responsabilité d'affirmations qu'il
      a, toutes, puisées dans des ouvrages antérieurs, en les contrôlant de son
      mieux chaque fois qu'il a pu, ou en nous faisant part des doutes qu'elles
      lui inspiraient."

32   "Si, au lieu d'écrire sa *Légende* en italien, il l'a écrite dans un honnête
      latin de sacristie, dont les humanistes de la Renaissance ont eu beau jeu à
      rallier la médiocrité, c'est que, sans doute, sous cette forme, il a su que
      son livre pourrait se répandre plus loin, et ouvrir à plus d'âmes la maison
      de Dieu" (pp. 18-19).

33 "Pour citer encore une expression de Bollandus, le tort de Vivès et des autres détracteurs de la *Légende Dorée* a été 'de vouloir critiquer ce qu'ils ne comprenaient pas et qu'ils ignoraient.' Ils ignoraient qu'un érudit du XIIIᵉ siècle ne disposait point des mêmes moyens d'information que ceux dont ils disposaient, trois ou quatre siècles plus tard: c'est-à-dire qu'il manquait de beaucoup de ceux qu'ils avaient, mais que, peut-être aussi, il en avait d'autres qui désormais leur manquaient" (pp. 20-21).

34 " . . . ne comprenaient pas, en effet, que des erreurs comme celles qu'ils signalaient dans la *Légende Dorée* n'avaient point, pour un lecteur catholique, la même importance que pour ce ministre calviniste qui hantait leurs rêves."

35 "Sous l'influence du protestantisme et du jansénisme, nombre d'excellents catholiques, alors, estimaient imprudent de trop prêcher au peuple la bonté de Dieu. . . . Les philosophes insistaient sur la différence essentielle de la bonté divine et de l'humaine. Et tous, d'une façon générale, ils s'efforçaient plutôt d'effrayer les hommes que de les rassurer. Peut-être, dans ces conditions, la *Légende Dorée* leur aura-t-elle paru trop consolante, je veux dire faite pour nous donner une notion trop inexacte de l'éternelle justice?"

36 Again relying on the combined testimony of the major catalogs for the research libraries of the United States, the British Library, and the Bibliothèque Nationale, one finds 9 editions in German, 1 each in Polish and modern Italian, 2 each in Dutch and modern Spanish, 3 in modern English, and 3 more in Caxton's slightly archaic language—a total of 21 (or 18) to set against the 18 modern French editions in this century. The inclusion of the Bibliothèque Nationale holdings does not bias the result; even without them, the preponderance of French editions is unmistakable.

37 Ernest C. Richardson, "The Influence of the Golden Legend on Pre-Reformation Culture History," *Papers of the American Society of Church History* 1 (1888): 237-48.

38 Idem, "Jacobus de Voragine and the Golden Legend," *Princeton Theological Review* 1 (1903): 267-81.

39 Hippolyte Delehaye, "Bulletin des publications hagiographiques," nos. 5-7, *Anal. Boll.* 22 (1903): 81. "Sauf ces réserves," Delehaye conclut, "l'introduction de M. de W. est instructive et agréable à lire."

40 "En effet, dans ses notes et ses 'recherches sur les sources,' feu le chanoine R. a accumulé les échantillons d'une érudition si déconcertante que c'est à se demander lequel des deux, de l'auteur ou de l'éditeur, a écrit au moyen âge" (ibid., p. 82).

41 The article in question, a review of Wyzewa's edition of the *Legenda,* is "The Golden Legend," *Church Quarterly Review* 57 (1903): 29-52. For

Delehaye's reaction, see "Bulletin des publications hagiographiques," nos. 67-71, *Anal. Boll.* 23 (1904): 325.

42   In fact, the anonymous critic does not just deplore the *Legenda* itself but also the old legends which it supposedly typifies, the ignorance of the whole period which cherished such literature, and the Catholic clergy who produced it. The breadth of his attack is well illustrated in his opening salvo: "We question whether it would be possible to meet with a volume of professedly Christian literature which transports the reader to an atmosphere more strangely different from that of our time than the *Golden Legend* of the Blessed Jacobus de Voragine. . . . [The author's] standard of holiness, his overpowering love of the marvellous, his entire lack of the critical faculty, his unhesitating adoption of the most incredible legends gathered indiscriminately from diverse sources, are but typical examples of the tone and spirit of the mediaeval monkish chronicler" ("The Golden Legend," pp. 29-30).

43   Thus, although he does not question Jacobus's authorship of the fanciful etymologies, Delehaye half approves of Wyzewa's decision to omit this potential source of merriment: "La plupart de ces interprétations exercent sur nous un effet irrésistible de bonne humeur, mais disposent mal à lire la légende. D'autre part, on manque d'un élément important pour juger de la mentalité et de la 'science' du bon Jacques de Voragine" ("Bulletin," 22:82).

44   "Ceux qui abordent la *Légende dorée* avec les préoccupations de l'historien et du critique se trouveront déroutés dès les premières pages, et ils seront exposés à exhaler leur mauvaise humeur à la manière de Vivès, de Melchior Cano, de Launoi et de beaucoup d'autres qui se sont placés pour la juger à un faux point de vue.
       "C'est ce que M. de W[yzewa] semble avoir parfaitement compris."

45   "Nous avons dit ici même (XXII, 81) comment l'attention du public a été attirée récemment sur le livre autrefois si populaire, puis si injustement oublié, de Jacques de Voragine. On continue à s'intéresser à la vieille Légende, et selon qu'on la replace dans son milieu et qu'on lui reconnaît son véritable caractère, ou qu'on la juge à un point de vue qui n'a pu être ni celui de l'époque ni celui de l'auteur, on exprime librement son enthousiasme ou son dédain" ("Bulletin," 23:325).

46   This and the subsequent quotations of Delehaye's book are from the translation by Donald Attwater, *The Legends of the Saints* (New York, 1962), pp. 180-81. In this instance, however, I have revised a little of Attwater's wording, substituting "accurately sums up" for his "is a perfect example of"; the original French version reads, "Bien longtemps on a traité la Légende Dorée, qui resume si exactement l'oeuvre hagiographique du moyen âge, avec un superbe dédain."

47   "Le livre est destiné à fournir au peuple des leçons et des exemples
      directement inspirés de la parole de Jésus-Christ. Si l'histoire n'est pas
      toujours bien exacte, à coup sûr, on y trouve le testament le plus
      authentique légué par douze siècles de christianisme." The author of the
      DTC's article on Jacobus is J. Baudot.

48   Alban Butler, *The Lives of the Saints,* ed. Herbert Thurston and Donald
      Attwater, 7 (London, 1932): 173-74.

49   Umberto M. Carmarino, "Giacomo da Varazze," *Bibliotheca
      sanctorum,* vol. 6 (Rome, 1965), cols. 424-25. Carmarino describes the
      Legenda as a "raccolta di narrazioni e leggende attinte alla S. Scrittura,
      ai SS. Padri, alle storie e alla tradizione orale, dove centinaia di creature
      viventi nella piú intima familiarità con Dio mostrano, in forma sensibile
      e concreta, la bellezza dell'ideale evangelico." In the final paragraph of
      Les légendes hagiographiques, Delehaye had written that the saints of
      legend "vivent, dès ici-bas, dans la familiarité de Dieu" and that "leur
      vie est, en effet, la réalisation concrète de l'esprit évangélique, et . . . rend
      sensible cet idéal sublime" (pp. 259-60).

50   The only exception I have found in the 78 subsequent volumes of the
      Analecta Bollandiana is a single sentence that appeared in 1929.
      Reviewing Paul Monceaux's *La vraie Légende dorée,* a collection of
      authentic accounts of early Christian martyrs, Maurice Coens expressed
      his agreement with Monceaux on the superiority of such documents to
      "la prestigieuse *Legenda aurea,* compilation d'anecdotes souvent
      suspectes et dont la naïveté va parfois 'jusqu'à la niaiserie'"(47:146).

51   "Dans les *Légendes hagiographiques* . . . , le P. Delehaye, peu suspect
      assurément de répudier le sens critique, . . . reprochait à l'humaniste
      Vivès d'avoir été trop dur à l'égard de J. de Varagine et terminait par ces
      mots: 'la légende, comme toute poésie, peut prétendre à un degré de
      vérité plus élevé que l'histoire.' M. Z[uidweg] n'admet pas cette
      appréciation. C'est pourtant celle des historiens qui ont étudié avec le
      plus de pénétration l'esprit du moyen âge, dont la *Legenda aurea* est une
      des productions les plus caractéristiques" (Baudouin de Gaiffier, in
      Anal. Boll. 61 [1943]: 315).
          See also 54 (1936): 441, where Richardson's glowing assessment of the
      Legenda is endorsed again, as it had been in Delehaye's 1904 review.

52   This notice, again by Gaiffier, is entitled "Légende dorée ou Légende de
      plomb?", given a page to itself, and placed among the major articles
      rather than the reviews; see *Anal. Boll.* 83 (1965): 350.

53   At the end of the nineteenth century Pierce Butler made a good start at
      reconstructing the history of the book and its reputation, in *Legenda
      aurea—Légende dorée—Golden Legend* (Baltimore, 1899), pp. 1-20, but
      remarkably little has been done to correct and extend Butler's research.
      Richardson's *Materials for a Life of Jacopo da Varagine* (4 vols. in 1

[New York, 1935]) is fatally flawed by Richardson's decision to publish his conclusions without documenting them. The relatively recent *Die Legenda aurea und ihr Verfasser Jacobus de Voragine* by Maria von Nagy and N. Christoph de Nagy (Bern and Munich, 1971) makes no pretense whatever to be a work of scholarship; the authors' stated purpose is just to revive the *Legenda* for a contemporary audience, and they tend to repeat the most enthusiastic claims for the book without questioning their validity. To my knowledge, in fact, only one scholarly monograph on the *Legenda* has ever been published: Jacobus J. A. Zuidweg's *De Werkwijze van Jacobus de Voragine in de Legenda aurea* (Oud-Beijerland, 1941), a doctoral dissertation which Gaiffier faulted on a number of grounds in the review mentioned above. A few substantial articles have appeared on such issues as the date of the *Legenda* and its use of particular sources; especially noteworthy is André Wilmart's "Saint Ambroise et la Légende dorée," *Ephemerides liturgicae,* n.s., 10 (1936): 169-206. Significantly, however, most of the scholars who have shed new light on the book during this century have done so as a byproduct of their research on other subjects. Besides Poncelet's seminal article on the legendary of Peter Calo, Dondaine's work on the legendary of Jean de Mailly, and Görlach's *Textual Tradition of the South English Legendary,* I should mention the massive edition of Jacobus's chronicle of Genoa by Giovanni Monleone (Rome, 1941), which begins with a systematic survey of Jacobus's life and the other writings attributed to him, and Helen C. White's *Tudor Books of Saints and Martyrs* (Madison, Wis., 1963), which presents some illuminating information on the later reputation of the *Legenda* in England.

54   *The Golden Legend of Jacobus de Voragine,* translated and adapted from the Latin by Granger Ryan and Helmut Ripperger (1941; rept. New York, 1969).

55   George V. O'Neill, "Biographical Introduction," *The Golden Legend: Lives of the Saints* (Cambridge, 1914), p. 8.

56   Richardson, *Materials for a Life of Jacopo da Varagine,* 1:55-56, 46-47.

Chapter 2: The Fall of the *Legenda* Reexamined

1   Seybolt, "Fifteenth-Century Editions of the *Legenda aurea,*" pp. 328-31.

2   Most dramatic are the data for Cologne, where there was an edition in 1470, new ones almost annually from 1476 to 1485, a gap of five years before the edition of January 5, 1490, and then silence. For Ulm, Seybolt's list shows a similar gap between the early editions (three before about 1481 and possibly another in 1482) and the last one in 1488. For Nuremberg the picture is less clear, since there is no such warning signal before the 1496 edition; but had publication of the Latin *Legenda* continued at anything like the original rate of three or four new editions

a decade, even the relatively incomplete catalogs on which we must rely for the sixteenth century would surely have registered some of them.

So far as our lists indicate, publication of the Latin *Legenda* may also have ceased at Basel before the end of the fifteenth century. The last edition cited by Seybolt belongs to 1495.

3 The only Spanish editions in any of our customary lists are the one published at Burgos around 1500 and a few in the twentieth century. Paul Meyer mentions another one, published at Barcelona in 1524 under the title *Flos sanctorum,* in "La traduction provençale de la *Légende dorée,*" *Romania* 27 (1898): 95. Seybolt found three verified editions of the Bohemian *Pasionál,* dated, respectively, 1475-79, c.1480, and 1495; the catalogs show the last of these and no other edition in this language until its reprint in 1927.

4 The catalogs, which as usual fall somewhat short of Seybolt's figures, show a total of twenty-seven fifteenth-century editions of the *Leben der Heiligen/Passionael* in High German, Low German, and Dutch; for the sixteenth century, however, the figure drops to eight editions in these languages. Taking them separately, one finds no fewer Low German editions (three) in the catalogs between 1501 and 1517 than between 1480 and 1500. In Dutch, however, there is a marked discrepancy between the eight editions attested before 1501 and the three thereafter. And in High German the catalogs show just two sixteenth-century editions, dated 1507 and 1517, as against no fewer than sixteen from the period between 1470 and 1500.

5 The catalogs show seven French vernacular editions between 1470 and 1490, five between 1491 and 1499, just one between 1500 and 1510, and then a revival which gradually runs down: four new editions in ten years (1511-20), followed by four in fifteen years (1521-35), and the last four in nineteen (1536-54). In the appendix to her article "Jean de Vignay: Un traducteur du XIVe siècle," *Romania* 75 (1954): 382-83, Christine Knowles provides a fuller listing of the French vernacular editions which shows the same pattern. Except for two editions whose dates cannot even be estimated from the meager information available, Knowles' list includes none which do not clearly belong either to the fifteenth century (twenty editions) or to the period from 1511 to 1554 (fourteen editions).

The defensive titles in the Latin editions and in a few vernacular ones are discussed in Chapter 3, below.

6 The catalogs show five Italian vernacular editions in the fifteenth century (c.1475, 1477, 1481, 1487, and 1494), five more between 1501 and 1520 (1503, 1505, 1511, 1514, and 1518), just one between 1520 and the beginning of the Council of Trent (1533), and six thereafter (1557, 1571, 1583, 1592, 1607, and 1613).

7 An unusually full and careful account of these events is found in Nicéron's *Mémoires,* 13 (Paris, 1730): 184-87; the original author of the

account Nicéron gives is identified as one Father le Pelletier, a canon of St. Jacques à Provins. See also the account by Jean de Launoy in his *Regii Navarrae gymnasii Parisiensis historia,* pt. 1 (Paris, 1677), pp. 704-5.

8   The source in question is Eugène Haag and Emile Haag, *La France protestante,* 4 (Paris, 1853): 557-59; in the second edition, revised by Henri Bordier (vol. 6 [Paris, 1888]), the article on Espence contains some major additions and qualifications. In a recent and more plausible interpretation by Donald Nugent, the fact that Espence was "hailed before the tribunal of the Sorbonne and compelled to retract several unorthodox remarks" is taken to illustrate the suspicions directed against Erasmian moderates in a contentious time; see *Ecumenism in the Age of the Reformation* (Cambridge, Mass., 1974), p. 134.

9   The originator of this claim may have been Jacques Auguste de Thou (1553-1617), a French statesman and great admirer of Espence who dramatized the injustice done when Espence was passed over for a cardinal's hat by ascribing no reason to his opponents except the minor flap over the *Legenda.* See book 16 of Thou's *Historia sui temporis;* in the French translation available to me, *Histoire universelle . . . depuis 1543 jusqu'en 1607* ([Paris], 1734), the relevant passage is found in vol. 2, pp. 623-24. Touron takes Thou's story as firm proof that "encore vers le milieu du seiziéme siécle la Légende avoit de grands défenseurs, même parmi les Savans" (*Histoire,* 1:597); Anfossi, *Memorie istoriche,* pp. 89-90, and the anonymous later Dominican account of Jacobus, "Le bienheureux Jacques de Voragine," p. 261, follow him closely.

10 Eric W. Kemp's *Canonization and Authority in the Western Church* (London, 1948) is full of fascinating detail about the early efforts to restrain and regulate the cult of the saints, including conciliar legislation against abuses like the veneration of false martyrs and the unauthorized translation of relics, and attempts by individual prelates to enforce the canons. Kemp also makes it clear, however, that such efforts were made only sporadically during the Middle Ages and even the Renaissance; evidently most authorities saw no need to intervene in the growth of a saint's cult unless it was arousing some troublesome controversy.

    In a more recent study, André Vauchez, *La sainteté en Occident aux derniers siècles du Moyen Age* (Rome, 1981), pp. 71-118, emphasizes the rarity with which the late-medieval papacy saw fit to canonize new saints, or even to initiate formal hearings on their lives and miracles; meanwhile, new cults continued to proliferate, few of them overseen by any higher authority than the diocesan bishop.

11 Kemp provides several nice examples of early medieval bishops who admitted new saints to the calendar on the strength of some unidentified relics and a vision (pp. 29-31). A number of other saints had their origins in mistakes of one kind or another. The historical Cecilia, for example,

may have done nothing more spectacular than found a church, but the location of her tomb apparently led a later generation of Christians to imagine her a martyr and concoct a legend which won wide acceptance; see Delehaye's *Etude sur le légendier romain* (Brussels, 1936), pp. 73-86. In other instances, a cultus might begin with nothing more solid than a popular romance which readers mistook for sacred history. Besides the famous case of Barlaam and Josaphat, who started as characters in a Buddhist legend, one recalls the apparently literary origins of such saints as Christopher and the allegorical sisters Faith, Hope, and Charity.

12   The point is memorably illustrated in the chapter of Delehaye's *Légendes hagiographiques* entitled "Le dossier d'un saint," which traces the legend of Saint Procopius from its original form, as set down by Eusebius, through a series of revisions so drastic that they presented the Middle Ages with a Saint Procopius who no longer bore the least resemblance to Eusebius's Palestinian martyr and was therefore considered a different person.

13   Hippolyte Delehaye, *Work of the Bollandists* (Princeton, 1922), esp. pp. 120-22, 146-47, 151-52.

14   Despite the personal conservatism of both Luther and Henry VIII with regard to such matters, their followers so quickly took a hard line against Catholic "idolatries" that statues and images of the saints were burned at Wittenberg as early as 1522 and the leading English shrines destroyed in 1538. As for the traditional reliance on the saints as intercessors, the Augsburg Confession in 1530 already foreshadowed Calvin's insistence that to invoke any saint was to violate the biblical teaching which named Christ the unique mediator between mankind and God.

15   See Pierre Féret, *La faculté de théologie de Paris et ses docteurs les plus célèbres, Epoque moderne,* 1 (Paris, 1900): 168-70. Espence himself seems not to have been present when his colleagues subscribed to the pledge (ibid., p. 239).

16   Perhaps the most persuasive testimony to this effect is that of Charles du Plessis d'Argentré, whose *Collectio judiciorum de novis erroribus* (Paris, 1724-36), 2:137-38, ascribes the convening of the tribunal to Espence himself and does not even bother to list the "inutiles" accusations of which he cleared himself on this occasion. Later authorities who have refused to take the accusations seriously include Féret (*La faculté de théologie de Paris,* 2:103) and A. Humbert (*DTC,* vol. 5, pt. 1 [1924], col. 604).

17   On this point the accounts in Nicéron's *Mémoires* and Launoy's *Regii Navarrae gymnasii Parisiensis historia* are again more thoughtful and more sensitive to the issues involved than most later sources.

18   As has already been noted, the Dominican defenders of Jacobus

responded with some heat to Baillet's allegations about Jacobus's personal character, but not to criticism of the book itself.

19   The rapidity with which Catholic scholarship matured, transcending the initial objective of refuting Protestants, is suggested by the progression from the *Annals* of Baronius around the end of the sixteenth century to the painstaking research in which the Maurists and the Bollandists were engaged by 1650.

20   There are convenient summary accounts of Launoy's life and writings in the *DTC* and in the *Dictionnaire des lettres françaises, XVIIe siècle* (Paris, 1954). The more detailed accounts in Nicéron's *Mémoires,* 32 (Paris, 1735): esp. 93-109, and Féret's *Faculté de théologie de Paris, Epoque moderne,* 5 (Paris, 1907): 5-9, 11-13, and 15-16, provide a good deal of additional information about his role in discrediting some of the old legends about the history of the church in France—and about the astounding barrage of angry pamphlets with which other churchmen attempted to protect them. As for the popular caricature of Launoy as the great "dislodger [*dénicheur*] of saints," the copious notes in Pierre Bayle's *Dictionaire historique et critique,* 5th ed. (Amsterdam, 1740), 3: esp. 64-65, report a number of current anecdotes and sayings on the subject; Féret (pp. 4-5, n. 5) supplies further examples.

21   Baillet, the son of a poor family, had only the formal education that could be provided in the schools at Beauvais, but in his capacity as librarian to the eminent Chrétien-François de Lamoignon (1644-1709) he studied a prodigious number of books, produced an analytical catalog of his patron's library that ran to 32 volumes in folio, and published substantial works of research on history and literary subjects; see, e.g., the account in Nicéron's *Mémoires,* 3 (Paris, 1729): 25-35. The works most pertinent here, his treatise *De la devotion à la sainte Vierge & du culte qui lui est dû* (Paris, 1694) and the more substantial *Vies des saints* (Paris, 1701), were sufficiently respectable to earn a lengthy and approving summary in Dupin's highly orthodox *Nouvelle bibliothèque des auteurs ecclésiastiques,* 18 (rept. Utrecht, 1731): 284-96. Another churchman's laudatory verdict on the *Vies des saints* is quoted in Nicéron's *Mémoires,* 10 (Paris, 1731): 128.

22   The *DTC,* which reports these reactions against Baillet's work in vol. 2, pt. 1, cols. 36-37, neglects to account for the fact that the *Vies des saints* was reissued in its entirety in 1715-16 (less than ten years after its first two volumes appeared on the Index) and again in 1724 and 1739. Apparently the ban was either lifted or ignored in France.

23   A brief but important commentary on the errors of Launoy and Baillet is found in Baudouin de Gaiffier's *Etudes critiques d'hagiographie et d'iconologie* (Brussels, 1967), pp. 298-302; the discussion, which explores the problems confronting all such scholars in the later seventeenth century, is aptly titled, "Entre Charybde et Scylla." As

Gaiffier notes, the view of Launoy as an excessively pitiless critic seems to have been shared by Daniel Papebroch, one of the great Bollandists of the early period, who described him as a "learned and irascible man" ("vir doctus et acer") who had won public notoriety by too passionately attacking commonly held beliefs about the saints (p. 301). For other scholars' assessments of Launoy, see Dupin's *Nouvelle bibliothèque,* 18:62, and the verdicts quoted in the *DTC.* As for Baillet, one need only note the contentiousness manifested in his criticism of the *Legenda,* which rapidly becomes an attack on the character of Jacobus and the integrity of the Dominicans of Baillet's own time.

24   "Habebat meliora scribenda (Divus Thomas) & subodoratus etiam, ut erat emunctae naris, aliquid incerti, aut minus verisimilis, ex medicorum praecepto, malum bene positum noluisset primus movere: atque ista longa traditione rata & firma, quae nihil obsunt fidei, prosunt etiam pietati, in disputationem revocare, credidisset pertinere ad illius generis quaestiones ab Apostolo damnatas, quae lites generant, non aedificationem."

    Bayle's dictionary, which supplies this quotation in note Q to its account of Launoy, identifies the source as the *Apologia Ordinis Praedicatorum*—presumably meaning Baron's *Libri quinque apologetici pro religione, utraque theologia, moribus ac juribus Ordinis Predicatorum* (Paris, 1666)—vol. 1, sec. 2:120-21.

25   "Je sçay bien que la pluspart de ceux qui aiment la paix et l'union de l'Eglise, desapprouvent ces disputes, et croyent qu'il est plus à propos de laisser les peuples dans leurs pieuses erreurs, que de les troubler par de vains scrupules, qu'on tâche d'imprimer dans leurs esprits" (quoted in Gaiffier, *Etudes critiques,* p. 301).

26   As the Bollandists have frequently pointed out, such falsifications could arise in a number of ways, not all of them nearly so deliberate and culpable as a modern reader might imagine. For a useful overview of the subject, see Gaiffier's "Mentalité de l'hagiographe médiéval d'après quelques travaux récents," *Anal. Boll.* 86 (1968): esp. 392-96.

27   Most of Launoy's own writings were published only in Latin, and in an eccentric and uncommonly difficult Latin, at that. Among the counterattacks by his opponents, however, were such vernacular pamphlets as François Gerson's *Saincte apologie pour sainct Denys Aréopagite, sainct Lazare, sainct Trophime, et autres saincts apostres des Gaules* (Paris, 1642) and Jean-Baptiste Guesnay's *Triomphe de la Magdeleine, en la créance et vénération de ses sainctes reliques en Provence* (1647; 2d ed., Lyons, 1657).

28   My principal source for this incident, the detailed account in Delehaye's *Work of the Bollandists,* pp. 122-37, is well worth reading at first hand. Gaiffier provides more documentation on the background to the quarrel and on the larger issues involved in *Etudes critiques,* pp. 302-6.

29   Delehaye reports a number of them and gives a general description of the line of argument adopted by Father Sebastian (*Work of the Bollandists,* pp. 124-28).

30   Ibid., p. 129. Delehaye notes that the printed sheet bearing this decree, in four languages, has been preserved in the Bollandists' library.

31   This is the chronological sequence in the most reliable accounts. Echard, however, neglects to indicate how much time passed between the destruction of the pamphlet and James Lacop's martyrdom, saying only, "ipseque priusquam cruci appenderetur impium suum libellum in ignem conjecit" (*Scriptores Ordinis Praedicatorum,* 1:456). And later defenders of Jacobus tend to convert this ambiguity into an improbable little drama whereby the martyr consigns the pamphlet to the flames as he ascends the very scaffold; see, e.g., Touron's *Histoire,* 1:596, and "Le bienheureux Jacques de Voragine," p. 261.

32   "Quo iconomachiae tempestas aliquot praecipua Belgii nostri loca pervasit, inter alios alibi multos, Lacopius quoque, Deo sic permittente, qui electis suis omnia cooperatur in bonum, ab haereticis misere seductus ac male persuasus, primum apud Fratres id monasterio linguam suam adversus Ecclesiae Catholicae sacrosancta dogmata juveniliter ac petulanter, ne dicam impie laxavit: moxque monasterii desertor, apud haereticos concionandi munus subivit; et libellum haereticum procaci stylo conscripsit, titulo Deflorationis aureae Legendae" (*Acta SS,* July, 2 [rept. Paris, 1867]: 819). Estius's account was first published in 1603.

33   On Estius's life and achievements, see e.g. the account by L. Salembier in the *DTC.* Salembier mentions the unusual care with which Estius's history of the Gorcum martyrs was researched and the respectful attention it won both from the authorities in Rome and from the Bollandists; he himself, however, notes one instance in which Estius overlooked an important piece of information.

34   "Dieu permit que l'opuscule ne fût pas publié" (Hubert Meuffels, *Les martyrs de Gorcum,* 3d ed. [Paris, 1922], p. 130).

35   "He had a quick and subtle mind, which he exercised diligently in the humanities and the study of languages" ("Prompto subtilique fuit ingenio; quod et humanioribus disciplinis, et linguarum studio diligenter excoluit" [*Acta SS,* July, 2:819]).

36   Such Protestant attacks as I have found belong to the period after 1560 and tend simply to exploit the existing notoriety of the *Legenda* in order to make a point about their real target, the church which had used it for so long; some representative instances are quoted in Chapter 3.

37   There are brief but informative accounts of Witzel's career in such standard sources as the *DTC* and the *New Catholic Encyclopedia* (New York, 1967). John Patrick Dolan provides a fuller picture of his life and ideas in *History of the Reformation* (New York, 1965), pp. 371-82, and

in an earlier study, *The Influence of Erasmus, Witzel, and Cassander in the Church Ordinances and Reform Proposals of the United Duchees of Cleve during the Middle Decades of the Sixteenth Century,* Reformationsgeschichtliche Studien und Texte no. 83 (Münster/Westfalen, 1958), esp. pp. 30-86.

38   Among the most useful sources on the career of Espence are Nicéron's *Mémoires,* 13:183-209, and Féret's *Faculté de théologie de Paris, Epoque moderne,* 1:231-40 and 2:101-17. For a fuller and more sympathetic view of Espence's role in the Colloquy of Poissy in 1561, see Nugent's *Ecumenism in the Reformation,* pp. 134-42 et passim.

39   The text of this proposal can be found in book 29 of Thou's *Historia sui temporis* (vol. 4, pp. 162-63, in the edition already cited). Worth noting is its testimony that the French proponents of compromise believed, like Witzel, that the solution lay in the knowledge of church history. Thus images of the Trinity are forbidden altogether, on the grounds that their use "est absolument condamné par l'Ecriture, les Conciles & les SS. Peres"; and veneration of the Cross—for which there are clear precedents in the patristic period—is explicitly permitted.

40   "Ne fût-ce qu'en faveur des faibles qui se scandalisent facilement" (Féret, *Faculté de théologie de Paris,* 1:239). The conference itself is described in more detail by Nugent in *Ecumenism in the Reformation,* pp. 190-98. Nicéron presents an entirely different version of the story, attributing the Faculty's intervention to some "Livre Anonyme sur le culte des Images" Espence had been accused of writing, and failing to mention the events at Saint-Germain; so does the brief summary in the *DTC.* But the joint testimony of Féret and Nugent seems quite convincing, not least because they cite different sets of early sources on this conference.

41   Although Vives' fame declined rather drastically after about 1650, the past century has seen a revival of interest in his work and its influence. Besides the vast bibliography in Spanish, one can find a surprising number of scholarly studies in German and at least a handful of important ones in English. Especially noteworthy are Robert P. Adams, *The Better Part of Valor: More, Erasmus, Colet, and Vives on Humanism, War, and Peace, 1496-1535* (Seattle, 1962), and the full-scale study of Vives' life and writings by Carlos G. Noreña, *Juan Luis Vives* (The Hague, 1970), whose express purpose is to "give Vives the familiarity and acclaim among English speaking people which he so justly deserves" (p. 14).

42   Noreña, *Vives,* esp. pp. 12-13, 175-99, and 275-99.

43   On this period of Vives' life, see Noreña, esp. pp. 113-20 and 128-31.

44   The account of Espence in the *DTC* notes simply that his moderate stance at the Etats d'Orleans in 1560 made him a target of attacks by

"catholiques intransigeants." Féret, *Faculté de théologie de Paris,*
2:109-11, provides a bit more information on the charges against him,
quoting several relevant passages from Espence's own *Apologie conten-
ant ample discours, exposition, response et deffense de deux conferences
avec les ministres* . . . (Paris, 1569). On the conflict between Witzel and
the forces that were victorious at Trent, one should read both Dolan's
account in *History of the Reformation,* pp. 381-82, and the more
complex and highly nuanced one by Emile Amann in the *DTC.*

45   The most accessible sources on Cano are the articles in Echard and
Quétif, *Scriptores Ordinis Praedicatorum,* 2 (1721): 176-78; Touron,
Histoire, 4 (1747): 193-204; and the *DTC,* the *Dictionnaire de
spiritualité,* and the *New Catholic Encyclopedia.*

46   "C'est le *De locis theologicis* qui a fait la réputation théologique de
Melchior Cano et l'a placé au premier rang des théologiens classiques.
Cette oeuvre, en effet, n'est pas seulement remarquable par la forme
littéraire qui l'égale aux plus belles productions de la Renaissance, ni par
la liberté d'esprit, la finesse de jugement, le sens critique et l'érudition de
son auteur; elle est surtout une création, et marque, à ce titre, une étape
dans l'histoire de la théologie" (*DTC,* vol. 2, pt. 2, col. 1539).

47   Edmond Vansteenberghe, *Le cardinal Nicolas de Cues* (Paris, 1920), p.
142.

48   The texts are edited by G. Meersseman in *MOPH,* vol. 18 (Rome, 1936);
for the entries on Jacobus, see p. 65, no. 65, and p. 74, no. 44.

49   As Poncelet pointed out ("Le légendier de Pierre Calo," p. 27, n. 2),
MS. Ff.V.31 in the University Library, Cambridge, which was copied in
1299, bears the title *Vite sanctorum auree compilate a quodam Fratre
Predicatore.*

50   The entry, no. 66, reads, "Fr. Iacobus de Voragine scripsit legendam
auream, sermones de tempore et de sanctis et de beata Virgine" (*MOPH*
18:29).

51   "Fr. Iacobus de Bonagine [*sic*], qui composuit plures sermones quibus
fratres utuntur communiter, fuit [archi]episcopus Ianuensis" (ibid., p.
9). Despite the unlikely spelling of the name, neither Meersseman nor
earlier authorities who studied this catalog seem to have had any doubt
that the Jacobus of this entry is the author of the *Legenda.*

52   "13. . . . fr. Thomas de Lentino composuit sermones bonos de
sanctis.
"14. Fr. Nicholaus de Byardo, Gallicus, sermones et distinctiones
utiles et morales, item summam de abstinentia.
"15. Fr. Iacobus de Voragine, Lombardus, vitas sanctorum novas et
grande opus sermonum, item Mariale.
"16. Fr. Nicholaus de Gorran, Gallicus, confessor regis Philippi,
postillas super Ecclesiasticum, super Matheum et super Lucam et super

epistolas Pauli valde aptas, item distinctiones bonas cum thematibus de dominicis et de sanctis.''

I quote from Thomas Kaeppeli's edition, *MOPH* 22 (1949): 36. This important catalog, entitled *De quatuor in quibus Deus Predicatorum Ordinem insignivit,* also lists Jacobus among the ''Prelati ecclesiarum de Ordine Predicatorum assumpti,'' mentioning his tenure as archbishop of Genoa and his earlier office as provincial prior for Lombardy, but not his writings. Given the modern legend that has grown up around Jacobus, it is perhaps worth mentioning that he is not listed among either the ''Magistri in theologia Parisius'' or the ''Predicatores gratiosi et famosi.''

53   Poncelet, ''Le légendier de Pierre Calo,'' p. 25. Poncelet refers to MS. A.564 at Rouen, which bears the title *Legenda sanctorum sub compendio a quodam fratre tradita.*

54   Ibid., p. 26. Echard, Touron, Anfossi, and ''Le bienheureux Jacques de Voragine'' also mention this early sign of dissatisfaction with the *Legenda.* Since Berengar's tenure as master general ran only from 1312 to 1317 or 1318, there is not much uncertainty about the date. On Berengar, see note 59, below.

55   ''Inpulit quoque me ad hoc ipsum obediencie meritum et astrinxit auctoritas superioris mei prelati, magistri ordinis Predicatorum, reverendi in Christo patris fratris Berengarii, qui, dum adhuc in ordine magisterio fungeretur, a quo interim in Compostellanum archiepiscopum est assumptus, vive vocis oraculo id ipsum michi imposuit et injunxit, absens quoque cohortatus est me sepius literis iteratis'' (general preface to Gui's *Speculum sanctorale,* as edited by Leopold Delisle in ''Notice sur les manuscrits de Bernard Gui,'' Appendix XX, *Notices et extraits* 27, pt. 2 [1879]: 423-24).

56   Ibid., pp. 274-86 and 436-37.

57   Poncelet, ''Le légendier de Pierre Calo,'' pp. 28-36, 38. I have omitted a few of the fourteenth-century compilations mentioned by Poncelet, either because their character is unclear from his description or because their contents are too limited to make them comparable with the *Legenda.* Guy Philippart's recent handbook, *Les légendiers latins et autres manuscrits hagiographiques* (Turnhout, Belgium, 1977), pp. 123-24, mentions three additional compilers of abridged legendaries in the fourteenth century, one of them a Dominican named Gerard de Wulich whose work may no longer be extant.

58   Gui's manual for inquisitors deals explicitly with each of these problems and additional ones as well. Delisle's ''Notice,'' Appendix XVII, pp. 402-15, reproduces the prefatory summary and table of contents found in two manuscripts of the manual.

59   Since Berengar (c.1262-c.1330) is relatively little known and tends to be
      omitted from the standard dictionaries of the church, some biographical
      information may be helpful here. By the time he was elected master
      general of the order, he had taught at several Dominican priories, been
      entrusted with the special independence and responsibilities of a
      preacher-general, earned the degrees of bachelor and master of theology
      at Paris, and served two terms as provincial prior for Toulouse—where
      Gui was already functioning as inquisitor. On Berengar's term as master
      general, which seems to have been marked by an unusual insistence on
      the religious knowledge needed by the friars, see D. A. Mortier, *Histoire
      des maîtres généraux de l'Ordre des frères Prêcheurs,* 2 (Paris, 1905):
      479-94, and William A. Hinnebusch, *History of the Dominican Order,* 2
      (New York, 1973): esp. 156-58. Worth noting are the measures he took
      to standardize Dominican teaching, establishing a system of close
      supervision over the lectors and writers of the order lest they depart from
      "the common doctrine of Thomas [Aquinas]" and "the common
      teaching of the Church" (Hinnebusch, p. 157). Other aspects of
      Berengar's career are covered a bit more fully in Echard and Quétif,
      Scriptores Ordinis Praedicatorum, 1:514-17.

60   Poncelet, "Le légendier de Pierre Calo," p. 36.

61   This two-volume legendary, entitled *Sanctuarium, seu Vitae Sanctorum,*
      was republished at Paris in 1910 with a new preface and a collection of
      early tributes to the excellence and importance of Mombrizio's works.

62   *Acta SS,* Jan., 1 (rept. Paris, 1867): xxi, col. 2.

63   "Aureas sanctorum vitas, post inclitam eorum vitam magnamque fidei
      constanciam, et virtutem atque bonorum operum usque in finem
      perseveranciam, summo sanctorum patrum studio investigatas, et
      codicibus atque apicibus studiosius commendatas, moderata presentis
      operis compendiositas conabitur explicare" (text from Delisle,
      "Notice," p. 421). So far as I know, it was Poncelet (p. 27) who first
      suggested that the opening words should be read as an allusion to
      Jacobus's book.

64   The first edition, entitled *De probatis sanctorum historiis,* was published
      in six volumes at Cologne (1570-75). The *DTC,* vol. 14, pt. 2, gives a
      useful assessment of its character and purpose, and also provides a
      wealth of information about the later editions, adaptations, and
      abridgements that extended the influence of this work across three
      centuries and much of the Western world.

Chapter 3: The Evaluation of Medieval Hagiography

1   "Il est Auteur de la Legende dorée, . . . dans laquelle il a ramasié sans
      critique & sans discernement quantité de faits la pluspart fabuleux"
      (Dupin, *Nouvelle bibliothèque des auteurs ecclésiastiques,* 10:85-86).

2   "La critique s'étant réveillée, & l'amour de la vérité ayant prévalu, cette Légende est tombée dans un grand mépris, à cause des Fables dont elle est remplie, & des Etymologies absurdes, par lesquelles commencent la plûpart des Vies. Il en faut moins acuser l'Auteur, que le mauvais goût de son siécle, où l'on ne cherchoit que le merveilleux." Touron, who quotes this passage at the end of his chapter on Jacobus (*Histoire,* 1:602-3), identifies the source as Fleury's *Histoire ecclésiastique* (1691-1723), bk. 89, n. 22.

3   See Delehaye's *Les légendes hagiographiques,* especially the chapter entitled "Classification des textes hagiographiques." My summary lumps together several categories in Delehaye's classification system without (I trust) falsifying his basic messages.

4   See esp. his second chapter, with its generalizations on the characteristics of the mass mind.

5   See, e.g., E. Catherine Dunn, "The Saint's Legend as History and as Poetry: An Appeal to Chaucer," *American Benedictine Review* 27 (1976): esp. 360-62.

6   The issues are laid out more comprehensively by Richard C. Trexler in a review article in *Speculum* 52 (1977): 1019-22.

7   Peter Brown, *The Cult of the Saints* (Chicago, 1981), pp. 12-20.

8   Benedicta Ward, *Miracles and the Medieval Mind* (Philadelphia, 1982), pp. 127-31.

9   All the details in my account are derived from Ward, pp. 82-88.

10 Vauchez, *La sainteté en Occident,* esp. pp. 215-20 and 257-87.

11 "La mort des saints, leurs funérailles, et leurs translations sont pour le peuple autant d'occasions d'avoir un contact direct avec le surnaturel et de se réjouir, dans le cadre d'une explosion de ferveur collective, pendant laquelle les oppositions entre les partis et les clans s'apaisent momentanément."

12 See, e.g., Vansteenberghe's summary of the ordinances of 7 February 1453 (*Nicolas de Cues,* pp. 141-42). The ordinances themselves were published in *Synodi Brixinenses, saeculi XV,* ed. G. Bickell (Innsbruck, 1880), pp. 33-38.

13 Vansteenberghe, *Nicolas de Cues,* p. 142; *Synodi Brixinenses,* pp. 45-46.

14 "Item ne populo praedicentur superstitiosa, quae in legenda lombardica habentur de S. Blasio, Barbara, Catharina, Dorothea, Margarita, etc." (*Synodi Brixinenses,* p. 41).

15 For the promises in question, see *Legenda aurea,* ed. Theodor Graesse, 3d ed. (Bratislava, 1890), pp. 168 (prosperity for anyone who annually offers a candle in a church named for Saint Blaise), 169 (maladies of the

throat healed for sufferers who call on Blaise), 402 (safe childbirth for women who call on Saint Margaret), 794 (Christ's own protection after death for those who honor the memory of Saint Catherine), 901 (remission of sins at the Judgment for those who honor the memory of Saint Barbara), and 911 (deliverance from earthly tribulations, including false accusations and poverty, and remission of sins at death for those who honor the memory of Saint Dorothea). Typically these guarantees are requested by the saint just before his or her martyrdom and ratified at once by a voice from heaven.

16   Thus, e.g., Echard, *Scriptores Ordinis Praedicatorum,* 1:456, reports that Espence said "Legendam auream Legendam esse ferream & rebus absurdis plenam." Launoy, *Regii Navarrae gymnasii Parisiensis historia,* p. 704, uses exactly the same wording in his account.

17   The fullest excerpts I have found are those in the second edition of the Haags' *La France protestante,* vol. 6, cols. 98-100. Most relevant here are the first three propositions Espence disavowed, two dealing with whether prayers should be addressed primarily to God or to the saints and the third with the offering of candles to saints.

18   Vives provides a helpful gloss for "ferrei oris" when, in the paragraph following his condemnation of Jacobus, he notes with regard to a number of other medieval hagiographers, "In illo suo Latino sermone, stilo sunt sordidissimo, ac spurcissimo, seu nullo potius, neque enim est stilus incondita illa barbarismorum et soloecismorum congeries" (Vives, *Opera omnia,* ed. Gregorio Mayáns y Siscar [1785; rept. London, 1964], 6:109). Concern with the style in which the old legends were written was not, of course, confined to the Renaissance; on the stylistic preoccupations of medieval hagiographers themselves, see, e.g., René Aigrain, *L'hagiographie* (Paris, 1953), p. 305.

19   "Nec in actis Sanctorum scribendis major est veritatis custodia, in quibus omnia oportebat esse exacta, et absoluta; unusquisque eorum acta scribebat ut in quenque erat affectus, ita ut animus historiam dictaret, non veritas: Quam indigna est Divis et hominibus christianis illa Sanctorum historia, quae *Legenda aurea* nominatur, quam nescio cur *auream* appellent, quum scripta sit ab homine *ferrei oris, plumbei cordis!* Quid foedius dici potest illo libro? O quam pudendum est nobis christianis, non esse praestantissimos nostrorum Divorum actus, verius, et accuratius, memoriae mandatos, sive ad cognitionem, sive ad imitationem tantae virtutis, quum de suis ducibus, de philosophis, et sapientibus hominibus tanta cura Graeci et Romani auctores perscripserint!" (*De disciplinis,* vol. 1, *De causis corruptarum artium,* bk. 2, ch. 6 [*Opera omnia,* 6:108]).

20   See especially his discussion of the usefulness of history in *De tradendis disciplinis,* bk. 5, ch. 1 (*Opera omnia,* 6:389-90). This discussion can

also be found in Foster Watson's translation, *Vives on Education* (1913; rept. Totowa, N. J., 1971), pp. 231-33.

21   See esp. *De tradendis disciplinis,* bk. 5, ch. 2 (*Opera omnia,* 6:400; Watson trans., pp. 248-49).

22   "Fuere, qui magnae pietatis loco ducerent, mendaciola pro religione confingere, quod et periculosum est, ne veris adimatur fides propter falsa et minime necessaria, quoniam pro pietate nostra tam multa sunt vera, ut falsa tamquam ignavi milites, atque inutiles, oneri sint magis quam auxilio" (*Opera omnia,* 6:400).

23   "Nominibus parco, quoniam hujus loci judicium morum etiam est, & non eruditionis tantum, in qua liberior potest esse censura. Nam quae morum est, haec debet profecto esse & in vivos cautior, & in mortuos reverentior. Certum est autem, qui ficte & fallaciter historiam ecclesiasticam scribunt, eos viros bonos atque synceros esse non posse, totamque eorum narrationem inventam esse aut ad quaestum, aut ad errorem, quorum alterum foedum est, alterum perniciosum" (Melchior Cano, *Opera,* ed. Hyacinth Serry [Bassano, 1746], p. 330).

24   "Justissima est Ludovici querela de historiis quibusdam in ecclesia confictis. Prudenter ille sane ac graviter eos arguit, qui pietatis loco duxerint mendacia pro religione fingere. Id quod & maxime periculosum est, & minime necessarium. Mendaci quippe homini ne verum quidem credere solemus. Quamobrem qui falsis atque mendacibus scriptis mentes mortalium concitare ad Divorum cultum voluere, hi nihil mihi aliud videntur egisse, quam ut veris propter falsa adimatur fides, & quae severe ab auctoribus plane veracibus edita sunt, ea etiam revocentur in dubium."

25   "[Eorum] uterque non tam dedit operam, ut res veras certasque describeret, quam ne nihil omnino praeteriret, quod scriptum in schedulis quibuslibet reperiretur. . . . Quamobrem boni licet ac minime fallaces viri, . . . apud criticos graves atque severos auctoritate carent."

26   "Negare non possumus, viros aliquando gravissimos, in divorum praesertim prodigiis describendis, sparsos rumores & excepisse, & scriptis etiam ad posteros retulisse. Qua in re, ut mihi quidem videtur, aut nimium illi sibi, aut fidelium certe vulgo indulserunt: quod vulgus sentiebant non tantum ea facile miracula credere, sed impense etiam flagitare. Itaque signa nonnulla, & prodigia sancti quoque memoriae prodiderunt, non quo ea libenter credidissent, sed ne deesse fidelium votis viderentur. . . . Nec ego hic libri illius auctorem excuso, qui speculum exemplorum inscribitur: nec historiae etiam ejus, quae Legenda aurea nominatur. In illo enim miraculorum monstra saepius, quam vera miracula legas: hanc homo scripsit ferrei oris, plumbei cordis, animi certe parum severi, & prudentis."

This passage has had a very odd history. Dupin mistranslated the last sentence (*Nouvelle bibliothèque,* 10:86), and several later sources follow him in applying the "miraculorum monstra" charge to the *Legenda.* Elsewhere, and especially in Dominican defenses of Jacobus, the tradition arose that Cano had never mentioned the *Legenda* at all, and Dupin was accused of having fabricated the whole quotation; see, e.g., Anfossi, *Memorie istoriche,* p. 92. Characteristically, Touron provides the most dispassionate and informative commentary on the matter (*Histoire,* 1:597-99). Touron applies to Jacobus Cano's critique of deliberate falsifiers, paraphrasing the argument with some care, but denies the existence of the explicit—and much less damaging—reference to Jacobus that occurs just a few paragraphs later in *De locis theologicis.* Thus he raises the possibility that Baillet may have been right when he charged (*Vies des saints,* vol. 1, col. 35) that some editor or editors of Cano's work had seen fit to remove these particular sentences from the text.

27   "Vidi pariter ac dolui, e nostrorum hominum memoria indignissimis modis eiectos, & ceu sepultos delitescere, per quos diuina Maiestas primum. . . sui notitiam atque uoluntatem manifestauit mortalibus, per quos edidit innumerabilia miracula, omnipotentiae suae propalam declarandae, per quos pereuntis mundi tenebras illuminauit, per quos mentium morbos sanauit, per quos miserabiliter errantes populos in uiam reduxit: per quos denique omnem prioris Adae calamitatem imminuit" (Georg Witzel, *Hagiologium* [Mainz, 1541], sig. 2).

28   Thus, e.g., he cites the *Ecclesiastical History* of Pseudo-Dionysius on the early Christian custom of honoring the martyrs' victories with ceremonies at their tombs and quotes two passages from the panegyric on Saint Athanasius by Gregory Nazianzen which affirm the rightness of celebrating the virtues of the saints as a form of praise to God and a personal inspiration to all Christians (*Hagiologium,* sig. 4ᵛ). The most extensive quotation from the Bible in his preface is the passage from Heb. 11:33-39 on the achievements of the Old Testament heroes commemorated for their faith (sigs. 4-4ᵛ).

29   "Volumus in coelum repente ab obitu rapi: sed interea uoluntatem patris, qui est in coelis, facere detrectamus, sufficere putantes: Domine, domine: credo, credo. Quin igitur, dum tempus est, dumque sapientia fores nostras pulsat, resipiscimus, & primum perspecto archetypo Christo seruatore, oculos uertimus ad exemplaria gregis, hoc est, sanctos episcopos ac martyres, qui nobiscum Christi eiusdem seruatoris uiuum, aeternumque corpus sunt."

30   "Laudemus uiros illos gloriosos, ac decantemus ipsorum opera bona, ut per ea is glorificetur demum, quo authore facta sunt omnia opera bona. Verum a laude statim progrediamur ad laudatorum uirorum imitationem, ne in nos quoque quadrare posse uideatur, quod de Demosthene

Plutarchus scripsit, Nimirum illum maiorum facta laudare potuisse, sed nequaquam imitari.''

31 "Ergo non pium modo, uerum etiam utile est, sibi quenquam Christianorum persuasum habere, Ecclesiam seruatoris nostri Opt. Max. temporibus multiplicis atque saeuissimae persecutionis, tam omnigenis miraculis, quam incomparabili magnanimitate mirabiliter claruisse.''

32 His convenient but incomplete "Catalogus authorum . . . quorum luculentis testimonijs usi in hoc opere sumus," at sig. 6ᵛ, includes such predictable favorites as the Bible, Eusebius, the *Tripartite History,* the *Vitae Patrum,* Greek Fathers of the church who composed panegyrics on the saints, and Latin ones whose homilies provided classic expressions of Christian teaching on the major feasts and commemorations of the liturgical year—alongside more surprising choices like the "author incertus" who wrote the life of Charlemagne, Latin poets ranging from Prudentius to Adam of St. Victor, a number of Renaissance humanists, and the contemporary liturgical reformer Francesco Cardinal Quiñones.

33 "His omnium nouissimus accessit, inter recentiores diligentior agiologus, Petrus de Natalibus praesul Equilinus. . . . Pergratae breuitati studuit Equilinus, & quam minimum intexuit mythologiae, quo commendatior eius apud nos fama est" (sig. 3).

34 "Longe melius Voragine de Ecclesia meritus est Petrus Lombardus, qui post Voraginem scriptitauit, multa mutuatus ad uerbum ex membranis ueterum: id quod conferenti inter se libros facile adparet" (sig. 3). Apart from the rather minor geographical error, the only apparent obstacle to the identification suggested is an explicit reference to Peter Calo's legendary some fifteen lines after this statement: "& ante [Petrum de Natalibus] Petrus Calo Venetus." Since Witzel here departs from his otherwise invariable practice of evaluating each hagiographer mentioned, the logical assumption is either that he deliberately substituted "Lombardus" for "Calo" in the first passage, for the sake of a rhetorical play with Jacobus's work, the "Lombardica," or that he had found a reference to Peter Calo in another source and did not connect him with the manuscript legendary he had actually seen and admired.

35 "Post, ut ad recentiores descendam, extitit Iacobus Voraginis praesul Genuensis, qui uixit Anno 1290. Verum quid is praestiterit, uel caeco perspicuum sit. . . . Mythologiae ille impensius indulget, quam ob rem in tantum contemptum abijt apud omnes cordatos. Hac profecto Lombardica hactenus nimium usae, seu abusae potius cathedrae sunt, contemptis interim, aut certe neglectis sanctorum actis, quae nobis Ecclesiastica historia, Eusebio Pamphilo authore, offerebat in Christi gregem diuulganda. Nec uulgares passim bibliothecae in monasterijs continent historicum quid de Sanctis praeter hanc unam Lombardicam, quam cur auream uocent, demiror.''

The sentence omitted is the one on "Petrus Lombardus" quoted and discussed in the preceding note.

36   Among the works published by Espence, in fact, were French translations of a sermon by Theodoret on the martyrs and another by John Chrysostom on the saints (1563) and a life of the early French Benedictine saint Godo or Gaon (1565).

37   BN *Cat.,* vol. 215, col. 138. The edition in question was published at Lyons by J. Lambany.

38   Ibid., col. 139. This title was used for at least the two editions printed in Paris by Jean Réal in 1549 and 1554.

39   "Legenda hec aurea nitidis excutitur formis claretque plurimum censoria castigatione: usque adeo, vt nihil perperam adhibitum semotumue: quod ad rem potissimum pertinere non videatur offendi possit." I quote from the edition of October 28, 1505, printed at Lyons by Nicholas de Benedictis for Jacques Huguetan (*NUC,* 275:452). All told, the *NUC* and the BN *Cat.* identify seven early-sixteenth-century editions at Lyons and one at Rouen with essentially the same title.

40   "Legenda sanctorum que lombardica historia dicitur: characteribus optimus cuditur: recenterque a mendis quam plurimis purgatur: cura eruditi viri Lamberti Campestri ordinis predicatorum" (Lyons: Constantine Fradin, 1516 [*NUC*]). According to the BN *Cat.,* the edition published at Caen by Laurentius Hostingue in 1518 bore the same title with the addition of "aurea" after "sanctorum."

41   "Ad vetustorum exemplarium fidem." This wording is found in the titles of at least four editions printed at Lyons between 1536 and 1546 (BN *Cat.,* vol. 215, cols. 132-33; *NUC,* 275:452).

42   Thus, for example, the final page of the edition dated August 17, 1519, printed at Lyons for Constantine Fradin by Guillaume Huyon, reads as follows: "Aurea legenda edita per . . . Jacobum de Voragine, . . . a mendis quam plurimis purgatis cura . . . Claudii de Rota . . . promotionis conventus Lugdunensis" (BN *Cat.,* col. 132).

43   "Legenda, vt vocant, sanctorvm. Nvnc demum summa cura diligentiaque Fr. Claudij à Rota . . . recognita, infinitisque mendis repurgata: adiectis denuo, praeter historiam Lombardicam, aliquot Sanctorum Sanctarumque uitis, antehac non excusis . . . ." The edition was printed by Guillaume Regnier for Eustace Barricatus; *NUC,* 275:453, notes that the name of Jacobus is not given until sig. B2.

44   "Legenda, vt vocant, sev Sanctorum sanctarumque vitae, ex variis historijs quam diligentissime collectae, ac secundum anni progressum opera Claudii a Rota digestae." Again the printer was Guillaume Regnier; the bookseller, Godefry Gailliandus, also of Lyons (*NUC,* 275:453).

45   Richard Hooker, *Of the Laws of Ecclesiastical Polity,* bk. 5, ch. 20, par.
      9 (Everyman's Library ed., 2:71-72).

46   Delehaye, *Work of the Bollandists,* pp. 13-14.

47   See Chapter 1, above.

48   "Le malheureux succès de [la *Légende dorée*] n'a pas peu contribué à
      décréditer dans l'opinion de certaines personnes la foi due aux plus
      respectables monuments. Le scepticisme moderne a mieux aimé
      condamner tous les miracles que de chercher à en approfondir un seul.
      Les protestants ont fait de cette légende une espèce de triomphe contre les
      Catholiques, comme si nous étions intéressés à la défendre. Ce n'est pas
      à eux que l'on en doit la première critique" (A. Sévèstre, *Dictionnaire de
      patrologie,* vol. 3 [Paris, 1854], col. 652).

49   Thomas Becon, "The Acts of Christ and of Antichrist," in *Prayers and
      Other Pieces of Thomas Becon, S.T.P.,* ed. John Ayre, Parker Society,
      vol. 4 (Cambridge, 1844), p. 519. The passage on "saints' lies" is from
      the same pamphlet, ibid., p. 535. Other references to the *Legenda* occur
      in the preface to Becon's "Comfortable Epistle to the Afflicted People
      of God" and in his "Humble Supplication for the Restoring of God's
      Word" (pp. 199-200 and 234).

50   John Jewel, "Defence of the Apology of the Church of England," part
      5, in *Works of John Jewel,* ed. John Ayre, Parker Society, vol. 26
      (Cambridge, 1850), p. 816.

51   "Opus quidem historiis Christianis accensendum, an potius ad fabulas
      Romanenses ablegandum? a cordatioribus etiam pontificiis (ut videmus)
      non sine gravi stomacho damnatum. Certe nugis nugacissimus [*sic*],
      fictis, ineptissimisque narrationibus refertissimum, quae non sine
      immenso Christianae religionis scandalo legi, multo magis defendi
      possunt" (William Cave, *Scriptorum ecclesiasticorum historia literaria,*
      2 [1698; rept. Basel, 1745]: 334).

52   Cruikshank spells out his purpose on page 2: "The design of this
      publication . . . is to expose the *modern* Catholic miracles by exhibiting
      to the world the *ancient* ones; and thereby to ridicule the monstrous and
      absurd pretensions to miraculous powers, which the church of Rome
      has, in all ages, set up. The *nature* of those miracles, which she declares
      were anciently wrought by her, indeed, sufficiently testify against their
      truth: the gross immorality of many of them, the ridiculous absurdity of
      others, and the shameless fraud, which is observable in all, prove beyond
      the possibility of doubt, that their origin is any thing but divine"
      (*Catholic Miracles* [London, 1825]).

53   For this reference I am indebted to Léon E. Halkin's article, "Hagiogra-
      phie protestante," *Anal. Boll.* 68 (1950): 458-59. The 1619 edition of
      Crespin's *Histoire des martyrs,* as reprinted by the Société des Livres
      Religieux de Toulouse in 1885, seems not to mention Jacobus's book

directly, but its "Preface monstrant une conformité des persecutions et des martyrs de ces derniers temps à ceux de la première Eglise" expresses such suspicion toward post-apostolic miracle stories—"ainsi que les Moines & Prestres oisifs en ont autres fois forgez de leurs idoles" (p. xliv, col. 2)—as to provide a likely gloss on what Crespin meant by "fables de *Légendes dorées.*"

54   On Foxe's efforts to distinguish his work from the *Legenda,* see also White's discussion in *Tudor Books of Saints and Martyrs,* pp. 136-40.

55   Thus the early title pages of Surius's own legendary assure the reader that the contents were drawn "partim ex tomis Aloysii Lipomani . . . partim etiam ex egregiis MSS codicibus, quarum permultae antehanc nunquam in lucem prodiere." Other prominent examples are Francis Verhaer's *Vitae Sanctorum, ex probatissimis authoribus, et potissimum ex Reverend. D. Aloysio Lipomano & R. P. Laurentio Surio* . . . (Antwerp, 1594) and Guillaume Gazet's *Histoire de la Vie, mort* . . . *et Miracles des Saints* (Rouen, 1610), which bears a complicated subtitle explaining its relationship to the works of such "autheurs approuvez" as Metaphrastes, Lippomano, Surius, Molanus, and Baronius.

56   Thus, e.g., the chronological surveys in Aigrain's *L'hagiographie* (pp. 323-28, 356ff.) show the term *legenda* or its derivatives used in the short titles of four important manuscript legendaries of the fourteenth century and in three other collections printed before or during the decline of Jacobus's own book: the *Légende de saints nouveaux* (1476 and 1477), Hilarion's *Legendarium nonnullorum sanctorum* (1494), and Capgrave's *Nova legenda angliae* (1516). Thereafter, Aigrain records only one such use of the term (in the Franciscan *Leggendario* by Benedict Mazzara, published late in the seventeenth century).

57   According to Emile Littré's *Dictionnaire de la langue française,* French Calvinists in the sixteenth century were already using *légende* pejoratively in reference to the biographies of such figures as Catherine de Medici and Espence's friend the cardinal of Lorraine, "ainsi dites à cause de la catholicité des personnages et des faits extraordinaires dont elles prétendent donner la clef." Aigrain, who suggests the connection between "la mauvaise réputation d'un trop grand nombre de ['légendes' des saints] auprès des historiens" and the term's general loss of respectability (*L'hagiographie,* p. 128), may have been thinking primarily of his native French; similar developments seem to have occurred, however, in Italian, German, and Dutch as well as in English.

58   Even more striking is the similar reference to Jacobus's book—by this time apparently the stuff of proverbs—in a letter by Lady Mary Wortley Montagu in 1740: "After this, you are obliged to me that I do not suspect [your popish priest] can persuade you into a belief in all the miracles in the Legend."

59   "The rest that foloweth of this story in the narration of Bede, as of
      drying up the River, as Alban went to the place of his execution: then of
      makyng a welspryng in the top of the hill, and of the fallyng out of the
      eyes of him that did behead him (with such other prodigious miracles
      mentioned in his story) because they seeme more legendlike, then
      truthlike: agayne, because I see no great profit, nor necessitie in the
      relation therof, I leave them to the free iudgement of the Reader, to
      thinke of them, as cause shall moue him" (Foxe, *Actes and Monuments*
      [London, 1576], p. 89, col. 2).

60   "Likewise it is sayd, that Eugenia . . . was assayled with sundry kyndes
      of death, first beyng tyed to a great stone & cast into Tyber, where she
      was caryed vp from drowning, then put in the hoate bathes, whiche were
      extincted, and she preserued: afterward by famishment in prison, where
      they say she was fed at the hand of our Saviour: all which Legendary
      miracles I leave to the Reader to iudge of them, as shall seeme good vnto
      him" (ibid., p. 74, col. 2).

61   Even the first citation under sense 6, "an unauthentic or non-historical
      story," might be read as another allusion to the particular book by
      Jacobus, this time linked with a particular book by Ovid: "That yee may
      know the Indians want not their Metamorphoses and Legends, they tell
      that a man . . . had a daughter, with whom the sunne was in love"
      (Samuel Purchas, 1613). The second likely citation, listed under sense 8,
      is a line from Giles Fletcher's *Wildgoose Chase* in 1621: "A glorious
      talker, and a Legend maker / Of idle tales."

62   Echard—on what authority, he does not say—asserts that Berengar
      ordered Gui "ut Legendam alteram ex sincerioribus actis colligeret ac
      ederet, quod & fecit" (*Scriptores Ordinis Praedicatorum,* 1:456).
      Touron, with his usual even-handedness, manages to suggest that other
      issues were involved: "Guidonis travailla sur des Mémoires plus fidéles,
      ou plus autentiques; il éxamina tout avec plus de soin, & choisit avec
      discernement" (*Histoire,* 1:596).

63   "Nichil enim intelligencie faciliorem parat aditum quam brevitas non
      obscura. Sanctorum . . . legendas veteres et novas relegens, et ex
      utrisque non nova cudendo, sed pociora eligendo, pretermissis apocrifis
      atque superfluis, quantum licuit, resecatis, veritate tamen et integritate
      hystorie semper salva, in unum colligere studui que dispersa invenieban-
      tur in multis" (Gui, general preface to *Speculum sanctorale,* ed. Delisle,
      in "Notice," p. 421). Gui goes on to mention the necessity of finding
      "autenticas scripturas et illas quas Romana ecclesia nequaquam suscipi
      prohibet," but without the emphasis he places on condensing them
      prudently.

64   "Ea igitur neccessitas laboris in presenti opere fuit quoniam in modernis
      compilationibus legende sanctorum veteres rerumque gestarum hystorie
      per ipsos compilatores, brevitati studentes, sic in plerisque decise sunt ut

videatur pars non modica detruncata; item de pluribus sanctis nulla prorsus habetur mencio in eisdem de quibus agitur in presenti.''

Peter Calo seems to have agreed; Poncelet, ''Le légendier de Pierre Calo,'' p. 32, quotes an excerpt from Calo's preface which declares his intention to transmit the old legends in a more complete and adequate form than his predecessors had tended to do.

65   ''Allexit vero animum meum ad subeundum laborem desiderium sciendi sanctorum illustres agones et insignia gesta virtutesque preclaras ac exemplares vitas et perfectionum semitas, ad proficiendum in via Dei, eorum exemplo, imitatione et doctrina, necnon ipsorum meritis michi suffragantibus viatori ad perveniendum ad patriam, in qua ipsi sine fine vivunt et regnant cum Christo qui est sanctorum omnium gloria et corona.''

66   Gui's own care to keep the saints subordinate to Christ is illustrated by the very plan of his legendary. Instead of simply following the liturgical calendar as most medieval legendaries did—and allowing the saints, through their sheer number, to assume more prominence than they deserve—Gui's *Sanctorale* is divided into four parts. The first, as he explains in his preface, is devoted to the feasts directly pertaining to Christ, ''qui est caput tocius ecclesie et causa omnium festivitatum dierum et temporum'' (ibid., p. 422), and—in subordinate ranks, following—to those celebrating the Virgin who bore him, the cross on which he suffered, the angels, all saints, all souls, and the dedication of a church. The second part of the legendary is reserved for New Testament saints, again ordered at least roughly by their importance. Only in the third and fourth parts, devoted respectively to martyrs and confessors, does Gui let his priorities be set by the calendar.

67   Delehaye, *Legends of the Saints,* trans. Attwater, p. 181.

68   Ibid.

69   See especially the colloquy entitled ''A Pilgrimage for Religion's Sake'' (''Peregrinatio religionis ergo'') in Craig R. Thompson's translation of the *Colloquies* (Chicago, 1965), pp. 285-312.

70   For a good overview of Foxe's practice with regard to signs and miracles, see White's *Tudor Books of Saints and Martyrs,* esp. pp. 164-67. Crespin's book devotes whole chapters to the ''Iugemens de Dieu'' that had fallen on various persecutors of the faithful.

71   Thus, e.g., Frederick Homes Dudden found it impossible to reconcile the contents of the *Dialogues* with Gregory's obvious intelligence in other areas: ''It is certainly astonishing that the clear-headed man who managed the Papal estates and governed the Church with such admirable skill, should have contributed to the propagation of these wild tales of demons and wizards and haunted houses, of souls made visible, of rivers obedient to written orders, of corpses that scream and walk'' (*Gregory*

the Great [London, 1905], 1:356). Arthur C. McGiffert's verdict goes further, invoking the "two-tiered model" of the church to explain and condemn the marvels in this book: "The significance of Gregory's treatment of [supernatural marvels] is not that he had anything new to impart but that he gave the popular belief in angels and demons in all its crudities and absurdities the support of his authority and thus raised it to the dignity of a part of the doctrinal system of the church" (*A History of Christian Thought* [New York, 1933], 2:158).

72   Gui's respect for this work can be seen from his own legendary, which reproduces Gregory's life of Benedict with great faithfulness, omitting almost nothing except the passages of dialogue between Gregory and his supposed interlocutor, "Peter." For Gui's legends of confessors (pt. 4 of the *Speculum sanctorale*), my source is Bibliothèque Nationale MS. latin 5406; the accounts of Benedict and Scholastica occupy, respectively, folios 66^v-74 and 38^v-39 in this manuscript.

73   Like Gui, Witzel uses an account of Scholastica (sigs. a.ii-a.ii^v) which is a complete transcript of Gregory's (*Dial.* II.33-34) except that a brief comment by "Peter" is omitted. For Benedict's own life, Witzel gives just a brief summary at the anticipated point in the liturgical year (sigs. f.iii-f.iii^v), directing interested readers to Gregory for a fuller picture; but in the final pages of the *Hagiologium* he suddenly finds more room and reproduces the prologue and first chapter of Gregory's account (sigs. Rr^v-Rr.ii^v), breaking off with another, stronger suggestion that the "pius presbyter" should read the entire legend in the *Dialogues*.

74   "Ille in historia Anglorum, hic in dialogis quaedam miracula scribunt vulgo jactata & credita, quae hujus praesertim saeculi Aristarchi incerta esse censebunt. Equidem historias illas probarem magis, si earum auctores, juxta praefinitam normam, severitati judicii curam in eligendo majorem adjunxissent. Sed quoniam modeste, & circumspecto judicio de tantis viris pronunciandum est, ne in his quidem duobus rejicienda sunt plurima. Pauca enim in eis possis arguere, quamvis historiam ecclesiasticam revocare ad severiora judicia contendas. Ac si necesse est in alteram peccare partem, omnia eorum probari legentibus, quam multa reprobari malo" (Cano, *De locis theologicis* 11.6 [Serry ed., p. 334]).

75   Georg Dufner, *Die Dialoge Gregors des Grossen im Wandel der Zeiten und Sprachen,* Miscellanea erudita 19 (Padua, 1968), provides a useful overview of the vernacular translations (pp. 13-45), as well as a detailed study of five versions in various Italian dialects. Interestingly enough, one of the Italian translations was made by Dominic Cavalca, a celebrated Dominican approximately contemporary with Gui.

76   J.J.A. Zuidweg's proposed edition of the *Legenda,* to be based on the best manuscripts, was eagerly awaited twenty years ago; but there seems now to be a consensus that the project is too vast for any individual to carry out. One recent step in the right direction is the establishment of a

card file to bring together all the information scholars have obtained on the various manuscripts and early printed editions of the *Legenda,* both Latin and vernacular; see the announcement by Konrad Kunze in *Anal. Boll.* 95 (1977): 168. The less famous legendaries of the period should not pose such formidable problems to would-be editors, but volunteers with the necessary qualifications seem to be few. It is not a great exaggeration, in fact, to call Antoine Dondaine the only important advocate of these works since Poncelet, in 1910. Thanks to Dondaine we have at least a trustworthy account of the more important manuscripts of the legendary by Bartholomew of Trent ("*L'epilogus in gesta sanctorum de Barthélemy de Trente*" [1971]) and a French translation of the legendary by Jean de Mailly (1947). For Bartholomew, Peter Calo, Bernard Gui, and the rest, only a few fragments have been printed, and those not always in sources of unquestionable reliability.

77   Graesse's major source, identified in his preface only by a reference to Ebert's *Allgemeines bibliographisches Lexikon,* is among the earliest editions of the *Legenda;* Seybolt lists it as number 6. Although the printer seems not to have been identified, Gaiffier identifies the place of publication as Basel (*Anal. Boll.* 76 [1958]: 470).

78   The point is illustrated by Witzel's ability in 1541 to lay hands on a text of Gregory's life of Benedict that differs hardly at all from those in modern critical editions. The variants in Gui's version are more numerous, but for the most part they are quite minor.

79   Pierce Butler's theory of a direct link between Jacobus and Vincent can presumably be laid to rest, since Dondaine has shown the likelihood that both authors used the earlier *Abbreviatio in gestis et miraculis sanctorum* by Jean de Mailly; Vincent simply borrowed Jean's abridged versions of various legends, whereas Jacobus borrowed and built on Jean's whole idea of a portable, inexpensive, conveniently ordered compilation of material on the saints. See Dondaine, "Le dominicain français Jean de Mailly et la *Légende dorée,*" esp. pp. 84-93. But even Dondaine, intent on showing that the *Abbreviatio* deserves some of the recognition traditionally accorded to the *Legenda,* sometimes exaggerates the similarities between the two; for example, he asserts that the vast majority of Jacobus's chapters "lui sont communs avec les *Gestes et miracles,* dans le fond, la forme et la langue, parfois à la lettre" (p. 91).

Chapter 4: The Richness of Gregory's *Dialogues*

1   The historical context in which the *Legenda* was written will be treated more fully below in Chapters 7-9. The date of the original version has been much debated, with a few scholars suggesting possibilities as late as 1288. But there was until the Second World War a manuscript in the Collection Salis at Metz that bore the date 1273; see, e.g., the *Catalogue général des manuscrits des bibliothèques publiques de France,*

Départements, 48 (1933): 392. This *terminus ad quem* agrees quite neatly with the final statement in the history of Lombardy that constitutes most of the *Legenda* chapter on Saint Pelagius ("Quo [Frederico] deposito et defuncto sedes imperii usque hodie vacat"), since it was not until 1273 that another claimant to the imperial throne was recognized by the papacy. After studying the records of Jacobus's life, however, Monleone concluded that the *Legenda* must have been written "durante la vita claustrale di frate Iacopo e probabilmente prima del 1267" (*Iacopo da Varagine e la sua Cronaca di Genova,* 1:101), and I am inclined to accept that view; Jacobus may have added a few chapters or parts of chapters later in his life, but the bulk of the work is much easier to understand if we assign it provisionally to the decade between 1257 and 1267. Richardson claimed to have found an extant manuscript dated 1265, but he unfortunately neglected to identify it, and Kaeppeli's recent list of manuscripts includes nothing dated before 1273.

2   Our information on Jacobus's early career is quite sparse; in fact, most of the undisputed details are derived either from Bernard Gui or from the scattered autobiographical comments in the chronicle of Genoa which Jacobus wrote toward the end of his life. Echard's summary (*Scriptores Ordinis Praedicatorum,* 1:454), which depends heavily on these two sources, seems relatively trustworthy: "He was born about 1230 and embraced the Dominican order as a youth in Genoa, in the year 1244. He became a man notable for piety, regular observance, learning, zeal for saving souls, prudence, and a talent for getting things done. He expounded Holy Scripture in various places and schools of the order. Then such was the grace of his speaking and the elegant refinement of his mother tongue that he preached from the more important pulpits of Italy during Advent and Lent and was everywhere heard with approbation and profit. He was elected to office in the order as a prior, and in 1267 he was advanced to the rule of the whole province of Lombardy—then undivided and very large—which, Bernard Gui informs us, he administered continuously and uninterruptedly for 18 years." ("Natus est circa MCCXXX & adolescens Januae in S. Dominici ordinem anno MCCXLIV amplexatus, vir evasit pietate, disciplina regulari, doctrina, salutis animarum studio, prudentia rerumque agendarum peritia clarissimus. Sacras apud suos litteras variis in locis & scholis interpretatus est, tum qua valebat dicendi gratia, linguaeque maternae puritate & elegantia, celebriora Italiae pulpita obtinuit per adventum & quadragesimam ubique cum plausu & fructu auditus. Suis etiam praefuit electus prior: anno vero MCCLXVII ad totius Lombardiae provinciae, quae unica tum & vastissima, regimen assumtus est, quam octodecim annis solidis & continuis administrasse docet Bernardus Guidonis.")

3   See the introduction to Father Vogüé's new critical edition of the *Dialogues,* Sources chrétiennes, vol. 251 (Paris, 1978), pp. 31-42.

4   The evidence on this score is presented in Chapter 5.

5   Here and throughout I ignore the presence of the subtler levels of
     allegorical meaning in the *Dialogues*. These have been discussed in
     various articles by Pierre Courcelle, Maximilien Mähler, and others, and
     there are many references to them in Father Vogüé's notes. For purposes
     of comparison with the *Legenda,* however, the only important meanings
     in Gregory's book are those capable of being grasped by a relatively
     unsophisticated, literal-minded reader—the kind of reader, that is, to
     whom Gregory descended through the questions given to his pupil Peter
     within the book.

6   See esp. the prologue to Book I, secs. 7-10, and note the full title of the
     work: *Dialogorum . . . libri quatuor de miraculis patrum Italicorum.*
     All my quotations from the *Dialogues* are based on Father Vogüé's
     edition, and my references to sections within chapters follow his
     numbering system.

7   "Sed quaeso te ut me aequanimiter feras, si ipse quoque apud te more
     Ecclesiastis nostri infirmantium in me personam suscepero, ut eisdem
     infirmantibus prodesse propinquius quasi per eorum inquisitionem
     possim" (IV.4.9). As Vogüé notes, this request marks a transition of
     sorts, from the reasonably well-informed questions a Peter might ask on
     his own account to questions designed to allay the doubts and
     misconceptions of the truly ignorant. The philosophy underlying this
     whole aspect of the *Dialogues* is eloquently expressed in Gregory's reply:
     "Cur condescendentem te infirmitati proximorum aequanimiter non
     feram, cum Paulus dicat: *Omnibus omnia factus sum, ut omnes facerem
     saluos?"*

8   The point is most explicit a little later in the text, when Gregory recounts
     Benedict's return to the wilderness after a first, unhappy experience as an
     abbot: "Tunc ad locum dilectae solitudinis rediit, et solus in superni
     spectatoris oculis habitauit secum" (ch. 3.5).

9   Boglioni's important study, "Miracle et nature chez Grégoire le Grand,"
     Epopées, légendes, et miracles: Cahiers d'études médiévales 1 (Mont-
     real, 1974): 11-102, sheds light on a number of issues beyond the
     Dialogues themselves. For our purposes the crucial section is the final
     one, entitled "La théorie grégorienne du miracle," pp. 70-102.

10   Ibid., p. 75.

11   "Isdem uero frater salubriter correptus erubuit, quia uenerabilis pater
     uirtutem omnipotentis Domini, quam admonitione intimauerat, miracu-
     lis ostendebat, nec erat iam ut quisquam de eius promissionibus dubitare
     posset, qui in uno eodemque momento, pro uitreo uase paene uacuo,
     plenum oleo doleum reddidisset."

12   I refer to the stories of the monk distracted from his prayers (ch. 4), the

monk wanting to return to the world (ch. 25), and the Arian persecutor Zalla (ch. 31).

13   "Quos ille protinus percontatus est, dicens: 'Vbi comedistis?' Qui responderunt, dicentes: 'Nusquam.' Quibus ille ait: 'Quare ita mentimini? Numquid illius talis feminae habitaculum non intrastis? Numquid hos atque illos cibos non accepistis? Numquid tot calices non bibistis?' Cumque eis uenerabilis pater et hospitium mulieris et genera ciborum et numerum potionum diceret, recognoscentes cuncta quae egerant, ad eius pedes tremefacti ceciderunt, se deliquisse confessi sunt. Ipse autem protinus culpam pepercit, perpendens quod in eius absentia ultra non facerent, quem praesentem sibi esse in spiritu scirent."

14   See esp. III.34.2.

15   "Mira sunt et multum stupenda quae dicis. Nam in aqua ex petra producta Moysen, in ferro uero quod ex profundo aquae rediit Heliseum, in aquae itinere Petrum, in corui oboedientia Heliam, in luctu autem mortis inimici Dauid uideo. Vt perpendo, uir iste spiritu iustorum omnium plenus fuit."

16   "Vir Domini Benedictus, Petre, unius spiritum habuit, qui per concessae redemptionis gratiam electorum corda omnium inpleuit. De quo Iohannes dicit: *Erat lux uera, quae inluminat omnem hominem uenientem in hunc mundum,* et de quo rursus scriptum est: *De plenitudine eius nos omnes accepimus.*"

17   The idea itself was not of course originated by Gregory; it is at least implicit in all the ancient and medieval legends (and they are legion) which report the recent occurrence of miracles like those in the Bible. Gaiffier provides a useful overview of the phenomenon in "Miracles bibliques et vies de saints," an article reprinted in his *Etudes critiques,* pp. 50-61.

18   "Sed ut tanta ualeat homo de terra, caeli et terrae conditor in terram uenit e caelo, atque, ut iudicare caro etiam de spiritibus possit, hoc ei largiri dignatus est, factus pro hominibus Deus caro, quia inde surrexit ultra se infirmitas nostra, unde sub se infirmata est firmitas Dei."

19   "Quod omnipotens Deus ex magnae pietatis dispensatione disponit, quia dum prophetiae spiritum aliquando dat et aliquando subtrahit, prophetantium mentes et eleuat in celsitudine et custodit in humilitate, ut et accipientes spiritum inueniant quid de Deo sint, et rursum prophetiae spiritum non habentes cognoscant quid sint de semetipsis."

20   Boglioni supplies a splendid gloss on this image, quoting a series of passages from Gregory's *Homilies on Ezekiel* which use the figure of embers for hidden saints, whose examples inflame only the few other men in direct contact with them; lamps, for those so distinguished by their gifts—and so generous in letting them be known—that they

"montrent aux pèlerins la lumière des bonnes oeuvres par leur vie et leur parole" ("Miracle et nature," pp. 95-96).

21   See esp. the introductory volume of Vogüé's edition, pp. 36-39.

22   "Nonnumquam uero ad augmentum mei doloris adiungitur, quod quorumdam uita, qui praesens saeculum tota mente reliquerunt, mihi ad memoriam reuocatur, quorum dum culmen aspicio, quantum ipse in infimis iaceam agnosco. Quorum plurimi conditori suo in secretiori uita placuerunt, qui ne per humanos actus a nouitate mentis ueterescerent, eos omnipotens Deus huius mundi laboribus noluit occupari."

23   I quote from p. 171 of Cuthbert Butler's *Western Mysticism* (1922; rept. New York, 1966), a book which conveniently brings together and translates a number of Gregory's important statements on the relationship between contemplation and action. For a definition of the "pure contemplative" which Benedict was not, one could hardly do better than the next paragraph of the same homily: "But the contemplative life is: to retain indeed with all one's mind the love of God and neighbour, but to rest from exterior action, and cleave only to the desire of the Maker, that the mind may now take no pleasure in doing anything, but having spurned all cares, may be aglow to see the face of its Creator; so that it already knows how to bear with sorrow the burden of the corruptible flesh, and with all its desires to seek to join the hymn-singing choirs of angels, to mingle with the heavenly citizens, and to rejoice at its everlasting incorruption in the sight of God."

24   Butler provides ample evidence on this score; see esp. the texts cited and partially reproduced on pp. 174-76 of his *Western Mysticism.*

25   "Haec namque singulariter uictima ab aeterno interitu animam saluat, quae illam nobis mortem Vnigeniti per mysterium reparat. . . . Quis enim fidelium habere dubium possit ipsa immolationis hora ad sacerdotis uocem caelos aperiri, in illo Iesu Christi mysterio angelorum choros adesse, summis ima sociari, terram caelestibus iungi, unum quid ex uisibilibus atque inuisibilibus fieri?"

26   "Tunc ergo uere pro nobis Deo hostia erit, cum nos ipsos hostiam fecerit. Sed studendum nobis est ut etiam post orationis tempora, in quantum Deo largiente possumus, in ipso animum suo pondere et uigore seruemus, ne post cogitatio fluxa dissoluat, ne uana menti laetitia subrepat, et lucrum conpunctionis anima per incuriam fluxae cogitationis perdat."

27   See, e.g., Butler's excerpts from *Moral.* XXX.8 (p. 178) and XXIII.38 (pp. 180-81) and from *Reg. past.* I.7 and II.7 (p. 179).

28   "Si sanctus uir contra se unanimiter conspirantes suaeque conuersationi longe dissimiles, coactos diu sub se tenere uoluisset, fortasse sui uigoris usum et modum tranquillitatis excederet, atque a contemplationis lumine mentis suae oculum declinasset, dumque cotidie illorum incorrectione

fatigatus minus curaret sua, et se forsitan relinqueret, et illos non inueniret.''

29   The actual term used here is *remoti,* presumably a bit of shorthand for the "continentes et tacentes . . . ab huius mundi actione remoti" to whom Gregory referred in the preceding homily. Butler's translation substitutes Cassian's word for monks, "renunciantes.''

30   This is the most unequivocal statement on the matter brought forth by Butler, but it is not quite an isolated case. See also the succeeding brief excerpts from *Hom. in Evang.* IX.5 and *Moral.* VI.55, and the longer and more interesting one from *Moral.* VI.57, which outlines some qualifications and disqualifications for contemplation based on individual temperament (pp. 187-88).

31   Gregory makes essentially the same point, in equally strong language, in *Hom. in Ezech.* II.2.15; Butler gives the relevant passage just before the one quoted in the text. See also his excerpts from *Hom. in Ezech.* II.2.11 (p. 173) and I.5.12 (p. 184).

Chapter 5: Gregory's Narrative in the *Legenda aurea*

1   See, e.g., the chapters on the passion and resurrection of Christ (pp. 223-45 in Graesse's 3d ed., from which all my quotations are taken), the Chair of Saint Peter (pp. 178-83), the Rogations (pp. 312-16), the Ascension and Pentecost (pp. 318-37), and the nativity of John the Baptist (pp. 356-64).

2   Poncelet himself seems not to have drawn this conclusion; in fact, he argued that both the title *Legenda* or *Legendae sanctorum* and the contents of Jacobus's book "semblent indiquer que Jacques s'est surtout proposé de mettre aux mains des fidèles un livre de lectures édifiantes, et non pas de composer un manuel à l'usage des prédicateurs" ("Le légendier de Pierre Calo," p. 24). In Dondaine's 1946 article "Le dominicain français Jean de Mailly et la *Légende dorée,*" however, one finds the *Legenda* characterized precisely as "une somme de prédication" (p. 82) and shown to be more, rather than less, sophisticated in its contents than Jean's compilation for parish priests. More recently, William A. Hinnebusch has described the *Legenda* as part of the "arsenal" of reference books compiled by the early Friars Preachers, classing it with such works as scriptural concordances, handbooks for confessors, and collections of illustrative material for use in sermons (*History of the Dominican Order,* 2 [New York, 1973]: 232).

3   "Cum plurimi sacerdotes sanctorum passiones et vitas non habeant et ex officio suo eas nec ignorare nec tacere debeant ad excitandam fidelium devotionem in sanctos, eorum maxime vitas qui in kalendariis annotantur succincte perstringimus, ut et libelli brevitas fastidium non generet, et

parrochiales presbyteros librorum inopia non excuset'' (quoted in Poncelet, "Le légendier de Pierre Calo," pp. 22-23).

4   The crucial wording from this preface reads as follows: "Habeatque Predicatorum ordo nec non et alii, qui sine fictione discere et sine invidia hec aliis communicare desiderant, velocius pre manibus quid de sanctis ad Dei laudem et proximorum hedificationes audientibus proponant'' (ibid., p. 16).

5   "Duodecim monasteria . . . [construxit], in quibus statutis patribus duodenos monachos deputauit, paucos uero secum retinuit, quos adhuc in sua praesentia aptius erudiri iudicauit.''

6   "Quidam monachus erat qui ad orationem stare non poterat, sed mox ut se fratres ad orationis studium inclinassent, ipse egrediebatur foras et mente uaga terrena aliqua et transitoria agebat. Cumque ab abbate suo saepius fuisset admonitus, ad uirum Dei deductus est, qui ipse quoque eius stultitiam uehementer increpauit, et ad monasterium reuersus uix duobus diebus uiri Dei admonitionem tenuit, nam die tertio ad usum proprium reuersus, uagari tempore orationis coepit.''

7   "Multis ad eum venientibus duodecim monasteria construxit. In uno autem illorum quidam monachus erat . . .''

8   " . . . quidam monachus erat, qui ad orationem diu stare non poterat, sed orantibus aliis mox foras exibat et aliqua terrena et transitoria agebat. Quod cum abbas illius monasterii beato Benedicto narrasset, ivit illuc . . .''

9   "Et extunc immobilis in oratione permansit, sicque antiquus hostis dominari non ausus est in ejus cogitatione, ac si ipse percussus fuisset ex verbere'' (*Legenda,* p. 206). The wording in the *Dialogues* is a bit fuller at the beginning but otherwise almost identical.

10 It is probably not just coincidence that the *Rule of Saint Benedict* authorizes the use of corporal punishment in cases of obstinacy if the brother in question has been twice admonished by his superiors in private and once in public, to no avail (ch. 23).

11 "Die igitur alia, expleta oratione, vir Dei monachum foris reperit, quem pro sui caecitate virga percussit et extunc immobilis in oratione permansit.''

12 "Cum uero iam omnipotens Deus et Romanum uellet a labore requiescere, et Benedicti uitam in exemplum hominibus demonstrare, ut posita super candelabrum lucerna claresceret, quatenus omnibus qui in domo sunt luceret, cuidam presbitero . . . per uisum Dominus apparere dignatus est, dicens . . .'' (*Dial.* II.1.6).

13 "Post hoc cuidam presbitero refectionem sibi in paschali solemnitate paranti dominus per visum apparuit dicens: tu tibi delicias praeparas et servus meus illo in loco fame cruciatur. Qui protinus surrexit . . .''

From "cuidam presbitero" on, this passage follows that in the *Dialogues* almost verbatim.

14   "Vicit itaque peccatum, quia mutauit incendium. Ex quo uidelicet tempore, sicut post discipulis ipse perhibebat, ita in illo est temptatio uoluptatis edomita, ut tale in se aliquid minime sentiret. Coeperunt postmodum multi iam mundum relinquere, atque ad eius magisterium festinare. Liber quippe a temptationis uitio, iure iam factus est uirtutum magister" (*Dial.* II.2.2-3). "Vicit itaque peccatum, quia mutavit incendium. Ab illo autem tempore nulla postmodum tentatio in ejus corpore pullulavit" (*Legenda,* p. 205).

15   "Tunc . . . , cum ille ad monasterium rediisset, elevatis oculis animam sororis suae in specie columbae coeli secreta penetrantem adspexit" (*Legenda,* p. 212). At this point Gregory added a description of his joyfulness and praise to God: "Qui tantae eius gloriae congaudens, omnipotenti Deo in hymnis et laudibus gratias reddidit, eiusque obitum fratribus denuntiauit" (*Dial.* II.34.1).

16   After recounting Benedict's orders for the burial of Scholastica in the tomb he had prepared for himself, Gregory (but not Jacobus) continues, "Quo facto contigit, ut quorum mens una semper in Deo fuerat, eorum quoque corpora nec sepultura separaret" (*Dial.* II.34.2). Although Jacobus retells the preceding story of the miraculous storm which forces Benedict to remain with Scholastica one night, he omits the details indicating that this is one in a regular series of visits between them, that they have spent many hours together in mutually enjoyable spiritual conversation, and that Benedict's refusal to stay even later is based on a sense of obligation to his monastery. The *Legenda* suggests only that Benedict's sister, who is not characterized or even named in the narrative, manages by her prayers, on one occasion shortly before her death, to obtain a longer visit with him than he was willing to grant.

17   Of Gregory's whole lengthy account, the *Legenda* retains only a summary description of the vision itself and the assertion that Germanus did in fact die at the very time Benedict saw his soul's ascent: "Quadam nocte dum servus domini Benedictus per fenestram conspiceret et dominum exoraret, vidit fusam lucem desuper cunctas noctis tenebras effugasse. Subito autem totus mundus velut sub uno solis radio collectus ante oculos ejus adductus est ibique animam Germani, episcopi capitalis, ad coelum deferri videns manifeste comperit postea, quod hora eadem a corpore migravit" (p. 212).

18   Omitted are the story involving a forbidden meal outside the monastery and the one about the monk who hid away some handkerchiefs he had received as a gift (*Dial.* II.12 and 19, respectively); the former story was discussed above, in Chapter 4.

19   "Thotila rex Gothorum experiri volens, utrum vir Dei prophetiae
      spiritum haberet, cuidam suo spatario vestimenta regalia tribuit eumque
      cum omni apparatu regio ad monasterium destinavit, quem [Benedictus]
      venientem conspiciens dixit: pone, fili, pone: hoc quod portas, non est
      tuum. Qui protinus in terram cecidit et quia tanto viri illudere
      praesumsisset, expavit."

20   "Gothorum namque temporibus, cum rex eorum Totila sanctum uirum
      prophetiae habere spiritum audisset, ad eius monasterium pergens, paulo
      longius substitit eique se uenturum esse nuntiauit. Cui dum protinus
      mandatum de monasterio fuisset, ut ueniret, ipse, sicut perfidae mentis
      fuit, an uir Domini prophetiae spiritum haberet, explorare conatus est"
      (*Dial.* II.14.1).

21   "Vir quidam duos flascones vini per quendam puerum ad eum misit, sed
      ille unum in via abscondit et alium detulit, vir autem Dei cum gratiarum
      actione accepit unum et descendentem puerum admonuit dicens: fili,
      vide ne de illo flascone, quem abscondisti, bibas, sed inclina eum caute et
      vide, quid intus habeat. Qui confusus valde ab eo exivit et reversus
      volens adhuc probare, quod audierat, cum flasconem inclinasset,
      protinus de eo serpens egressus est."

22   In the *Dialogues* (ch. 23.4-5) Benedict was informed of the excommuni-
      cation by the nuns' former nurse, who regularly offered an oblation on
      their behalf and applied to him, in her grief, when she saw their bodies
      leaving the church. The *Legenda* mentions her offerings and her role as a
      witness, but omits the details suggesting her emotions and the saint's
      desire to comfort her. Also omitted is Gregory's conclusion, which
      emphasized the spiritual meaning of Benedict's intervention ("Qua ex re
      indubitanter patuit, quia, dum inter eos qui communione priuati sunt
      minime recederent, communionem a Domino per seruum Domini
      recepissent"). Thus the emphasis falls simply on the visible miracle and
      on the power of Benedict's oblation to accomplish what all the nurse's
      oblations could not.

23   "Sed sicut nonnullis solet nobilitas generis parere ignobilitatem mentis,
      ut minus se in hoc mundo despiciant, qui plus se ceteris aliquid fuisse
      meminerunt, necdum praedictae sanctimoniales feminae perfecte lin-
      guam sub habitus sui freno restrinxerant, et eundem religiosum uirum,
      qui ad exteriora necessaria eis obsequium praebebat, incautis saepe
      sermonibus ad iracundiam prouocabant.
          "Qui cum diu ista toleraret, perrexit ad Dei hominem, quantasque
      pateretur uerborum contumelias enarrauit. Vir autem Dei haec de illis
      audiens, eis protinus mandauit, dicens: 'Corrigite linguam uestram,
      quia, si non emendaueritis, excommunico uos'" (*Dial.* II.23.2-3).

24   This change may reflect the suspicion that had become attached, by the
      time of the *Legenda,* to such informal versions of the religious life as
      Gregory had depicted. But surely late-medieval notions of propriety

could have been satisfied, and the original issues of pride and ingratitude preserved, by transforming the helpful layman into a female servant or lay sister.

25   "Non longe ab ejus monasterio duae sanctimoniales feminae ex nobili genere erant, quae linguam non restringebant, sed eum, qui iis praeerat, incautis sermonibus saepe ad iracundiam provocabant. Qui cum hoc viro Dei retulisset, mandavit iis dicens: restringite linguam vestram, alioquin excommunicabo vos."

26   "PETRVS. Iste uir diuinitatis, ut uideo, etiam secreta penetrauit, qui perspexit hunc clericum idcirco diabolo traditum, ne ad sacrum ordinem accedere auderet" (*Dial.* II.16.3). Peter's inferences are not always correct, but this one is implicitly affirmed as the dialogue proceeds.

27   "Clericus quidam, qui a dyabolo vexabatur, ad virum Dei, ut sanaretur, adductus est, cumque ab eo dyabolum expulisset, ait: vade et de caetero carnes non comedas nec ad sacros ordines accedas: quacumque autem die ad sacros ordines accedere praesumseris, juri dyaboli mancipaberis. Cum vero hoc aliquo tempore custodiisset, sed minores suos sibi praeponi in sacris ordinibus cerneret, verba viri Dei quasi ex longo tempore oblitus postposuit atque ad sacrum ordinem accessit. Quem mox, qui eum reliquerat, dyabolus tenuit eumque is vexare, quousque animam ejus excuteret, non cessavit" (*Legenda,* p. 208).

28   In a reversal of the usual pattern, the *Legenda* appends to this story a statement describing the thanksgiving of the boy and his family ("et de hoc immensas gratias Deo obtulerunt") and another suggesting the spiritual fruit borne by the miracle ("et postmodum dictus puer in bonis operibus perseverans in domino feliciter obdormivit" [p. 210]). The latter detail may have its origins in a later section of the *Dialogues* (IV.49.2-3) which recounts the blessed death of a monk named Antony; an Antony was cited as Gregory's source for this healing story, and the *Legenda* presents the story as if it were Antony himself (rather than a servant of his father's) who had been cured. The logic behind the *Legenda*'s reference to the boy's later holiness, when it characteristically omits such conclusions from the disciplinary stories, will become clearer as we proceed; see especially the last section of Chapter 8, below.

One of the other cures ascribed to Benedict was a posthumous miracle (*Dial.* II.38.1). The remaining cure and exorcism omitted from the *Legenda* are found, respectively, in chs. 27.3 and 30.1 of Gregory's account.

29   I refer to the story in which Benedict provides money for an indebted layman (*Dial.* II.27.1-2) and the one in which he dispels the illusion of a fire that was terrifying his followers (*Dial.* II.10).

30   "Alio quoque tempore Gothus quidam pauper spiritu ad conuersa-

tionem uenit, quem uir Domini Benedictus libentissime suscepit''
(II.6.1).

31   "Itaque, ferro perdito, tremebundus ad Maurum monachum cucurrit
Gothus, damnum quod fecerat nuntiauit, et reatus sui egit
paenitentiam'' (II.6.2).

32   "Quadam vice dum circa monasterium viri Dei quidam cum falcastro
vepres abscideret, ferrum de manubrio prosiliens in quendam [lacum]
profundum cecidit, cumque de hoc ille nimis angustaretur, vir Dei
manubrium in lacu posuit et mox ferrum ad suum manubrium usque
enatavit.''

33   See above, Chapter 4, n. 15.

34   "Ex his autem monasteriis . . . tria sursum in rupibus montis erant, et
ualde erat fratribus laboriosum semper ad lacum descendere, ut aquam
haurire debuissent, maxime quia ex deuexo montis latere erat graue
descendentibus in timore periculum. Tunc collecti fratres ex eisdem
tribus monasteriis ad Dei famulum Benedictum uenerunt, dicentes:
'Laboriosum nobis est propter aquam cotidie usque ad lacum descendere, et idcirco necesse est ex eodem loco monasteria mutari.'
    "Quos blande consolatus dimisit, et nocte eadem cum paruo puerulo
nomine Placido . . . eiusdem montis ascendit rupem, ibique diutius
orauit.''

35   "Ex his monasteriis tria sursum in rupibus montis erant, quae deorsum
cum magno labore aquas hauriebant, cumque fratres illi virum Dei saepe
rogarent, ut monasteria sua mutaret, quadam nocte cum quodam puero
montem adscendit, ubi diutius orans . . . .''

36   "'Valet enim omnipotens Deus etiam in illo montis cacumine aquam
producere, ut uobis laborem tanti itineris dignetur auferre''' (*Dial.*
II.5.3); "valet enim dominus inde vobis aquam producere'' (*Legenda,*
p. 206).

37   In Graesse's edition (pp. 209-10) this story occupies a bit more than 32
lines. The only other story even approaching this length in the *Legenda*
account is that about the envious priest Florentius, who attempts to harm
Benedict and his disciples and is punished with a sudden and violent
death just as he seems to have defeated the saint (pp. 206-7; 25 lines).
More typically, the *Legenda* devotes no more than 15 lines, and
sometimes as few as 5, to a given anecdote from the *Dialogues.*

38   "Cumque fratres parietem paulo altius aedificarent, antiquus hostis viro
Dei apparuit et quia ad laborantes fratres pergeret, indicavit, qui
protinus iis per nuntium misit: fratres, caute vos agite, quia ad vos
spiritus malignus venit. Vix autem nuntius verba complevit et ecce
parietem antiquus hostis evertit et quendam puerum monachum ruina
contrivit. Sed vir Dei puerum mortuum et laceratum in sacco ad se
adduci fecit et oratione sua ipsum resuscitans operi praedicto restituit.''

In Gregory's version the disaster was followed by reactions that showed its meaning to the community: "Contristati omnes ac uehementer adflicti, non damno parietis, sed contritione fratris. Quod uenerabili patri Benedicto studuerunt celeriter cum graui luctu nuntiare" (ch. 11.1). And after the body was brought to Benedict, there was enough additional detail to underline both the urgency of the saint's prayers and the wondrousness of the resurrection itself (ch. 11.2).

39   Nor am I completely alone in finding such patterns in the *Legenda*. A decade ago, in an article entitled "La justice immanente dans la 'Légende dorée'" (*Epopées, légendes, et miracles* [1974], pp. 135-47), Giselle Huot-Girard surveyed the fates of various kinds of malefactors in the *Legenda* and concluded that the lessons driven home are very harsh indeed: "Le règne de Dieu se maintient par la crainte, la terreur; la vérité luit par la force. C'est le Dieu de l'Ancien Testament, le Dieu justicier, le Dieu vengeur, qui réapparaît dans la *Légende dorée*" (p. 147).

40   Charles F. Altman, "Two Types of Opposition and the Structure of Latin Saints' Lives," *Medievalia et Humanistica*, n.s., 6 (1975): 1-11. My own distinction between adversarial and inclusive patterns in saints' legends owes a good deal to Altman's brief but thought-provoking discussion of the structures he differentiates as "diametrical" and "gradational."

41   There is a helpful overview of the classes of miracles conventionally used in these passions, with some critical comments on their effect, in Delehaye's *Les passions des martyrs et les genres littéraires* (Brussels, 1921), pp. 287-303. Sometimes, as Delehaye points out, these passions go so far as to have God strike the persecutors with physical blindness or some other affliction before they have managed to execute the martyrs—but to no avail. Even when such a malefactor is miraculously healed by one of the saints he is victimizing, he is practically never converted, or even persuaded to spare the life of the saint who has healed him.

42   The connections between the martyrs' own ordeal and their subsequent power to heal are much subtler and more interesting than I have had space to indicate; see esp. pp. 75-85 in Brown's *Cult of the Saints.*

43   As Guy Philippart recently put it, "L'édition hagiographique du bas moyen âge était minée par un traditionalisme pesant qui se mesure à la permanence, à travers mille ans d'histoire, de genres sans doute adaptés aux premiers siècles de la période, mais qui l'étaient de moins en moins. Permanence, c'est peu dire. Les *best-sellers* du IXᵉ siècle sont encore ceux de 1200, voire, à peine rhabillés dans les *Abbreviationes,* ceux de 1500: ce sont les Passions des martyrs. Ces récits—souvent épiques et fabuleux—ont continué de véhiculer une représentation antique du saint, une morale et une théologie désaccordées d'avec les aspirations et les croyances renouvelées" (*Les légendiers latins,* p. 47).

44   A quick survey of the *Legenda*'s hagiographical contents yields the
      following figures: 95 chapters whose principal figures are martyrs; 22 on
      apostles, bishops, and popes who did not undergo martyrdom; 24 on
      non-martyred hermits, monks, and recluses; and a mere 11 on confessors
      who represent other conditions of life. I have counted each saint only
      once, although several of them are celebrated in more than one chapter,
      and have not included the "legendae superadditae" which Graesse
      relegates to a sort of appendix in his edition.

Chapter 6: Jacobus as a Teacher

1   Richardson, *Materials for a Life of Jacopo da Varagine,* 2:41-43.

2   "Benedictus autem religiosus et pius puer, cum nutricem suam flere
      conspiceret, eius dolori conpassus, ablatis secum utrisque fracti capisterii
      partibus, sese cum lacrimis in orationem dedit. Qui ab oratione surgens,
      ita iuxta se uas sanum repperit, ut in eo fracturae inueniri uestigia nulla
      potuissent. Mox autem nutricem suam blande consolatus, ei sanum
      capisterium reddidit, quod fractum tulerat."

3   "Incepit a compassione: Gregor. 'Benedictus religiosus, & pius puer,
      cum nutricem suam flere conspiceret, ejus dolori compassus' est. Et ideo
      meruit divinam miserationem: *Beati misericordes, quoniam ipsi
      misericordiam consequentur.* Incepit a devota oratione, quia capisteri-
      um fractum, devota oratione sua redintegravit. Et ideo meruit a Deo
      magnam fiduciam, & securitatem: *Oratio humiliantis se penetrabit
      nubes, [. . .] & non discedet, donec aspiciat Altissimus.*
          All my quotations and page references from Jacobus's sermons are
      based on *Reverend. ac Illustr. Archiepiscopi Januensis P. F. Jacobi de
      Voragine ordinis Praedicatorum Sermones aurei de praecipuis sanc-
      torum festis, et laudibus Deiparae Virginis,* ed. Rudolph Clutius, vol. 2
      (Augsburg and Cracow, 1760); see pp. 107-8 for the quotation above. I
      have added quotation marks to set off passages borrowed verbatim from
      Gregory and have inserted the scriptural references. The four- or
      five-digit identification numbers cited for this and Jacobus's other
      sermons on the saints are those given by Johannes Baptist Schneyer in his
      invaluable *Repertorium der lateinischen Sermones des Mittelalters für
      die Zeit von 1150-1350,* part 3 (Münster Westfalen, 1971), pp. 246-66.

4   "Quam Benedictus flere conspiciens partes capisterii accepit et ab
      oratione surgens integre solidatum invenit."

5   The latter sort of audience was presumably the normative one by
      Dominican standards, since the early Friars Preachers focused so much
      of their attention on the urban areas where learning flourished. When
      Dominic dispersed his first disciples from southern France, he sent a
      significantly large proportion of them to the university cities of Paris and
      Bologna, where they could both learn and attract other students to the
      order. And his successors extended this kind of outreach; see, e.g., the

contemporary testimonies cited by William A. Hinnebusch in his *History of the Dominican Order,* 1:313-15.

6   "Ut se muniret contra daemonum malignitatem, qui animabus insidiantur."

7   "Quidam moriuntur jacentes, quia a bonis operibus vacaverunt: Quidam prostrati, qui per peccatum corruerunt: Quidam claudi, qui fidem sine operibus habuerunt: Quidam ab infirmitate sanati, qui post peccatum ad poenitentiam reverterunt: Quidam erecti sicut viri sancti, qui a peccato liberati sunt bonis operibus pleni, & intentione recti."

8   "Possunt haec verba, quae locutus est Dominus ad Abraham, convenire beato Benedicto, & cuilibet religioso, in quibus Dominus quemlibet nostrum ad tria hortatur.

     "Primo ad mundi contemptum . . .
     "Secundo Dominus hortatur ad religionis ingressum . . .
     "Tertio ponit religionis fructum . . ."

9   "Luna tamen non lucet, quando terra interponitur, quia ordo monasticus multum tenebratur, quando terrena cupiditate aspergitur."

10 "*Benedictus in filiis.* . . . sed modo potest conqueri: *Filios enutrivi, & exaltavi, ipsi autem spreverunt me.* Facti sunt et degeneres filii, quia regulares observantias contemnunt, & praelationibus, & abbatiis intendunt. Temporalia indebite consumunt, non Dei honorem, sed proprium favorem attendunt."

11 The Clutius edition reads "electione" rather than "lectione," an apparent misprint which I have corrected on the authority of a fifteenth-century edition of Jacobus's sermons which is presently in the Beinecke Library at Yale (*Sermones de sanctis* [Strassburg: Johann Grüninger, July 14, 1484], sig. 8).

12 "Devotius vixit, tota enim vita sua fuit in oratione, & ideo merebatur exaudiri . . . ; fuit in lectione, & ideo merebatur sapientia divina impleri. . . . Fuit in contemplatione, & ideo merebatur caelestibus revelationibus adimpleri. . . . Fuit in efficaci locutione, & ideo merebatur ab auditoribus exaudiri. Gregor. Dum enim sibi cibum deferebant 'corporis, ab ejus ore [. . .] alimenta deferebant vitae.'"

    Benedict is credited with preaching again in the second sermon ("Ipse enim per suam praedicationem, & regulam multos filios generavit" [p. 109]), and in the third there is a bit of allegorical imagery which sounds very much like an allusion to the distinctive black-over-white habit worn by the Friars Preachers: "Religio igitur tunc est bona, quando est nigra per asperitatem: Boni enim religiosi denigrant se per humilitatem exterius, sed dealbant se interius per puritatem" (p. 110). On the brethren's fondness for just such allegorical interpretations of their habit, see Hinnebusch, *History of the Dominican Order,* 1:339-40 and 366, n. 3.

13 "Sanctus Benedictus de mundo tenebroso venit ad desertum poeniten-
    tiae; & de deserto poenitentiae pervenit ad gustum caelestis gratiae; & de
    gustu gratiae, pervenit ad contemplationem visionis divinae."
        Similarly, the third sermon emphasizes the private, contemplative side
    of the religious life, referring several times to the spiritual blessings
    obtained "in deserto" (pp. 110-11).

14 As one might expect, Benedict's simultaneous renunciation of further
    book-learning goes almost unmentioned in Jacobus's sermons. At the
    beginning of the first sermon, Jacobus quotes most of Gregory's
    statement on the saint's actual decision against the value system of his
    parents, but he retains no suggestion of the surrounding context, which
    explicitly set education against wisdom: "Incepit a paupertate, Gregor.
    'Despectis [. . .] studiis, relicta domo, rebusque patris, [. . .] sanctae
    conversationis habitum quaesivit'" (p. 107; cf. *Dial.* II.Prol.). Indeed,
    this sermon goes on to depict Benedict as a scholar. In the second and
    third sermons (pp. 109 and 110) Jacobus depicts Benedict's flight to the
    wilderness as a rejection of riches, honors, home, and "carnalis
    affectio" for his family—but not of studies.

15 In the first sermon Jacobus draws specifically on the *Dialogues* only for
    the five virtues from Benedict's early life (three of which have to do with
    his withdrawal from worldly concerns and rewards), for the details on his
    preparation for death, and for some illustrations of his miraculous
    power (discussed later in this chapter). The longest and most detailed
    section of the second sermon recounts Benedict's victories over the devil,
    the flesh, and the world, again drawing most of its illustrations from the
    preface and first two chapters of Gregory's account. And the central
    theme of the third sermon, as mentioned above, is renunciation of the
    world for the religious life.

16 For once Jacobus has his reference wrong; the quotation actually comes
    from the prologue to Part III of Gregory's *Regula pastoralis* (PL 77.49),
    and Gregory attributes it to his Greek predecessor Gregory Nazianzen.
    In emphasizing this particular bit of advice for preachers, Jacobus
    echoes the treatise on preaching (*De eruditione praedicatorum*) by the
    fifth Dominican master general, Humbert of Romans, which cites the
    same passage and a good deal more in the same vein from the *Regula
    pastoralis;* see, e.g., the Blackfriars translation, ed. Walter M. Conlon
    (London, 1955), pp. 70-71. Humbert's treatise spells out a number of
    the assumptions about preaching that underlie Jacobus's practice.

17 "Non enim una & eadem instructio est omnibus facienda, sed secundum
    qualitatem auditorum formanda, sicut ostendit Greg. in libro Moral.
    dicens: Saepe aliis officiunt, quae aliis prosunt. Nam plerumque herbae,
    quae animalia reficiunt, alia occidunt: & levis sibilus equos mitigat,
    catulos instigat; & medicamentum quod huic morbum imminuit, alteri
    vires auget; & panis qui vitam fortium roborat, parvulorum necat."

18   Sherry L. Reames, "Saint Martin of Tours in the *Legenda aurea* and Before," *Viator* 12 (1981): esp. 148-49, 152-55.

19   These lessons are particularly evident in sermons 582 and 583 S81, both devoted to the theme of Martin's perfect conformity with the *regulae* prescribed for his successive states of life.

20   "Quamvis enim mulieribus sit inhibitum officium praedicationis, quibusdam tamen sanctis virginibus fuit officium praedicandi a Spiritu S. concessum, quadam praerogativa gratiae singularis."

21   Thus one argument for Catherine's superiority to other virgins, in the same sermon, is that she converted not just "homines populares" but queens and princes, not just "homines simplices, & illiteratos" but rhetoricians and philosophers (p. 366).

22   "Aliae [virgines] habuerunt aliquam sapientiam a Deo infusam, haec autem praeter sapientiam infusam fuit studiis omnium liberalium artium erudita. Aliae contentae erant simplici eruditione; de hac dicitur, quod per varias conclusiones syllogismorum allegorice, discrete, & mystice cum Caesare disputavit" (p. 366).

23   Another preacher might have found it impossible to derive the traditional lesson about obedience from this portion of the *Vita S. Martini,* since the only prominent superior is Julian the Apostate and the emphasis falls on Martin's moral stand against his orders. But Jacobus rises to the occasion with some neatly ambiguous wording: "Exhibebat . . . superioribus subjectionem, sicut Juliano Imperatori, in his, quae non essent contra Deum" (no. 582 S81, p. 355; cf. no. 583 S81, p. 356).

24   "Describitur autem justitia, quod sit virtus reddens unicuique jus suum, scilicet Deo obedientiam, superiori reverentiam, pari concordiam, inferiori disciplinam, inimicis patientiam, miseris & afflictis compassionem operosam, & sibi sanctimoniam."

     I hesitated over the translation of "disciplina" here because Jacobus proceeds to illustrate it, a few lines later, with references to forceful correction, not just teaching: "Quarto [Thomas] dedit subditis disciplinam, unde dicitur de eo: Sapientia qua praeditus erat, in Ecclesia malignorum prohibebat insultus. *Stultitia colligata est in corde pueri, & virga disciplinae fugabit eam* [Prov. 22:15]."

25   "Ex illa enim regula docentur Monachi . . . quantum ad Praelatos sit obedientia devota, ideo dicitur: *Vir & mulier sibi bene consentientes;* tunc enim Praelatus, qui per virum, & subditus qui per mulierem intelligitur, bene sibi consentiunt, quando Praelatus sapienter regit, & subditus humiliter obedit."

26   "Prima, quoniam Christus assumturus erat carnem in sexu virili, ut ipsum sexum honoraret et ampliorem sibi gratiam faceret, voluit, ut puer citius formaretur et mater citius mundaretur. Secunda ut, quoniam mulier plus peccavit quam vir, sic et aerumnae ejus ab aerumnis viri

duplicatae sunt exterius in mundo, sic ut duplicari debuerunt interius in utero. Tertia vero per hoc intelligi detur, quod mulier quodammodo plus fatigavit Deum quam vir, ex eo quod amplius deliquit'' (p. 159).

27   ''Quarto [pulchritudinem virginalem conservavit] per suspectae familiaritatis vitationem; non enim habebat familiaritatem, nisi cum personis sanctis, sicut cum Urbano Episcopo, & cum pauperibus, quos ipsa nutriebat; nam secundum Chrysost. Periculum magnum est mulieribus devotis familiaritatem habere cum viris, duplici de causa. Una est quia mulieres sunt incautae & molles. . . . Virginibus autem est majus periculum, sicut dicit idem, triplici de causa; quia scilicet sunt incautae, & quia sunt molles, & quia sunt inexpertae. . . . Viduis vero est maximum periculum . . .''

28   ''Secundo habuit pulchritudinem, unde dicitur quod erat incredibilis pulchritudinis, & omnium oculis admirabilis videbatur. Pulchritudo autem mulieribus est causa ruinae. . . . Quinto passa est magnam sollicitationem; sollicitata quidem fuit magnis muneribus, & terroribus. Multae enim mulieres sunt, quae muneribus obediunt, & terroribus cedunt'' (no. 591 S85, pp. 365-66). Sermon 359 S18, on Saint Agnes, contains a more extended and emphatic set of generalizations about the ordinary female inability to overcome such ''impedimenta castitatis'' as youth, beauty, a noble suitor, the lure of presents, and the fear of suffering (p. 68).

29   ''Quarto [Beata Catharina] habuit libertatem, & securitatem, quia sui, & suorum domina remanserat. Nimia autem libertas, & securitas in muliere est periculosa. *Filiae tibi sunt, serva corpus illarum, & non ostendas hilarem faciem tuam ad illas* [Ecclus. 7:26]'' (no. 591 S85, p. 366).

30   ''Legitur in historia Ecclesiastica, quod cum in Niceno concilio diversi Episcopi diversos libellos Constantino praesentassent, ut ipse inter eos judicaret, omnes libellos in ignem projecit dicens: Deus vobis potestatem dedit de nobis judicare, & ideo a vobis recte judicamu[r]: Vos autem non potestis ab hominibus judicari: Vos enim nobis a Deo dati estis dii, & conveniens non est ut homo judicet deos, sed ille de quo dicitur; *Deus stetit in synagoga Deorum.*''
     Here Jacobus is quoting, with a few omissions, from Rufinus's continuation of the *Ecclesiastical History,* bk. I, ch. 2 (PL 21.468).

31   ''Corpus autem S. Thomae fuit organum Spiritus Sancti, Margarita Dei, & hostia Christi: ipsi autem persecutores fuerunt canes, ideo non debuerunt tangere organum Spiritus sancti; & quia erant porci, non debuerunt conculcare Margaritam Dei . . . & quia persecutores erant profani, ideo non debuerunt contrectare hostiam Christi. Corpus ergo B. Thomae a ministris Dei tantum tangi debuit, postquam tanquam sacra hostia immolatum fuit: nam & in veteri lege hostia Deo immolata non tangebatur, nisi manibus sacerdotum.''

32   See, respectively, sermon 582 S81 (p. 355), the end of 584 S81 and the beginning of 585 S81 (p. 358), and the second division of the long initial point in 584 S81 (p. 357). The first and most striking of these classification systems recurs with variations in the *Legenda* chapter on Saint Martin (pp. 744-45) and in Jacobus's sermons on such saints as Agnes (no. 360 S18, pp. 69-70), Peter Martyr (no. 431 S31, p. 162), and Francis (no. 558 S73, pp. 324-25).

33   "Secundo fuit ab hominibus amatus, & hoc propter multa beneficia, & miracula, quae inter eos fecit."

34   "Mira enim virtus de illo exibat, scilicet ab oculis suis, quando ligatum vidit ab hostibus, mox a vinculis est solutus. Mira a manibus suis, quia vas in quo erat potus venenatus, signo crucis confregit. Mira ab ore ejus, scilicet quando dixit monialibus, quae linguam suam non cohibebant: excommunica eas. Mira a corde suo, quia absentia, ut praesentia cognoscebat" (p. 108).

35   "Quosdam enim retinuit in vita a diabolica tentatione, sicut monachum, qui in oratione stare non poterat: Quosdam vero in morte, diabolica oppressione, sicut monachum, quem diabolus a ruina parietis oppresserat: Quosdam post mortem . . . ."

36   "Utebatur enim doctrinis, exemplis & etiam miraculis. Quidam enim erant inscii & ignari, & quantum ad istos utebatur bonis, & utilibus doctrinis, ut eos instrueret. Quidam erant insipidi & indevoti, & quantum ad istos utebatur gratiis & exemplis, ut indevotos attraheret. Quidam vero erant duri & obstinati, & quantum ad istos utebatur miraculis, ut eos converteret."

37   Severus, *Dialogues* II.4.

38   "Tertio placuit [Deo] in statu Pontificali. Duo enim sunt quae faciunt Praelatum esse perfectum, scilicet perfectio sanctitatis & dignitas potestatis" (no. 582 S81, p. 355). The resurrections are cited twice in the ensuing discussion, figuring both among the proofs that Martin "habuit magnam potestatem" and, less predictably, in an argument that he "habuit vitam sanctam" because he had received the Holy Spirit as the first apostles did.

39   "Tertio habuit gratiae manifestationem. . . . Manifestabat enim quod placuit Deo in statu laicali per Christi approbationem, cum dixit: Martinus adhuc catechumenus hac me veste contexit. In statu monachali per trium mortuorum resuscitationem: in statu pontificali per globi ignei appositionem" (no. 584 S81, p. 358).

Chapter 7: Saint Ambrose and the Enemies of the Church

1   For this text I have used the edition by Michele Pellegrino, *Vita di S. Ambrogio* (Rome, 1961), adding the conventional chapter numbers for ease of comparison with other versions.

2   *Vita Ambr.* 10.48 and 11.54; cf. the *Legenda,* p. 255.

3   "Quidam haereticus acerrimus disputator et durus et inconvertibilis ad fidem cum audiret Ambrosium praedicantem, vidit angelum ad aures ejus loquentem verba, quae populo praedicabat. Quo viso fidem, quam persequebatur, coepit defendere."

4   Jacobus omits just two of the punitive stories from the *Vita:* the one about the heretics fatally injured after they failed to keep their promise to debate publicly with Ambrose (*Vita Ambr.* 5.18), and the one in which Count Stilicho's soldiers are wounded by wild beasts just after they have seized a prisoner claiming sanctuary in a church (*Vita* 8.34).

5   L. Elliott Binns, *The History of the Decline and Fall of the Medieval Papacy* (1934; rept. Hamden, Conn., 1967), p. 98.

6   All the quotations in the remainder of this paragraph are taken from vol. 2 of Hinnebusch's *History of the Dominican Order.*

7   Perhaps it is just coincidence that Hinnebusch mentions the *Legenda* a mere two sentences after the arsenal image, but one would like to think he saw the connection.

8   Even more telling is the way Jacobus deemphasizes this issue when he deals with a saint like Martin of Tours, whose heroic example as a bishop was most vividly illustrated in his efforts to convert the still-pagan countryside—and when, in the Dominic chapter and elsewhere, he characterizes the mission of the Order of Preachers.

9   Even the chapter on James the Lesser, which recounts the siege and destruction of Jerusalem in grisly detail, shows noticeable restraint for a medieval narrative of its kind. Among the important Jews present at the martyrdom of James is a priest "ex filiis Rahab" who tries to intervene on his behalf; and the "populus" is credited with the desire to punish his murderers (*Legenda,* p. 298). Jacobus's account goes on to emphasize the proofs of God's desire to save the Jews, rather than see them punished for rejecting Christ (pp. 298-99). The message that Jews are human beings capable of redemption is reinforced elsewhere in the *Legenda* by Jacobus's tendency to retell stories in which they are converted, rather than condemned, by miracles; see, e.g., pp. 27-28 (two posthumous miracles of Saint Nicholas that result in such conversions), 78 (the conversion of Saint Sylvester's Jewish opponents), 125-26 (the Jewish physician beloved and finally converted by Saint Basil), and 608-9 (two stories in which Jews are converted by the miraculous blood that flows from images of Christ).

10   The implications of Jacobus's selectivity in the *Legenda* account are explicitly reaffirmed in his second sermon on Ambrose, which credits the saint with having defended the church "a tribus persecutoribus. Primo a violentia tyrannorum. . . . Secundo defendit ipsam a fraudulentia Haereticorum. . . . Tertio defendit Ecclesiam a malitia daemonum" (no.

422 S4, p. 152). Even more striking is the prominence of the same enemies in Jacobus's model sermons on Pope Sylvester—a prominence quite unexpected, since the triumphs actually celebrated in the Sylvester legend are the conversion of the emperor Constantine and a victorious debate with the Jews. In sermon 343 S13 Jacobus seizes the opportunity for a vivid lesson against the "error pravitatis haereticae," outlining the rise of the Arian heresy after Sylvester's death, its refutation at Nicaea, and the horrible death of Arius himself ("nefando ore, quo Christum blasphemavit, viscera sua evomuit" [p. 51]). And in sermon 344 S13 Jacobus manages to work in demons and secular rulers as well, by digressing from Sylvester's own career to his successors' responsibility to guard the flock from wolves: *"Ego scio quoniam intrabunt post discessionem meam lupi rapaces in vos non parcentes gregi* [Acts 20:29], & ideo ipsum a luporum morsibus custodiatis. Et intelliguntur lupi daemones, haeretici, & tyranni: Debent quidem praelati custodire Ecclesiam a morsibus daemonum per orationem assiduam. . . . A morsibus haereticorum per sanam doctrinam. . . . A morsibus tyrannorum per firmam constantiam" (p. 52).

11 "Quinto in orationis instantia, unde dicitur de eo et habetur in libro XI hystoriae ecclesiasticae: Ambrosius adversum reginae furorem non se manu defensabat aut telo, sed jejuniis et continuatis vigiliis, sub altari positus per obsecrationes defensorem sibi atque ecclesiae Deum parabat." The reference is to the first book of Rufinus's continuation of the *Ecclesiastical History* by Eusebius, ch. 16 (PL 21.524).

12 "Notandum, quod beatus Ambrosius in multis commendabilis fuisse videtur, primo in liberalitate, quia omnia, quae habebat, pauperum erant, unde refert de se ipso, quod imperatori petenti basilicam sic respondit et est in decreto XXIII qu.VIII: convenior etc., si a me peteret, quod meum esset, id est fundum meum, argentum meum et hujusmodi meum, non refragarer, quamquam omnia, quae mea sunt, pauperum sunt. . . . Tertio in fidei firmitate, unde dixit, cum imperator peteret basilicam, et est in eodem capitulo: prius est, ut animam mihi quam sedem auferat." Cf. Gratian's *Decretum* C. 23, q. 8, ch. 21 (PL 187.1254, 1256).

13 "Quo bello ecclesiae murum ac turrim validissimum pulsabat Ambrosium. In ejus quoque praefatione sic de eo cantatur: tanta Ambrosium virtute solidasti, constantiae tanto munere coelitus decorasti, ut per eum exclusa torquerentur daemonia, Arianorum impietas propulsa tabesceret ac secularium principum colla tuo jugo subacta redderentur humilia."
The preface in question, only part of which Jacobus quotes here, is found in the mass commemorating the baptism of Ambrose (November 30) in the so-called Ambrosian rite traditionally used at Milan; a full text is given in *Das ambrosianische Sakramentar von Biasca,* ed. Odilo

Heiming, vol. 1 (*Corpus Ambrosiano Liturgicum* 2 [Münster Westfalen, 1969]), p. 8.

14   *Legenda,* pp. 256-57; cf. the *Decretum,* ch. cited (PL 187.1254-56). The ultimate sources are Ambrose's epistle 20, to Marcellina (PL 16.996-99), and his "Sermo contra Auxentium" (PL 16.1008, 1012, and 1018). Jacobus's version focuses even more narrowly on the legal issue than the *Decretum* does, and does not retain the statements affirming the possibility of a constructive relationship between the emperor and the church.

15   *Legenda,* pp. 257-58; cf. Cassiodorus-Epiphanius, *Historia ecclesiastica tripartita* IX.30.3-25 (ed. Rudolph Hanslik, Corpus scriptorum ecclesiasticorum latinorum 71 [Vienna, 1952], pp. 541-45). The major changes in Jacobus's selective abridgement have to do with the character of Theodosius, whose piety and spiritual perceptiveness are no longer shown, and the nature of his relationship with Ambrose, which predictably becomes more adversarial. Jacobus's lack of interest in the pastoral dimension of the story is perhaps most strikingly exhibited at the end, when he neglects even to mention the nature of the public penance to which Theodosius consented.

16   The motif finds its most sustained and dramatic expression in Ambrose's initial speech to Theodosius at the door of the church: "Quibus igitur oculis aspicies communis domini templum? Quibus calcabis pedibus sanctum illius pavimentum? Quomodo manus extendas, de quibus adhuc sanguis stillat iniustus? Quomodo huiusmodi manibus suscipies sanctum domini corpus? Qua praesumptione ore tuo poculum sanguinis pretiosi percipies, dum furore sermonum tantus iniuste sit sanguis effusus? Recede igitur, recede, ne secundo peccato priorem nequitiam augere contendas" (Cassiodorus, IX.30.8-9 [pp. 541-42]). Except for the fourth question, whose absence from a late-medieval version is not surprising, this portion of the dialogue is repeated almost verbatim in the *Legenda* (p. 257), where it naturally looms even larger than in Cassiodorus because so much of the surrounding material has been abbreviated and simplified.

17   "Cum igitur reconciliatus ecclesiam intrasset et intra cancellos staret, requirit Ambrosius, quid ibi exspectaret. Cui cum diceret, se perceptionem sacrorum ministeriorum exspectare, ait Ambrosius: o imperator interiora loca tantum sacerdotibus sunt collocata, egredere igitur et hanc exspectationem cum caeteris communem habe, purpura namque imperatores facit non sacerdotes. Cui imperator protinus obedivit. Cum ergo Constantinopolin reversus extra cancellos staret, mandavit eidem episcopus, ut intraret, et ille ait: vix discere potui, quod differentia sit imperatoris et sacerdotis, vix enim veritatis inveni magistrum, Ambrosium namque solum novi vocari pontificem."

Cf. Cassiodorus, IX.30.26-30 (pp. 545-46). Here again Jacobus's abridgement has both simplified the issue and increased the apparent opposition between the emperor and the saint. The original thrust of the story was summed up in the way Theodosius responded to Ambrose's words: "Tunc fidelissimus imperator etiam hanc traditionem animo gratanti suscipiens remandavit: 'Non audaciae causa intra cancellos mansi, sed in Constantinopolitana urbe hanc consuetudinem esse cognovi. Unde ago gratias pro huiusmodi medicina.' Tali ergo tantaque et praesul et imperator virtute clarebant" (IX.30.28-29).

18   "Cui Ambrosius ait: etsi ego indignus tanto sacerdotio, tibi tamen non convenit in qualemcunque sacerdotem manus injicere, unde timere debuisti judicium Dei, ne tibi aliquid contingat."

19   "Et tu quidem venies ad ecclesiam nec clausis ianuis invenies qua ingrediaris." The version in the *Legenda,* p. 253, is a bit ambiguous grammatically, but clearly means the same thing.

20   "Alius etiam gladium ferens ad cubiculum usque pervenit, ut interficeret sacerdotem; sed cum elevasset manum, districto gladio, dextera obrigente remansit. Tunc se missum a Iustina postquam confessus est, brachium quod inique cum extenderetur obriguerat sanatum est confessione."

21   "Alius quidam nocte ejus cubiculum adiit, ut gladio ipsum necaret, prece ac pretio a Justina inductus, sed cum dextra gladium elevasset, ut ipsum percuteret, continuo aruit manus ejus."

22   In the *Vita* his punishment comes on the first anniversary of his attempt on Ambrose.

23   "Innumeras insidias a Justina imperatrice [Ambrosius] pertulit, muneribus et honoribus adversus eum populum excitante. Cum ergo multi eum in exsilium pellere niterentur, unus eorum caeteris infelicior in tantum furorem excitatus est, ut juxta ecclesiam domum sibi locaret ac in ea quadrigam paratam haberet" (*Legenda,* p. 251). In the *Vita* the story also began with a general statement on Justina's efforts, but the man was not introduced until the moral issues had been clarified further: "Sed infirmorum animi talibus promissis decipiebantur: promittebat enim tribunatus et diversas alias dignitates his qui illum de ecclesia raptum ad exilium perduxissent. Quod cum multi conarentur, sed Deo praesule perficere non valerent, unus infelicior ceteris, nomine Euthymius, in tantum furorem . . . ."

24   "In eodem carpento inpositus de eadem domo ipse ad exilium destinatus est, reputans sibi iusto iudicio Dei id in se esse conversum, ut in eo carpento dirigeretur ad exilium quod ipse paraverat sacerdoti. Cui non minimum solatii sacerdos praebuit, dando sumptus vel alia quae erant necessaria" (*Vita Ambr.* 4.12). Jacobus discards most of the "reputans" clause, with its suggestion of moral awakening on the

culprit's part, and replaces the reference to consolation with a more impersonal formula when he mentions Ambrose's gesture.

25   "Sed Dei judicio ipso die, quo eum rapere arbitrabatur, in eadem quadriga de eadem domo in exsilium pulsus est. Cui tamen Ambrosius reddens bona pro malis, sumptus et necessaria ministravit."

26   "Quidam aruspex daemones advocabat et ipsos ad nocendum Ambrosio transmittebat, sed reversi daemones renuntiabant, quod non solum ad ipsum, sed nec etiam ad fores domus suae appropinquare valebant, quoniam ignis insuperabilis omne illud a[e]dificium communiret, ut etiam longe positi urerentur" (*Legenda,* p. 252).

27   "Ad excitanda odia populorum in episcopum cacumen tecti ecclesiae conscendens medio noctis sacrificaverit. Sed quanto instantius et sollicitius opera maligna exercebat, tanto magis amor populi circa fidem catholicam et Domini sacerdotem convalescebat" (*Vita Ambr.* 6.20).

28   "Quidam aruspex Innocentius nomine non tamen opere, cum in causa maleficiorum a iudice torqueretur, aliud quam interrogabatur fateri coepit; clamabat enim ab angelo maiora tormenta sibi adhiberi eo, qui custodiret Ambrosium."

29   "Praedictus vero aruspex cum a judice propter quaedam maleficia torqueretur, clamabat amplius ab Ambrosio se torqueri."

30   "Cum quidam vir quoddam flagitium perpetrasset et coram eo adductus fuisset, dixit Ambrosius: oportet illum tradi Sathanae in interitum carnis, ne talia deinceps audeat perpetrare. Quem eodem momento, cum adhuc sermo esset in ore ejus, immundus spiritus discerpere coepit." The *more* of Graesse's edition is obviously a mistake for *in ore,* the reading of the *Vita.*

31   Dolan's *History of the Reformation* gives a pertinent account of Erasmus's own program for ecclesiastical concord, emphasizing his arguments for moderation and flexibility so that the necessary reforms might be achieved without forcing anyone "into a religion that repels him" (p. 370); Witzel's work toward the same end is described in the ensuing pages (371-82). Vives, who had seen members of his own family victimized by the Inquisition in Spain, was even more sensitive to the costs of intolerance than most of his fellow humanists. In fact, a fundamental tenet of his whole philosophy was the need to rise above the kind of partisan instinct that would defend the claims of one's own group, be it family or class or nation, at the expense of truth and the common good. On this aspect of his thought, see, e.g., the little collection of excerpts from his works published in French by Alain Guy, *Vivès; ou, L'humanisme engagé* (Paris, 1972), nos. 2, 13, 17, 21, 24, 26-28, and 30.

32   "Ottone deposito Fridericus, Heinrici filius, eligitur et ab Honorio coronatur. Leges optimas pro libertate ecclesiae et contra haereticos

edidit. Hic super omnes divitiis et gloria abundavit, sed iis in superbia abusus fuit, nam tyrannidem contra ecclesiam exercuit, duos cardinales vinculavit, praelatos, quos Gregorius IX. ad concilium convocaverat, capi fecit et ideo ab ipso excommunicatur. Denique Gregorius multis tribulationibus pressus moritur et Innocentius quartus natione Januensis concilium apud Lugdunum convocans ipsum imperatorem deposuit. Quo deposito et defuncto sedes imperii usque hodie vacat.''

The historical record is not nearly so simple as this passage suggests, of course. For one thing, Gregory had excommunicated Frederick in 1239 and may well have intended to depose him at the very council which was prevented, in 1241, by Frederick's capture of the cardinals and other prelates who were travelling to it. Nor did Frederick submit to the decree of deposition when it was finally proclaimed in 1245; rather, the last years of his life were marked by an increasingly bold and ruthless kind of warfare against the papacy and its allies. The monumental modern biography by Ernst Kantorowicz (*Frederick the Second, 1194-1250*, trans. E. O. Lorimer [1931; rept. New York, 1957]) sides with Frederick almost as unabashedly as the *Legenda* sides with the popes, but it sheds a good deal more light on the great symbolic issues that were bound up in the struggle, as well as on the practical grounds for the popes' enmity to this particular emperor.

33   Although the question of the *Legenda*'s date cannot be conclusively resolved until much more work has been done with the thirteenth-century manuscripts, enough has been learned about the sources behind it to create a scholarly consensus that 1255 is an unrealistically early estimate. As it happens, some of the strongest evidence in this regard is found in the chapter on Dominic, which repeatedly draws on two sources which were themselves first compiled between 1256 and 1260. Since this "late" material is sometimes quite thoroughly interwoven with Jacobus's borrowings from the earlier accounts of Dominic, one cannot easily dismiss it as an addition after the fact. And of course there is very little likelihood that the Dominic legend was omitted from Jacobus's original plan for the *Legenda*—as, say, the legends of Francis and Elizabeth of Thuringia might have been—and supplied in a later recension.

34   Brian Tierney, *The Crisis of Church and State, 1050-1300* (Englewood Cliffs, N. J., 1964), p. 141. See also Kantorowicz, *Frederick the Second,* esp. pp. 621-24, and C. W. Previté-Orton in the *Cambridge Medieval History,* 6 (1929): 176.

35   Tierney provides an English translation of the dramatic letter in which Frederick made this proposal to the kings of Christendom (pp. 145-46), along with a brief assessment of its significance (pp. 141-42). See also Kantorowicz, *Frederick the Second,* pp. 615-19.

36   Antoine Dondaine, "La hiérarchie cathare en Italie," *Archivum fratrum praedicatorum* 19 (1949): 280-312, and 20 (1950): 234-324.

37   Ibid., 20:285, n. 14.

38   See, e.g., the *Cambridge Medieval History,* 6:145 and 151-55 (the role of
      the Lombard League early in the war against Frederick), 163-64 and 166
      (the political situation at Frederick's death), and 168-71 (the impedi-
      ments to Innocent's goals thereafter.

39   The nature of this campaign is spelled out with unusual clarity in Henri
      Maisonneuve's *Etudes sur les origines de l'Inquisition,* 2d ed. (Paris,
      1960), pp. 307-15. Maisonneuve also supplies a good deal of informa-
      tion on the earlier history of the Inquisition in Lombardy; see esp. pp.
      243-57.

40   "Verum cum pestis haeretica in Lombardiae provincia pullularet et
      multas jam civitates contagione pestifera infecisset, summus pontifex ad
      pestem dyabolicam abolendam diversos inquisitores de ordine praedica-
      torum in diversis Lombardiae partibus delegavit. Sed cum apud
      Mediolanum haeretici non solum multi numero, sed etiam saeculari
      potentia acuti fraudulenta eloquentia et pleni dyabolica scientia reside-
      rent . . . ."

      Since this passage is used to introduce the final mission of Peter of
      Verona, or Saint Peter Martyr, the pope in question is presumably
      Innocent IV and the year 1251.

41   ". . . summus pontifex sciens et intelligens beatum Petrum virum esse
      magnanimum, qui ab hostium multitudine non paveret, animadvertens
      quoque ejus constantem virtutem, per quam adversariorum potentiae
      nec in modico cederet, cognoscens etiam ejus facundiam, per quam facile
      haereticorum fallacias detegeret, non ignorans insuper ipsum in divina
      plene sapientia eruditum, per quam frivola haereticorum argumenta
      rationabiliter confutaret, ipsum tam strenuum fidei pugilem et tam
      indefessum domini bellatorem in Mediolano et ejus comitatu instituit, et
      inquisitorem suum auctoritate concessa plenaria ordinavit."

42   "Petrus per martirium haereticos multos convertit. Quamvis enim
      egregius doctor et fidei pugil haereticorum dogma pestiferum in vita sua
      plurimum eradicaverit, post mortem tamen suam ejus meritis et
      coruscantibus miraculis fuit adeo exstirpatum, ut quam plurimi errorem
      suum relinquerent et ad gremium sanctae ecclesiae convolarent, ita ut
      civitas Mediolanum et comitatus ejusdem . . . purgata est" (*Legenda,* p.
      282).

43   Thus the number of Dominicans serving as inquisitors in Lombardy was
      raised to four and then eight during the 1250s, and each of them seems
      ordinarily to have been accompanied and assisted by a *socius,* or
      travelling companion, from the order, a deputy, at least one notary, and
      a small army of legal advisers and minor functionaries. In theory at
      least, the bishop of the diocese in question also involved himself in the
      proceedings.

44   On these developments, see A. S. Turberville in the *Cambridge Medieval History,* 6:719-22, and Maisonneuve, *Origines de l'Inquisition,* esp. pp. 315-28.

45   Despite its age and strong Protestant bias, Henry Charles Lea's *History of the Inquisition of the Middle Ages* (1888; rept. New York, 1958) is probably still the best source on this subject; see vol. 2, esp. pp. 218-38.

46   "Plures etiam de iis maximi et famosi praedicatores ordinem sunt ingressi, qui usque nunc cunctos haereticos et fautores fervore mirabili persequuntur."

47   "Secundo defendit [Ecclesiam] a fraudulentia Haereticorum; & hoc fiebat tribus modis. Primo judiciis, eos per saeculare brachium coercendo. *Si tibi voluerit persuadere frater tuus,* &c. Et infra: *Neque parcat ei oculus tuus,* &c. *sed statim interficias."*

      Jacobus's failure to support this assertion with any citation from the life or writings of Ambrose suggests (not surprisingly) that he was unable to find one. In reality, Ambrose was vehemently opposed to the idea that the church might implement the code of Deuteronomy against heretics; see, e.g., his letters 24.12, 25, and 26 (Benedictine numbering), PL 16.1039-46. On the extent to which other authorities from the patristic period, notably Augustine, laid the groundwork for the late-medieval Inquisition, the discussion in Joseph Lecler's *Toleration and the Reformation,* trans. T. L. Westow (London, 1960), 1:32-64, is particularly clear, precise, and even-handed.

48   The principal orthodox doctrines driven home in these instances concern the sacrament of baptism (sermon 342 S13, p. 50), the dual nature of Christ and the genuineness of his sufferings on the cross (no. 430 S31, p. 161), the reality of Purgatory and the efficacy of masses and other good works for the dead (*Legenda,* pp. 728-39), and the holiness of John the Baptist and—again—the sacrament he instituted (*Legenda,* esp. pp. 358-63). The *Legenda* chapters on Christ's advent, nativity, circumcision, passion, resurrection, and ascension also place considerable emphasis on points denied by the Cathars in particular, including the literal incarnation of Christ and the holiness of the Old Testament and its law. Since virtually all the contemporary heretics rejected the authority of the Catholic clergy, insisting that a true apostle of Christ neither embraced earthly wealth and power nor practiced persecution, Jacobus's authoritarian stories about the saints could of course be used against them as well. Among the most pertinent sources on these heresies are the *summae contra haereticos* attributed to Jacobus's fellow Dominicans Anselm of Alessandria, Peter Martyr, Moneta of Cremona, and Rainerius Sacconi. Substantial excerpts from all four and further bibliographical information can be found in the handy sourcebook by Walter L. Wakefield and Austin P. Evans, *Heresies of the High Middle Ages* (New York, 1969).

49   Jacobus relates a briefer version of this highly dramatic story at the
      beginning of sermon 516 S60 and follows it with a polemical interpreta-
      tion of David's vengeance on the Ammonites for their shameful
      treatment of his messengers (2 Kings 10). By putting the two stories
      together, Jacobus manages to draw a conclusion which endorses the use
      of physical as well as spiritual force against "tyranni" who persecute the
      clergy: "Sed & David qui interpretatur manu fortis, id est bonus
      Praelatus debet habere audacem animum, ut tales non timeat; debet
      habere imperiosum verbum, ut scilicet eos reprehendat & excommunica-
      tioni subjiciat, & debet habere hujusmodi Praelatus fortem manum, ut
      etiam per brachium saeculare si opus fuerit, eos coerceat" (pp. 269-70).
      This whole sermon is noteworthy for its explicitly negative messages
      about the relationship between laymen and religious.
          The sort of polemical weapon a preacher could devise from exempla
      about the saints' moral authority, if he combined them with Old
      Testament stories of vengeance, is suggested again in Jacobus's sermon
      356 S17; under the heading of the "gladius justitiae" which good men
      wield against bad, he cites Pope Fabian's rebuke to the emperor Decius
      and Exodus 32:27, a text in which God commands the Levites to wield
      literal swords in a great bloodbath against the Israelites who have
      abandoned his worship for that of the golden calf (p. 65).

50   See esp. pp. 143-45, 309-10, 365-66, and 570-72 of the *Legenda.*

51   See the end of Chapter 5, above.

52   Hinnebusch, *History of the Dominican Order,* 1:88. In the next
      paragraph Hinnebusch confirms that this strategy was retained by later
      popes and their legates, and by at least one more generation of friars who
      preached in Lombardy. A subsequent volume of his history is
      apparently to treat the matter in some detail.

Chapter 8: Saint Augustine and the Holy Life

1   Kaeppeli provides a brief but useful bibliography on the *Tractatus* in his
      Scriptores Ordinis Praedicatorum, 2:369, citing twelve manuscripts in
      which this brief work survives, an early printing, and a recent edition in
      an American dissertation. The tradition about Jacobus's having
      memorized Augustine is mentioned, with varying degrees of skepticism,
      by such authorities as Echard (*Scriptores Ordinis Praedicatorum* 1:458),
      Touron (*Histoire,* 1:585), and Richardson (*Materials,* 2:83).

2   The material in question runs from the end of fol. 159^v to the first
      column of fol. 163 in Bibliothèque Nationale MS. latin 5406, and
      includes all the passages of selective quotation from the *Confessions* and
      the *Soliloquies* which Jacobus cited to illustrate Augustine's virtues after
      conversion, a number of abridged testimonies from Possidius on the
      same theme, and all but one of the miraculous events that Jacobus
      derived from other sources; only for the translation of Augustine's

remains to Pavia (fols. 161v-162) does this part of Gui's chapter draw on a more detailed source. Although Gui has reordered the excerpts and edited them somewhat, they parallel the *Legenda* so consistently in both content and wording that there cannot be much uncertainty about his immediate dependence on it. He separates these additions from his account of Augustine's life (fols. 155v-159v) with the following statement: "Hec ex gestis que digessit Possidonius [*sic*] sunt accepta: ea vero que sequntur collecta sunt aliunde, nam & ipse Augustinus plura de se ipso conscripsit in libro confessionum, ubi de malis suis coram Deo humiliter se accusat, & de donis & beneficiis divinis gratias agit." Despite the ascription to Possidius, the principal source behind Gui's own account is the *Confessions,* whose narrative content he presents in an abridgement that is more detailed and much less revisionary than Jacobus's.

3   See especially the comments of Claude d'Espence, Melchior Cano, and Georg Witzel, quoted above in Chapter 3. The same charge was made by such Protestant spokesmen as Thomas Becon and John Jewel.

4   For the Latin *Vita* I have relied on the revised text by Herbert T. Weiskotten (Princeton, 1919). The echoes mentioned here occur in the *Legenda* account of Augustine's parentage and education (p. 549); cf. *Vita Aug.,* ch. 1.

5   The Augustine chapter itself contains an emphatic statement, not paralleled in the *vita,* about the need for confession and the Eucharist before one dies: "Denique dissolutione corporis appropinquante hoc memoriale docuit, nullum videlicet hominem quantumcunque excellentis meriti sine confessione et eucharistia debere transire" (p. 559). In sermon 524 S63 Jacobus repeats this point about the Eucharist (p. 282) and also affirms the role of baptism among the causes of Augustine's blessedness: "Beatus autem Augustinus, quem Christus genuit per Ambrosii doctrinam, & Baptismi gratiam, & lachrymarum matris abundantiam" (p. 283). Other chapters of the *Legenda* that lay some stress on the importance of baptism include those on Saints Sylvester (pp. 72, 75), Sebastian (p. 111), Christina (p. 420), Mamertinus (pp. 580-81), Remy or Remigius (p. 659), and Cecilia (pp. 772-74). Lessons about the sanctity of the Eucharist and its importance, especially as part of one's preparation for death, are far more numerous.

6   "In liberalibus artibus sufficienter edoctus fuit, adeo ut summus philosophus et rhetor luculentissimus haberetur. Nam libros Aristotelis et omnes libros liberalium artium, quoscunque legere potuit, per se didicit et intellexit, sicut in libro confessionum testatur dicens: omnes libros, quos liberales vocant, tunc nequissimus malarum cupiditatum servus per me ipsum legi et intellexi, quoscunque legere potui."

Jacobus has extracted this statement from the question which opens sec. IV.16.30 of the *Confessions:* "Et quid mihi proderat, quod omnes libros . . .?" (*Confessionum libri tredecim,* ed. Martin Skutella, vols. 13-14 of *Oeuvres de Saint Augustin* [Paris, 1962]).

7   "Quem Augustinus in sua adolescentia, dum adhuc gentilis et philosophus esset, genuerat."

8   "Item in eodem [libro]: quicquid est de arte loquendi et disserendi, quicquid de dimensionibus figurarum et de musicis et de numeris, sine magna difficultate nullo hominum tradente intellexi. Scis, tu domine Deus meus, quia celeritas intelligendi et discendi acumen donum tuum est, sed non inde sacrificabam tibi, verum quia scientia sine caritate non aedificat, sed inflat."

     Again Jacobus's source is *Conf.* IV.16.30; the largest verbal difference here is Jacobus's "discendi" where Skutella's text has "dispiciendi."

9   "In errorem Manichaeorum, qui Christum phantasticum fuisse affirmant et carnis resurrectionem negant, incidit et in eo per annos IX, dum adhuc adolescens esset, permansit. Ad has etiam nugas adductus est, ut arborem fici plorare diceret, cum ab ea folium vel ficus tolleretur" (*Legenda,* pp. 549-50). For this detail see *Conf.* III.10.18. Among the more important effects deplored by Augustine himself are blindness to the very nature of God and of goodness (III.6.10ff.), blasphemy (e.g., IV.16.31), and spiritual pride (V.10.18 et passim).

10   See, e.g., the accounts in Hinnebusch's *History,* vol. 1, of Dominic's special efforts to recruit university students (pp. 61-62), the background of Reginald of Orleans and the other learned men he attracted to the order (pp. 59, 64-65), and the emphasis on academic training and promise in the later recruiting campaigns by Jordan of Saxony and Humbert of Romans (pp. 313-15).

11   "Immisit dominus in mentem ejus, ut ad Simplicianum, in quo lucebat lux, divina scilicet gratia, pergeret, ut sibi aestus suos secum conferenti proferret, quis esset aptus modus vivendi ad ambulandum in via Dei, in qua alius sic, alius sic ibat" (*Legenda,* p. 551). Here Jacobus is condensing the account in *Conf.* VIII.1.1-2.

12   "[Augustinus] ceteris suspensior aderat, ne quid vel pro ipsa vel contra ipsam haeresim diceretur. Et *provenit Dei liberatoris clementia sui sacerdotis cor pertractantis,* ut contra illum errorem incidentes legis solverentur quaestiones, atque ita edoctus sensim atque paulatim haeresis *illa miseratione divina* eius ex animo expulsa est" (*Vita Aug.,* ch. 1; emphasis mine). "Erat autem valde in praedicatione suspensus, ne quid contra ipsam Manichaeorum haeresin vel pro ipsa diceretur. Quadam enim vice contra illum errorem Ambrosius diutius disputavit et ipsum apertis rationibus et auctoritatibus confutavit, ita ut error ille a corde Augustini penitus pelleretur" (*Legenda,* pp. 550-51).

13   "An uero tu, deus misericordiarum, sperneres cor contritum et humiliatum uiduae castae ac sobriae . . . , bis die, mane et uespere, ad

ecclesiam tuam sine ulla intermissione uenientis, non ad uanas fabulaš et aniles loquacitates, sed ut te audiret in tuis sermonibus et tu illam in suis orationibus? . . ." (*Conf.* V.9.17).

14   Thus from the passage quoted in part in note 13, Jacobus retains nothing except the image of Monica's dedication ("Quolibet autem die, mane et vespere, ad ecclesiam ibat et pro filio orabat" [*Legenda,* p. 550]). He gives a much fuller account of her prophetic dream, relating both her conversation with the young man who promises that Augustine will eventually stand on the same "regula" where she is standing and her subsequent argument with Augustine about the dream's meaning (ibid.); gone, however, are the whole surrounding context, which explicitly praised God for having heard and consoled Monica, and even the narrative details which made it clear that the young man was a messenger from heaven. The ensuing story about the impatient bishop's answer is yet more depersonalized, as Jacobus retells it; and the one about Augustine's departure for Rome mentions only Monica's despairing cries to God, not the way they will be answered (ibid.).

15   "Adveniente vero paschali tempore Augustinus, cum esset annorum XXX . . . meritis matris et praedicatione Ambrosii sacrum baptisma suscepit" (*Legenda,* pp. 552-53). Here again one notes the absence of any reference to God's personal agency in the conversion.

16   The phenomenon is quite evident in both Jacobus's chapter and sermons on Martin of Tours, as I have shown previously ("Saint Martin of Tours in the *Legenda aurea,*" esp. pp. 148 and 156-59), and in his account of Dominic. Several additional examples are cited below in Chapter 10.

17   "Cum igitur esset annorum XIX et quondam librum cujusdam philoso-phi, in quo vanitas mundi contemnenda et philosophia appetenda dicebatur, perlegeret, ex hoc quidem liber plurimum placuit, sed quia nomen Jesu Christi, quod a matre imbiberat, ibi non erat, dolere coepit" (*Legenda,* p. 550; cf. *Conf.* III.4.7-8). Jacobus places this passage after his comments on Augustine's fall into Manichaeanism, reversing the order in the *Confessions* as if to suggest that Cicero presents a relatively enlightened alternative to that heresy.

18   "Cum te primum cognoui, tu assumsisti me, ut uiderem esse, quod uiderem, et nondum me esse, qui uiderem. et reuerberasti infirmitatem aspectus mei radians in me uehementer, et contremui amore et horrore: et inueni longe me esse a te in regione dissimilitudinis, tamquam audirem uocem tuam de excelso: 'cibus sum grandium: cresce et manducabis me. nec tu me in te mutabis sicut cibum carnis tuae, sed tu mutaberis in me.'"

The English version in the text is from *Confessions,* trans. John K. Ryan (Garden City, N. Y., 1960).

19   "Simplicianus autem coepit eum hortari, ipse quoque se ipsum hortari et
      dicere: quot pueri et puellae intra ecclesiam domini Deo serviunt, et tu
      non poteris, quod ist[i] et iste, an vero ist[i] et iste in se ipsis possunt et
      non in Deo suo? Quid in te stas et non stas? Projice te in eum et excipiet
      te et salvabit te" (*Legenda,* p. 551). From "tu non poteris" on, this is
      the speech of Continence in *Conf.* VIII.11.27, with a few omissions to
      adapt it to its new context.

20   "Horum exemplis Augustinus vehementer exarsit ita, quod socium suum
      Alipium tam vultu quam mente turbatus invasit et fortiter exclamavit:
      quid patimur, quid audimus? Surgunt indocti et coelum rapiunt et nos
      cum doctrinis nostris in infernum demergimur, an quia praecesserunt,
      pudet sequi et non pudet nec saltem sequi?"
         The direct discourse here closely follows *Conf.* VIII.8.19, except that
      Augustine described himself and Alypius as "sine corde" as well as
      learned, and lamented that they were wallowing in flesh and blood
      ("ecce ubi uolutamur in carne et sanguine"); Jacobus's image of their
      sinking into hell is obviously simpler and more dramatic. The English
      version in the text is adapted from Ryan's translation of the
      Confessions.

21   "Displicebat enim ei, quidquid agebat in saeculo, prae dulcedine Dei et
      decore domus ejus, quam dilexit."

22   "Aperuitque statim codicem apostolicum et conjectis oculis ad primum
      capitulum legit: induimini dominum Jesum Christum" (*Legenda,* p.
      552). Worth noting here, once again, is the way the original moral issue
      has been excised. In the *Confessions* the scriptural exhortation was
      quoted more fully, and it explicitly addressed Augustine's besetting sin
      of sensuality: "Non in comisationibus et ebrietatibus, non in cubilibus et
      inpudicitiis, non in contentione et aemulatione, sed induite dominum
      Iesum Christum et carnis prouidentiam ne feceritis in concupiscentiis"
      (VIII.12.29).

23   The *Legenda* account of this miracle (p. 552) begins with a paraphrase
      from the section of the *Soliloquies* (I.12.21) where the toothache is
      mentioned, but the major source is *Conf.* IX.4.12.

24   "Protinus autem in fide catholica mirabiliter confirmatur, spem omnem,
      quam habebat in saeculo, dereliquit. . . . Quanta autem dulcedine divini
      amoris extunc frueretur, ipse in hoc libro confessionum aperit."
      Jacobus's source for the first two points here may well have been
      Possidius; cf. the *Vita Aug.,* chs. 1(end)-2.

25   Jacobus's selectivity here is particularly clear in his excerpt from *Conf.*
      IX.2.3, which substitutes first-person singular forms for all Augustine's
      references to the community of which he was a part, and at the end of his
      excerpt from IX.4.11: "Legebam totum psalmum illum et ardebam, qui
      fueram latrator amarus et caecus adversus litteras de melle coeli mellitas

et de lumine tuo luminosas et super scripturas hujusmodi tabescebam" (*Legenda,* p. 553). What Jacobus has excised here is Augustine's expression of concern for those still enslaved to the error from which he himself has been liberated: "Legebam et ardebam *nec inueniebam, quid facerem surdis mortuis, ex quibus* fueram, pestis, latrator amarus et caecus aduersus litteras de melle caeli melleas et de lumine tuo luminosas, et super *inimicis scripturae* huius tabescebam" (emphasis mine).

26   English version adapted from Ryan's translation of *Conf.* IX.1.1. Except for the omission of "et redemptor meus" after "adjutor meus," Jacobus's version of this passage agrees almost verbatim with the original.

27   Like the Manichaeans of Augustine's time, the Cathars of the late Middle Ages seem to have minimized the problem of sin, defining salvation as a matter of extricating one's soul from the evil world in which it had somehow become imprisoned. And of course they tended to reject the idea of the Incarnation, on the premise that God's nature would have been sullied by actual contact with the flesh, and honored as "perfecti" those who had liberated themselves, by strict abstinence, from most of the carnal instincts and pleasures that kept man entrapped in this world. On these aspects of Cathar teaching, see, e.g., the excerpts from the accounts by Rainerius Sacconi and Bernard Gui in Wakefield and Evans' *Heresies of the High Middle Ages,* esp. pp. 330-34 and 379-82, and the more sympathetic overview in Wakefield's introduction, pp. 41-50.

28   *Solil.* I.10.17. For this work I have used the Benedictine edition of the Latin text and the English translation by Thomas F. Gilligan. The two are printed side by side in Gilligan's *Soliloquies of Saint Augustine* (New York, 1943).

29   "Quantumlibet velis eam pingere atque cumulare bonis omnibus, nihil mihi tam fugiendum quam concubitum esse decrevi" (*Solil.* I.10.17).

30   "R. Non ego nunc quaero quid decreveris, sed utrum adhuc lucteris, an vero jam ipsam libidinem viceris. Agitur enim de sanitate oculorum tuorum.
      "A. Prorsus nihil hujusmodi quaero, nihil desidero: etiam cum horrore atque aspernatione talia recordor" (ibid.).

31   "B[eatus] vero Augustinus aut tales inordinatas affectiones in memoria non habebat, aut in horrore, aut in aspernatione habebat. Unde cum ratio in libro soliloquiorum ipsum interrogasset: Nonne te delectat uxor casta, pudica, pulchra, morigerata, & dives? respondit: Quantum-cunque mulierem depinxeris, atque de bonis omnibus cumulaveris, nihil mihi tam fugiendum, quam concubitum decrevi. Dehinc ratio: non quaero quid decreveris, sed utrum adhuc alliceris. Et respondit: prorsus nihil in hujusmodi quaero, nihilque desidero, sed etiam cum horrore &

aspernatione talia recordor'' (sermon 521 S63, p. 278). One interesting change is that the ideal wife described by Ratio was also to be educated (''litterata''), or at least intelligent enough to be easily taught; Jacobus's version makes her ''casta'' instead.

32 ''Post conversionem fuit piissimus, quod patet, quia divitias contemnebat, honores respuebat, voluptates abhorrebat. Quantum ad divitias: ideo in libro soliloquiorum, quem in primordio suae conversionis fecit, ipsum interrogari fecit dicens: Divitias nullas cupis? Et ipse respondit: Haec quidem nec nunc primum, nam cum 20. [sic] annos agam, 14. anni sunt ex quo ista cupere destiti, porro unus liber Ciceronis mihi facile persuasit, nullo modo esse divitias appetendas. Quantum ad honores interrogat dicens: Quid honores? [respondit:] fateor eos pene his diebus cupere destiti. Quantum vero ad voluptates interrogat ratio dicens: Quid uxor? respondit: Quantumcunque eam mihi depinxeris, nihil magis fugiendum quam concubitum decrevi. Deinde subjungit dicens: Quid de cibis? respondit: Sive de cibo & potu caeteraque corporis voluptate nihil interroges, tantum ab eo peto quantum mihi valetudinis opem conferre potest'' (sermon 522 S63, p. 280). Like the exchange on marriage, the questions and answers on wealth, honors, and food are all drawn from Solil. I.10.17. Only with regard to honors, however, did Augustine neglect to add qualifications and explanations which Jacobus has omitted.

33 In this version (Legenda, p. 566), Augustine's answer on wealth includes a qualifying clause after ''ista cupere destiti'' (''nec aliud in his praeter necessarium victum cogitavi''), the exchange on marriage is a bit more detailed—and closer in wording to the Soliloquies—than the one in the first sermon, and baths are listed along with food and drink—again, following the Soliloquies—in Augustine's final answer. Both the order and the remaining contents of the long passage in the Legenda are closely approximated in the second sermon.

34 ''Notandum, quod, cum tria sint, quae a mundanis hominibus appetuntur, scilicet divitiae, deliciae et honores, vir iste sanctus tantae perfectionis exstitit, quod ipse divitias contemsit, honores respuit, voluptates abhorruit.''

35 John Moorman's History of the Franciscan Order from Its Origins to the Year 1517 (Oxford, 1968) provides a good introduction to both the ideals of Francis himself and the struggles among his followers. Also worth consulting on Franciscan poverty and the issues it raised is the detailed discussion in Gordon Leff's Heresy in the Later Middle Ages, 1 (New York, 1967): 1-16, 51-255.

36 Marie-Humbert Vicaire, ''La pauvreté évangélique dans la 'conversion pénitentielle' des prêcheurs,'' in Vicaire's Dominique et ses prêcheurs (Fribourg, 1977), pp. 269 et passim.

37   Ibid., pp. 275-76. Vicaire's source for this story, on which I have also drawn, is Jordan of Saxony's *Libellus de principiis Ordinis Praedicatorum,* sec. 73, published in *MOPH,* vol. 16 (1935).

38   On the first three dangers, see Humbert's *Treatise on Preaching,* ed. Walter M. Conlon (London, 1955), pp. 116-17, 143-47. As for the company of seculars, Humbert's warnings range from the explicit statement that "it is exceedingly difficult to remain for a long time among seculars without suffering [spiritual] harm" (p. 118) to general lessons against succumbing to the influence of the world (e.g., pp. 125, 134)—or to the influence of "the wicked" or "heathens" with whom the preacher is thrown into contact (p. 123).

39   Thus, e.g., Humbert places a good deal of emphasis on an interpretation of 1 Corinthians 6:4 attributed to Gregory the Great, which assigns "inferior persons" to temporal affairs and saves preachers for "the ministry of higher things" (*Treatise,* p. 145). A few pages earlier Humbert uses an interpretation of Lamentations 4:1 which appeals even more directly to the preacher's pride: "The gold [of the preacher's state] . . . becomes dim by mixing in completely human affairs; the holiness of the life is soiled; the beautiful color is lost when the public esteem for those who were judged as good religious diminishes. For when one who is dressed in a holy habit permits himself to become immersed in worldly affairs, it is as if he were to lose caste in the eyes of men, and the respect which they had for him were to vanish" (p. 143).

40   Ibid., pp. 83-84.

41   Vicaire makes this point explicitly (pp. 268-69).

42   Gui's note, preserved in the margin of MS. 490 in the municipal library at Toulouse, is among his additions to the official record of the provincial chapter convened in that city on September 8, 1254. According to Douais' *Acta capitulorum provincialium Ordinis fratrum Praedicatorum* (Toulouse, 1894), it reads as follows: "De manu fratris Stephani de Salanhac inveni scriptum in dorso rotuli sic: Petat Magister a papa quod de oratione beati Dominici tollatur *temporalibus,* et dicatur *spiritualibus proficiat incrementis,* quia in oratione beati Francisci petitur terrena despicere, et in nostra petuntur dari; et dicatur: Deus, qui ecclesiam tuam beati Dominici confessoris tui illuminare dignatus es meritis et doctrinis, concede ut eius intercessione spiritualibus proficiat incrementis et gaudiis perfruatur eternis. Per Dominum" (p. 58, n. 3).

43   Significantly enough, Jacobus's model sermons on Dominic make even more of this virtue than do the sermons on Augustine. Dominic too is praised for having despised worldly riches, pleasures, and honors (sermon 493 S54, p. 236), but that is just the beginning. In the first section of the same sermon, Jacobus suspends his customary enthusiasm for learning long enough to credit Dominic with having despised

"philosophica dogmata," as well as "terrena" in general, and to draw an uncharacteristic lesson about the "lex vanitatis" that rules philosophers. In another striking passage, he explicitly presents Dominic's renunciations as a means of transcending the ordinary human condition: "Nec fuit [Beatus Dominicus] contentus esse solummodo homo rationalis, quia omnibus mundanis & terrenis abrenuntiabat, sed fuit homo Angelicus, quia ab omni carnali delectatione abstinuit. Et fuit homo divinus, quia totus per amorem in Deum transivit de sobrietate viae superveniens ad satietatem patriae" (sermon 495 S54, p. 239). And when he applies to Dominic Paul's statement about the world's being crucified to him, and he to it (Gal. 6:14), the central motif is not the saint's humble participation in Christ's suffering, but his sublime disdain for the things of this world: "Mundus quippe sibi crucifixus est, quia ipsum mundum & omnia mundana, & terrenas cupiditates vilipendit & despexit. Et ipse mundo crucifixus est, quia de mundo non fuit reputatus, nec mundus de ipso curabat" (sermon 491 S54, p. 235).

44   "Quare autem institutum sit, ut festivitates sanctorum in terris agamus, . . . quarta [ratio] est propter exemplum nostrae imitationis; cum enim eorum festivitas recensetur, ad eorum imitationem provocamur, ut scilicet eorum exemplo terrena contemnamus et coelestia desideremus" (*Legenda,* p. 720).

45   "Vincentius quasi vitium incendens vel vincens incendia vel victoriam tenens. Ipse enim incendit, id est, consumsit vitia per carnis mortificationem, vicit incendia suppliciorum per constantem poenarum perpessionem, victoriam tenuit mundi per ipsius despectionem. Vicit enim tria, quae erant in mundo, scilicet falsos errores, immundos amores, mundanos timores, quos vicit per sapientiam, munditiam et constantiam. De quibus dicit Augustinus: ut cum omnibus erroribus, amoribus et timoribus vincatur hic mundus, sanctorum martiria docent et docuerunt."

46   "Tertii, qui in purgatorium descendunt, sunt, qui lignum, foenum et stipulam secum ferunt, qui scilicet circa suas divitias infra tamen Deum carnali tenentur affectu. Affectiones enim carnales, quibus dediti sunt, domibus, conjugibus, possessionibus, ita tamen, ut nil Deo praeponant, illis tribus significantur, qui secundum suos amandi modos vel diutius ut lignum vel minus ut foenum vel minimum ut stipula cremabuntur. Qui ignis, sicut dicit Augustinus, etsi aeternus non sit, miro tamen modo est gravis, excellit enim omnem poenam, quam unquam passus est aliquis in hac vita; nunquam in carne inventa est tanta poena, licet mirabilia martires passi sint tormenta."

47   *Vita Aug.,* esp. chs. 6-7, 9, 11-12, 14, 16-18, 21, and 30.

48   Thus Augustine's preaching in place of Bishop Valerius is mentioned on p. 554, but only in the context of the custom it violated; a few lines later, Jacobus refers in passing to his victorious debates with Fortunatus and

other heretical teachers (cf. *Vita. Aug.,* chs. 5-7). Only once in a very long chapter does Jacobus give any emphasis to Augustine's role as a teacher: "A multis ecclesiis invitabatur et ibi verbum domini praedicabat et multos ab errore convertebat. Aliquando a proposito digressionem facere consueverat in praedicatione et tunc dicebat, Deum hoc ad profectum salutis alicujus ordinasse, sicut in quodam Manichaeorum negotiatore patuit, qui in praedicatione quadam Augustini, ubi ipse digressionem faciens contra hunc errorem praedicaverat, conversus fuit" (p. 558; cf. *Vita Aug.,* ch. 15).

49 "In his quoque quae ecclesia habebat et possidebat intentus amore, vel implicatus non erat, sed maioribus magis et spiritalibus suspensus et inhaerens rebus, aliquando seipsum ad illa temporalia ab aeternorum cogitatione relaxabat et deponebat. Quibus ille dispositis et ordinatis, tamquam a rebus mordacibus ac molestis, animi recursum ad interiora mentis et superiora faciebat, quo vel de inveniendis divinis cogitaret, vel de iam inventis aliquid dictaret, aut certe ex iam dictatis atque transcriptis aliquid emendaret. Et id agebat in die laborans, et in nocte lucubrans. . . . Nam fabricarum novarum nunquam studium habuit, devitans in eis implicationem sui animi, quem semper liberum habere volebat ab omni molestia temporali. . . . Interea dum ecclesie pecunia deficeret, hoc ipsum populo Christiano denunciabat, non se habere quod indigentibus erogaret" (*Vita Aug.,* ch. 24).

50 "In his quoque, quae in ecclesia possidebat, intentus amore vel implicatus non erat, sed die ac nocte de scripturis et de rebus divinis cogitabat. Fabricarum quoque novarum nunquam studium habuit, [devitans] in iis implicationem sui animi, quem semper liberum habere volebat ab omni molestia corporali, ut libere vacare posset continuae meditationi et assiduae lectioni" (*Legenda,* p. 557).

51 "Et erat tamquam illa gloriosissima Maria, typum gestans supernae Ecclesiae, de qua scriptum est, quod sederet ad pedes Domini, atque intenta eius verbum audiret: de qua soror conquesta, quod ab eadem circa multum ministerium occupata non adiuvaretur, audivit: *Martha Martha, meliorem partem Maria elegit, quae non auferetur ab ea* [Luke 10:41-42]." These statements follow immediately after "nocte lucubrans" in the passage quoted in n. 49.

52 *City of God* XIX.19, trans. Marcus Dods, in *A Select Library of the Nicene and Post-Nicene Fathers,* ed. Philip Schaff et al. (1887; rept. Grand Rapids, Mich., 1956).

53 See Chapter 4, above.

54 *Summa theologiae* II-II^{ae}, q. 184, a. 7, ad. 2.

55 Humbert of Romans, *Treatise,* p. 142.

56 On Martin, compare Sulpicius Severus's *Vita S. Martini,* esp. chs. 11-17

and 23-25, with the account of Martin's episcopacy in the *Legenda,* pp. 743-48. On Dominic, see Chapter 9, below.

57   Among the numerous figures in the *Legenda* who make this symbolic gesture are Saint Lucy and her mother (p. 30), Saint Antony (p. 104), Aglaë the former mistress of Saint Boniface (p. 318), the martyrs Gervase and Prothase (p. 354), Gallicanus, a convert of the soldier saints John and Paul (p. 365), Saint Praxed and her sister (p. 407), and the Seven Sleepers (p. 435). The chapter on Saint John the Evangelist contains a long exemplum on the importance of thus renouncing one's earthly wealth (pp. 57-59).

58   See Chapter 6.

59   "Prima autem vita scilicet contemplativa consistit in devota oratione, in divinorum revelatione, & in Dei laudatione."

60   "Secunda vita, scilicet actuosa consistit in carnis maceratione, eleemosynarum largitione, & utili occupatione. . . . Tertium [Ambrosius] habuit, quia semper, aut praedicabat aut scribebat, aut orabat."

61   The same logic stands out in sermon 493 S54, whose theme is the perfection attained by Dominic himself. Here too Jacobus cites the terms from the *City of God,* even asserting explicitly that the *vita composita* is the most excellent. But instead of actually applying Augustine's definitions to the life of Dominic, the sermon promptly substitutes a schema which has nothing to do with an ideal of usefulness to others. The lowest level of perfection, which Dominic reached as a layman, is said to consist in obedience to the precepts; the second, which he reached as a canon regular, means the addition of the counsels. And the highest level, manifested in Dominic's life as a "vir Apostolicus," is not defined as the addition of apostolic service, but as the renunciation of even more than the counsels require.

62   The authority cited for this detail is Honorius of Autun (d. 1152); see PL 172.995 for his brief reference to the tradition.

63   "Post hoc assumtis Nebr[i]dio et Euodio et matre ad Africam remeabat, sed cum essent apud Hostiam Tyberinam, pia mater ejus defuncta est. Post cujus mortem reversus est Augustinus ad agros proprios, ubi cum his, qui sibi adhaerebant, jejuniis et orationibus Deo vacabat, libros scribebat et indoctos docebat."

64   "Contra hoc quod uoluit, in uirtute omnipotentis Dei ex feminae pectore miraculum inuenit. Nec mirum quod plus illo femina, quae diu fratrem uidere cupiebat, in eodem tempore ualuit. Quia enim iuxta Iohannis uocem *Deus caritas est,* iusto ualde iudicio illa plus potuit, quae amplius amauit" (*Dial.* II.33.5). Jacobus's version of the story (p. 212) omits this whole ending.

65   Humbert himself attempts to counter this temptation in the following passage from his treatise: "A brother, it is said [in the *Vitae patrum*], having learned that his mother had come to visit him, refused to receive her and had her told that he was content to see her in the next world. Does not the Psalmist say: 'Forget thy people and thy father's house?' (Ps. 44:11.) Why, then, do we visit so often those whom we ought to forget?" (*Treatise,* pp. 116-17). Jacobus gives a more detailed version of the same anecdote in the *Legenda,* p. 803.

66   *On Christian Doctrine* I.22, trans. D. W. Robertson, Jr. (Indianapolis, 1958). Section IV.12.18 of the *Confessions* begins with another statement of the same idea: "If you find pleasure in bodily things, praise God for them, and direct your love to their maker, lest because of things that please you, you may displease him. If you find pleasure in souls, let them be loved in God. In themselves they are but shifting things; in him they stand firm; else they would pass and perish. In him, therefore, let them be loved, and with you carry up to him as many as you can" (Ryan's translation).

67   The major exceptions to this rule occur in chapters about groups of martyrs, who are often connected by family ties and tend to encourage one another to stand fast and die bravely. Toward members of their families who are either pagan or too worldly to share their ideals, on the other hand, the saints of the *Legenda* exhibit a lack of sympathy that sometimes appears quite brutal; see, e.g., Christina's treatment of her parents (pp. 419-20), the condemnations of their married sister by Bernard and his brothers (p. 532), Perpetua's fierce farewell to her grieving family (pp. 798-99), and Pastor's refusal to concern himself with the welfare of his imprisoned nephew (p. 803).

68   "Tantae autem puritatis et humilitatis fuit, ut ipsa etiam minima peccata, quae apud nos nulla vel minima reputantur, in libro confessionum de his confiteatur et de his coram Deo humiliter se accuset."

69   The problem is illustrated with special power in Augustine's chapter on the pleasures of the eyes (*Conf.* X.34.51). He finds it impossible, he confesses, not to be affected during all his waking hours by the ever-changing splendors of the visible world. And he distrusts this response, fearing that he may be so beguiled by such beauty as to forget its relationship to his true good: "The eyes love fair and varied forms and bright and beauteous colors. Let not such things possess my soul: may God who made these things good, yea, very good, may he possess it. He is my good, not they" (Ryan's translation).

70   "In eodem quoque libro de confessionibus accusat se de ipsa modica delectatione, quam aliquando in comedendo sentiebat, dicens . . ."

71   In *Conf.* X.32.48 Augustine himself expressed the belief and hope that he was immune to the attractions of sweet odors; Jacobus abridges this

brief discussion without altering its essential content (*Legenda,* p. 556). With regard to church music, on the other hand, Augustine acknowledged the danger of excessive severity, contending that it would surely be wrong to reject a pleasurable gift which can be spiritually useful (X.33.49-50); Jacobus retains nothing from this chapter except two statements which reinforce his own message about Augustine's distrust of pleasure: "De auditu confitetur dicens: voluptates aurium tenacius me implicaverant et subjugaverant, sed resolvisti et liberasti me. Cum mihi accidit, ut me amplius cantus, quam res, quae canitur, moveat, poenaliter me peccare confiteor et tunc mallem non audire cantantem" (p. 556). And from the whole discussion of food and drink, Jacobus selects two short excerpts on Augustine's struggle against the temptations they pose and a longer passage in which the saint deplores the fact that pleasure inevitably accompanies the process of satisfying hunger (p. 556; cf. *Conf.* X.31.44). Here what Jacobus skips over, most notably, is Augustine's emphasis on the generosity of God and the goodness of his creation (see esp. X.31.46).

72   "Quid est hoc, fili, quod loqueris? Putas, quod, si tale quid facere possem, mihi hoc ipsum non conferrem?" Jacobus's version of this story is a bit simpler and more dramatic than the one in *Vita Aug.,* ch. 29, where the petitioner was a relative of the sick man and there was no attempt to render Augustine's actual words.

73   "Ecce ergo quantae charitatis fuit potius illi aegro ad eum venienti, quam sibiipsi charitatem voluit impendere. Nec mirum, quia desiderabat transire ad Deum."

74   "Laudabat quoque plurimum illos, quibus moriendi desiderium inerat" (*Legenda,* p. 557). The supporting examples brought forward here are three stories about bishops from ch. 27 of the *Vita,* none of which actually celebrated quite the kind of virtue that Jacobus tries to extract from them. The central issue in each story was whether the holy man, already on his deathbed, was ready to depart from this life whenever God might decree. In the first and most detailed story, moreover, Possidius explained that what Augustine held up for admiration was the humility with which the bishop (Ambrose) expressed himself at this juncture.

75   Thus Jacobus has Augustine call his followers together during the terrible siege of Hippo and make the following announcement: "Ecce rogavi dominum, ut aut nos ab his periculis eruat aut patientiam tribuat aut me de hac vita suscipiat, ne tot calamitates videre compellar"; the next sentence explains his final illness, which began just three months later, as God's answer to the third part of this petition (p. 559). The version of this story in *Vita Aug.,* ch. 29, is superficially similar, but there are two significant differences. In Possidius's version the prayer sounds much less selfish because it does not just express Augustine's own longing for deliverance; Possidius explains that the saint taught this

prayer to his followers, who joined with him in offering it on their own behalf and that of their fellow bishops and the other residents of Hippo. And God's response, Possidius suggests, was eventually to deliver the city, as well as to let Augustine die: "Nam et sibiipsi et eidem civitati quod lacrimosis depoposcit precibus, in tempore impetravit."

76   Thus, e.g., sermon 491 S54 enumerates four kinds of vice to which "Prelati" are subject—pride, "levitas" and inconstancy, carnal desire, and "terrenorum cupiditas"—and demonstrates how thoroughly Dominic overcame them (pp. 234-35). Sermon 515 S60 contrasts the holiness of Saint Bernard with the worldly ambitions of "mali Religiosi" (pp. 268-69). Jacobus's message about secular-minded churchmen is even clearer in sermon 524 S63, when he deals with Augustine's example as a bishop: "Tertio fulsit in statu Pontificali. In quo sex radiis fulsit a quibus alii Episcopi consueverunt privari. Primo enim removit a se omnem suspectam familiam. . . . Secundo removit a se omnem ambitionem & pompam, tam in vestibus quam in vasis. . . . Tertio removit a se omnem cupiditatem & avaritiam. . . . Quarto ad pauperes habuit magnam liberalitatem. . . . Quinto in cibo & potu ipse habuit magnam parcitatem. . . . Sexto nullam habuit ad suos consanguineos carnalitatem" (p. 282).

77   Pierre Courcelle's *Recherches sur saint Ambroise: "Vies" anciennes, culture, iconographie* (Paris, 1973) reproduces three late-medieval illustrations of this story, which apparently became quite popular, and suggests that Jacobus himself originated it (pp. 188-89, 197). As we have seen, however, Jacobus ordinarily eschews invention of this kind. Since he introduces the story with the vague attribution "ut ajunt" (*Legenda*, p. 253), one ought perhaps to infer that he derived it from an oral tradition instead of a book. Bernard Gui tells the same story (Bibliothèque Nationale MS. latin 5406, fol. 82, col. 2), but his wording is so nearly identical with Jacobus's that he may well have borrowed it from the *Legenda* itself.

78   "Surgite et hinc quantocius fugiamus, quia dominus non est in loco isto. Festinate, filii, festinate nec in fugiendo moram facite, ne nos hic divina ultio apprehendat et in peccatis illorum pariter nos involvat."

79   "Ecce fratres, quam misericorditer Deus parcit, cum hic adversa tribuit, et quam severe irascitur, cum semper prospera elargitur."

80   "Si enim Deus tantum punit illos, qui habent vitam sanctam, quantum puniet & illos, qui habent vitam iniquam? *Si justus in terra recipit malum, quanto magis impius, & peccator.* Si tantum punit illos, in quibus benedicitur, quantum puniet illos in quibus blasphematur?" Either Jacobus himself or his text of the Vulgate has added the word *malum* to the proverb.

81 Boglioni makes this point quite strongly, concluding that Gregory had no interest in the natural world at all, save as a symbolic setting for the moral drama in which man is engaged ("Miracle et nature," p. 20)—or even in human nature, apart from the issues of sin and grace (p. 50).

82 Besides the five examples mentioned by Nicholas (see Chap. 3, above, at n. 14), unequivocal promises of the saints' assistance occur in the chapters on Saint George (p. 264) and Saint Leonard (p. 691). In these chapters, as in all but one of the others usually attributed to Jacobus himself, the promises are either limited to relief from a specific earthly plight like imprisonment or dangerous childbirth, or worded so generally that they can and probably should be read as implying just spiritual assistance. The odd exception is the chapter on Saint Blaise, which does not sound like Jacobus's work because it promises healing to anyone who invokes the saint (p. 169) and even earthly prosperity to those who offer an annual candle in his honor (p. 168).

83 See, e.g., pp. 516-17 (sec. 7), 592 (sec. 5), 593 (sec. 8), and 686 (the conclusion of the Dagobert story) in the *Legenda*.

84 On this story see Chapter 5, above, at n. 28.

85 Among the clearest examples are the stories involving Constantia (*Legenda*, p. 116), the persecutor of Longinus (p. 203), the daughter of Archemius (p. 344), the soldier resurrected by Mary Magdalene (p. 415), the daughter of Rufus (p. 418), the sinful monk resurrected for penance (p. 460), the plowman healed by Hippolytus (pp. 503-4), the penitent woman saved from execution (pp. 594-95), and the soldier's wife healed by Palmatius (p. 687). A few additional stories about resurrections for the purpose of penance are mentioned above in n. 83.

86 Although Graesse's edition has the old man lamenting "quod corpus Christi videre non poterat," the context obviously demands "corpus sancti," and this is indeed the reading in the most accessible manuscript of the *Legenda*, MS. 9 in the Winchester College (Warden and Fellows' Library) Medieval Manuscript Collection, published by World Microfilms, London.

87 See, e.g., the cases of Julian of Auvergne (p. 141), George (p. 262), Adauctus (p. 575), Adrian (pp. 597-98), and Euphemia (p. 620).

88 "Pater autem corpus filii coram altari beati Dominici collocans lamentari coepit et dicere: beate Dominice, laetus veni ad te, en tristis redeo, cum filio veni et orbatus recedo; redde mihi, quaeso, filium meum, redde mihi laetitiam cordis mei. Et ecce circa [noctis] medium puer revixit et per ecclesiam ambulavit" (*Legenda*, pp. 479-80).

Jacobus's source, the life of Dominic by Constantine of Orvieto, sec. 72, ends the story as follows: "Circa noctis medium puer revixit, lac suxit et per ecclesiam ambulavit, tandemque ad domum propriam a parentibus est incolumis cum letitia reportatus" (*MOPH* 16:339).

89   "Omnis ab eo spes curationis abscessit. Deo igitur et beato Dominico se
      devovens cum se filo, de quo fienda erat candela, totum mensus esset in
      longum, coepit etiam corpus, collum et pectus cingere. Cum tandem
      genu filo ambiente cinxisset, invocato ad quamlibet mensurationem
      nomine Jesu et beati Dominici continuo se alleviatum sentiens exclama-
      vit: ego sum liberatus. Exsurgens et prae gaudio lacrymans sine aliquo
      fulcimento venit ad ecclesiam, in qua corpus sancti Dominici
      quiescebat" (*Legenda,* pp. 480-81).
          The story would sound less strange if Jacobus had not omitted so
      much of the passage preceding the miraculous climax; cf. the version in
      Peter Ferrandus's life of Dominic, sec. 52 (*MOPH* 16:250-51), which was
      evidently reproduced without change in Jacobus's immediate source, the
      life by Constantine of Orvieto.

90   "In eadem provincia Ungariae matrona quaedam ad honorem beati
      Dominici missam disponens facere celebrari sacerdotem hora debita non
      invenit, quapropter candelas tres ad hoc paratas manutergio mundo
      involvit et in quodam vase reposuit, aliquantulum autem devertens et
      postea rediens candelas flammis patentibus ardere vidit. Currentes
      omnes ad tam grande spectaculum tamdiu ibidem trementes et orantes
      steterunt, donec sine laesione manutergii penitus exarserunt."
          In this instance, Jacobus has not omitted anything important; the
      version in sec. 91 of Constantine's account (*MOPH* 16:347) is equally
      pointless. The problem will be discussed further in the next chapter.

Chapter 9: The Legacy of the Founder

1   The problem is most acute with regard to certain parallels between the
      Legenda account and a revised version of the *Vitae fratrum* which, if one
      accepts the reasoning of Berthold Altaner, must postdate the death of
      Gerard de Frachet in 1271; see Altaner's *Der hl. Dominikus: Unter-
      suchungen und Texte* (Breslau, 1922), esp. pp. 149 and 152-53. Altaner's
      conclusion that the *Legenda* must have been compiled after 1271 is
      questionable, of course, since a manuscript that survived into our own
      century was dated 1273 (see above, Chapter 4, n. 1).

2   The major early sources on Dominic's life are conveniently brought
      together in *MOPH,* vol. 16 (Rome, 1935); for Jordan's account, edited
      by H. C. Scheeben, see pp. 1-88 of that volume.

3   It may well be true, as Jordan suggests, that the brethren were originally
      reluctant even to have a saint of their own. William A. Hinnebusch
      relates this attitude quite logically to their self-abnegation as mendicants:
      "Followers of the humble Christ should not boast of holy relics that lay
      in their midst, exploit their Founder to gain advantage for themselves,
      give wagging tongues a chance to say that greed prompted their piety"
      (*History,* 1:107).

4   For these three recensions of the liturgical life I have relied throughout on the texts in *MOPH,* vol. 16; the editors are M. Hyacinth Laurent (Peter Ferrandus, pp. 195-260), H. C. Scheeben (Constantine, pp. 261-352), and Angelo Walz (Humbert, pp. 353-433).

5   For the date of Jacobus's birth, it is hard to improve on Echard's "circa MCCXXX." In his chronicle of Genoa, Jacobus describes the great eclipse of the sun in 1239, commenting that he was still a boy ("annos pueriles ageremus") when he witnessed it.

6   Vicaire mentions Constantine's use of some "récits miraculeux envoyés par divers couvents à la demande du chapitre général de 1245" (*Dominique et ses prêcheurs,* p. 48). The preface Humbert attached to the *Vitae fratrum* refers in more detail to the call issued by the general chapter that was held at Paris in 1256; see the text, ed. Benedict M. Reichert, in *MOPH,* 1 (1896): 4.

7   Humbert, preface to *Vitae fratrum, MOPH* 1:4.

8   "Cum autem multis discretis fratribus opus illud legentibus placuisset et dignum approbacione iudicarent, Nos tandem de approbacione multorum discretorum ac bonorum fratrum illud inter fratres duximus publicandum. Nolumus tamen quod extra Ordinem tradatur sine nostra licencia speciali" (ibid., pp. 4-5).

9   Dondaine, "Le dominicain français Jean de Mailly," pp. 65-66. To my knowledge, Jean's account of Dominic has been printed only twice: in Marie Dominique Chapotin's *Les dominicains d'Auxerre* (1892) and in the relatively recent French translation of the *Abbreviatio* by Dondaine, *Abrégé des gestes et miracles des saints* (Paris, 1947), pp. 304-13. I have relied throughout on Dondaine's text.

10 Poncelet, "Le légendier de Pierre Calo," p. 15, gives an unequivocal 1244 as the date of Bartholomew's *Epilogus in gesta sanctorum;* Altaner says 1245; and Kaeppeli, in the recent *Scriptores Ordinis Praedicatorum medii aevi,* vol. 1, places it between 1245 and 1251, the year of Bartholomew's death. Since Bartholomew's retelling of the Dominic legend adopts almost none of the innovations found in Constantine's recension of the liturgical life, which became the official one in 1248, the earlier part of this period seems the more likely.

    For Bartholomew's version of the legend the closest thing to a critical edition seems to be that of Altaner in *Der hl. Dominikus,* pp. 230-39. Where the readings of the manuscript Altaner chose to follow are obviously inferior to those in his own corpus of variants or in the *Acta SS,* Aug., 1 (1733; rept. Paris, 1867): 556-58, I have silently emended his text from those sources.

11 Marie Humbert Vicaire, "'Vesperus' (L'étoile du soir) ou l'image de saint Dominique pour ses frères au XIIIᵉ siècle," in *Dominique et ses prêcheurs,* pp. 280-304.

12 Vicaire, p. 288; Hinnebusch, *History,* 1:105 and 118, n. 191. The
    passage in question comprises the last few lines of sec. 92 in Jordan's
    Libellus: "'Well,' he said, 'divine mercy has kept me until now in purity
    of the flesh; yet I must confess that I have not escaped this imperfection,
    that my heart delights more in conversing with young women than in
    addressing old ones.'" ("'En,' inquit, 'usque ad hanc horam in carnis
    incorruptione misericordia me divina servavit; nec tamen hanc me
    imperfectionem evasisse confiteor, quin magis cor meum afficiant
    iuvencularum colloquia, quam vetularum affatus.'") The text of the
    ordinance deleting these lines is also reproduced in *MOPH,* vol. 16 (p.
    200, n. 24).

13 The story appears in Jordan's *Libellus,* secs. 56-58, but Jean's version is
    much closer to that of Peter Ferrandus (secs. 33-37).

14 Again Jean's source seems to be Peter Ferrandus (sec. 42); neither this
    story nor the following one about the legate occurs in the original
    account by Jordan.

15 "Nous ne rapportons pas ces faits par manière d'approbations de devins
    et de sortilèges, car autre chose est de présumer la connaissance des faits
    à venir en les devinant par un art diabolique, autre chose est, dans le
    doute et quand la prudence humaine fait défaut, d'espérer une réponse
    divine à une prière confiante. Les saints et les pères consultaient le
    Seigneur dans la nécessité, c'est pourquoi les juifs réclamaient toujours
    des signes" (*Abrégé,* p. 311). Cf. Peter Ferrandus, sec. 44.

16 Where Jordan and Peter Ferrandus say simply that the Virgin showed
    Reginald the "habitum ordinis (Predicatorum)," in Bartholomew's
    account she shows him the "habitum ordinis, quo nunc [*or* nostri] fratres
    predicatores utuntur" (sec. 12). And Bartholomew proceeds to explain
    that it was this vision, when related to Dominic, that led to the order's
    abandonment of the surplice worn by canons in favor of the habit that
    became the brethren's special trademark. As Hinnebusch notes
    (*History,* 1:343), Bartholomew's explanation of the habit enjoyed wide
    currency in the order, especially after it was endorsed by such authorities
    as Bernard Gui. But it did not become part of the official legend in the
    mid-thirteenth century; both the later liturgical lives follow Peter
    Ferrandus instead of Bartholomew.

17 "Honorius itaque [papa] ordinem confirmavit et ne pusillus grex timore
    quateretur, revelacionibus et miraculis cepit eos Deus consolari. Nam
    quidam, qui frater Dominicus simplex dicebatur, a quadam illecebrose
    temptatus inter duos rogos accensos et vicinos se proicit et nil lesus
    miseram convertit."
    Bartholomew apparently derived the story of Brother Dominic (but
    not the link with Honorius and the approval of the order) from Jordan's
    Libellus, sec. 50.

18   "[Duo fratres] pro Domino incarceratam visitaverunt; quorum illa iuvenilem eleganciam intuens hesitare cepit, vix tales aut similes immaculatos ab hoc seculo posse custodiri. Anxiatur pro talibus et devote oranti astitit regina, merencium consolatrix, protectrix suorum, virgo Maria et inenarrabile pallium, quo circumamicta videbatur, coram anxia expandens, pro quibus erat sollicita iuxta se astantes ostendit dicens: Ne sis pro hiis anxia aut horum similibus, quia mei sunt et mihi eos servabo. Merito tanta spe fulciti, clamant assidue: Vita dulcedo et spes nostra, salve."

19   Compare sec. 21 of Constantine's recension, reproduced as Humbert's sec. 30, with the earlier account by Peter Ferrandus (sec. 27); for Jacobus's version, see *Legenda,* pp. 468-69. The second life of Saint Francis by Thomas of Celano, compiled a year or so before Constantine's recension of the Dominic legend, uses a very similar story to show Innocent's receptiveness to the goals of Francis and his followers: "The lord pope . . . recalled a certain vision he had had a few days before, which, he affirmed, under the guidance of the Holy Spirit, would be fulfilled in [Francis]. He had seen in his sleep the Lateran basilica about to fall to ruin, when a certain religious, small and despised, propped it up by putting his own back under it lest it fall. 'Surely,' he said, 'this is that man who, by his works and by the teaching of Christ, will give support to the Church'" (ch. 11, sec. 17, trans. Placid Hermann, in *St. Francis of Assisi: Writings and Early Biographies,* ed. Marion A. Habig [Chicago, 1973], pp. 377-78).

20   "Obitum comitis Montis fortis sanctus previdit Dominicus arbore sibi perpulchra in visu apparente, in qua multitudo avium quiescebat, sed succisa corruit et aves disperguntur. Dispersit igitur et ipse paucos, quos habuit fratres et multi appositi sunt ad eos" (Bartholomew, sec. 9). Cf. Jordan, secs. 46-47, and Peter Ferrandus, sec. 31.

21   "Dum igitur Romae in ecclesia sancti Petri pro [dilatatione] sui ordinis exoraret, gloriosos principes apostolorum Petrum et Paulum ad se venientes adspexit, quorum primus Petrus videlicet baculum, Paulus vero sibi librum tradere videbantur addebantque dicentes: vade, praedica, quia a Deo ad hoc ministerium es electus. Moxque in momento temporis videbatur ei, quod filios suos per totum mundum dispersos adspiceret incedentes binos et binos." Cf. Constantine, sec. 25. Again Humbert also follows Constantine.

22   "Sic ait: mater mea, quid possum vel debeo amplius iis facere? Misi patriarchas et prophetas et parum se emendaverunt. Veni ego ad eos, deinde misi apostolos et me et illos occiderunt. Misi martires et confessores et doctores nec illis acquieverunt."

      In Reichert's text of the *Vitae fratrum* I.1.2-3 one finds the first two visions in a slightly longer form with numerous small differences in order and wording; the sense, however, is almost the same as that in the *Legenda*.

23   "Sed quia non est fas, ut tibi aliquid denegem, dabo iis meos praedicatores, per quos valeant illuminari et mundari, si non autem, veniam contra illos."

"Ad votum tuum adhuc hanc cum iis misericordiam faciam, quod praedicatores meos iis mittam, qui eos moneant et informent, et si se non correxerint, amplius iis non parcam."

24   "Cui illa: tempera, fili, furorem et paulisper exspecta, habeo enim fidelem servum et pugilem strenuum, qui ubique discurrens mundum expugnabit et tuo dominio subjugabit."

Reichert's text of the *Vitae fratrum* gives a significantly different account of the dialogue between Christ and Mary in this third vision story. Christ does not relate the three spears to particular human vices, as he does in the *Legenda;* and the solution proposed by the Virgin makes Dominic sound more like a missionary, bent on converting mankind to Christ, than like the conquering warrior of Jacobus's version: "Sicut tu scis qui omnia nosti; hec est via per quam eos ad te reduces. Habeo unum servum fidelem quem mittes in mundum, ut verba tua annunciet, et convertentur et te querent omnium salvatorem" (I.1.4).

25   "Tu es socius meus, tu pariter curres mecum, [strenuus] simul et nullus adversarius praevalebit."

26   James A. Weisheipl provides a useful overview of the antimendicant controversy of the 1250s, elucidating both its particular origins at the University of Paris and its larger importance for the work of the new orders, in *Friar Thomas d'Aquino: His Life, Thought and Works* (New York, 1974), pp. 80-92.

27   On this sort of error, which often arose out of sheer enthusiasm for Mary, see the survey of thirteenth-century Mariology in Hilda Graef's *Mary: A History of Doctrine and Devotion,* 1 (London, 1963): 365-92.

28   "Beatus Dominicus, dux et pater inclitus Predicatorum, qui appropinquante mundi termino, quasi novum sydus emicuit, ex Hyspanie partibus, villa que dicitur Calaroga, Oxomensis diocesis, oriundus fuit. Sane decebat ut qui olim Luciferum in tempore suo produxerat, Vesperum quoque, advesperascente iam die, super filios terre consurgere faceret ab occasu."

29   "Multifarie multisque modis olim Deus electos ad eternum invitans convivium, novissime diebus istis, id est hora undecima, misit servum suum dicere invitatis ut venirent, quia parata sunt omnia. Servum hunc ordinem Predicatorum sanctus interpretatur Gregorius novissimis dirigendum temporibus ad humanas videlicet mentes de vicino adventu iudicis commonendas. Novum enim ordinem Predicatorum aliquando fore scriptura premonuit."

Cf. Constantine, sec. 4, and Humbert's prologue. The "Gregorius" of this passage is Gregory the Great, whose *Homilia in Evangelia* XXXVI (PL 76.1267) does indeed identify the summoning servant as a "praedicatorum ordo" and the hour of the feast as the end of the world. The actual context, however, leaves no doubt that Gregory was explaining his own mission as a preacher, in what he believed to be the final times, rather than prophesying the emergence of a new religious order.

30 "Missus igitur hora cene, id est diebus novissimis, ordo novus, novus, inquam, pariter et antiquus, novus institutione, antiquus auctoritate, novus, immo novissimus spatio, primus autem officio" (Peter Ferrandus, sec. 1; cf. Humbert's prologue).

31 One noteworthy source behind these allegorical justifications of the order is Gregory IX's bull canonizing Dominic, also conveniently reproduced in *MOPH,* 16:190-94, which uses the vision of Zacharius as a key text in interpreting the whole history of the church and in relating not only the Dominicans, but also the Franciscans, to more traditional religious orders.

32 The classic example is William's own *De periculis novissimorum temporum,* a diatribe first issued in March 1256 which apparently continued to circulate despite its solemn condemnation by Pope Alexander IV in October of the same year.

33 It should be noted, however, that Jacobus follows Bartholomew's version of this story, asserting—as the liturgical lives do not—that the Virgin actually chose the brethren's habit (*Sermones,* pp. 235-36). The influence of Bartholomew is even more evident at the corresponding point in the *Legenda* (p. 473), where Jacobus reproduces some of Bartholomew's wording about the habit.

34 "Tertio iste Ordo fuit a Matre Dei impetratus. . . . Nam cum quidam sanctus vir ante istius Ordinis institutionem instaret orationi, vidit beatam Virginem Mariam pro humano genere exorantem, cui ait Christus: Quid possum amplius facere? Misi Patriarchas & Prophetas & parum se emendaverunt, veni & ego ad eos. Deinde misi Apostolos & me & eos occiderunt: Misi etiam Martyres & Confessores ac Doctores, & nec illis acquieverunt. Sed, quia non est fas, ut aliquid tibi denegem dabo eis Praedicatores meos."

35 Jacobus's acquaintance with Bartholomew's account of Dominic is suggested not only by the parallel cited in n. 33, but also by the inclusion in the *Legenda* account of a brief vision story for which only Bartholomew, among all the early sources we know, provides a precedent; in this instance, moreover, Bartholomew's wording is reproduced fully and exactly (see below, n. 50). It is also worth considering the possibility that Jacobus was imitating Bartholomew

when he began this and other chapters of the *Legenda* with allegorical etymologies of the saints' names. Bartholomew is not the only possible influence here; indeed, one side-benefit of studying the early accounts of Dominic is the discovery that such etymologies were considered sufficiently edifying to be included in two of the three liturgical lives of the founder (see Peter Ferrandus, sec. 14, and Humbert, sec. 15). But Bartholomew's example is particularly relevant because he places this material at the head of his account, as if recommending it to the special attention of the preachers who would use his book. The prefaces for which Jacobus would receive so much ridicule, in later centuries, differ only in being longer and more detailed.

Jacobus's debts to the account of Dominic by Jean de Mailly are harder to single out, especially when one has no text of the latter in the original Latin. But there is not much doubt that Jacobus knew the *Abbreviatio* well and used it as one of his models when he compiled the *Legenda.*

36   "Il les réunit tous et leur dit sa résolution de les disperser dans les divers pays, malgré leur petit nombre. Il leur fit élire comme abbé frère Matthieu, par qui ils seraient tous gouvernés, lui-même se proposant d'aller prêcher la foi aux nations païennes."

37   "Certains des frères partirent pour l'Espagne, d'autres pour Paris, d'autres enfin pour Bologne, où, dans le dépouillement d'une extrême pauvreté et par la vertu de Dieu, ils se multiplièrent en grand nombre."

38   "Au matin, le bienheureux Dominique vint prendre des nouvelles du malade et celui-ci lui répondit qu'il était en bonne santé; et comme l'homme de Dieu pensait qu'il parlait de l'état de son âme, Réginald insista qu'il s'agissait bien de la santé du corps, et il lui raconta en détail l'apparition dont il avait été favorisé."

39   "Les ayant prévenus et exhortés à résister courageusement au démon, saint Dominique les vit quand même tous l'abandonner, à l'exception de trois. Mais le saint homme ne se découragea pas dans sa prière pour eux, et après peu de temps, mus par l'esprit de Dieu, ils revinrent presque tous."

In both this story and the preceding one, Jean's emphases are very close to those of Peter Ferrandus, secs. 35 and 40.

40   "Pour héritage, il ne légua pas aux frères de richesses terrestres, mais les trésors de la grâce céleste, c'est-à-dire qu'il leur demanda de vivre dans la charité, de conserver l'humilité, de posséder la pauvreté volontaire, défendant avec la plus grande énergie à quiconque d'introduire les possessions temporelles dans l'Ordre, menaçant de la malédiction de Dieu et de la sienne propre celui qui souillerait la pauvreté de l'Ordre de la poussière des richesses."

41   Cf. Peter Ferrandus, from sec. 46 (*Boll.* 48) to the end. Peter orders the
      scenes in a less natural way, recounting Dominic's translation before his
      legacy and the vision of his ascent to heaven, and his account provides
      many opportunities to demonstrate Dominic's power as heavenly
      patron—including 27 stories about posthumous healings—which Jean
      neglects to utilize.

42   "Convocatis itaque XII fratribus spondet securissime se post mortem
      corporis utiliorem ordini fore quam in vita" (Bartholomew, sec. 19).
      These details are also to be found in the account by Peter Ferrandus: the
      twelve brethren in sec. 46 (*Boll.* 48) and the promise of posthumous
      assistance in sec. 50. More surprisingly, they occur also in Jordan's
      Libellus, secs. 92-93.

43   "Deinde Tolosam veniunt, ubi tunc legato Romane ecclesie cum multis
      prelatis concilium celebrante contra hereticos de consilio dicti episcopi
      Dydachi et sancti Dominici omnes pompas superfluas abiciunt et in
      paupertate pauperem Christum predicant" (Bartholomew, sec. 3).

44   "Episcopus Tolosanus Fulco sanctum Dominicum diligens sibi et suis
      redditus bonos dedit et insuper de consensu capituli sextam partem
      omnium decimarum tocius dyocesis sue." Cf. Jordan, sec. 39, and Peter
      Ferrandus, sec. 26.

45   "Sic et dominus Wilhelmus tunc Mutinensis, nunc autem Sabinensis
      cardinalis episcopus mores sancti Dominici explorans se in fratrem
      ordinis ab eo petiit recipi. [Cui] sanctus annuens eidem tamquam patri
      ordinis negocia recommisit; quod idem episcopus ferventer observat
      usque in hodiernum diem" (Bartholomew, sec. 17).

46   "Sanctus nempe Dominicus, dum esset in Yspania, vidit in visione
      draconem inmanissimum fratres, qui secum venerant, absorbere. Unde
      factum est, ut tribus exceptis omnes alii abscederent, quos dum
      persuasionibus sanctis retinere non posset, orando reduxit" (sec. 14).

47   "Denique venerabilis vir Dominicus plus de divina gracia quam de
      humana sapiencia presumens, fratres, quos ad predicandum mittebat,
      sedulis oracionum suffragiis prosequebatur" (sec. 18). Cf. Peter
      Ferrandus, sec. 41.

48   Salimbene, *Cronica,* trans. G. G. Coulton, in *From St. Francis to Dante,*
      2d ed. (rept. Philadelphia, 1972), pp. 26-27. Although Salimbene's
      chronicle belongs to the 1280s, the Dominicans must have been aware
      before 1250 that some such skeptical gossip about their founder was in
      the air, since Constantine's recension already includes cautionary tales
      about a Franciscan and a laywoman who scoffed at Dominic's memory
      (see the text below at n. 55).

49   One striking example of medieval tastes in such matters is the fate of
      Eadmer's life of Anselm, an exceptionally fine record of a saint's actual
      behavior and conversation which failed to earn anything like the acclaim

accorded to more conventionalized and wonder-filled legends. R. W. Southern sheds considerable light on the larger issues, as well as this one case, in *Saint Anselm and His Biographer* (Cambridge, 1963), esp. pp. 320-36.

50   "Pater effulgens . . . dissolucionem sui corporis novit imminere. Vidit enim iuvenem pulcherrimum, hiis verbis se vocantem: Veni, dilecte mi, veni ad gaudia, veni."
     This is the vision mentioned in n. 35 above which Jacobus seems to have borrowed from Bartholomew. It is introduced a little differently in the *Legenda* ("Sui autem corporis dissolutio sibi in visione monstrata est" [p. 478]), but for the vision itself Jacobus gives almost an exact transcript of Bartholomew's wording.

51   "Claruit eisdem temporibus sanctus Franciscus, qui ordinem fratrum minorum instituit et tanta caritate huic sanctus Dominicus coniunctus fuit, ut idem velle et idem nolle esset utrique. Dilatantur ergo sub isdem patribus duo ordines."

52   "Hic postea Bononie, Parisius et alibi Jesu Christo plurimos attraxit et post pauca in pace quievit" (Bartholomew, sec. 12). The theme of fruitful love is more prominent here, and the historical complexities less so, than in the accounts by Jean (p. 310) and Peter Ferrandus (secs. 36-37).

53   "Nycolaus Anglicus, sicut ipse vidi, a gravi multiplici paralisi curatus coram nobis omnibus astantibus tamquam cervus exiliit letus et gaudens. Alios etiam paraliticos diversimode infirmos diversimode curatos probatum est. . . . Febricitantes plurimos votis ad eum emissis Jesus Christus meritis servi sui Dominici liberavit. Corruptos in intestinis plurimos suis meritis Christus Jesus reintegravit. Tres desperatos et morti deditos sicut probatum et approbatum est, vite restituit et sanitati. Puerum pro mortuo a cunctis habitum per plures dies voto ad sanctum Dominicum facto restituit Christus vite presenti. Mutorum quatuor approbatorum et multorum aliorum linguas absolvit. Cecis visum restituit et surdis auditum."

54   I quote from Hinnebusch, *History,* 1:109. For the corresponding passage in the original Latin, see *MOPH* 16:193.

55   "Cum matrone quedam, que in ecclesia fratrum missarum interfuere sollemniis, domum redirent, invenerunt mulierem quandam domus sue sedentem pre foribus et filantem. Quam cum verbis caritativis arguerent, quare in festo tanti patris a servili opere non cessasset, illa protinus indignanti animo et turbata facie dixit eis: 'Vos, que estis bizote fratrum eius, festa colite sancti vestri.' Statimque oculi ipsius in tumorem cum pruritu conversi sunt, et ex ipsis ceperunt vermes protinus scaturire; ita quod vicina quedam, quam ad se perterrita convocavit, decem et octo

vermes eduxit ex eius oculis in instanti. Quapropter contrita spiritu ad ecclesiam beati Dominici cum eiulatu cucurrit. . . .''

56   Humbert, Appendix, secs. 57 and 59. Since Walz does not reproduce them in his edition, just citing the corresponding sections of Constantine's account, they are presumably unchanged.

57   Among the posthumous miracles in Constantine's account, e.g., one finds twenty-seven healings that were previously recounted by Peter, six new stories of resurrection, and over a dozen more healings (secs. 72-90, 92-118, 121). Humbert apparently retains all these beneficent miracles, and he adds two more healing stories (Appendix, secs. 58 and 61).
      Worth noting as an indication of Jacobus's distance from his Dominican predecessors is the extent to which their very ordering of these posthumous miracles affirms the importance of the practical benefits conferred by them. Peter Ferrandus and Bartholomew use an order dictated almost entirely by the type and severity of the maladies cured; and the later liturgical lives arrange the major set of additional miracles, those reported from Hungary, so that the resurrections come first, followed in turn by bodily cures and exorcisms (Constantine, secs. 71-90; Humbert, Appendix, secs. 37-55).

58   Constantine, sec. 91; Humbert, Appendix, sec. 56. Jacobus's version of this story, a reasonably accurate condensation of Constantine's version, is quoted at the end of Chapter 8, above.

59   Constantine, sec. 45; Humbert, sec. 49. Cf. the *Legenda,* pp. 474-75.

60   Constantine, sec. 56; Humbert, sec. 60 (p. 417). This anecdote, which seems to affirm the desirability of bodily health, predictably does not find its way into the *Legenda.*

61   Constantine, secs. 41-44; Humbert, secs. 45-48.

62   Peter Ferrandus, secs. 31-32; cf. the *Abrégé,* p. 308. Bartholomew condenses this part of the legend without mentioning the plans of Dominic himself, but the remainder of his account leaves no doubt about the breadth of the mission assumed by the order.

63   Constantine, sec. 51; cf. Humbert, sec. 53. Vicaire gives an illuminating critical discussion of this story and its background in *Dominique et ses prêcheurs,* pp. 46-57. At the beginning of the same article (pp. 36-43), Vicaire surveys the later tradition that identified Dominic with the Inquisition. One noteworthy point is the key role played by Bernard Gui, who, on the basis of Constantine's story and his own misinterpretation of two official documents, clothed this tradition in an aura of scholarly respectability that went unquestioned for centuries. Subtler but even more important, because it runs counter to modern expectations, is the body of evidence suggesting that Gui and later Dominicans, down to at least the seventeenth century, felt that their founder's status

was enhanced rather than diminished by his supposed role as the first inquisitor.

64   Thus, e.g., Jordan concludes that the miracle "monstravit aperte et fidei veritatem et eius, qui libellum conscripserat, sanctitatem" (sec. 25); the conclusions of Peter Ferrandus (sec. 15), Jean de Mailly (*Abrégé*, p. 306), Bartholomew (sec. 4), and Constantine (sec. 15) all echo the same points.

65   Altaner and others have traced this second version of the story back to Peter Vallis Sarnensis, *Historia Albigensium,* ch. 7 (PL 213.555-56). Humbert himself identifies his source as the "gesta nobilis et nominati viri Simonis comitis Montis Fortis" (sec. 17).

66   "Stupentibus qui aderant, unus ceteris durior ait illis: 'Proiciatur in ignem iterum et tunc experiemur plenius veritatem.' Proicitur iterum, iterum resiliit incombusta. Quod videns ille durus et tardus ad credendum dixit: 'Iterum tertia vice proiciatur, et tunc sine dubio rei exitum cognoscemus.' Proicitur tertio, nec tunc quidem comburitur, sed integra ab igne resilit et illesa. Heretici autem visis tot signis nec tunc ad fidem voluerunt converti, sed in sua manentes malitia, districtissime sibi invicem inhibuerunt, ne miraculum illud per narrationem alicuius ad nostrorum notitiam deveniret."

67   See, e.g., the stories of the novice tempted to return to the world and the disobedient lay brother possessed by a demon (*Legenda,* pp. 470-71). Despite the great brevity with which Bartholomew summarizes these stories (sec. 14), his versions bring out the theme of fatherly care as Jacobus's do not. So do the full-length variants of both stories in the *Vitae fratrum,* II.11 and 22.

68   I do not mean to suggest that Jacobus abandons his usual principles in order to encourage the veneration of Dominic. All told, his chapter on Dominic retells just three of the six resurrections from Constantine's account and three of the forty posthumous cures, and the promises implicit in these stories are deemphasized because Jacobus nearly always focuses on the supernatural details at the expense of the human ones. Jacobus adds one new posthumous healing: Dominic visits a nun who has been seriously ill for several months and provides her with a healing ointment after he has questioned her to make sure that she desires health only in order to serve God better (pp. 481-82; cf. the *Vitae fratrum* II.36). Themes other than healing also receive a good deal of emphasis in Jacobus's collection of posthumous miracles; besides the story about the candles, he makes room for two revelations of Dominic's ascent to heaven, a good deal of detail about the miraculous fragrance emanating from the tomb, the gruesomely vivid punishment of the laywoman who scoffed at devotion to Dominic, and a long final story (pp. 482-83) in which a worldly-minded student in Bologna becomes a Dominican as the result of an allegorical vision.

69 *Legenda,* pp. 477-78. Jacobus's version of this story seems to be a combination of two stories that had long been current among the brethren; cf. the end of Bartholomew's sec. 14, where there is a fragment from each story, and the *Vitae fratrum* II.15-16, where both stories are retold at length.

70 "Missus igitur Reginaldus Bononiam praedicationi ardenter instabat et fratrum numerus excrescebat. Post hoc autem missus [Parisius] non post multos dies in domino obdormivit" (*Legenda,* p. 473). For the less anticlimactic ending of the story in the earlier abridgement by Bartholomew, see above, n. 52. The achievements of Reginald predictably receive more emphasis in Jordan's *Libellus* (see esp. secs. 58 and 63) than in any of the later accounts. But even the liturgical life by Constantine, which foreshadows Jacobus's narrowing of focus at this point (sec. 33), contains a good deal more detail on Reginald's preaching than Jacobus elected to retain. And had Jacobus turned to Humbert's recension, as he does for other details in the legend, he would have found a much stronger affirmation of Reginald's impact on the citizens of Bologna (sec. 35).

71 "Hic fuit in ordine valde religiosus et lector in ordine plurimum gratiosus. Qui tandem moriens cum jam oculos clausisset et fratres eum migrasse crederent, ille apertis oculis fratres circumspiciens ait: dominus vobiscum. Quibus respondentibus: et cum spiritu tuo, adjunxit: fidelium animae per memoriam Dei requiescunt in pace, et sic protinus ille in pace quievit."

72 I refer to one story from the *Vitae fratrum,* discussed immediately below, and the three stories from Constantine's account. Constantine supplements the general rubric in sec. 40 with several reminders of Dominic's resemblance to the first apostles, most notably the explicit link with Peter at the end of the boatman story (sec. 43). Although in Jacobus's retelling of the boatman story Dominic still describes himself as a "discipulus Christi," the only reference to the purpose of the saint's travels is the adversarial-sounding one from the *Vitae fratrum* II.13: Dominic's second miraculous entrance past closed doors occurs "cum in conflictu haereticorum . . . fuisset" (*Legenda,* p. 471).

73 "In eisdem partibus Tolosanis accidit, quod cum beatus Dominicus, qui causa predicacionis discurrebat frequenter, transiret vado fluviolum, qui vocatur Aregia, in medio eius libri, quos in sinu portabat, cum se succingeret, ceciderunt. Qui Deum laudans venit ad domum cuiusdam bone matrone, nuncians ei suorum perdicionem librorum."

74 "Cui cum dixisset suorum amissionem librorum, cepit dicta matrona de hoc non modicum contristari. Cui dixit beatus Dominicus: Ne dolearis, mater, quia oportet nos pariter portare omnia, que contra nos deus ordinare disposuit." Reichert cites this addition in his corpus of variants, *MOPH* 1:69.

75 "Cum in partibus Tolosanis quoddam flumen transiisset, libri ejus nullum habentes conservatorium in fluvium ceciderunt, die autem tertia quidam piscator ibi hamum projiciens, cum magnum piscem se prehendisse putaret, libros ipsos extraxit penitus sic illaesos, ac si in aliquo armario fuissent cum omni diligentia custoditi."

76 "O quanta munditiae puritate ejus caro pollebat, cujus odor tam mirabiliter sordes mentis purgabat" (*Legenda,* p. 471); cf. the *Vitae fratrum* II.27.

77 "Pergens autem cum praedicto episcopo Tolosam deprehendit hospitem suum haeretica pravitate corruptum, quem ad fidem Christi convertit . . ." The remainder of the sentence repeats Constantine's rather hollow suggestion of numerous conversions to follow: "et quasi quendam primitiarum manipulum futurae messis domino praesentavit" (*Legenda,* p. 467). What Jacobus fails to retain here is Constantine's reference to the "benigna simul et evangelica" kind of persuasion with which Dominic won this man (sec. 12).

78 Besides Constantine's new story of this kind, discussed immediately below, Jacobus retells the traditional one about the strict Lenten fast whereby Dominic won over some women who had been misled by the pretended virtue of the Cathars (*Legenda,* p. 468; cf. Constantine, sec. 19).

79 "Praedicante eo aliquando quaedam matronae ab haereticis depravatae ejus pedibus provolutae dixerunt: serve Dei, adjuva nos. Si vera sunt, quae hodie praedicasti, diu mentes nostras errorum spiritus excaecavit" (*Legenda,* p. 475). Cf. Constantine, sec. 48.

80 In Constantine's version the women's initial speech continued, after the portion retained by Jacobus: "'Nam istis, quos tu hereticos vocas, nos autem bonos homines appellamus, usque in hodiernum diem credidimus et adhesimus toto corde. Nunc autem in medio fluctuamus. Serve Dei, adiuva nos, et ora ad dominum Deum tuum, ut notam nobis faciat fidem suam, in qua vivamus, moriamur et salvemur.'"

81 "Tunc vir Dei, stans aliquamdiu et intra semetipsum orans, post aliquantulum dixit eis: 'Constantes estote et exspectate intrepide; confido in domino Deo meo, quod ipse, qui neminem vult perire, iam ostendet vobis, quali domino hactenus adhesistis.'"

82 "Quibus ille: constantes estote et exspectate paulisper, ut videatis, quali domino adhaesistis."

83 "Predicante aliquando viro Dei Dominico in partibus Tolosanis, contigit quosdam hereticos captos et per eum convictos, cum redire nollent ad fidem catholicam, tradi iudicio seculari. Cumque essent incendio deputati, aspiciens inter alios quendam Raymundum, de Grossi nomine, ac si aliquem in eo divine predestinationis radium fuisset intuitus: 'Istum' inquit officialibus curie, 'reservate, nec aliquomodo cum ceteris

comburatur.' Conversusque ad eum blandeque alloquens: 'Scio,' inquit, 'fili mi, scio, quod adhuc licet tarde bonus homo eris et sanctus'" (Constantine, sec. 51).

84   Jacobus omits the "ac si . . . fuisset intuitus" clause when he abridges the portion of the story quoted in the preceding note; in the ensuing account of Raymond's conversion his only major omission is the clause that attributes this happy result to the grace of God ("tandem vero Dei gratia illustratus relictis tenebris ad lumen venit" [Constantine, sec. 51]).

85   "Cum in partibus Tolosanis quosdam haereticos convicisset et illi essent incendio deputati, inspiciens inter eos quendam Raymundum nomine, ait ministris: istum servate, ne aliquo modo cum caeteris comburatur. Conversusque ad eum blandeque alloquens: scio, inquit, fili mi . . ." (*Legenda,* p. 475).

86   On two occasions Dominic's prayers call forth a personal response from heaven, but the *Legenda* does not attribute either response to God himself. In the Reginald story, as Jacobus presents it (pp. 472-73), one sees only the Virgin's care for the order; in Constantine's version of the same story, God was explicitly credited with having inspired in Reginald the ideal of preaching that drew him toward the order in the first place (sec. 30), with revealing the Virgin's first healing visit to Dominic (sec. 32), and with extending the revelation to a third witness (sec. 32). Constantine's account of Dominic's commissioning vision also suggested that the saint's prayer was heard and answered directly by God: "Cum igitur vir Dei Dominicus esset Rome et in basilica sancti Petri *in conspectu Dei* orationem suam pro conservatione et dilatatione ordinis, quem per ipsum dextera eius propagabat, effunderet, *facta manu domini super eum* gloriosos principes Petrum et Paulum ad se subito visione quadam imaginaria venientes aspexit" (sec. 25; emphasis mine). In Jacobus's retelling (quoted above, n. 21) both references to God's immediate involvement have vanished; although the apostles still say that God has chosen Dominic as their successor, the saint's personal access to him is no longer affirmed.

87   See esp. the stories about Dominic's lost books (discussed above), the second resurrection and the miraculously provided bread (Constantine, secs. 36-37; *Legenda,* pp. 473-74), Dominic's conversation with the Cistercian prior before Conrad joins the order (Constantine, sec. 58; *Legenda,* p. 476), and the final legacy.

88   Compare the last eight lines of p. 476 in the *Legenda,* which contain Jacobus's hints of these themes, with secs. 60 and 62 in Constantine's account.

89   Cf. Constantine, secs. 61-62. Jacobus's interest in examples of extreme self-chastisement can also be seen in a number of his chapters on other saints. Thus, e.g., he credits Mary Magdalene with having devised an

immolation (*holocaustum*) of herself for every pleasure she had enjoyed in her earlier life (p. 408); Macarius, with having endured six months of nakedness and suffering in the desert to punish himself for killing a flea (p. 102); Germain of Auxerre, with having maintained a thirty-year regimen of astonishing severity and joylessness, apparently to atone for the worldly life he had led before his election as a bishop (pp. 448-49); Gregory and Bernard, with having carried mortification of the flesh so far that it destroyed their health (pp. 189 and 533).

90   "Denique circumstantibus fratribus et quasi inconsolabiliter de tanti patris destitutione dolentibus, dulciter consolans eos confidenter adiunxit: 'Ne vos mea, filii, corporalis turbet discessio, nullatenus dubitantes, vos utiliorem me mortuum habituros quam vivum.' Grandis sane sed non vana fiducia, sciebat enim nimirum, cui crediderat, et de reposita sibi corona glorie certus erat, qua percepta tanto fieret ad impetrandum potentior, quanto in potentia domini iam securior introisset" (Constantine, sec. 63). Cf. Humbert, sec. 64. Jacobus, whose wording shows his dependence on Constantine's account here, retains only the statement by Dominic and an abridged version of the sentence introducing it (*Legenda,* p. 478).

91   "Testamentum condidit dicens: haec sunt, quae vobis tanquam filiis haereditariis jure possidenda relinquo, caritatem habete, humilitatem servate, paupertatem voluntariam possidete."

92   "Testamentum condidit quale decebat pauperem Christi, divitem in fide et coheredem regni quod repromisit Deus diligentibus se. Testamentum, inquam, non terrene pecunie sed gratie, non materialis suppellectilis sed spiritualis virtutis, non terrene possessionis sed celestis conversationis. Denique quod possederat, hoc legabat. 'Hec sunt . . .'"

93   "In huius inquam triplicis proprietate thesauri summopere universos filios heredes instituit, per quam nimirum illius regni, quod repromisit Deus diligentibus se, secum fierent coheredes" (Constantine, sec. 63).

94   Peter Ferrandus, sec. 50 (*Boll.* 49); *Abrégé,* p. 312. Only Bartholomew, whose whole summary of the final scene between Dominic and his followers runs to less than five lines of print, fails to mention spiritual wealth at this point (sec. 19)—but he also omits the curse reinforcing poverty, so that his version does not create the effect of harshness which one sees in the *Legenda.*

95   "Illud vero, qua potuit, districtione prohibuit, ne quis unquam in suo ordine possessiones induceret temporales, maledictionem Dei omnipotentis et suam terribiliter imprecans ei, qui praedicatorum ordinem terrenarum divitiarum pulvere praesumeret maculare." This wording is taken almost verbatim from Constantine until the very end; the last five words, with their image of wealth as dust that would defile the order,

seem to be Humbert's (sec. 65), altough Peter Ferrandus, sec. 50, and the
Abrégé, p. 312, use the same image.

96   Unlike the accounts of all his predecessors, Jacobus's account of the
original preaching mission in southern France does not even mention the
key strategy of apostolic poverty (*Legenda,* p. 467; cf. esp. Constantine,
sec. 14), and the closest he comes to repairing this omission in the
remainder of the legend is when he has Dominic declare to the boatman,
in a story which no longer mentions preaching, that "discipulus Christi
esset nec aurum vel pecuniam deportaret" (p. 474).

97   See above, Chapter 4, n. 1.

98   One of the two critical pieces of evidence here is the prologue to
Jacobus's collection of sermons on the saints, which begins as follows:
"Rogatus ut post compilatas legendas sanctorum aliquam quoque de
ipsis sanctis facerem compilationem" (Kaeppeli, *Scriptores Ordinis
Praedicatorum medii aevi,* 2:359). The other is his apparently chrono-
logical listing of his works in the *Chronica civitatis Ianuensis* (ed.
Monleone, vol. 2, pp. 404-5). The list starts with the *Legenda*
("Legendas Sanctorum in uno volumine compilavit"), then proceeds in
turn to cite three collections of sermons (those on the saints mentioned
first), the *Mariale,* and the chronicle of Genoa itself.

99   Despite the requirements spelled out in the Constitutions of the order,
the reception of a youth below the age of eighteen was not a rare
occurrence in the thirteenth century. Hinnebusch, *History,* 1:283-84,
cites a number of ordinances and admonitions from the period which
make it clear that the age requirement was rather flexible in practice,
especially for promising candidates, and that local superiors sometimes
ignored it altogether.

Chapter 10: On the *Legenda* as a Medieval Best-Seller

1   Dondaine has suggested that the *Legenda* might have been preferred to
the *Abbreviatio* because it offered a broader and less regional selection
of saints, or because it supplemented the hagiographical material proper
with more scholarly disquisitions on various points of doctrine and
tradition. But he himself does not seem to have been thoroughly
satisfied with either of those explanations; see, e.g., the introduction to
his translation of the *Abbreviatio,* p. 18.

2   My brief summary of Vauchez's findings about what he calls "official"
sanctity in *La sainteté en Occident aux derniers siècles du Moyen Age*
(Rome, 1981) by no means suggests the enormous scope and richness of
his book, which all serious students of medieval hagiography ought to
read. Since the present study was virtually finished before I encountered
Vauchez's work, I have simply attempted in this final chapter to show
the most obvious connections between his findings and my own.

3   Vauchez demonstrates, in fact, that there were extended periods during which the only requests for canonization that had any chance of success were those championed by at least one of the great mendicant orders, the French monarchy, or the house of Anjou; for the details, see pp. 87-98 of his study.

4   "Non sufficit quod in uno fuerit gloriosus vel semel tantum, sed quod in multis et multotiens, imo quod continue eius vita fuerit gloriosa" (Innocent IV, *In quinque libros decretalium,* quoted by Vauchez, p. 602, n. 51.)

5   One result of this change was the growing emphasis in the dossiers of new saints on the testimony of their confessors; another, Vauchez suggests, was the tendency for the supporters of earlier saints to revise their biographies to eliminate signs of human frailty, as Bonaventure did with Saint Francis and as the Order of Preachers had already done with Saint Dominic (pp. 601-2).

6   "Vita eius non fuit solum vita hominis sed supra hominem" (quoted by Vauchez, p. 606, n. 67). Vauchez's next three footnotes document the conversion of this statement into a criterion by which later saints were judged.

7   Thus Vauchez notes, e.g., that healings constituted a very small fraction of the miracles attributed to these saints during their lifetimes; much more common were supernatural signs showing God's favor toward the saints themselves and proofs of their power over the elements (pp. 588-90).

8   The low esteem in which parish priests were generally held is suggested by the fact that no other representative of this class was canonized during the Middle Ages; moreover, even Saint Yves was portrayed in the iconography of the time as a judge and advocate for the poor, rather than as a parish priest.

9   The gap between the official criteria for sanctity and the priorities of most late-medieval Christians is illustrated even more strikingly by the lack of popular enthusiasm for most of the other saints canonized in the fourteenth and fifteenth centuries; as Vauchez notes, the majority of laymen and many of the clergy continued to prefer more old-fashioned and less narrowly spiritual kinds of saints than the "great clerks" in Rome did (pp. 484-88).

10   Vauchez concludes, in fact, that the late-medieval bishops who won the favorable attention of the papacy were distinguished above all "par la vigueur avec laquelle ils ont lutté contre les empiétements du pouvoir laïc pour défendre les droits et les privilèges de leur Église, ou encore par l'exercice efficace d'une autorité qui s'affirme en multipliant les sanctions et les excommunications" (p. 456).

11   The four female mystics in question were Dauphine of Puimichel
      (d. 1360), Dorothy of Montau (d. 1394), Saint Bridget of Sweden
      (d. 1373, canon. 1391), and Saint Catherine of Siena (d. 1380, canon.
      1461).

12   Thus, e.g., the diocesan synod of Angers in 1293 expressed concern over
      the public's declining interest in the cult of Saint Maurice, the traditional
      patron of their city and cathedral. And Salimbene indignantly charged
      that the secular clergy were promoting questionable new cults in a
      deliberate attempt to compete with the mendicant orders and their
      famous saints (Vauchez, p. 159, n. 1).

13   This was a very real problem, as Vauchez demonstrates in his account of
      "local sanctity" in the late Middle Ages (esp. pp. 105-15 and 161-62),
      and of course it ran directly counter to the goal of uniform belief and
      practice, directed from Rome, that was being pursued by the papacy. In
      this context, it is not hard to see the potential appeal to conservative
      churchmen of a single, simplified legendary, dominated by ancient and
      well-established saints, which could be disseminated throughout the
      Western church.

14   Besides noting the relatively egalitarian implications of the official
      canonizations in the late twelfth and early thirteenth centuries, Vauchez
      places a good deal of emphasis on the initiative apparently taken by
      laymen, especially in Italy, with regard to the selection of new saints. In
      fact, he portrays the cult of the saints as an important battleground in a
      generalized struggle for power within the church. The untaught
      multitudes, he asserts, were beginning to reshape Christianity in
      accordance with their own aspirations (p. 154), and the clergy were so
      moved by this threat that they came together in a solid front against it:
      "Au delà des conflits, qui occupent le devant de la scène, entre
      Mendiants et séculiers ou entre partisans et adversaires de la monarchie
      pontificale, se crée une Sainte-Alliance des clercs, unanimes pour ne
      laisser aux laïcs qu'un rôle marginal et pour rejeter la foi des humbles,
      qui étaient en majorité des incultes" (p. 160).

15   One might well look both for significant marginalia and for major
      alterations in the text—additions, abbreviations, and so on—which
      suggest something about the particular audience or purpose for which a
      given manuscript was produced. Nor should one disregard the numerous
      manuscripts which contain just a few excerpts from Jacobus's book; the
      particular excerpts chosen and the kinds of material with which they are
      juxtaposed may turn out to be instructive.

16   See, e.g., MSS Bodley 389, fols. 220^v-227; Lambeth Palace 221, fols.
      48-58; Salisbury Cathedral 167, fols. 7^{v}ff.; Trinity College (Cambridge)
      B.15.1, fols. i-iv; and Winchester College 9, fols. 2^v-15^v.

17 Paul Meyer claimed to have found at least one, and perhaps as many as three, anonymous French translations from the *Legenda* that were produced before 1300 ("Notice du MS. Med.-Pal. 141 de la Laurentienne," pp. 3-4).

18 I venture this generalization after reading half a dozen chapters from the Vatican MS. (Barb. 2300) of Bartholomew's work, besides the published chapter on Dominic.

19 "Si les anges ne l'avaient pas visité et fortifié, son pauvre corps humain n'aurait pu soutenir longtemps un tel supplice. Mais celui qui avait conservé vivant Jonas dans le ventre du monstre marin soutint Eusèbe dans son réduit." For this and the other passages cited in the present chapter, I was able to verify the accuracy of Dondaine's edition by comparing it with the text in Vatican MS. latin 1198.

20 "Ses vêtements et ses chaussures, son lit étaient simples, tout en demeurant en rapport avec son état; on n'y trouvait aucun luxe comme aucune négligence exagérée, excès si fréquents parmi les hommes. 'Les hommes, disait-il, ont coutume de se glorifier insolemment en ces choses, soit par excès, soit par défaut, et dans les deux cas ils recherchent leur propre intérêt, non celui de Jésus-Christ' " (*Abrégé,* pp. 361-62). Cf. the *vita* by Possidius, ch. 22.

21 The most dramatic example I have noticed is the discourse to the newly married couple in the chapter on Thomas the Apostle (*Legenda,* pp. 34-35).

22 "Agnes virgo prudentissima . . . XIII. anno aetatis suae mortem perdidit et vitam invenit. Infantia quidem computabatur in annis, sed erat senectus mentis immensa, corpore juvencula, sed animo cana, pulchra facie, sed pulchrior fide. Quae dum a scholis revertitur, a praefecti filio adamatur. Cui ille gemmas et divitias innumerabiles promisit, si consensum ejus conjugio non negaret. Cui Agnes respondit: discede a me fomes peccati, nutrimentum facinoris, pabulum mortis, quia jam ab alio amatore praeventa sum. . . . [I]llum amo, qui longe te nobilior est et genere dignior, cujus mater virgo est, cujus pater feminam nescit, cui angeli serviunt."

23 Even his chapter on Petronilla, which looks almost identical to Jacobus's on first reading, contains a few details which qualify the message that illness and an early death are the blessings that every devout father should desire for his daughters.

24 "La bienheureuse Agnès naquit à Rome, de parents riches et nobles. A l'âge de treize ans, un jour qu'elle revenait de l'école, elle fut remarquée par le fils du préfet; charmé par sa beauté, il la désira pour épouse. Agnès repoussa toutes ses prières et tous ses cadeaux; elle ne voulait pas, disait-elle, faire l'injure à son fiancé de violer ses noces éternelles et de l'abandonner, lui si puissant, si riche et si beau."

25   Other gratuitous insults that stand out in the *Legenda* include Agatha's
      contemptuous remarks about the gods in which her judge believes (p.
      171), Margaret's gibes at the prefect who is having her tortured (p. 401),
      Christina's invective against her father (pp. 419-20), and Cecilia's attacks
      on her judge and everything he stands for (p. 776). Jean does not retell
      the Christina legend at all, and his versions of the other three are
      noticeably more restrained than those in the *Legenda*.

26   Among the saintly laywomen discussed by Vauchez, Dorothy of Montau
      (d. 1394) and Saint Francesca Romana (d. 1440) exhibited the most
      remarkable symptoms of this aversion; for the details, see *La sainteté,*
      esp. p. 443, n. 500, and p. 445, n. 506.

27   Thus he finds a new tendency in the fourteenth and fifteenth centuries to
      ask the saints for temporary cures rather than lasting ones: the
      momentary resurrection of an infant to permit baptism, for example, or
      the momentary restoration of sight to a blind person who desired only to
      see the consecrated Host (*La sainteté,* p. 553). And from the fourteenth
      century on, it apparently became rather common for pious Christians to
      seek out living saints without expecting or hoping to obtain anything at
      all except the privilege of witnessing some sign of the saints' supernatural
      gifts (p. 555).

Principal Works Cited

Primary Sources and Early Commentaries (through the Renaissance)

Acta canonizationis S. Dominici. Ed. Angelo Walz. *MOPH* 16 (1935): 91-194.

Acta capitulorum provincialium Ordinis fratrum Praedicatorum: Première province de Provence, Province romaine, Province d'Espagne (1239-1302). Ed. Célestin Douais. Toulouse, 1894.

Ambrose of Milan. *Epistolae.* PL 16.875-1286.

Augustine of Hippo. *City of God.* Trans. Marcus Dods. A Select Library of the Nicene and Post-Nicene Fathers, ed. Philip Schaff et al., 1st ser., vol. 2. 1887; rept. Grand Rapids, Mich., 1956.

———. *Confessions.* Trans. John K. Ryan. Garden City, N.Y., 1960.

———. *Confessionum libri tredecim.* Ed. Martin Skutella. Vols. 13-14 of *Oeuvres de Saint Augustin.* Paris, 1962.

———. *On Christian Doctrine.* Trans. D. W. Robertson, Jr. Indianapolis, 1958.

———. *Soliloquies.* Trans. and annotated by Thomas F. Gilligan. New York, 1943.

Bartholomew of Trent. *Epilogus in gesta sanctorum.* Vatican MS. Barberini latin 2300.

———. "[Legenda] Dominici confessoris" from the *Epilogus.* Ed. Berthold Altaner. In *Der hl. Dominikus,* pp. 230-39.

Becon, Thomas. *Prayers and Other Pieces.* Ed. John Ayre. Parker Society, vol. 4. Cambridge, 1844.

Cano, Melchior. *De locis theologicis.* In *Melchioris Cani . . . Opera,* ed. Hyacinth Serry, pp. 1-457. Bassano, 1746.

Cassiodorus, Flavius Magnus Aurelius, and Epiphanius. *Historia ecclesiastica tripartita.* Ed. Rudolph Hanslik. Corpus scriptorum ecclesiasticorum latinorum, 71. Vienna, 1952.

Constantine of Orvieto. *Legenda S. Dominici.* Ed. H. C. Scheeben. *MOPH* 16 (1935): 261-352.

Crespin, Jean. *Histoire des martyrs, persécutez et mis à mort pour la vérité de l'Evangile, depuis le temps des apostres jusques à present* (1619). 3 vols. Rept. Toulouse, 1885-89.

Estius, William. "Historia martyrum Gorcomiensium." *Acta SS,* July, 2 (1867 rept.): 754-838.

Foxe, John. *Actes and Monuments of These Latter and Perilous Dayes.* London, 1576.

Gerard de Frachet. *Vitae fratrum Ordinis Praedicatorum, necnon Cronica Ordinis ab anno MCCIII usque ad MCCLIV.* Ed. Benedict M. Reichert. *MOPH,* vol. 1 (1896).

Gratian. *Decretum.* PL, vol. 187.

Gregory I (the Great). *Dialogues.* Ed. Adalbert de Vogüé. Sources chrétiennes, vols. 251, 260, 265. Paris, 1978-80.

———. *Homilia in Evangelia.* PL 76.1075-1314.

———. *Regulae pastoralis liber.* PL 77.13-128.

Gui, Bernard. General Preface to *Speculum sanctorale.* Ed. Leopold Delisle. In "Notice sur les manuscrits de Bernard Gui," Appendix XX, pp. 421-24.

———. *Speculum sanctorale,* Part Four. Bibliothèque Nationale MS. latin 5406.

Gui, Bernard, and Stephen de Salanhac. *De quatuor in quibus Deus Predicatorum Ordinem insignivit.* Ed. Thomas Kaeppeli. *MOPH,* vol. 22 (1949).

Humbert of Romans. *Legenda S. Dominici.* Ed. Angelo Walz. *MOPH* 16 (1935): 353-433.

———. *Treatise on Preaching (De eruditione praedicatorum).* Trans. Dominican students of the Province of St. Joseph; ed. Walter M. Conlon. London, 1955.

Jacobus de Voragine. *The Golden Legend.* Trans. and adapted by Granger Ryan and Helmut Ripperger. 1941; rept. New York, 1969.

———. *Legenda aurea, vulgo Historia lombardica dicta.* Ed. Theodor Graesse. 3d ed. Bratislava, 1890.

———. *Sermones aurei de praecipuis sanctorum festis, et laudibus Deiparae Virginis.* Vol. 2. Ed. Rudolph Clutius. Augsburg and Cracow, 1760.

Jean de Mailly. *Abbreviatio in gestis et miraculis sanctorum.* Vatican MS. latin 1198.

———. *Abrégé des gestes et miracles des saints.* Ed. and trans. Antoine Dondaine. Paris, 1947.

Jordan of Saxony. *Libellus de principiis Ordinis Praedicatorum.* Ed. H. C. Scheeben. *MOPH* 16 (1935): 1-88.

Mombrizio, Bonino. *Sanctuarium, seu Vitae Sanctorum.* Milan, before 1480; rept. Paris, 1910.

Paulinus of Milan. *Vita S. Ambrosii.* Ed. Michele Pellegrino. Rome, 1961.

Peter Ferrandus. *Legenda S. Dominici.* Ed. M. Hyacinth Laurent. *MOPH* 16 (1935): 195-260.

Pignon, Lawrence, et al. *Catalogi et Chronica, accedunt Catalogi Stamsensis et Upsalensis scriptorum O.P.* Ed. G. Meersseman. *MOPH,* vol. 18 (1936).

Possidius, bishop of Calama. *Sancti Augustini vita.* Ed. Herbert T. Weiskotten. Princeton, 1919.

Rufinus of Aquileia. *Historia ecclesiasticae libri duo.* PL 21.461-540.

Salimbene, Ognibene di Guido di Adamo. *Cronica.* Trans. and adapted by G. G. Coulton. In *From St. Francis to Dante.* 2d ed. 1907; rept. Philadelphia, 1972.

Sulpicius Severus. *Dialogues*. PL 20.183-222.

——. *Vita S. Martini*. Ed. Jacques Fontaine. Sources chrétiennes, vols. 133-35.

Surius, Laurence. *De probatis sanctorum historiis*. 6 vols. Cologne, 1570-75.

Synodi Brixinenses, saeculi XV. Ed. G. Bickell. Innsbruck, 1880.

Thou, Jacques, Auguste de. *Histoire universelle . . . depuis 1543 jusqu'en 1607, traduite sur l'édition latine de Londres.* . . . 16 vols. [Paris], 1734.

Vives, Juan Luis. *De disciplinis*. Vol. 6 of *Joannis Ludovici Vivis Valentini Opera omnia* . . ., ed. Gregorio Mayáns y Siscar. Valencia, 1785; rept. London, 1964.

——. *De tradendis disciplinis* (Part 2 of *De disciplinis*). Trans. Foster Watson. In *Vives on Education*. 1913; rept. Totowa, N.J., 1971.

——. [Excerpts from various works]. Trans. Alain Guy. In *Vivès; ou, L'humanisme engagé*. Paris, 1972.

Wakefield, Walter L., and Austin P. Evans, eds. *Heresies of the High Middle Ages: Selected Sources Translated and Annotated.* . . . New York, 1969.

Witzel, Georg. *Hagiologium, seu de Sanctis ecclesiae: Historiae Divorum toto terrarum orbe celeberrimorum, e sacris Scriptoribus, summa fide ac studio congestae.* . . . Mainz, 1541.

Modern Scholarship and Criticism

Aigrain, René. *L'hagiographie: Ses sources, ses méthodes, son histoire*. Paris, 1953.

Altaner, Berthold. *Der hl. Dominikus: Untersuchungen und Texte*. Breslau, 1922.

Altman, Charles F. "Two Types of Opposition and the Structure of Latin Saints' Lives." *Medievalia et Humanistica*, n.s., 6 (1975): 1-11.

Anfossi, Filippo. *Memorie istoriche appartenenti alla vita del beato Jacopo da Varagine dell'Ordine de' Predicatori, arcivescovo di Genova*. Genoa, [1816].

Baillet, Adrien. *Vies des saints, composées sur ce qui nous est resté de plus authentique et de plus assuré dans leur histoire*. Vol. 1. 2d ed. Paris, 1704.

Baudrillart, André. "La psychologie de la *Légende dorée*." *Minerva* (Paris) 5 (1902): 24-43.

Bayle, Pierre. *Dictionaire* [sic] *historique et critique*. 5th ed. Amsterdam, 1740.

"Le bienheureux Jacques de Voragine, Archevêque de Gênes (1230-1298)." *L'année dominicaine*, 7 (Paris, 1895): 253-62.

Boglioni, Pierre. "Miracle et nature chez Grégoire le Grand." *Epopées, légendes, et miracles: Cahiers d'études médiévales* (Montreal) 1 (1974): 11-102.

Bolland, John. "Praefatio generalis in vitas SS." *Acta SS*, Jan., 1 (1643; rept. Paris, 1863): ix-lxi.

Broussolle, J. C. "La *Légende dorée*." *L'université catholique*, n.s., 44 (1903): 327-57.

Brown, Peter. *The Cult of the Saints: Its Rise and Function in Latin Christianity.* Chicago, 1981.

Brunet, Gustave. "Notice préliminaire." In *La Légende dorée par Jacques de Voragine,* trans. G[ustave] B[runet], 1:1-9. Paris, 1843; rept. 1906.

Butler, Cuthbert. *Western Mysticism: The Teaching of Augustine, Gregory, and Bernard on Contemplation and the Contemplative Life.* 2d ed. 1927; rept. New York, 1966.

Butler, Pierce. *Legenda aurea—Légende dorée—Golden Legend: A Study of Caxton's Golden Legend with Special Reference to Its Relations to the Earlier English Prose Translation.* Baltimore, 1899.

The Cambridge Medieval History. Ed. H. M. Gwatkin et al. 8 vols. New York, 1911-36.

Cave, William. *Scriptorum ecclesiasticorum historia literaria, a Christo nato usque ad saeculum XIV. . . .* 2 vols. 1688-98; rept. Basel, 1741-45.

Courcelle, Pierre. *Recherches sur saint Ambroise: "Vies" anciennes, culture, iconographie.* Paris, 1973.

Delehaye, Hippolyte. "Bulletin des publications hagiographiques," nos. 5-7. *Anal. Boll.* 22 (1903): 81-83.

———. "Bulletin des publications hagiographiques," nos. 67-71. *Anal. Boll.* 23 (1904): 325-26.

———. *Etude sur le légendier romain: Les saints de novembre et de décembre.* Brussels, 1936.

———. *Les légendes hagiographiques.* Brussels, 1905.

———. *The Legends of the Saints.* Trans. Donald Attwater. New York, 1962.

———. *Les passions des martyrs et les genres littéraires.* Brussels, 1921.

———. *The Work of the Bollandists through Three Centuries, 1615-1915.* Princeton, 1922.

Delisle, Leopold. "Notice sur les manuscrits de Bernard Gui." *Notices et extraits des manuscrits de la Bibliothèque Nationale et autres bibliothèques* 27, pt. 2 (1879): 169-455.

Dolan, John Patrick. *History of the Reformation: A Conciliatory Assessment of Opposite Views.* New York, 1965.

Dondaine, Antoine. "Le dominicain français Jean de Mailly et la *Légende dorée.*" *Archives d'histoire dominicaine* 1 (1946): 53-102.

———. "L'*Epilogus in gesta sanctorum* de Barthélemy de Trente." In *Studia mediaevalia et mariologica P. Carolo Balić O F M septuagesimum explenti annum dicata,* pp. 333-60. Rome, 1971.

———. "La hiérarchie cathare en Italie." *Archivum fratrum Praedicatorum* 19 (1949): 280-312; 20 (1950): 234-324.

Dudden, Frederick Homes. *Gregory the Great: His Place in History and Thought.* 2 vols. London, 1905.

Dupin, Louis-Ellies. *Nouvelle bibliothèque des auteurs ecclésiastiques. . . .* 20 vols. in 8. Paris, 1688-1715; new ed., Utrecht, 1730-31.

Echard, Jacques, and Jacques Quétif. *Scriptores Ordinis Praedicatorum recensiti, notisque historicis et criticis.* 2 vols. Paris, 1719-21; rept. Turin, 1961.

Féret, Pierre. *La faculté de théologie de Paris et ses docteurs les plus célèbres: Epoque moderne.* 7 vols. in 4. Paris, 1900-1910.

Gaiffier, Baudouin de. *Etudes critiques d'hagiographie et d'iconologie.* Subsidia hagiographica no. 43. Brussels, 1967.

———. "Mentalité de l'hagiographe médiéval d'après quelques travaux récents." *Anal. Boll.* 86 (1968): 391-99.

"The Golden Legend." *Church Quarterly Review* (London) 57 (1903): 29-52.

Görlach, Manfred. *The Textual Tradition of the South English Legendary.* Leeds Texts and Monographs, n.s. 6. Leeds, 1974.

Haag, Eugène, and Emile Haag. *La France protestante; ou, Vies des protestants français.* . . . 10 vols. Paris, 1846-59.

———. *La France protestante.* 2d ed. Rev. Henri Bordier. 6 vols. in 12. Paris, 1877-88.

Hinnebusch, William A. *History of the Dominican Order.* Vol. 1, *Origins and Growth to 1500.* Vol. 2, *Intellectual and Cultural Life to 1500.* New York, 1966-73.

Huot-Girard, Giselle. "La justice immanente dans la 'Légende dorée.'" *Epopées, légendes, et miracles: Cahiers d'études médiévales* (Montreal) 1 (1974): 135-47.

Kaeppeli, Thomas. *Scriptores Ordinis Praedicatorum medii aevi.* Rome, 1970-.

Kantorowicz, Ernst H. *Frederick the Second, 1194-1250.* Trans. E. O. Lorimer. 1931; rept. New York, 1957.

Kemp, Eric W. *Canonization and Authority in the Western Church.* London, 1948.

Knowles, Christine. "Jean de Vignay: Un traducteur du XIVᵉ siècle." *Romania* 75 (1954): 353-83.

Launoy, Jean de. *Regii Navarrae gymnasii Parisiensis historia.* 2 vols. in 1. Paris, 1677.

Lea, Henry Charles. *History of the Inquisition of the Middle Ages.* 3 vols. 1888-1922; rept. New York, 1958.

Lecler, Joseph. *Toleration and the Reformation.* Trans. T. L. Westow. 2 vols. London, 1960.

Leff, Gordon. *Heresy in the Later Middle Ages: The Relation of Heterodoxy to Dissent c.1250-c.1450.* 2 vols. New York, 1967.

Mähler, Maximilien. "Evocations bibliques et hagiographiques dans la vie de saint Benoît par saint Grégoire." *Revue bénédictine* 83 (1973): 398-429.

Maisonneuve, Henri. *Etudes sur les origines de l'Inquisition.* 2d ed. Paris, 1960.

Mâle, Emile. *L'art religieux du XIIIᵉ siècle en France: Etude sur l'iconographie du moyen âge et sur ses sources d'inspiration.* Paris, 1898.

———. *The Gothic Image: Religious Art in France of the Thirteenth Century.* Trans. Dora Nussey. 1913; rept. New York, 1972.

Meyer, Paul. "Notice du MS. Med.-Pal. 141 de la Laurentienne." *Romania* 33 (1904): 1-7.

Monleone, Giovanni. "Studio introduttivo." In *Iacopo da Varagine e la sua Cronaca di Genova dalle origini al MCCXCVII,* vol. 1. Rome, 1941.

Moorman, John. *History of the Franciscan Order from Its Origins to the Year 1517*. Oxford, 1968.

Mortier, Daniel A. *Histoire des maîtres généraux de l'Ordre des frères Prêcheurs*. 8 vols. Paris, 1903-20.

Nicéron, Jean Pierre, et al. *Mémoires pour servir à l'histoire des hommes illustres dans la république des lettres*. . . . 43 vols. in 44. Paris, 1729-45.

Noreña, Carlos G. *Juan Luis Vives*. International Archives of the History of Ideas, no. 34. The Hague, 1970.

Nugent, Donald. *Ecumenism in the Age of the Reformation: The Colloquy of Poissy*. Cambridge, Mass., 1974.

O'Neill, George V. "Biographical Introduction." In *The Golden Legend: Lives of the Saints*, pp. 1-14. Cambridge, 1914.

Philippart, Guy. *Les légendiers latins et autres manuscrits hagiographiques*. Typologie des sources du moyen âge occidental, fascs. 24-25. Turnhout, Belgium, 1977.

Poncelet, Albert. "Le légendier de Pierre Calo." *Anal. Boll.* 29 (1910): 5-116.

Reames, Sherry L. "Saint Martin of Tours in the *Legenda aurea* and Before." *Viator* 12 (1981): 131-64.

Richardson, Ernest Cushing. "The Influence of the Golden Legend on Pre-Reformation Culture History." *Papers of the American Society of Church History* 1 (1888): 237-48.

———. "Jacobus de Voragine and the Golden Legend." *Princeton Theological Review* 1 (1903): 267-81.

———. *Materials for a Life of Jacopo da Varagine*. 4 vols. in 1. New York, 1935.

Roze, J.-B. M. [Preface.] In *La Légende dorée de Jacques de Voragine: Nouvellement traduite en français*, 1:v-xxvi. Paris, 1902.

Schneyer, Johannes Baptist. *Repertorium der lateinischen Sermones des Mittelalters für die Zeit von 1150-1350*. Beiträge zur Geschichte der Philosophie und Theologie des Mittelalters 43. Münster Westfalen, 1969-.

Sévèstre, A. *Dictionnaire de patrologie; ou, Répertoire historique, bibliographique, analytique, et critique des saints pères, des docteurs, et de tous les autres écrivains des douze premiers siècles de l'Eglise*. 5 vols. (Vols. 20-23 bis of Migne's *Nouvelle encyclopédie théologique*.) Paris, 1851-59.

Seybolt, Robert Francis. "Fifteenth-Century Editions of the *Legenda aurea*." *Speculum* 21 (1946): 327-38.

———. "The *Legenda aurea*, Bible, and *Historia scholastica*." *Speculum* 21 (1946): 339-42.

Southern, Richard W. *Saint Anselm and His Biographer: A Study of Monastic Life and Thought, 1059-c.1130*. Cambridge, 1963.

Tierney, Brian. *The Crisis of Church and State, 1050-1300*. Englewood Cliffs, N.J., 1964.

Touron, Antoine. *Histoire des hommes illustres de l'Ordre de saint Dominique*. 6 vols. Paris, 1743-49.

Vansteenberghe, Edmond. *Le cardinal Nicolas de Cues (1401-1464): L'action, la pensée*. Paris, 1920.

Vauchez, André. *La sainteté en Occident aux derniers siècles du Moyen Age, d'après les procès de canonisation et les documents hagiographiques.* Bibliothèque des Ecoles françaises d'Athènes et de Rome 241. Rome, 1981.

Vicaire, Marie-Humbert. *Dominique et ses prêcheurs.* Studia Friburgensia, n.s., 55. Fribourg, 1977.

Ward, Benedicta. *Miracles and the Medieval Mind: Theory, Record, and Event, 1000-1215.* Philadelphia, 1982.

White, Helen C. *Tudor Books of Saints and Martyrs.* Madison, Wis., 1963.

Wilmart, André. "Saint Ambroise et la *Légende dorée.*" *Ephemerides liturgicae,* n.s., 10 (1936): 169-206.

Wyzewa, Teodor de. "Introduction." In *La Légende dorée,* 1:9-25. 1902; rept. Paris, [1960].

Zuidweg, Jacobus J. A. *De Werkwijze van Jacobus de Voragine in de "Legenda aurea"* (with a summary in French). Oud-Beijerland, 1941.

Index

Abraham, 104-5

Abridged legendaries. *See* Legendaries, abridged

Acta Sanctorum, 11, 33, 34

Active life: defined by Gregory, 81, 153; defined in Jacobus's sermons, 153

Active service to others: in the *Legenda,* 150-51, 152; Augustine cited on, 151; Gregory cited on, 152; Thomas Aquinas cited on, 152; in Jacobus's sermons, 153, 280n61; in dossiers of late-medieval saints, 199-200, 201

Adeodatus, Augustine's son, 137, 154

Adrian, Saint, 162

Agatha, Saint, 132, 304n25

Agnes, Saint, 206-7, 260n28

Albigensians. *See* Cathars

Altman, Charles F., 98

Alypius, Augustine's friend, 141, 154

Ambrose, Saint: special importance to Jacobus, 7, 114, 120, 121-22, 125-26, 129-30, 191; sponsored cult of the saints, 46; confrontations with emperors, 119, 120, 121; as portrayed in Jacobus's sermons, 130, 153; as Augustine's teacher, 138-39, 154; and the Tuscan landowner, 159; opposed the use of coercion against heretics, 269n47. *See also* Paulinus, life of Ambrose

Ambrosian liturgy, 7, 121

Anastasia, Saint, 132, 205

Andrew, Saint, 132

Anfossi, Filippo, 16

Anselm, Saint, 292n49

Antimendicant controversy, 1250s, 171, 173

Antoninus, Saint, 53

Antony, Saint, 132

Apollonia, Saint, 162

Arians, 117, 121, 122, 132, 205

Arius, 263n10

Attila the Hun, 131

Augsburg Confession, 225n14

Augustine, Saint: attitude toward miraculous cures, 47, 66; special importance to Jacobus, 135, 138, 145-46, 149, 150; *Rule,* 138; on the continuity between nature and grace, 143, 156; on objects of worldly desire, 144-45; portrayal in Jacobus's sermons, 145-46, 161, 283n76; on contemplation and action, 151; on human relationships, 154, 155-56; on charity, 156; appreciation of nature, 157-58, 281n69; portrayal by Jean de Mailly, 206. *See also* Possidius, life of Augustine

—*Confessions:* impediments to his conversion, 137-38; communications between Monica and God, 139; portrayal of God, 139-40; first mystical experience, 140; conversion of Victorinus, 141; Augustine's spiritual state after conversion, 142-43; Monica's death, 154; on the problems posed by earthly pleasures, 157, 281n71

—*Soliloquies,* 144-45

Bacon, Francis, 61

Baillet, Adrien, 14, 15, 31, 32, 36, 217n23, 226n21, 227n23, 236n26

Barbara, Saint, 160, 234n15

Baron, Vincent, 32-33

Bartholomew of Trent, legendary of: surviving MSS, 3; intended audience and

313

Bartholomew of Trent *(continued)*
use, 86; account of Dominic, 165, 167, 168-69, 174-75, 177-78, 179-81, 183, 184; general characteristics, 168, 181, 198, 204; date, 286n*10;* influence on the *Legenda,* 290nn *33, 35,* 293n*50*
Becon, Thomas, 59-60
Bede, 53, 55, 67
Bellarmine, Robert, 58-59
Benedict, Saint: kinds of miracles recorded at his shrines, 99; *Rule,* 108, 250n*10.* *See also* Gregory the Great, Saint, life of Benedict
Berengar of Landorra, 40, 41, 62-63, 64, 232n*59,* 241n*62*
Bernard, Saint, 131, 161, 281n*67,* 283n*76,* 299n*89*
Bible, printed editions before 1501, 4
Blaise, Saint, 233n*15,* 284n*82*
Boglioni, Pierre, 76
Bolland, John: defense of saints' legends, 11-14, 59; scholarly criteria, 13-14, 21, 22, 25-26, 68; cited by Wyzewa, 18-19; vantage point on the *Legenda,* 57-62 *passim;* mentioned, 21, 42
Bollandists, Society of, 14, 20, 23-24, 31, 33-34, 42, 56, 69, 226n*19*
Bonaventure, Saint, 301n*5*
Boniface VIII, Pope, 199
Bridget of Sweden, Saint, 302n*11*
Brown, Peter, 46-47, 66, 67
Butler, Pierce, 221n*53*

Calvin, John, 31, 37, 225n*14*
Cano, Melchior: career, 38; *De locis theologicis,* 38-39; on falsifications in hagiography, 52-53, 56; on Vincent of Beauvais, 53, 62; on Bede and Gregory the Great, 53, 67; explicit criticism of the *Legenda,* 53-54, 62, 236n*26;* mentioned, 21, 31, 42, 65, 88
Canonization. *See also* Saints, selection of
—by tradition, 30
—local, in late Middle Ages, 198, 202, 224n*10,* 302nn *13, 14*
—papal: relative rarity in Middle Ages, 30, 224n*10;* Papebroch's history of, 34; political implications in late Middle Ages, 198, 202-3, 301n*3;* new criteria after 1270, 199, 200, 201, 301nn *9, 10*

Carmelites: dispute with Bollandists, 33-34
Carranza, Bartholomew de, 38
Cassiodorus, *Tripartite History,* 121-22
Cathars, 41, 127-28, 144, 175, 183, 188, 269n*48,* 275n*27*
Catherine de Medici, Queen of France, 37, 240n*57*
Catherine of Alexandria, Saint, 107, 109, 259n*21,* 234n*15*
Catherine of Siena, Saint, 302n*11*
Cave, William, 60, 135, 136
Caxton, William, 4, 11, 205
Cecilia, Saint, 108-9, 224n*11,* 304n*25*
Celestine V, Pope, 200
Charity: in the *Legenda,* 142-43, 152-53, 156, 208n*57;* as defined by Augustine, 156, 281n*66. See also* Active service to others; Pastoral care
Charles de Guise, Cardinal of Lorraine, 37, 240n*57*
Charles of Blois, Duke of Brittany, 209
Chaucer, Geoffrey, 4
Christ: as uniting contemplation with action, 83; as Judge, 170-71, 173
Christina, Saint, 281n*67,* 304n*25*
Cicero, 140, 273n*17*
Constantine I, Emperor, 109
Constantine of Orvieto, life of Dominic, 165, 169-70, 172, 182, 183-84, 188, 190, 191, 192, 193
Contemplative life: Gregory cited on, 81, 83, 84, 152, 248n*23;* Jacobus cited on, 105-6, 151, 153; Augustine cited on, 151; in dossiers of late-medieval saints, 199-200, 201-2
Contemptus mundi: in the *Legenda,* 140, 144, 146, 158; in lives of late-medieval saints, 200; in Jacobus's sermons, 277n*43*
Counter-Reformation, 29, 42
Credibility. *See* Hagiography, criteria for
Crespin, Jean, 60-61, 66, 239n*53*
Cruikshank, George, 60, 239n*52*
Cult of the saints: extent of regulation by church authorities, 30, 202, 203, 204, 224n*10;* Protestant reaction against, 31, 35, 37, 66, 225n*14;* Enlightenment verdict on, 46; sponsorship in the early church, 46-47; social and religious functions, 47, 48, 49; sponsorship in Middle

Ages, 47-49. *See also* Canonization; Miracles

Cusa, Nicholas of. *See* Nicholas of Cusa

Dauphine of Puimichel, 202, 302n*11*

Delehaye, Hippolyte: sympathy with the *Legenda*'s admirers, 20-21; scholarly activities in early 20th century, 21; usual criteria for saints' legends, 22, 45; influential defense of the *Legenda*, 22-24; embraces folklore theory, 45-46; describes archetypal saint's legend, 64-65, 67, 89; mentioned, 25

Deuteronomy, Code of, 130, 269n*47*

Diego of Osma. *See* Dominic legend

Doctrinal soundness. *See* Hagiography, criteria for

Dominic, Saint: in Jacobus's sermons, 110, 112, 277n*43*, 280n*61*, 283n*76*; preaching mission in Lombardy, 128, 133; missionary ideal, 147; role of poverty, 147; measures used against heresy, 183; major achievements, 188-89. *See also* Dominic legend

Dominicans, early: catalogs of illustrious members, 39-40; missionary activity, 73, 119; ideals, 105, 118; character, 118-19; role in the Inquisition, 128, 129, 268n*43*; efforts to recruit learned men, 138, 256n*5*, 272n*10*; penitential conversions to the order, 147; uncompromising stance against worldliness, 147-49; rivalry with Cistercians, 148; proposal to revise official prayer, 148-49; rivalry with Franciscans, 148-49, 178-79; revisions of the Dominic legend, 164-66, 169-70, 178-79, 182-85, 194-95, 286n*6*, 287n*12*; charges by their enemies and detractors, 169, 172, 173, 178-79, 292n*48*; use of eschatological prophecy, 171-73; allegorical interpretation of the habit, 257n*12*; minimum age requirement, 300n*99*

Dominic legend: the saint's posthumous miracles, 162-63, 177, 180-81, 292n*41*, 294n*57*, 295n*68*; role of Diego of Osma, 165-66, 175, 177, 185; cure of Reginald of Orleans, 167, 168, 176, 180, 186; proofs of heavenly favor toward the Order of Preachers, 167, 168-71, 173;

Dominic as a precursor of Judgment, 171-72; on the order's apostolic mission, 175, 176, 177, 180, 186, 300n*96*; Dominic as model preacher, 175-76, 177, 180, 181, 183, 184, 187, 189, 190, 296n*72*, 297nn *77, 78*; Dominic as father and patron, 176, 177-78, 179-80, 185-86, 192; Dominic's final legacy to his followers, 177, 192-93, 299n*94*; road miracles, 183, 186-88; Dominic as inquisitor, 183-84, 191, 294n*63*; Dominic and the heretics, 183-85, 188-91

Donation of Constantine, 109

Dondaine, Antoine, 127, 128, 197, 204, 244nn *76, 79*, 300n*1*

Dorothea, Saint, 160, 234n*15*

Dorothy of Montau, 302n*11*, 304n*26*

Du Cange, Charles, 33

Dudden, Frederick Homes, 242n*71*

Dupin, Louis-Ellies, 15, 44, 236n*26*

Eadmer, life of Anselm, 292n*49*

Echard, Jacques, 14, 35, 228n*31*, 241n*62*, 245n*2*

Edification. *See* Hagiography, criteria for

Education: Renaissance trends in, 37-38, 42; emphasized by early Dominicans, 105, 118, 138, 256n*5*, 272n*10*; in Jacobus's sermons, 107, 258n*14*, 259n*21*; in the *Legenda*, 137; in dossiers of late-medieval saints, 199, 200

Elizabeth of Thuringia, Saint, 201

Elzéar of Sabran, Saint, 201-2

Erasmus, 13, 36, 37, 38, 41, 42, 66, 126, 266n*31*

Espence, Claude d': controversial Lenten sermons in 1543, 29-30, 31, 51, 224n*8*; criticism of the *Legenda*, 30, 50-51; attempts to reunify the church, 37, 229nn *39, 40*; attacked by less moderate Catholics, 38, 229n*44*; concern with lay education, 56-57; hagiographical works, 238n*36*

Estius, William, 35-36, 228n*33*

Eucharist, 82, 163, 209, 271n*5*

Eusebius, *Ecclesiastical History,* 12, 56; Rufinus's continuation of, 109, 120

Eusebius, Saint, 205-6

Eustace, Saint, 159

Fabian, Saint, 131

Family bonds: treatment in the *Legenda*, 90, 154, 155, 281nn *65, 67*, 304n*25;* in Humbert's treatise, 148, 155, 281n*65;* in Jacobus's sermons, 258n*14*

Fleury, Claude, 45

Fleury, shrine of Benedict, 99, 132

Flight from the world. *See* Separation from the world

Folklore theory of saints' legends, 45-46

Foxe, John, 61, 66, 241

Francesca Romana, Saint, 304n*26*

Franciscans, 147, 148-49, 178-79, 199, 201

Francis legend, revisions of, 288n*19,* 301n*5*

Francis of Assisi, Saint, 147, 171, 178, 180

Frederick II, Emperor, 73, 126-27, 128, 131, 185, 267n*32*

Frideswide, Saint, 47-48

Fulk, Bishop of Toulouse, 177-78

Gaiffier, Baudouin de, 23, 25

George, Saint, 131, 132

Gerard de Frachet. *See Vitae fratrum*

Germain of Auxerre, Saint, 131, 299n*89*

Giles, Saint, 161

God: revealing himself through the saints, 54, 84; as teacher, 75, 76, 80, 112, 139; as inflicter of punishment, 77, 122, 123, 124, 126, 132, 159; humble descent to raise man up, 80, 139-40, 160; as Judge, 82, 159-60, 193; as Creator, 155-56, 157, 281n*69;* as wanting no one to perish, 189, 190

Görlach, Manfred, 214n*4*

Gorcum martyrs, 34-35

Graesse, Theodor, 68, 69, 244n*77*

Gratian, *Decretum,* 120, 264n*14*

Gregory the Great, Saint: functional definition of miracles, 76; definition of the active life, 81; on contemplation as against action, 81-84; on preaching to different audiences, 106; in the *Legenda,* 132, 152, 299n*89;* and Augustine, 150, 160; on human relationships, 155; on the lesser goods of this life, 160; cited as prophesying the Order of Preachers, 172; apparent lack of interest in nature, 284n*81*

—*Dialogues:* Cano's verdict, 53, 67,

243n*74;* treatment by Witzel, 55, 67, 243n*73;* issue of credulity or superstition, 67, 74, 76, 242n*71;* and the criteria for hagiography, 67-68; reputation over the centuries, 68; translations, 68, 243n*75;* text little changed during Middle Ages, 69, 244n*78;* general occasion and purpose, 73, 75; hybrid genre, 74, 75; intended audience, 74, 103; role played by Peter, 75, 79-80, 246n*7;* Gregory's self-portrayal, 75, 81; portrayal of God, 80, 82-83, 84, 160; on the Eucharist, 82

—life of Benedict: pattern of withdrawal and return, 75-76, 81; the saint's impact on others, 76, 78, 80, 81, 91, 247n*20;* practical functions of the miracles, 77-78; parallels to Biblical miracles, 79; analogies between the saint and all Christians, 79, 80; special importance of his example, 81, 84; treatment in Gui's legendary, 243n*72;* mentioned, 175

Gregory IX, Pope: warfare with Frederick II, 126, 127, 267n*32;* bull canonizing Dominic, 181-82, 290n*31*

Gregory of Tours, 66

Gui, Bernard: career and general outlook, 40, 41; on Jacobus's achievements, 40, 231n*52;* on the real "golden legends," 42-43; criticism of the *Legenda,* 62-63; expectations from hagiography, 64; as Dominican historian, 148, 287n*16,* 294n*63*

—*Speculum sanctorale:* why compiled, 40, 62-63, 241n*62;* surviving MSS, 40-41; apparent borrowings from the *Legenda,* 136, 270n*2,* 283n*77;* too scholarly to become popular, 204; general design, 242n*66;* treatment of Gregory's life of Benedict, 243n*72;* treatment of Augustine's *Confessions,* 270n*2*

Guy de Châtres, 41

Hagiography, ancient and medieval: reputation in 17th century, 12, 58-59; origins of apocryphal traditions, 30, 33, 224n*11,* 227n*26;* historical criticism of, 31-32; reactions against historical criticism, 32-34, 36; loss of status in 16th century, 43, 54, 58; reputation during

Enlightenment, 44; promotional functions, 49; conventions, 52, 65, 98, 179

Hagiography, criteria for: historicity, 44-45, 51, 62, 63; edification, 49, 64-66; doctrinal soundness, 50-51, 54, 64; Latin style, 51, 234n*18;* credibility, 51-54, 55, 56, 64, 65, 179; moral usefulness, 52, 54-55, 64, 65; conformity with the Gospels, 65; reassurance, 67; and Gregory's *Dialogues,* 67-68; and the *Legenda,* 97

Hedwige of Silesia, Saint, 201

Henry of Cologne, 147

Henry of Treviso, Blessed, 48-49

Henschenius, Godfrey, 34

Heretics: in the *Legenda,* 96, 118, 122-23, 128-29, 188-91; in Jacobus's sermons, 262n*10. See also* Arians; Cathars; Manichaean heresy; Waldenses

"Heroic virtue" as a criterion for canonization, 199

Hilary, Saint, 161

Hinnebusch, William A., 119, 133

Historicity. *See* Hagiography, criteria for

Homebon of Cremona, Saint, 201

Honorius III, Pope, 126, 133, 168

Hooker, Richard, 58

Humanism, Renaissance, 42, 64

Humbert of Romans: on books as weapons, 119; *Treatise on Preaching,* 147-48, 152, 155, 258n*16,* 277nn *38, 39,* 281n*65;* life of Dominic, 165, 169, 172, 182, 183, 184-85, 189, 191, 192-93; preface to *Vitae fratrum,* 165, 173

Impeccability as a criterion for canonization, 199, 301n*5*

Incarnation, 80, 139-40, 160

Index of prohibited books, 32, 34

Innocent III, Pope, 169, 201, 288n*19*

Innocent IV, Pope: warfare with Frederick II, 126, 127, 129, 267n*32;* launches Inquisition in Lombardy, 128; definition of sanctity, 199

Inquisition, Spanish, 34, 266n*31*

Inquisition in 13th-century Lombardy, 128, 129, 130, 185, 268n*43*

Jacobus de Voragine: reputation for saintliness, 15, 216n*18;* supposed Italian translation of Bible, 15, 217n*20;* official beatification, 16; life and career, 73, 165, 193-94, 231n*52,* 245n*2,* 286n*5;* doctrinal teaching against heresy, 130, 269n*48; Tractatus de libris a beato Augustino editis,* 135; general outlook, 194, 195; chronology of his works, 300n*98*

—*Legenda aurea:* etymological prefaces, 12, 44, 45, 149, 216n*15,* 220n*43,* 290-91; treatment of healings and resurrections, 93-94, 96, 97, 118, 158, 161, 253n*28,* 284n*85,* 295n*68;* proportion of martyrs among its saints, 98, 256n*44;* pictorial style, 102; consistency of emphases, 114, 133-34; treatment of paganism, 119, 262n*8;* treatment of Jews, 119-20, 262n*9;* account of Frederick II, 126; account of heretics' influence in Milan, 128; account of Peter Martyr and the Inquisition, 128-29; apparent dualism, 144

—*Legenda aurea,* emphases: the saints' power, 88, 89, 91, 92, 93, 97, 124, 125, 133, 190; saints as solitary individuals, 90, 94-95, 153-54, 155, 188, 189, 195; vindications against adversaries, 91, 92, 93, 96, 97, 126, 131; confrontations with heretics, 96, 118, 122-23, 128-29, 188-91; the inferiority of women, 108; confrontations with secular rulers, 120, 121-22, 126, 129, 131; prerogatives of the clergy, 122, 125-26, 129; miracles of retribution, 122-25, 132, 262n*4;* saints as punishers of wrongdoing, 124-25, 129-30, 191; separation from the world, 138, 142, 143-44, 146, 151, 152-53, 193, 194, 280n*57;* apparent remoteness of God, 138-39, 140-41, 142, 143, 190, 191-93, 273nn *14-16,* 298n*86;* encouragements to despise earthly things, 144, 146, 149-50, 157-58, 159, 160-62, 280n*57;* on Purgatory and Hell, 149-50, 159; saints' eagerness to die, 158, 159, 162, 192, 282nn *74, 75;* the necessity of penance, 160; feats of anti-natural virtue, 161-62; importance of virginity, 161-62, 206, 207, 303n*21;* the supernatural in its purest form, 162-63; polemic on behalf of the Order of

—*Legenda aurea*, emphases (*continued*)
Preachers, 169-71, 173; saints' penitential austerities, 192, 298n*89*; importance
of the sacraments, 271n*5*; saints against
their families, 281nn *65, 67*, 304n*25*
—*Legenda aurea*, history: probable date of
compilation, 126-27, 193-94, 244n*1*,
267n*33*, 285n*1*, 300n*98*; intended audience and use, 74, 85-86, 87, 103, 112,
113, 130, 132-33, 194-95, 205, 249n*2*;
surviving Latin MSS, 3-4, 203; vernacular translations and adaptations, 4, 86,
204, 207-8, 214n*4*; additions by later
authors, 160; medieval indexes to,
203-4, 302n*16*; early editions (Latin), 4,
5, 27-28, 29, 57-58, 214n*8*, 222n*2*; early
editions (vernacular), 5, 28-29, 57, 223;
theories about its success, 14, 17, 18,
197-98, 203, 204, 207, 300n*1*; probable
effects on late-medieval audiences,
208-9, 304n*27*; reputation among Dominicans in late Middle Ages, 39-40, 41;
reputation in 16th century, 57-58, 60-61,
136, 160; Protestant attacks on, 20,
59-60, 220n*42*, 228n*36*, 239n*52*; reputation among Dominicans in 18th and
19th centuries, 14-15, 16; modern editions (vernacular), 5, 16-17, 18, 19-20,
24-25, 219n*36*; modern editions (Latin),
68, 243n*76*, 244n*77*; modern reputation,
5, 23, 24; current state of scholarship,
7-8, 24, 68-69, 197, 203-4, 207-8,
221-22, 243-44
—sermons on the saints: characteristic
differences from the *Legenda*, 101-3,
113, 130, 173-74, 205; relative sophistication of style, 102, 103; kind of
audience implied, 103, 110, 113; treatment of miracles, 103, 110-13, 158;
allegorical interpretations of Scripture,
104, 105, 108, 270n*49*; lessons on preparing for death, 104, 271n*5*; on the
special calling of monks and friars,
104-6, 153; criticisms of worldly churchmen, 105, 158-59, 283n*76*; on the hierarchy of states within the church,
106-10; on the special calling and status
of preachers, 107; on the prerogatives of
bishops and other prelates, 107, 109,
112-13; on the inferiority of women,

108-9, 260n*28,*276n*31*; on the superiority of priests to laymen, 109-10; justifications of force against heretics and other
malefactors, 130, 191, 259n*24*, 270n*49*;
on Augustine's contempt for earthly
things, 145-46, 158; on God as punisher
even of the righteous, 159; proofs of
heavenly favor toward the Order of
Preachers, 173-74; on secular rulers as
persecutors of the church, 262n*10*; on
the perfection attained by Dominic,
280n*61*

Jean de Mailly, *Abbreviatio in gestis et
miraculis sanctorum:* surviving MSS, 3;
as model for the *Legenda*, 69-70,
244n*79*; intended audience and use, 86;
account of Dominic, 165, 167, 169,
174-77, 179, 181, 183, 184, 193; suitabil-
ity for use by laity, 167-68, 181, 204-7;
virtues chosen for emphasis, 175-76,
177, 205-7; realistic limitation of the
saints' power, 176, 179, 205-6

Jean de Vignay, 4, 205
Jewel, John, 60
Jews: in Paulinus's life of Ambrose, 119; in
the *Legenda*, 262n*9*
John the Baptist, Saint, 269n*48*
Jordan of Saxony, account of Dominic,
164, 165-66, 184, 287n*12*
Julian the Apostate, Emperor, 131
Juliana, Saint, 132
Justina, Empress, 120, 121, 123, 124

Lacop, James, 34-35, 36, 228nn *31, 35*
Launoy, Jean de, 21, 31, 32, 33, 36, 37,
226n*20*, 227n*23*
Learning. *See* Education
Legend(a): original meanings of the term,
61, 86; loss of favor as a title for
hagiographical works, 61, 240n*56*;
development of pejorative meaning in
English, 61-62, 240n*58*, 241nn *59-61*;
development of pejorative meaning in
other languages, 240n*57*
Legenda aurea. See Jacobus de Voragine,
Legenda aurea
Legendaries, abridged, 3, 40, 41, 197, 204,
231n*57*, 244n*76*
Leo, Saint, 131
Lippomano, Luigi, 61

Lombardy, political situation in 13th century, 126, 127-28, 129, 133
Louis, Saint, 199
Louis of Anjou, Saint, 199-200

Macarius, Saint, 299n89
McGiffert, Arthur C., 243n71
Mâle, Emile, 17, 18, 24-25, 85
Manichaean heresy, 137-38, 140, 157, 272n9, 275n27
Margaret of Antioch, Saint, 234n15, 304n25
Martin of Tours, Saint: character and ideals in *Vita S. Martini*, 107, 262n8; transformed in Jacobus's sermons, 107, 259n23; miracles as used in Jacobus's sermons, 110, 112-13
Martyrs: treatment in the *Legenda*, 98, 131-32, 162, 205, 206, 207, 281n67, 304n25; preponderance in late-medieval legendaries, 98, 255n43; treatment in Jean's *Abbreviatio*, 205-6, 207, 304n25
Mary, Saint. *See* Virgin Mary, Blessed
Mary Magdalene, Saint, 298n89
Mass. *See* Eucharist
Maurists, 226n19
Mauritius, Emperor, persecutor of Gregory the Great, 132
Mendicants: contrasts with earlier religious orders, 146-47; charges against them in 13th century, 172, 173. *See also* Antimendicant controversy, 1250s; Dominicans; Franciscans
Miracle stories: regarded with suspicion in 16th century, 55, 239n53; pedagogical effectiveness, 74
Miracles: role in a saint's dossier, 65; treatment in Jacobus's sermons, 103, 110-13, 158; Biblical types in saints' legends, 247n17
—acts of retribution: in early Protestant hagiography, 66, 242n70; punishing actual persecution of the saints, 77, 123-24, 132; punishing disrespect for the saints, 93, 99, 118, 123, 182; punishing infringements on church property, 99, 132; punishing excessive earthly prosperity, 159
—healings and other acts of mercy: social and religious meanings, 47, 48, 65-66;

valued by Augustine, 47, 66; defended by Witzel, 66; downplayed by Jacobus, 93-97, 111, 118, 158, 161, 162, 253n28, 295n68; role in passions of martyrs, 98, 255n42; usual preponderance in shrine collections, 99; included in Paulinus's life of Ambrose, 117, 118; temporary cures for spiritual purposes, 161, 284n85, 304n27; in Bartholomew's account of Dominic, 180-81; in other versions of the Dominic legend, 294n57; infrequent in dossiers of late-medieval saints, 301n7
—signs: proving saints' virtue and favor with God, 90, 96, 110, 112-13, 118, 179-80, 184, 187-88, 201, 202; proving the blindness and perversity of the saints' enemies, 98, 131, 184-85, 189, 255n41; proving saints' power over nature, 110-11, 261n32, 301n7
—supernatural valued for its own sake, 162-63, 183, 304n27
Mixed life (*vita composita*): defined by Jacobus, 153; as a model for the laity, 201
Mombrizio, Bonino, 42
Monastic virtues: in Jacobus's sermons, 105-6, 153; in dossiers of late-medieval saints, 201-2, 209
Monica, Saint, 136, 139, 154
Monleone, Giovanni, 193, 222n53, 245n1
Monte Cassino, shrine of Saint Benedict, 99
More, Henry, 61
More, Thomas, 37, 38
Moses, 95, 96, 125

Nagy, Maria von, 222n53
Neoplatonists, 140
Nicholas of Cusa: finds "superstitiosa" in the *Legenda*, 39, 50, 160, 233n15; universalist philosophy, 41; concern with lay education, 41-42, 50; effort to reform diocese of Brixen, 50

Order of Friars Minor. *See* Franciscans
Order of Preachers. *See* Dominicans
Oudin, Casimir, 3
Oxford, shrine of Saint Frideswide, 47-48

Papebroch, Daniel, 34, 227n23
Paris, University of. *See* Sorbonne faculty
Pastor, Saint, 281n67
Pastoral care: in Gregory's life of Benedict, 77-78, 81, 82, 84, 87, 89, 90, 94, 96, 97; elsewhere in Gregory's writings, 83, 152; in Paulinus's life of Ambrose, 117; in Humbert's *Treatise on Preaching,* 152; in Jacobus's sermons, 153; in the official Dominic legend, 188; in lives of late-medieval saints, 199, 200
Paulinus, life of Ambrose, 117, 119, 120, 121, 122-24, 125
Penitence as a means of sanctification, 198, 201
Penitential practices: in the *Legenda,* 192, 298n89; in dossiers of late-medieval saints, 199, 200, 209
Perpetua, Saint, 281n67
Peter Calo, legendary of, 41, 56, 204, 237n34, 242n64
Peter Comestor, 12
Peter Ferrandus, life of Dominic, 165, 167, 168, 171-72, 182, 183, 184, 193
Peter Lombard, 12
Peter Martyr (Peter of Verona), Saint, 128-29, 185
Peter Natal, *Catalogus sanctorum,* 41, 42, 55, 62, 204
Peter of Morrone, Saint. *See* Celestine V, Pope
Peter the Exorcist, Saint, 159
Petronilla, Saint, 161-62, 303n23
Pickworth, William, 41
Pignon, Lawrence, 39
Poncelet, Albert, 213n1
Portian Basilica (Milan), 117, 120, 121
Possidius, life of Augustine, 136, 138-39, 150, 151, 282nn 74, 75
Primus, Saint, 131
Procopius, Saint, 225n12
Purity: in the *Legenda,* 157, 158, 161, 162, 188, 206; in dossiers of late-medieval saints, 200, 201-2. *See also* Separation from the world; Virginity

Quétif and Echard. *See* Echard, Jacques

Reginald of Orleans. *See* Dominic legend

Renunciation of the world. *See* Separation from the world
Richardson, Ernest C., 20, 25, 101, 221n53, 245n1
Rosweyde, Héribert, 58
Roze, J.-B. M., 18, 20
Rufinus, continuation of the *Ecclesiastical History,* 109, 120
Ryan, Granger, and Helmut Ripperger, 24-25

Saint-Germain-en-Laye, France: Colloquy in 1562, 37
Saints, cult of the. *See* Cult of the saints
Saints, late-medieval: as penitents, 198, 201; as defenders of church property and clerical prerogatives, 201, 209, 301n10; as punishers of wrongdoing, 201, 301n10
—selection of: preferred social classes and occupations, 17, 198, 201, 202-3, 256n44, 301n8; types canonized between 1190 and 1270, 198, 201; types canonized between 1270 and 1450, 199-202. *See also* Canonization
Saints' legends. *See* Hagiography
Salimbene, 179, 302n12
Scholastica, Saint, 90, 155, 251n16
Sebastian, Saint, 159, 205
Sebastian de Saint-Paul, 34
"Secular arm," 129, 130, 191
Separation from the world: in Jacobus's sermons, 105-6, 145-46, 153, 158, 258nn 14, 15, 277n43, 280n61; in the *Legenda,* 138, 142, 143-44, 146, 151, 152-53, 193, 194, 280n57; earlier tradition of, 146-47; in Humbert's treatise, 147-48, 277nn 38, 39; importance to 13th-century Dominicans, 147-49; in dossiers of late-medieval saints, 200, 201-2
Sévèstre, A., 59
Simplicianus, Augustine's visit to, 138, 141
Sorbonne faculty, 30, 31, 32, 37
Stephen of Salanhac, 40, 148
Stilicho, Count, 125
Sulpicius Severus, 112
Surius, Laurence, *De probatis sanctorum historiis,* 43, 61
Sylvester, Saint, 109, 111, 132, 263n10

Theodosius I, Emperor, 117, 119, 121-22, 129
Theophilus legend, 25
Thomas Aquinas, Saint, 32, 152, 156, 199, 200
Thomas of Canterbury, Saint, 109-10, 132
Thomas of Cantilupe, Saint, 200-1
Totila, king of the Ostrogoths, 91
Touron, Antoine, 15, 35, 224n9, 236n26, 241n62
Treviso, Italy: cult of Henry of Treviso, 48-49
Tripartite History. See Cassiodorus, *Tripartite History*
"Two-tiered model" of the church, 46, 243n71

Valentine, Saint, 50
Valentinian II, Emperor, 120, 121
Vauchez, André, 48-49, 198-203 *passim,* 207, 209, 300n2, 301-2, 304
Vedastus, Saint, 161
Via media, 36-38, 229n39, 266n31
Vicaire, Marie-Humbert, 147, 165, 171, 173, 184
Victoria, Francis de, 38, 42
Victorinus, conversion of, 141
Vincent of Beauvais, 12, 53, 55-56, 62, 70, 244n79
Virgin Mary, Blessed: as special patron of the Order of Preachers, 167, 168, 170-71, 173, 174, 287n16, 290n33; as chief intercessor for mankind, 170-71
Virginity: in the *Legenda,* 161-62, 206, 207, 303n21; in dossiers of late-medieval saints, 202, 209, 304n26; in Jean's *Abbreviatio,* 206-7, 303n23
Vitae fratrum, 165, 170, 171, 173, 174, 187, 188
Vitus, Saint, 131
Vives, Juan Luis: general stature and reputation, 13, 229n41; errors, according to Wyzewa, 19; verdict on the *Legenda,* 29, 51-52, 126; career and principles as an educator, 37-38, 266n31; expectations from hagiography, 51, 52; warning against falsifications and their consequences, 52, 56; mentioned, 11, 21, 22, 23, 31, 57, 65, 88, 117

Waldenses, 41, 107, 127
Ward, Benedicta, 47-48, 99, 132
White, Helen C., 222n53
William of Saint-Amour, 171, 173
Withdrawal from the world. *See* Separation from the world
Witzel, Georg: Bolland's reply to, 11-13; career and ecumenical goals, 36, 266n31; scholarly credentials, 36-37; conflict with less moderate Catholics, 38, 230n44; purposes of his own legendary, 54-55, 56, 57; defense of hagiography in general, 54-55, 236n28; verdict on Peter Natal, 55, 62; defense of miracles, 55, 66; treatment of Gregory's life of Benedict, 55, 67, 243n73; verdict on Vincent of Beauvais, 55-56; on the *Legenda* and its continued use, 56, 62, 126; on "Petrus Lombardus," 56, 237n34; list of preferred sources, 237n32; mentioned, 29, 31, 117
Wortley Montagu, Lady Mary, 240n58
Wyzewa, Teodor de, 18-20, 23, 25, 101

Yves Hélory, Saint, 199, 301n8

Zacharius, vision of, 173, 174, 290n31
Zuidweg, Jacobus J. A., 23, 222n53, 243n76